Haunted Heartland

HAUNTED HEARTLAND

Beth Scott & Michael Norman

BARNES
&NOBLE
BOOKS
NEW YORK

This edition published by Barnes & Noble, Inc.,
by arrangement with Stanton & Lee Publishers, Inc.

1992 Barnes & Noble Books

ISBN 0-88029-614-3

Printed and bound in the United States of America

M   20   19   18   17   16   15   14

Contents

Preface

"The oldest and strongest emotion of mankind is fear, and the oldest and strongest kind of fear is fear of the unknown."

H. P. Lovecraft

"We—or our primitive forefathers—once believed that the return of the dead, unseen forces, and secret injurious powers were realities, and were convinced that they actually happened. Nowadays we no longer believe in them, we have surmounted those modes of thought; but we do not feel quite sure of our new beliefs, and the old ones still exist within us ready to seize upon any confirmation."

Sigmund Freud

"Incomprehensible? But because you cannot understand a thing, it does not cease to exist."

Pascal (1670)

Within a wisp of time in the geological calendar, humanity has moved from Pascal's cautious acceptance of entities unseen to the pervasive skepticism of the "supernatural," characterized by the twentieth century. A nuclear Armageddon, deadly acid rain from the skies, or an explosive political crisis pose more of a threat today than hobgoblins in white linen or fatal spells cast by witches on broomsticks. These latter fears have gone the way of dragons and knights, elves and unicorns, or (dare we say it) Scotland's Nessie and the Himalaya's ephemeral snowman. All are part of our collective myth but hardly the stuff of reasoned, adult discourse.

Ours is the age of science, not black magic. It is the era of civilized understanding of those forces that once confounded our ancestors. While the catatonic child or the epileptic adult were previously shunned, or perhaps even put to death by their neighbors who declared them to be possessed by the devil, we wince at such savagery nowadays, knowing full well that "it couldn't happen now."

Whereas ancient men and women feared what they did not understand, we now seek to understand what we once feared. The ancients attributed every natural event, and all human dysfunction it might be added, to an unexplainable act of the gods. We, on the other hand, believe that science can explain physical events such as eclipses, earthquakes and volcanic eruptions.

And so it is with belief in the supernatural—we have all the answers. The witches of Salem? Crazy, harmless old women singled out for retribution by vengeful teenage girls. The possessed? Nothing but a group of disconsolate people who were most likely schizophrenic. Ghosts? Obviously the product of over-active imaginations fueled by alcohol.

Likewise, Houdini proved that mediums were fraudulent, that the crystal ball was nothing more than a come-on for the gullible. There is nothing "over there," on the other side of this existence, that plagues the living. Ghosts, poltergeists, the walking dead and haunted houses are pure myth and should be herded into the same corral of fantasy as unicorns and saucermen. There's absolutely nothing to them.

But are *you* sure of this? Totally certain?

Freud knew that old ways die slowly. To feel a slight chill as you walk past a graveyard late at night is to doubt all that you have been told of reality and superstition.

And that's why we have written this book. What follows is a compendium of the unbelievable and fantastic: ghosts, haunted houses, possession and exorcism, vanishing people and ships, spontaneous combustions, mystery lights, automatic writing and premonitory dreams.

It is the world of the supernatural. The stories contradict everything that is rational and scientific. You are about to journey into a world filled with people and events out of step with what we believe.

Perhaps even more startling is the fact that each of these stories originated in the so-called "sedate" American Middle West. From ghostly mansions in Ohio to a Nebraska classroom lost in time, and from haunted manganese mines in northern Minnesota to ancient specters wandering the Ozark hills of Missouri, we hope to lay to rest once and for all the notion that hauntings occur only in moss-draped southern plantations or shuttered, clapboard cottages on the Maine coast.

You'll meet inhabitants of the unseen world who are frightening, some who are charming and others so peculiar as to defy description. And there is no geographical limitation to their activities—a rural farmhouse, suburban ranch home or country road all provide the ideal abode for ghostly shenanigans.

The line between myth and "reality" in these stories is sometimes thin. For instance, some of the stories, while purportedly based on actual events, seem to be rooted in the folklore of a region. In the Ozarks, for example, many ghost stories have been orally told and re-told for generations while other tales fall more within the realm of parapsychology since they deal with people who have experienced strange and perplexing supernatural encounters.

Are the stories that follow true? We honestly don't know. And, quite frankly, that is not the point of the book. What matters most, we believe, is that these stories have been *told* by the people involved as if they were true. The tales are passed along as accounts of what happened to ordinary, living people.

Our primary objective is to make available in one collection those stories of Midwest supernatural phenomena that are generally unavailable to the reading public. We have collected stories from remote and diverse sources; many originally appeared in books or periodicals of limited circulation. Other stories, primarily the contemporary accounts, have never before appeared in print.

In our preparation however, we discarded many of the ghost tales that we had originally unearthed. There were several reasons for this, including a lack of material about the original event, doubts as to the accuracy of the story's sources, and a desire to include only those tales that we felt best represented the accounts told in the various midwestern states. For instance, there are possibly hundreds of legends concerned with mysterious female phantoms who wear long, black dresses and roam American towns large and small, yet we have included only a few of them here. To include more would be repetitious since the phantom's activities are oddly similar despite their geographical separation.

Finally, we must emphasize that we are *not* parapsychologists or ghost hunters. All these stories are told from a distance—it is not our intention to investigate the hauntings or other peculiar phenomena. We're simply writers dealing with a subject that interests us. We offer you these true stories, imaginatively told, purely as entertainment, a slight detour, if you will, as you speed your way through the "real world."

A book of this scope could not have been written without the cooperation and assistance of many people. We would like to especially thank our Stanton & Lee editors Doug Bradley, Mark Lefebvre, Meg Saart and Betty Durbin for their patience and wisdom; Martha Mattingly, *Firehouse Magazine*, New York; Mary Margaret Fuller, editor, *Fate*; Laurel G. Bowen, Curator of Manuscripts, Illinois State Historical Society, Springfield; Fiora Fuhrmann, Lake Zurich, Illinois; Chicago Historical Society; Edith T. Piercy, Chief

Librarian, Rockford *Register Star*, Rockford, Illinois; E. G. Brady, Jr., Librarian, *Commercial Appeal*, Memphis, Tennessee; Cathy Hess, Assistant Head Librarian, The Indianapolis *Star/News*; Patricia A. Harris, Curator, Michigan City Historical Society, Inc., Old Lighthouse Museum, Michigan City, Indiana; Dorothy Rowley, Associate Curator, and staff, La Porte State Historical Society, La Porte, Indiana; Tina Bucuvalas, Archivist, and staff, Folklore Institute, Indiana University, Bloomington; Eric Pumroy, Indiana Historical Society Library, Indianapolis; Robert K. O'Neill, Ronald L. Baker, Indiana State University, Terre Haute; Deborah Griesinger, Curator, Ham House Museum, Dubuque County Historical Society, Dubuque, Iowa; Lowell R. Wilbur, Librarian, Iowa Department of History & Archives, Des Moines; Jane Norman, reporter, Des Moines *Register*; William E. Koch, Folklorist and Associate Professor of English (retired), Kansas State University, Manhattan; Jane Abernathy, Topeka, Kansas; Kay Tice, Librarian, Greely County Library, Tribune, Kansas; John Cumming, Director, Clarke Historical Library, Central Michigan University, Mount Pleasant, Michigan; Philip La Ronge, Archives Assistant, Wayne State University, Detroit; Paul Sporn, Associate Professor of English, Wayne State University, Detroit; Janet L. Langlois, Assistant Professor and Director, Department of English Folklore Archive, Wayne State University, Detroit; Elizabeth Bright, Librarian, Iron Range Research Center, Chisholm, Minnesota.

Also: Dorothy M. Murke, Librarian, Minneapolis History Collection, Minneapolis Public Library and Information Center; Hazel H. Wahlberg, Roseau County Historical Museum and Interpretive Center, Roseau, Minnesota; Sandra Peddie, St. Paul *Pioneer Press*; Jack LaZebnik, Professor of English, Stephens College, Columbia, Missouri; Mrs. Ellis (Hester) Jackson, Secretary, Webster County Historical Society, Marshfield, Missouri;

Thomas P. Sweeney, M.D., Springfield, Missouri; Si Colborn, Monroe County *Appeal*, Paris, Missouri; Anne P. Diffendal, Manuscripts Curator, Nebraska State Historical Society, Lincoln; Robert B. Smith, Editor-in-chief, *Ohio Magazine*, Columbus; Jannette K. Hemsworth, Alumni Office, Denison University, Granville, Ohio; James L. Murphy, Reference Librarian, Archives-Library Division, The Ohio Historical Society, Inc., Columbus, the family of David K. Webb; Nancy Steen, Popular Culture Librarian, Bowling Green State University, Bowling Green, Ohio; Great Lakes Historical Society, Vermillion, Ohio; Cleveland Public Library; Richard W. Heiden, Milwaukee, Wisconsin; Michael Kluever, Wausau, Wisconsin; Sue Kurth, Beloit *Daily News*, Beloit, Wisconsin; Superintendent, Big Foot Beach State Park, Lake Geneva, Wisconsin; Tom Hollatz, The Lakeland *Times*, Minocqua, Wisconsin; Tim Ericson, Archivist, University of Wisconsin-River Falls; Mary Abdoo, Mineral Point, Wisconsin.

To those whose stories are told in this book and the many other people whose names must be kept anonymous we thank you for brushing up against the "other side" and thus providing substance to a most elusive subject.

Michael Norman
Beth Scott
October, 1985

In certain instances, the names and places contained in the following stories have been changed to protect the identities of those involved. Although all the material in this book is based on "true" incidents, the authors have, in some cases, expanded upon the original circumstances to create scenes which may not have actually taken place. In all cases, however, the hauntings have occurred in the manner described. These are, after all, ghost stories. And ghosts are notorious for not leaving behind a written record of their activities.

Haunted Heartland

Chapter I.
Illinois

"Her name is Mary ... the most beautiful and evasive ghost in Chicago ... a captivating, blue-eyed, flaxen-haired girl in her late teens. On those occasions when she chooses to be seen, she wears the long, off-white ballgown and dancing shoes in which she died ... in 1934 ...

... For the past fifty years her appearances have become accepted by residents of the southwest section of Chicago ..."

Resurrection Mary from "HAUNTED CHICAGO"

HAUNTED CHICAGO

The ghosts that walk the neighborhoods of Chicago are not necessarily those of old-time politicians or Depression-era gangsters. The hauntings in the Windy City are more likely those of ordinary men and women who, for one reason or another, cannot leave Chicago. From the apparition of a beautiful girl who strolls Archer Road to the city room of the late *Chicago American* to a firefighter who left his permanent mark on an old firehouse, Chicago ghosts are a lively ... er, deadly ... congregation of departed souls.

RESURRECTION MARY

The most beautiful and evasive ghost in Chicago is a captivating, blue-eyed, flaxen-haired girl in her late teens. On those occasions when she chooses to be seen, she wears the long, off-white ballgown and dancing shoes in which she died ... in 1934. And she loves to dance at the Willowbrook Ballroom.

Her name is Mary, or more precisely Resurrection Mary, after the cemetery in which she is restlessly entombed, Resurrection Cemetery, 7200 S. Archer Road, in suburban Justice, Illinois. No one knows her real name, or at least it has never been revealed. Old cemetery records do indicate that a Polish girl of about Mary's age and description is buried there.

Resurrection Mary died in an automobile accident in 1934 on her way home from a night of dancing at the old O. Henry Ballroom, now renamed the Willowbrook. For the past fifty years her appearances have become accepted by residents in that southwest section of Chicagoland. A song has even been written about her, "The Ballad of Resurrection Mary."

Mary first made her presence known in 1939, five years after her death, when motorists complained that a mysterious girl in a formal gown tried to jump onto the running boards of their automobiles. In some cases, she hitched rides to the O. Henry Ballroom. On those occasions, no one suspected that Mary was anything but mortal. She would dance all night with some of the single men who frequented the night spot, but she was always quiet and vague about where she lived. "Aloof" was the word used most often by her dancing partners. Her escorts would later say her skin was icy cold.

After the last dance, Mary would ask for rides, and she would direct her impromptu beaus to head north on Archer Avenue. She usually disappeared from the vehicle as it passed Resurrection Cemetery. Most of the time she didn't bother with the formality of opening the door. But Mary was not always discourteous—she kissed at least one man goodnight.

At other times, Mary asked the driver to stop just short of the cemetery, got out of the car and vanished as she ran *through* the locked cemetery gates. That's when her escort knew he was with Resurrection Mary.

The young girl was also seen *in* the cemetery. On one occasion, a man was passing the graveyard late at night when he happened to glance toward the locked gates. A young woman peered back at him through the iron bars. He thought she might have been locked in when the cemetery closed at dusk, and he left to phone police. By the time officials arrived the girl was gone. A curious sight, however, was revealed in the policeman's spotlight when it shone on the gate. Two bars had been spread apart. Directly at the curve of each bar, the outlines of two feminine hand prints were embedded in the metal! The misshapen bars were quickly replaced.

Resurrection Mary has been especially active since Resurrection Cemetery was renovated ten years ago. One of the more recent, and detailed, accounts of her activities appeared in a Chicago newspaper.

A cab driver was returning to the tollway after dropping off a fare in Palos Park. It was a few minutes past midnight on a snow-swept January night. The cabbie was driving up Archer Avenue when he saw a coatless girl standing near the entrance to the Old Willow Shopping Mall.

The man thought that the girl had encountered car trouble, so he stopped to help. She climbed in the front seat, a strikingly beautiful girl dressed in a white gown with black patent leather dancing shoes fashioned with a thin strap over her delicate arch.

The mysterious passenger told the driver that she had to get home and gestured northward. The cab driver later recalled that the young woman was vague, giving unclear answers as he asked her questions. He thought that perhaps she may have had a few too many drinks. The only thing she said which he clearly remembered was, "The snow came early this year."

After the pair had traveled several miles up Archer Avenue, the girl shouted, "Here!" The cabbie pulled to the curb and looked out his window at the area toward which the girl had pointed. A small shack was all he saw. But when he looked back toward the girl, she was gone. Vanished. The car door had never opened!

The shack was located directly across the street from Resurrection Cemetery.

MORE HAUNTED CEMETERIES

At least two other Chicago-area cemeteries have occasioned peculiar events.

A "magic house" occasionally appears in a shroud-like mist on the rutted trail leading to the abandoned Bachelor Grove Cemetery, west of Crestwood in Rubio Woods Forest Preserve. The house floats into view only rarely. People who have seen the place describe the same scene: a porch swing sways gently on a large, wood-colonnaded front porch. The two-story house is vaguely Victorian with a faint glow of light seeping through heavily-curtained windows.

No house was ever known to have been built on that property. And no one has ever reported entering the home. At least, no one has ever left the house to report on its "occupants."

Bachelor Grove Cemetery also features a "ghost light." Eyewitnesses say a blue orb often bounces across the cemetery on clear, moonlit nights. Its origins are also unknown.

Tombstones in the weed-choked cemetery have also been rearranged on occasion. However, a coven of witches reportedly meets in the cemetery, and the vandalizing of the grave markers has been attributed to them.

Holy Sepulchre Cemetery, between 111th and 115th Streets, west of Cicero Avenue, contains the grave of a young girl who is rapidly taking on religious prominence.

Mary Alice Quinn died at the tender age of fourteen in 1935. She was a quiet, pious child. Mary is buried beneath a tombstone marked Reilly, and was believed to have had healing powers. Before her death, she reportedly cured several people of various afflictions.

Pilgrims who believe in Mary Alice's ability to heal have made their way to her grave in the hope her spirit can mend their various ills. It is easy to find her resting place ... the grave gives off the scent of roses though there are no such flowers nearby!

THE HULL HOUSE DEVIL BABY

The three elderly Italian women chattered amiably as they scurried along the sidewalk on an early spring morning in 1913. They kept closely together, not daring to lose sight of one another, their pocketbooks clutched tightly against their ample bosoms. Should any one of the hundreds of strangers they passed that day have been asked to identify their mission, the answer might have been that the ladies were on their way to church, or the market, or perhaps to visit a favorite daughter-in-law. But that was as far from the truth as the women were from their native Sicily.

The trio turned the final corner and paused. Their destination lay a few yards away. The women looked at one another. Should they continue, they silently quizzed each other. Absolutely, came the unanimous reply, for it wasn't every day that they would be able to see a living Devil Baby at Chicago's famous Hull House!

The Hull House receptionist greeted them, sat the women down, and, as gently as possible, told them that there was *no* Devil Baby. The story was all gossip. The women insisted they knew what they were talking about and proceeded to describe the peculiar toddler in great detail—pointed ears, a very short tail and cloven hoofs. Furthermore, the child could speak from the moment he was born; with his first breath he had cursed his father! The infant even grabbed the cigar out of his father's mouth and smoked it. And somehow the baby had acquired a red automobile in which to ride around Chicago!

Fantastic as it sounds, Hull House was inundated with thousands of similar requests to see the Devil Baby before the episode was finally laid to rest six weeks later. Letters, telephone calls and personal visits by the curious fully taxed the resources of Hull House. A group of people from Milwaukee wrote offering to organize a "delegation" to visit Hull House for an opportunity to view the child—they even volunteered to pay whatever price might be asked for the privilege!

Hull House has been a Chicago landmark since Jane Addams and Ellen Starr founded the settlement house for the city's large influx of immigrants in the late 1880s. Although Hull House moved to new quarters in 1963, the original structure, built in 1856 as the home of Charles J. Hull, has been preserved as a memorial to Addams and Starr, and the hundreds of volunteers who provided personal, educational and recreational opportunities to generations of immigrants, poor people and the homeless.

It is not clear what prompted the origin of the Devil Baby legend in those first months of 1913. The reason for the birth of a baby with the features and demeanor of Satan seemed to vary with the religion and ethnic background of each inquisitive visitor. Italian, Irish and Jewish versions of the peculiar child have been documented, each bearing strong moral implications. The "lesson" seemed to be: Don't question the teachings of your religion or family; to stray from the fold was to invite horrible retribution.

For example, the Irish version of the story reflected a strong Catholic influence:

An Irish girl failed to confess to a priest that she had had an affair with a man before she married her husband. For this transgression, she was punished by being forced to give birth to the Devil. The woman's shocked husband took the infant to Hull House.

Despite the child's grotesque appearance, several workers at Hull House decided to have him baptised.

But, when they unwrapped the infant's swaddling clothes, they were empty. A fiendish laugh erupted from the back of the church. The startled group turned to see the baby dancing away across the empty pews.

The Italian account also emphasized the dangers inherent in ignoring Church law:

A young Italian woman committed the grievous sin of marrying an atheist, despite the protests of her family. A few months later and pregnant with her first child, she hung a painting of the Virgin Mother on the bedroom wall. When her husband returned from work that night, he ripped the picture from its frame, and burned it. He shouted that he would rather have the Devil himself in the house than a holy picture. His loose tongue was an invitation to Satan. The evil one implanted himself in the unborn child. At his birth, the couple's weird child ran and talked, skipping around the kitchen table, shaking his finger at his "father." The woman's fearful husband took it immediately to Hull House and left it on the steps.

And there were at least five Jewish versions of how the Devil Baby came to be born, including:

- The youngest daughter of a very pious Jewish family supposedly married a gentile *without* her parents' approval or knowledge. When her father heard of the girl's marriage, he exploded in a rage—"I would rather have the Devil as a grandchild than a gentile as a son-in-law!" That indiscreet remark came to pass, for his daughter soon gave birth to the Devil child. The horrible offspring was deposited at Hull House since the young mother had been attending classes there.
- Two young women had gone to see the play "Faust" shortly before one of them was due to give birth. A neighbor of one of the women reported that the

pregnant woman had looked too intensely at the "stage" devil, thereby adversely affecting her offspring. Sure enough, her newborn infant was the spitting image of Mephistopholes. A visiting nurse, assigned to look after the unwed mother, took the demonic child to Hull House.

Orthodox Jewish belief was at the center of another version of the Devil Baby tale, as it relates to the tradition of *pinyin ha-ben*. This held that when a first son is born, the child must be redeemed by its parents' paying a fee to the rabbi one month following the boy's birth. Allegedly, a young Jewish mother had been asked if her offspring was indeed her first child. The woman said yes, hiding the fact that she had given birth out of wedlock some years earlier. For that sin, she paid dearly—her next child was Satan.

What caused such a bizarre story to gain credence in the ethnic neighborhoods of Chicago? How could sensible people believe that a Devil Baby actually existed?

Part of the answer can be found in an appreciation of the lives of the immigrant matrons who fervently believed and passed on the tale. Surrounded as they were by a foreign culture, these women clung tenaciously to the ways of the Old World. Miracles, curses and the supernatural were considered possible in the cultures they brought with them to America.

The existence of a Devil Baby, for example, seemed perfectly normal to these women whose family, home, religion, traditions and superstitions were the cornerstone of their lives. If a woman questioned the teachings of her elders, dared to marry outside her religion or station in life, or in any way disrupted the pattern of behavior expected of her, the penalties were harsh.

Jane Addams, the founder of Hull House, understood what motivated these women. She wrote of the Devil Baby uproar:

"During the weeks of excitement . . . it was the old women who really seemed to have come into their own, and perhaps the most significant result of the incident was thc rcaction of the story upon them. It stirred their minds and memory as with a magic touch, it loosened their tongues and revealed the inner life and thoughts of those who are so often inarticulate. They are accustomed to sit at home and to hear the younger members of the family speak of affairs quite outside their own experiences in a language they do not understand."

To the hundreds who made their way to Hull House, the pilgrimage may have been the one great adventure in their lives. They took no part in the life of the city, rarely venturing farther than their local church or synagogue. They were sequestered in a way difficult for present generations to comprehend.

Day after day, sometimes with their own children in tow, the women trudged up the steps to Hull House, inquiring about the Devil Baby. They all had heard a version of its birth.

One old woman from the city's poorhouse likewise had heard the tale. At nights she lay awake under a thin wool blanket thinking but one thought—somehow she must get to Hull House to see this child. Although she was badly crippled, and penniless, she knew a kindly bartender in a tavern across the street who could help her. One morning she hobbled to the saloon and asked for a dime so that she could visit Hull House and see the mysterious child. In return, she promised to deliver a full description of its hideous features to the bartender.

She got her dime and the bartender and the streetcar conductor lifted her aboard the trolley. At Hull House, the woman nearly collapsed from exhaustion.

She told the receptionist of her mission. She explained
that her own grandmother had been able to see into the
future. Furthermore, she herself had correctly predicted
the deaths of several members of her own family.

The old woman's eyes shone. If she could only see
this child, she insisted, she would be able to narrate
perfectly the circumstances surrounding its birth.

The kindly workers at Hull House postponed telling
her the truth for as long as possible. The old woman
seemed to be brought to a plane of joy she had probably
never before experienced. The thought that she might be
able to provide insight into the reasons for the Devil
Baby's appearance seemed to give her a reason to live.

Tea and cakes were served while she rattled off her
numerous reasons for wanting to see the child. At last,
she was told the truth.

The poor soul seemed to shrivel, a destitute and
forlorn old lady living only through the graces of the
city's charity.

Who started the rumor of the Devil Baby?

No one knows.

Was there ever any basis for the story?

Probably not. Perhaps a child had been born with
some horrible birth defect and taken to Hull House for
care. If so, there is no record to indicate who the child
was or whatever became of him or her.

Despite the lack of evidence, however, for a month
and a half in the spring of 1913, a Devil Baby did exist
at Hull House—if only in the fertile imagination of the
old, the superstitious and the lonely.

THE TELLTALE HAND

Each city in America has its tales of heroic firefighters,
public servants whose lives are often sacrificed to protect
the public they serve. Chicago is no different. The files

of the Chicago Fire Department are filled with the names of those who have died in the line of duty, and of the fires which have claimed them.

Of course, every American school child knows of Mrs. O'Leary and her errant, lantern-kicking cow whose actions triggered the conflagration which nearly destroyed the city. But one of the strangest cases in Chicago fire history does not concern a particularly spectacular or long-remembered fire. Although there was a tragic loss of ten lives, including eight firemen, the events which unfolded *after* the fire make the story chilling.

Francis X. Leavy ... Frank to his fellow firefighters ... seemed melancholy, preoccupied, as he raised the soapy rag to clean the winter's dirt from another window in the firehouse at 13th and Oakley. It was Good Friday, April 18, 1924. Leavy was scheduled to work that day and Easter, according to a recently-posted work schedule. Leavy was a thirteen-year veteran of the force, dedicated to his profession, but disturbed by being away from his wife Mary and young children, June and Frank. They would understand, of course, but that didn't assuage Leavy's gloom as he struggled to concentrate on cleaning the windows in the firehouse.

The cold winter and late spring had taken its toll on the spirits of the men at Engine Company 107 and Truck Company 12. They were thankful that on this day they could leave the large, red doors of the firehouse open as they went about spring housecleaning.

Leavy's friend, Edward McKevitt, was concerned about his comrade's dour expression. He walked over to Leavy. Was there a problem? he asked. Leavy's shoulders sagged. "This is my last day on the fire department," he replied. The soapy palm of his left hand rested on the window glass while he continued to wipe at the window with the wet cloth in his other hand.

McKevitt was surprised. Earlier that morning, Leavy seemed happy and content, talking about his future plans. Whether it was working on the Easter holiday, or concern about a big fire spreading in the Union Stockyards, McKevitt didn't know.

For several hours a ticker-tape type device—the "big joker" it was termed—had been rat-a-tat-tatting messages to the company about the four-alarm stockyard blaze. The machine was the firehouse's link with other firehouses. The stockyard's fire was extremely serious. Leavy's company was far enough away not to have been called, but if the fire grew any worse they might have to respond. And, worse yet, if a blaze erupted in another part of the city, Leavy's company might not be able to count on back-up support because of the large number of units already fighting the stockyard blaze.

Suddenly, the "big joker" clicked out a message from alarm box 372, nearly two miles across the city. Several minutes later, Engine Company 107 and Truck Company 12 were ordered to report to a fire at Curran Hall, an imposing four-story brick and stone edifice southwest of the Loop.

Frank Leavy, Edward McKevitt and their fellow firefighters clambered aboard the pumper and truck for the harrowing ride through congested streets to the fire. There were few traffic lights in 1924; intersections were scenes of impossible congestion. Street cars, horse-drawn wagons, automobiles and pedestrians all vied for the right-of-way. The screaming fire engines left a trail of bewildered citizenry and frightened horses.

Curran Hall was engulfed in flames. The building housed a number of small businesses. The heaviest smoke seemed to be pouring from the upper floors.

Truck 12's crew was ordered onto the roof to chop a hole to ventilate the upper floor. Firefighters could then reach the center of the fire.

Frank Leavy and the men on Engine 107 were told to make their way to the second floor. On their hands and knees, the men groped their way up to a stairwell through the choking smoke. There were no oxygen masks in those days. The men coughed and vomited all the way. Once they reached the second floor, the men had to take turns going out onto the fire escape for fresh air.

The minutes passed slowly. It seemed the firefighters were gaining the advantage over the flames. Suddenly, a cry rang out, "Get out! Get out!"

Supervisors on the ground saw what the men inside could not—the outside wall was crumbling. Leavy and the others scrambled to the fire escapes and started down. But it was too late. The wall caved in with a sickening crunch like a giant roll of thunder.

Hoses split, sending streams of water exploding in all directions. Ladders snapped in two, like so many matchsticks, and firefighting equipment was buried under an avalanche of bricks and mortar. And the frantic firefighters making their way to safety disappeared under the lethal shower of building materials.

Frank Leavy never had a chance. He was only partway down the fire escape when the wall collapsed. Hours later the bodies of eight firefighters were pulled from the rubble. While almost all the firemen-victims were battered beyond recognition, the face of Frank Leavy was the only one recognizable among the fatalities.

The next day, Holy Saturday, Edward McKevitt slumped in his chair as he tried to explain to his fellow firefighters what had happened the day before. It was not easy—eight of his cohorts were dead; twenty other firefighters were injured, two critically. And yet, McKevitt found himself the most troubled by Frank Leavy's premonition of death—"This is my last day on the fire department."

As McKevitt glanced around the fire station, trying to understand the senseless events, his gaze rested on the window Leavy had been washing the day before. His eyes focused on what seemed to be a blemish on the window. He rose and looked closely at it . . . the unmistakable outline of a man's hand, Frank Leavy's hand! McKevitt clearly remembered Leavy resting his palm against it as he wiped the window less than twenty-four hours earlier!

"My God! It's Leavy's hand," McKevitt muttered, almost to himself. The men who had been listening to McKevitt gathered around the strange impression.

McKevitt told them of how he had seen Leavy place his left hand in that very spot only the day before. The image which remained on the glass was that of a left hand, its fingers outstretched, just the type of mark that would have been made by a hand drenched in water and soapy suds.

McKevitt rubbed at the window with a sponge from the bucket Leavy had been using. The mark would not go away. The harder McKevitt wiped, the more obvious it became that Leavy's handprint would not go away. Other men tried to wipe it off. They all failed. Ammonia, strong soaps, and even a razor blade failed to dislodge the image. One firefighter went outside, thinking the print was not on the inside of the window. His intense scrubbing was futile.

By early the following week, the story of the firehouse at 13th and Oakley and its mysterious handprint had spread through the city, fueled by several newspaper stories. Soon, other firefighters, newspaper reporters, neighbors and curiosity seekers showed up at the station's big red doors for a look at Leavy's handprint.

An expert from the Pittsburgh Plate Glass Company, the manufacturers of the window, was called in to solve the problem. He used a special, highly reliable chemical compound to clean the window. But Leavy's handprint remained.

A city official compared a copy of Leavy's thumbprint to the thumb mark on the window. He said that they matched!

As the weeks and months passed, a steady stream of the curious continued to show up at the fire station. Firefighters regularly washed the windows, including Leavy's handprint, knowing full well that the image would not go away. Suggestions were periodically made to replace the glass, but the firefighters usually objected, saying it wasn't right to tamper with the "unknown."

Over the years, the firehouse at 13th and Oakley saw dozens of firefighters stay within its walls, and then go on to other assignments. Leavy's handprint always remained. It was the custom for older firemen to tell the story of Frank Leavy to the new men. Newspaper reports occasionally resurrected the oddity, bringing a new horde of curiosity seekers.

Curiously, Frank Leavy's widow, Mary, and his children never came to look at the handprint, even though Frank, Jr. followed in his dad's footsteps and became a fireman on April 18, 1945 . . . the twenty-first anniversary of his father's death!

Did the window pane actually contain Leavy's ghostly handprint? Or, was the image a defect in the glass which, when viewed from certain angles, resembled a man's hand?

It is impossible to answer those questions today. However, there is no evidence to suggest that the defect was ever noticed until *after* Frank Leavy's tragic death.

Some firemen were convinced the print was supernatural. Others suggested that Leavy's frightening premonition of death caused a bodily chemical to mix with his perspiration causing the indelible stain. No one has ever satisfactorily explained what caused the grim legacy of a dead fireman.

And what happened to the window with Frank Leavy's handprint? That is perhaps strangest of all. On April 18, 1944 . . . twenty years *to the date* on which Leavy died . . . a newspaper boy threw a rolled-up newspaper toward the firehouse. The missile struck Leavy's window, shattering it into thousands of pieces.

RED ROSE

Newspaper reporters are usually tough characters not given to hysteria or a belief in things supernatural. Objectivity is the cornerstone of their profession, a world of hard information supported by physical evidence.

Ann Marsters was just that kind of reporter. She worked for the old *Chicago American*, one of William Randolph Hearst's newspapers. Before that, she was a pioneer woman sportswriter for Hearst's *Boston American*. Marsters was not gullible. She had met too many press agents, charlatans and phonies in her career as a newspaperwoman to be taken in by fraud.

That's why she was assigned to write a series of articles on Lily Dale, the famed home of the American Spiritualist Movement, in New York state. The year was 1942. Interest in life-after-death, the heart of the spiritualist's belief, was heightened by World War II—whenever mass death occurs, particularly in time of war, newspapers and other periodicals scramble to find what belief there may be in the "hereafter."

What Ann Marsters found in Lily Dale would change forever her belief in such things as spirits and ghosts. And the proof would occur in the busy city room of the *Chicago American*.

Back in the mid-nineteenth century, the Fox sisters—Margaretta, Catherine and Katie—purported to be able to communicate with a spirit in their Hydesville, New York home. They called him Mr. Splitfoot, the spirit of a peddler who had been murdered and buried in the basement by the previous occupants of the house.

The girls claimed they could communicate with him through a series of rappings. Katie, eleven years old in

1847, worked out a code for talking with her mysterious "friend."

Over a period of time other manifestations of the haunting occurred. Furniture moved unassisted across the floors, beds rocked and doors slammed shut by themselves. In the most grisly scenario of all, the murder of the peddler was re-enacted, replete with screams, falling bodies and the sound of a corpse being dragged down the basement stairs.

The eldest daughter, Catherine, decided to exploit the mysterious hauntings and the belief in spiritualism was born.

Was there ever any proof to support the claim that a murder was committed in the Hydesville house? During their lifetimes the girls were subjected to a good deal of ridicule. Their claims were consistently debunked by scientists and, later, by magicians who said they could duplicate the mysterious sounds. Yet, in 1904, the *Rochester Democrat and Chronicle* trumpeted in a front-page story the discovery of a body, or the bones of one at any rate, beneath the foundation of the Fox sisters' old house.

Rain had weakened one of the basement's stone walls. Sections of the granite had fallen away, revealing a false wall. In the space between the false wall and the original foundation a human skeleton was found. It may have been that of the murdered peddler.

The girls' followers were not shaken when it was revealed that many of the so-called rappings had been caused by their cracking the joints in their big toes. The re-enactment of the peddler's death, and some of the rappings, were still unexplained, the devoted maintained.

The Fox sisters' Hydesville home was eventually moved to Lily Dale, a town situated in north-central Chautauqua County near Lake Erie, southwest of Buffalo. During the winter, the village's population numbered fewer than 300 persons, but as many as 2,000 persons came each summer to study spiritualism at Lily Dale, the mecca of the spiritualist movement.

So it was that in the summer of 1942 Ann Marsters was given the opportunity to investigate Lily Dale, then at its zenith as a spiritualist center. Her assignment was to interview Ralph Pressing, the editor of the spiritualist newspaper, *Psychic Observer*, and to sit in on some séances.

Could the spiritualists in Lily Dale really communicate with the dead? Ann Marsters' editors back in Chicago said the world awaited her answer.

As a good reporter, Marsters "went to Lily Dale with an open mind—not to write an exposé but to give an honest account of what I saw and heard. And I took along a staff photographer to make a pictorial record of my experiences," she later recalled.

What Marsters saw was a mixture of obvious sham and truly puzzling occurrences. She visited various sessions, all conducted as "experiments" in spirit communication, yet transacted in darkened rooms which made examinations for hidden gadgetry extremely difficult. From table rappings to trumpets floating through the air emitting disembodied voices to "materializations" of ghosts, the reporter witnessed many strange events. She dismissed some of them outright, but others raised questions in her mind. Could any of the communications be genuine? In some of the sessions, Marsters was addressed by voices from various deceased loved ones. She doubted if the voices were from the dead, and certainly not from her relatives.

But then Ann Marsters met Red Rose, an Indian spirit. The two became acquainted during a séance led by Ann Taylor, one of the better-known mediums at Lily Dale. Red Rose was Marsters' "spirit guide," a kind of helper from "the Beyond" assigned to assist Ann in contacting other spirits so they, too, might communicate with the living.

In a mixture of pidgin English and contemporary slang, Red Rose talked to the audience. At one particular session, Red Rose suddenly told Marsters, "You put a safety pin in the lining of your coat. Lazy!"

Marsters was flabbergasted. She had found a tear in her coat a few minutes before leaving her hotel room for the séance and didn't have time to mend it. Instead, she temporarily fixed the split with the safety pin. No one had seen her repair the coat . . . except perhaps Red Rose? The experience nagged at Marsters' hardened objectivity for days to come.

After she returned to Chicago a few days later, Marsters had a series of seven articles about Lily Dale to complete. She decided against including her own experience with Red Rose, fearing her editor would delete it. Too unbelievable.

Marsters did her writing at home. She completed her first article on a Friday and a copy boy came to collect the original manuscript and a carbon copy.

"Be sure to deliver these to the Sunday editor in person!" Marsters emphasized. Her series was due to begin on Sunday. A heavy advertising campaign was underway to promote her findings about life-after-death.

On Saturday her editor phoned. She was late with her copy for Sunday. Where was the first article? he demanded.

Marsters couldn't believe she had heard him correctly. Surely he had received the article yesterday from the copy boy. Marsters even identified the youngster by name. No, her editor said. He hadn't seen the story.

The editor interrogated the boy, short of giving him the "third-degree." The distraught youngster clearly remembered collecting the copy from the reporter, but had absolutely no knowledge of what he did with it afterward! Nothing succeeded in jogging his memory.

The editor phoned back. Marsters would have to rewrite the story. She wailed in rebuff. There was no way she could remember the story line-for-line and, besides, there was hardly time to finish the piece for Sunday. The deadline was only a few hours away.

Marsters decided instead to go to the newsroom herself in the belief she could determine what had happened to the manuscript.

She stood at the editor's desk in a state of absolute panic. What to do? Then she remembered Red Rose. Surely if the little spirit had found a safety pin in her coat she might be able to help the reporter find the missing manuscript.

"Oh, Red Rose, please try to help me!" Marsters silently pleaded.

And then, without conscious deliberation, Marsters walked across the busy city room to a table next to the pay telephone. She opened one of the phone books. Inside was the missing manuscript!

Ann Marsters never could explain or remember the reason why she went to that telephone directory in the *Chicago American* newsroom that day. And Lily Dale remains to this day the center of the American Spiritualist Church, descended upon each summer by thousands of people anxious to attend group séances, private psychic readings and demonstrations of psychic healing. Perhaps somewhere within that 172-acre village there dwells the spirit of Ann Marsters' "guide," Red Rose.

Of all the ghosts in this chapter, only Resurrection Mary still walks the Chicago streets. The rest have made brief appearances and then gone on to their permanent home, wherever that may be. They are all ordinary specters, if that is the right phrase, since they don't include among their numbers any of Chicago's more prominent, departed citizens. It's not that the shades of the mighty don't linger along Michigan Avenue or Maxwell Street, only that they haven't been seen . . . yet.

A Temperate Ghost Story

The founder of the Women's Christian Temperance Union (WCTU), Frances E. Willard, is remembered as an outspoken foe of alcohol and a champion of women's rights. Not at all the sort of person to believe in such things as ghosts. Until her death in 1898, however, Miss Willard related the following eerie story to anyone who ever brought up the subject of hauntings:

Belle Milner was a friend of the Willard family who had contracted a racking cough, possibly tuberculosis, in mid-1880. For nearly a year she suffered its debilitating effects before her doctors told her that she must move from smoggy Waukegan, Illinois, to the drier, cleaner climate of the American Southwest or else face certain death.

On a humid morning in the late summer of 1881, Belle Milner carefully packed her trunks in the bedroom of her family's modest home. She studied each artifact in the tidy room before she wrapped it and packed it away for the long train trip west. The hot sun filtered through the drawn drapes and fell across the hardwood floors. Those curious specks called dust angels floated about the room as she emptied a closet.

Belle was desperately weak. Any sustained effort made her cough, so that by midmorning she was slumped in an armchair next to the bed.

The street noises seemed to recede as she closed her eyes. A slight rustling sound and the momentary darkening of the sunlight seeping around the corners of the drapes made her sit up. Belle turned to face the window. The figure of Mary Willard, Frances Willard's sister, stared back.

Mary was wearing a light, salmon-colored dress. Her auburn hair, brushed low over her forehead, shimmered as sprays of sunlight fell across her face. She was as Belle had last seen her in 1862! She couldn't help but think that Mary looked as bright and as cheery as she had when the girls had last shared a schoolgirl confidence two decades before.

Strangely, no words passed between the women. Belle was never sure just how long Mary Willard had "visited" her, but she estimated it was at least ten minutes. Belle sensed that Mary had "stopped by" to say farewell and comfort her friend. Belle knew that the Southwest held her only salvation, yet she was leaving her family and friends for what was then still referred to as the "Wild West." Although nothing was spoken, Belle understood that Mary was trying to tell her, "Go ahead. Your health is all that matters. Don't think of the past. Look to the future."

At length, the shadowy figure of Mary Willard faded away, as if a light were being dimmed until it was extinguished, Belle later recalled.

Belle Milner briefly related parts of the story to only a few close acquaintances, but not even Frances Willard could ever pry all the details from her.

And no wonder. Mary Willard had died nearly nineteen years before she "visited" Belle Milner! Yet her message was for naught—the arid desert proved a tragically short respite for Belle who died just two years after her move from Waukegan.

THE OLD SLAVE HOUSE

David Rodgers was grateful to have escaped the imposing southern mansion that morning before Halloween in 1978.

It had been a long night for the young man from Harrisburg. He had become the first person to successfully challenge the ghosts of black slaves that haunt the dismal attic of the Old Slave House built, ironically, near Equality, Illinois.

With the consent of the house's owner, George M. Sisk II, Rodgers had entered the attic at eight o'clock the previous evening. Although he heard a lot of strange noises, Rodgers did not encounter any of the spectral forms that had caused at least 150 previous ghost-challengers to flee the former slave quarters on the mansion's third floor. Rodgers walked out of the house just after daybreak the following morning.

David Rodgers had heard the tales connected with the place—about the rushing forms and horrific screams that had driven two tough Marine veterans from the house in 1966; of how the air chilled as a visitor moved up the narrow, steep staircase to the third floor; and of how the wife of the owner saw vague forms disappear just beyond her range of vision.

But Rodgers also saw a good story. He was a television reporter for WSIL-TV in Harrisburg. During an earlier program, he had challenged Sisk to allow him to spend the night in the attic. After some hesitation Sisk agreed. Both men knew that no one except a slave had ever survived a night on that infamous third floor where men, women and children had been held in bondage by one of Illinois' most evil citizens.

John Hart Crenshaw, who built Hickory Hill, came from a fine old American family, but his sense of decency became perverted in his rush for wealth. His parents moved to Gallatin County after their home in New Madrid, Missouri, was destroyed in the great earthquake of 1811. The Crenshaws settled on Eagle Creek, near one of the many salt deposits prevalent in that area near the Saline River. John's father, William, died when the boy was a teenager, leaving him to support his mother and six siblings. John went to work in the salt refinery. It was hard, backbreaking work that caused the young man to grow sullen and resentful. He had, however, no other options . . . not then.

But some time after John Crenshaw's marriage to Sinia Taylor in 1817, his life began to change. Because Illinois prohibited slavery and encouraged each man to gain an independent living, it became increasingly difficult to hire laborers, especially for the salt works. The government, recognizing this fact, permitted employers to lease slaves from owners in slave territory and bring them to Illinois to work.

Crenshaw quickly saw his opportunity to become a wealthy man—he would become an employer. He leased several salt springs from the government and received permission to lease slaves from owners in Kentucky and Tennessee to work them.

By 1834, John Crenshaw had amassed a fortune. He owned three furnaces used in reducing salt water to crystals, a mill on the North Fork of the Saline River and nearly 30,000 acres of land. Now he could afford to give his wife the home of her dreams. Before the year was out, Crenshaw had begun construction of Hickory Hill. As the house took shape on a high, wind-swept hill near Equality, the owner's lust for money and power grew. When the house was completed four years later, in 1838, Crenshaw began kidnapping free black men and women. Some were destined to work for him in the salt works or in the fields; others would be sold into slavery.

Some historians say the house was carefully planned with this aim in mind. From the outside it appears to be of pseudo-Greek revival design with upper and lower verandas supported by massive columns, extending the width of the house. Not readily seen are the peculiar innovations, such as a carriageway that actually enters the house. Black men, women and children were said to have been brought into the house in carriages and then hustled up the back staircase to be imprisoned in cold, dark attic cells scarcely larger than horse stalls. This arrangement precluded curious neighbors and visitors from learning the true purpose of the house.

Another legend maintains that a secret passageway once connected the house to a nearby creek. Slaves would be brought up the Ohio River by boat to the Saline River. They would be transferred to smaller craft on the Saline, moved upriver by night to a point near Hickory Hill and then brought through the secret passage into the house.

But Crenshaw could not amass slaves fast enough. He soon began a breeding program that provided him with additional slaves to sell on the southern market. A pregnant woman, or one with a child, brought several hundred dollars more than a single slave.

"Uncle Bob," a giant of a black man, was chosen for his stamina and virility to sire the children. Confined as he was in a barren and unheated cell only slightly larger than the tiny cells in which other slaves were kept, he serviced frightened young female slaves who were brought to him. He supposedly fathered 300 babies!

The cells opened off both sides of the hallway twelve feet wide and fifty feet long. Each cell had a narrow doorway and a window with bars across it. The window overlooked the hall, the only ventilation coming from windows in the front and rear gables of the house. Iron rings attached to the floor secured the imprisoned slaves. Today, the rings are gone, but pieces of chains, shackles and a whipping post remain to bear testimony to the cruelties inflicted upon helpless men and women in this attic torture chamber where many were born and many died.

In 1842, Crenshaw was accused of selling into slavery a family of free blacks who owed him services. He went to trial, but was not convicted, possibly because of his financial and political eminence. But public sentiment went against him; his mill was burned.

John Hart Crenshaw died in 1871, and his wife, Sinia, ten years later. They are buried in Hickory Hill cemetery. Their deaths brought to an end a most shameful era in Illinois history.

Today, thousands of visitors tour Hickory Hill which, since Crenshaw's death, is almost always called the Old Slave House. Owner George Sisk II and his wife, Janice, operate it as a museum and tourist attraction. It is also their home. The house has been in the Sisk family for nearly eighty years. George and his wife have restored the outside and the first and second floors as their living quarters. They do not go up to the attic, but visitors do. They see remnants of the hideous cells, various instruments of torture and scarred markings on the wooden framework where cell doors once hung. One window remains barred. Some tourists return ashen-faced to report that they heard shuffling feet and whimpering cries; most feel uneasy.

They all want to know if Sisk believes that the house *is* haunted. Yes, he thinks it is. He claims that he does *not* believe in ghosts, but he respects them.

In the late 1920s the Benton, Illinois *Post-Dispatch* featured a story on the Old Slave House written by an exorcist named Hickman Whittington. Whittington was supposedly in splendid health when he visited the attic of the house. A few hours later he was dead.

George Sisk told psychic investigators Richard Winer and Nancy Osborn Ishmael that he believes that Whittington died of fright, that something in Hickory Hill scared him to death. What was it?

Sisk doesn't know. Perhaps it was the same thing that terrified the two Marines thirty-five years later. They were sitting in the attic at one o'clock in the morning when suddenly a kerosene lantern—their only source of light—began to flicker. A terrible moan shook the walls. Voices came from everywhere—human voices speaking unintelligible words. Swirling forms bore down upon the Marines. The light went out and from the darkness came bloodcurdling screams. In a panic they had never experienced in battle, the servicemen leaped down the stairs.

Mrs. Sisk understands that panic. She will not stay alone in the house. She was so frightened of the place in the early years of her marriage that she temporarily left her husband. And she had to quit taking baths in the evening because a voice would yell, "Janice!" She'd hurry from the bathroom, but no one was ever there. Mrs. Sisk still complains of the icy chill that pervades the rooms, even on warm days. And she and her husband both feel they're being constantly observed.

The house, from its hilltop position, is buffeted by winds. Is it just the wind rattling the windows and whipping under the eaves that creates a "presence?" Or do the voices of those doomed slaves still cry out in anguish? And why was David Rodgers, the television reporter, the only one to withstand their lamentations?

HATTIE'S PLAYMATE

Little Hattie Bennett was only twelve years old when her "friend," a girl her own age, brought notoriety to her family on the outskirts of East St. Louis in 1870.

Hattie's pal dressed in a simple blue merino dress trimmed with fur. Her shoulders were always covered with a cloak, even on the hottest of summer days. A bonnet was drawn tightly around her light brown curly hair, allowing just a hint of cascading ringlets to frame her cherubic face.

The girls talked often, sharing the confidences and guarded secrets so common in children of that age.

There was only one problem. Hattie's playmate was a ghost.

Just when the mysterious child first moved into the Bennett house is unclear. Vital Bennett, his wife Julia and their children, including Hattie, the youngest, lived on the old Belleville Road, about two miles from East St. Louis. The simple frame home contained just two downstairs rooms, a combination kitchen and living area and a separate bedroom. A loft, reached by a narrow, rough-hewn ladder, served as the children's bedroom.

A child often conjures up some invisible playmate to help pass the lonely hours when parents and older brothers and sisters have little time for her. But rarely do these imagined companions speak or cavort around the house on their own. Hattie's friend was different; among other things she was mischievous—she would yank coats and caps from wall pegs and toss them to the ground, only to replace them later. She scratched in the loft, as if her fingers were running across the rough plaster. And sometimes she could be heard, her disconcerting "voice" drifting through the small home, at times barely audible, while on other occasions it resounded clearly. The disembodied voice could also answer questions with the tone and syntax of a child. Sometimes it carried on a dialogue with visitors. At other times only Hattie could hear her speak.

The story of the ghost on Belleville Road soon spread beyond the Bennett household. A Catholic priest, one Father Zabel of the "Catholic Institute," expressed the firm opinion, after a visit, that whatever was present in the house was an "evil spirit."

A reporter for one St. Louis newspaper, drawn to the house in the hope of uncovering some trickery for his readers, came away so distraught and unnerved that he could only furnish his editors with a "disjointed memoranda" of the visit.

The mayor of East St. Louis, Col. Jarrolt, journeyed to the house with a group of businessmen and offered the only written account of the haunting. Part of his diary excerpt follows:

"Taking a seat in the neatly furnished parlor, and feeling ourselves at home, we laid our things outside and hung our outer garments on a nail. Engaged for a moment, we turned around, and our garments had disappeared. What had become of them? No one could tell; only they were gone.

"Entering into a conversation with 'the spirit,' we were told who we were, where we came from, and what our business was. Little Hattie, the child of Mr. Bennett, is the only person who can see the wonderful specter, whom she defines as being a child about twelve years of age . . .

"Clothes, articles of furniture, barrels of flour, and in fact, every movable object within the house had been moved from its position. Doors are opened, unhung and removed; lights blown out are relighted and garments on the family are repeatedly pulled."

Over the course of the year, Hattie's playmate made numerous forays about the house, often in the presence of visitors who trekked out from the city to witness the "wonderful specter."

There is no written record of any formal investigation of the phenomena, nor of when the ghost child finally took her leave. The identity of the mysterious visitor forever remained a secret.

Was little Hattie playing these tricks? Or, perhaps, was one of the other children?

Whether Hattie's playmate was a product of her own imagination, a trick played on unsuspecting adults by the children, or a genuine ghost, one thing is certain—she added the Bennett family name to the odd history of American hauntings.

GHOST STORIES FROM ADAMS COUNTY

The most ambitious chronicler of regional Illinois folklore was Harry Middleton Hyatt, a history professor at Culver-Stockton College in Canton, Missouri. Hyatt spent decades collecting oral legends from the people of Adams County, Illinois, and the ghost stories he compiled are timeless. Most of the tales are anonymous, yet they all provide insight into the kinds of legends passed down through the generations.

Quincy, the Adams County seat, sits on the Mississippi River directly across from northeast Missouri. Although Missouri was ostensibly a part of the Union during most of the Civil War, Southern sympathies were common, particularly among those people whose ancestors had migrated to northern Missouri from the South prior to the outbreak of the War. Thus, Quincy was often the unwilling host to rebel soldiers and sympathizers during the Civil War.

One such house that legend says harbored Southern soldiers was located at Second and Vermont streets in Quincy. It was known for decades after the War as the "Old Rebel House" and it had the reputation for being haunted.

One particular story about the house centers upon a family who lived in it during the 1880s. A mother and three children were occupying the top floor, while the woman's married daughter and son-in-law were living downstairs. A long veranda stretched the length of the second floor on the house's east side with doors opening onto the porch from nearly every room.

One day, the mother left the house for work and, as was her custom, locked all the doors going onto the porch. The only way into or out of her apartment was through the downstairs apartment. No sooner had she left than her eldest son and youngest daughter fell to arguing over who would rock their baby brother's cradle. Suddenly, a door going onto the porch opened. Both of the children looked up to see a man.

"It looked like the devil to us," the girl recalled years later. "The man looked just like the picture you see of the devil. We just stood there and stared."

The specter lurched over to the banister of the stairs going down to their sister's apartment. Their mother had hung several handmade quilts over the banister and the "devil" proceeded to take the quilts and throw them to the floor. He then picked them up and repositioned them on the hand railing. Next the mysterious visitor turned toward the children, but, before reaching them, he abruptly changed direction and exited through the door he had come in.

The children began to holler, bringing their sister rushing up the stairs. They explained what had happened and pointed to the door through which the "devil" had made his entrance and exit. The sister found the door locked. She then gave the children a sound spanking.

After their mother returned, the children repeated the tale and again it was disbelieved. Another spanking followed.

Nevertheless, the two children steadfastly clung to their story that the "devil" had visited the "Old Rebel House" until the day they died. There are many people in that part of the country who still believe the children's story.

Another Quincy building, Madison School, and its location possess a history of mysterious occurrences. Years before the school was built at Twenty-sixth and Maine streets, a house stood on that location and, supposedly, a woman was murdered there. The killers, whose identities were never discovered, apparently grabbed the woman at the top of a staircase, dragged her screaming down the steps, and stabbed her until her cries were stilled. A trail of blood snaked across the oak floors as they dragged her lifeless form into a closet beneath the staircase.

Families who later lived in the house could never get the blood off the floor. They finally resorted to covering the crimson stains with rugs. No one ever used the closet.

One family claimed they constantly heard the sound of something traveling up and down the stairs; they said that it sounded like a dog. Allegedly, the murdered woman owned a bulldog who accompanied her everywhere. Also, doors on the east side of the house unexpectedly flew open, even if they were locked.

Eventually, the house was torn down to make way for Madison School. But it seems likely that the strange occurrences have not ceased—the school nearly burned to the ground in 1982 during a fire whose origin has never been established!

Burton Cave, set about four miles east of Quincy, has been a popular spot for area picnickers for well over a century. And while today fewer groups find their way to the cavern, not many of the visitors realize that Burton Cave is the subject of a most curious legend.

The story takes place in the mid-1880s, when a group of young people from Quincy, intent on a leisurely Sunday picnic and an afternoon's exploration of Burton Cave, lounged in a shaded meadow not far from the cave's entrance. A thunderstorm cut short their picnic, however, and their cave exploration began earlier than expected.

The suddenly blackened sky made the soggy passage toward the cave difficult. A few persons had candles cupped in their hands, using the light to avoid becoming entangled in exposed tree roots.

A few yards from the cave, the group was startled to see a dark-robed figure spring from the cave and scurry away. The quick glimpse provided little clue to the person's identity, especially since a hood covered his head, shielding his face. Likewise, long sleeves extended over his hands, and the hem of the gown dragged on the ground.

The picnickers cautiously moved forward, deciding that the fleeting stranger was less of a danger than the wild storm raging outside.

Inside the cave, the group paused. None had ever been in the cave before. From somewhere there emerged a faint glow. The source seemed to be a ledge several yards away. They walked on. The prone figure of a woman, garbed completely in white, was laid out as if prepared for a funeral. Candles burned near her head and feet. She seemed to be lifeless. The suddenly silent band of picnickers quickly retreated, streaming out of the cave and running toward their wagons.

Later, the county sheriff, several deputies and two members of the picnic group returned to the cave. But no trace of a body could be found. Indeed, it seemed as if no one, save the frightened group of young people, had been in Burton Cave for a very long time.

The identity of the "dead" woman, the fleeing figure in black and the reason for the strange bier have remained mysteries, tucked away forever in the darkness of Burton Cave.

The young family was tired that morning as it approached the abandoned cabin near Kingston, Illinois. The road was dusty and the mules pulling the wagon full of the family's meager possessions needed rest.

"We'll stay here for a time," the father said, nodding toward the sturdy dwelling. His wife readily agreed.

"Maybe I can find some work at that farm down the road," he continued.

He unhitched the team as his wife carried their sleeping infant into the house. The place needed a thorough cleaning, but at least it had a roof and a solid floor. After they had unloaded what they would need that night, the man told his wife he would go to the spring nearby and get water for them and the horses.

No sooner had he begun to fill the buckets than he heard a scream from the cabin. He rushed back to find his wife in the yard, clutching the startled baby.

"This house is haunted!" she stammered. "Just as soon as we got in the house, an old ghost with a cane came in the door. He walked around us, then went out the door."

Her husband was not impressed. "You just imagined it."

He went back into the cabin with his trembling young wife. A complete search failed to locate any other person.

After lunch was over, the father left to look for work.

"That is my house," the farmer who lived next door said when the young man told him that he needed work and would like to stay in the cabin. "If you'll stay five years, I'll deed you the house. But," he added ominously, "no one stays there more than one night. You come back in the morning if you still want work."

Meanwhile, the ghostly old man was paying another visit to the cabin. As before, he seemed to materialize in the main room and walked around and around. When the woman started crying, however, he seemed disturbed. The ghost stopped his pacing and spoke, "Don't be afraid, I'll not harm you." With that, he vanished.

Upon her husband's return, the young wife insisted that they must leave. Although he had been given a hint that the place was haunted, the husband persuaded his wife that it *could* have been her imagination. They stayed the night and nothing further happened.

Early the next morning, after her husband had left for work and the morning dishes were put away, the ghostly old man returned.

"Lady, I will not hurt you. I'm here for a reason," he intoned. The woman cowered in a corner with her child clutched to her bosom. "I have come to do you good," he continued. "My wife and I were murdered here for our money. Only they did not get it. I want you and your husband to do three things for me. We are buried out there in a cave. I want you to dig us up and bury us in the graveyard on the hill and mark the place."

With that he led the terrified woman into the cellar and marked a spot on the dirt floor. "Dig here and you will find some money."

He motioned her to follow him outside. At the southeast corner of the house he made a mark on the ground. "And here you will find more money and the deed to this house. It is yours if you do what I tell you. Do you see that cave over there? That is where we are."

With that the specter vanished.

By now the woman's terror had faded, having been replaced by overwhelming curiosity. She took a shovel into the basement and began to dig. A few inches below the dirt floor, she uncovered a pitcher full of money.

She dusted off the ancient container and put it on a shelf. There was more money inside than she had ever seen before.

"I've made more money than you today," she announced proudly when her husband returned that afternoon. The story of the man's mysterious visit unfolded. The couple dug into the ground outside the house. A metal trunk rested beneath the surface filled with coins and the deed to the house.

The next morning the deceased couple's bones were removed from the dank cave and reburied in a nice pine coffin in the cemetery on the hill. The husband fashioned a headstone to mark the grave of the mysterious man whose ghost had brought him and his wife a most welcome gift.

It is rare that one man should spend his life collecting folklore from a single county, as Harry Hyatt did in Adams

County. He found hundreds of legends, from folk remedies to witchcraft, in a few square miles of western Illinois. The ghost stories in this section are only a few of the more detailed accounts Hyatt has recorded.

Those who shared their tales with Harry Hyatt firmly believed them to be true. Whether or not they are true belies the point of the stories, namely that for a span of time in that particular corner of the heartland the legends were accepted as fervently as any event in real life.

The legends are faded now, these folk tales having been passed down now through countless generations. But the ghosts present a different sort of challenge, for they still linger in Adams County.

ELVIRA

The Opera House has been a landmark for nearly a century, towering above a quintessentially Midwestern town square in the lovely, old northern Illinois community of Woodstock. Victorian homes stretch outward from the square, which is dwarfed by the four-story theater, crowned by a story-and-a-half belfry.

Still used by the community for theatrical presentations, the Woodstock Opera House has hosted some of the brightest names in modern American stage history—Geraldine Page, Paul Newman, Betsy Palmer, Shelley Berman and Tom Bosley.

The Opera House is also the host to the ghost of a tragic young actress. Her desire to appear on the theater's stage around the turn of the century was thwarted when she wasn't cast in a role she coveted. The actress ran from the stage, climbed the winding staircase to the belfry and threw herself from a tower portal to the sidewalk six stories below.

The actress's ghost—known as Elvira to those at the theater—has a peculiar effect upon young women who seek roles in Opera House productions—more than one actress has had an uncontrollable desire to climb those same belfry tower steps! At the very top, on the same landing from which Elvira committed suicide, the women move hypnotically toward the window ledge, seemingly mesmerized by the view from the height. In each instance, the women have been pulled back from the precipice by someone who noticed their peculiar errand.

Elvira herself has been seen on several occasions. A member of the Opera House's board of directors told friends the beautiful ghost had golden hair cascading to below her slim waist. A filmy dancing gown enveloped her.

Despite her peculiar affect on young actresses, Elvira seems to be more prankish than foul. Props move mysteriously, or change location for no explainable reason. Scenery flats have been known to fall, even though they are securely tied down.

Seat 113 is Elvira's favorite vantage point in the auditorium. On several occasions actors and stagehands have noticed that particular chair in a down position, even though it is spring-loaded and should rest upright when not in use. Later examinations of the seat have found nothing wrong with it. A muffed line, or forgotten cue, will also bring a low, deep sigh from Elvira's "seat."

One of the most unnerving experiences in the Opera House is reported to have occurred in the 1940s when young Shelley Berman, the popular comedian, was acting there in summer stock. It was late at night, and Berman was working on some scenery when a noise from the darkened auditorium caught his attention. He turned to see several seats—including 113—in the down position, as if a number of people had entered the theater and sat down. Berman jumped from the stage and rushed to the seats, but by the time he arrived they had returned to their correct, upright position.

The Opera House's productions usually play to standing-room-only audiences. Seemingly, Elvira the ghost hasn't harmed attendance, probably because her appearances are infrequent and, to most people's knowledge, she hasn't actually harmed anyone. If anything, playgoers may be intrigued at the prospect of witnessing a performance *not* on the scheduled program ... by an actress dead for eight decades.

THE GHOSTS OF EGYPT

The table-flat prairie of central Illinois gradually rises to the south into the hills and hollows of the land known as "Little Egypt." The legends of how the region received its uniquely romantic nickname vary, but it probably started when a businessman gave the name Cairo (pronounced KAY-roh) to Illinois' southernmost city. The man said the area reminded him of old Egypt—a Xenia and a Karnak are located nearby.

Egypt is roughly triangular in shape, stretching across the lower midsection of Illinois from East St. Louis to Lawrenceville, and southward to Cairo, at the confluence of the Ohio and Mississippi Rivers.

The rocky, clay soil is inhospitable to agriculture. Until recently the economy was largely dependent upon the dozens of coal mines scattered across the region. Tourism, however, has now become the prime industry, centered around the 250,000-acre Shawnee National Forest, beautiful 43,000-acre Crab Orchard National Wildlife Refuge, home of wintering Canadian Geese and Crab Orchard Lake, known worldwide for its fine bass fishing.

The people of Egypt are also rich in folklore. In fact, Egyptians are known as some of the firmest believers in ghostly superstitions of any regional group in the world.

Folklorist Richard M. Dawson has written that "the ghost ... tale carries such conviction in southern Illinois towns, where it is widely known and accepted by the neighborhood, that it becomes local legend."

The selections which follow reveal the antics of some of Egypt's most famous spirits and haunts.

DUG HILL

The most notorious ghost in southern Illinois haunts a road cut through a hill about five miles west of Jonesboro on State Highway 146. The "Dug Hill Road" was constructed by early residents so they could drive more easily to a Mississippi River landing only a few miles distant.

Details vary on how the area became haunted. Most old-timers agree that a Civil War-era incident may account for the ghostly legends, but few agree on the details. One common story maintains that a provost marshall named Welch was ambushed and murdered near Dug Hill by Union Army deserters sometime in 1865.

There are two versions of the Welch story, each similar in many respects, but varying in the number of deserters plotting revenge against the marshall:

- In the first account, Welch arrested two or three deserters and turned them over to army authorities in nearby Jonesboro. But, the garrison received word that a peace treaty was signed a few days earlier at Appomattox Courthouse, Virginia. The men were released. On his way home that evening, Welch had to pass through Dug Hill. The deserters lay in ambush for their captor, and when he rode by, shot him through the head. Authorities later found his body. His horse was tied nearby. No one was ever apprehended for the murder, but soon thereafter people in the neighborhood began seeing Welch's ghost.

- The second story varies in that a dozen deserters formed a plot against Welch, who had arrested them all at one time or another for desertion during the Civil War. One of the plotters befriended Welch and rode with him toward Dug Hill to make sure he would pass the spot where his co-conspirators lay in ambush. Another of the men loaded all but two rifles with blank cartridges. The bushwhackers selected the guns at random. As Welch neared the point of ambush, his "friend" made an excuse to leave and Welch rode on. He was cut down as he passed through Dug Hill below some bushes in which the men had hidden.

But while the details about the Dug Hill Road's background vary, the fact that the road is haunted has never been questioned. In fact, one night many years ago, a wagoneer was passing Dug Hill when he saw a body lying in the road. He pulled his horses to a halt and leaped out. When he knelt down to lift the stranger, his arms went right through the stranger's body! The wagoneer backed up a few paces, scratched his head and closed his eyes. After he opened them, he could see that the body was still in the road.

Again he tried to lift the body, but again he touched only the road where the "corpse" appeared to be resting. By this time the man was scared nearly senseless and leaped back into the wagon. He cracked his whip, and as the wagon rushed forward he could feel the wheels thump over the "body". He never looked back.

Another legend centering upon Dug Hill has the *ghost* driving a wagon in a most peculiar manner. The following account was given some years ago to folklorist Charles Neely by John H. Treece who lived in nearby Jonesboro:

"A feller by the name of Bill Smith ain't jest exactly in his right mind; he's sort o' half idiot, I guess. He's still a-livin' at Jonesboro, and you might see him on the street. If you'd ask him about it, he'd tell you the same thin' I'm a-tellin' you if he'd talk to you.

"Bill was a-haulin' off corn one day. It's been a long time ago. He'd hauled off three loads of corn that day and was a-goin' home after dark. He had to pass through Dug Hill for he lived in the bottoms. He'd jest about got half-way down the hill, goin' west, when the neck-yoke of one of his horses come off, and Bill had to stop the wagon right there on the grade and git out to fix the yoke.

"The ground was froze hard, for it was in December when he was a-haulin' the corn off. And that wagon that come over the roads done a heap of rattlin' on account of the shape they was in. You could hear the wagon comin' a long way off.

"As Bill was down there a-fixin' the yoke, he 'eared the awfullest racket a man ever did 'ear. It sounded like some drunk man a-drivin' an empty wagon over the road as fast as the horses could go. Bill thought maybe it was one of his buddies that was a-haulin' off corn with him, comin' home drunk. It scared Bill to death nearly, for he knowed that there wasn't enough room for the wagon to git by on account of the road bein' so narrow, and Bill knowed he couldn't git out of the way. It looked like him and his horses might git killed. Bill looked back up the hill and hollered as loud as he could, but it didn't do no good. The racket kept gittin' nearer and nearer. Bill didn't know what to do. He knowed that the driver couldn't stop the wagon in time.

"The noise was on the brink of the hill. Bill looked up, and he realized that the noise of the wagon was in the air above him and not on the road a-tall.

"Bill looked up in the air, and he seed comin' over the crest of the hill a heavy pair of black horses a-pullin' a heavy wagon with side-boards. A man was a-settin' in the wagon a-drivin.' The horses were a-runnin' up there in the air jest like they was on the ground, and the wheels of the wagon was a-turnin' jest like they was on the ground, and the wagon was makin' a awful lot of racket like a wagon does when it's drove over rough, froze ground. The wagon and team passed right over Bill's head and struck the crest of another hill, and Bill couldn't see it any more, but he 'eard the noise of the wagon after it had got two miles away!"

THE BOGER

In southern Illinois, the bogeyman is known as the boger or boger-man. The character is heard but seldom seen and is usually used to quiet obstinate children as in, "The boger-man will get you if you don't watch out!" One of the few times the boger has shown itself is revealed in this tale:

It was twilight when Frank Corzine passed through Dug Hill on the way to fetch old Doc Russell. Corzine's wife was sick with cholera. As he neared the crest of the hill, he saw the figure of a giant of a man walking some thirty yards behind him. Suddenly, the hulking figure was a few feet behind Corzine and stayed there.

Corzine spurred his horse, who needed very little prodding, and raced all the way to Doc Russell's house some 300 yards down the road.

Corzine was breathless and pale as he dismounted at Russell's door. The doctor emerged from the house and asked Corzine what had happened. He saw that the horse was trembling and shaking as if it had been ridden hard . . . or scared.

Corzine haltingly told of his encounter with the boger. Much to his surprise, the doctor said yes, he too had seen the boger-man only a few nights before and went on to describe the very same figure Corzine had encountered—a very large man, between nine and eleven feet tall, wearing black pants, a white shirt and a scarf draped about his neck.

Doc told Corzine that he couldn't come to see his wife that night ... he was too scared of the boger. Doc Russell did rouse some neighbors to accompany Corzine back home. The boger didn't show himself again ... at least that night he didn't.

THE DEVIL'S BAKE OVEN

A few miles north of Grand Tower, Illinois, on the Mississippi River, is a small, rocky promontory used for centuries as a landmark by river travelers. The Devil's Bake Oven is its unique name. It is a short distance north of another protuberance known locally as the Devil's Backbone.

Since the 1670s, French explorers, British soldiers, American fur traders, keelboatmen, steamboaters and river pirates have been guided by the rock outcroppings. They marked the eastern terminus of a stone ledge beneath the muddy waters of the Mississippi which caused boatmen troubles before the damming of the river. On their trips upstream, flatboatmen had to leave their crafts and walk along the shore, pulling their vessels behind them with long tow lines. Going downstream, they repeated the same procedure, only they had to hold their keelboats back lest they break loose and crash through the rapids.

River pirates also infested the area of the river near the Devil's Bake Oven and Devil's Backbone. They launched surprise attacks on keelboats with canoe-like pirogues camouflaged by tree branches and marsh grass as river flotsam. Passengers and crewmen were murdered, or left stranded on the desolate shore. Merchandise, not suitable for instant consumption or eventual bartering to pioneer outposts or Indians, was dumped in the river.

Piracy on the river vanished not because the brigands were driven out by the authorities, but only after a large number of settlements made the pirates' activities more perilous. But in the latter part of the nineteenth century, the Devil's Bake Oven became more than just a geographic landmark.

An iron foundry was constructed on the hill, and several large homes were built for the factory's managers, including a beautiful two-story structure for the superintendent of the furnaces—traces of the house's foundation can still be seen on the eastern side of the hill, near its summit. But all is not as it seems on the mound known as the Devil's Bake Oven. It is haunted by the ghost of the young daughter of a foundry superintendent.

The girl was young and beautiful and sheltered from the harshness of life by her doting parents. Yet, she had many suitors longing for her hand in marriage. Her father was strict; he carefully screened his delicate daughter from the rougher men who hoped to capture her heart. But, as so often happens, the girl fell in love with the wrong man—a dashing, handsome young fellow who was, unfortunately, quite irresponsible. He enjoyed the finer things in life, but didn't always have the funds available to pay for his largesse.

The girl's father strongly disapproved of the man his daughter loved with all her heart. He forbade her from seeing him; he confined her to the house for long periods of time. Whether from grief over her lost love, or some other equally serious malady, the young lady soon fell ill and died.

Visitors to the Devil's Bake Oven's rocky point soon after the girl's death told stories of a misty female figure who would float across the path up the mound and disappear into the dense brush. The pale moonlight would shine upon a form that many persons swore resembled the girl. And, on storm-swept nights when black clouds swirled overhead and streaks of lightning split the sky, pitiful, horrifying wails would turn into screams that shattered even the bravest man's spirit. Long after the superintendent's house was razed and the timbers used to build a railway station, the girl's ghost continued to mourn for her lost lover.

A bridge now passes over the Mississippi River near the Devil's Bake Oven, carrying natural gas lines from Missouri. The bridge tower on the Illinois side is near the south edge of the Devil's Bake Oven, a few yards north of the Devil's Backbone. There is little to remind the modern visitor of the incredible tapestry of history that unfolded below the Bake Oven's stony summit. And of the bereaved young maiden who returns in death to search eternally for her roguish beau.

THE PHANTOM FUNERAL

Between the hours of eleven and midnight on the night of Friday, July 4, 1986, three passers-by on a road near Prairie du Rocher, Illinois, may be able to see what no mortal has seen for nearly one hundred years—a phantom funeral procession making its way from ancient Fort De Chartres, near the Mississippi River, to a nearby cemetery. But we must go back in time to the *last* century to discover the origins of this most unusual tale.

On the Fourth of July, 1889, a woman named Mrs. Chris and a neighbor lady were keeping vigil over the body of Mrs. Chris's dead baby. It was nearly midnight, the air stifling hot as they rocked on the front porch of the house.

Suddenly, the neighbor noticed in the distance a shadowy procession of people and wagons coming down the road. Wagons rolled into view, silhouetted against the full moon, their drivers unseen in the darkness. No driver or wagon carried a light or any other visible indication of their origin or intended destination. The only clue to their purpose was a casket that was being transported in a low wagon. As the entourage drew closer,

Mrs. Chris and her friend became certain that it was indeed a funeral procession.

The women were astonished—although they counted nearly forty wagons, followed by thirteen pairs of horsemen, the enormous cavalcade did not make a single sound! The horses' hooves were battering against the earth, clouds of dust rolled from under the wagon wheels and the riders seemed to be talking to each other. Yet not a sound reached the ears of the witnesses, save the soft rustling of nearby trees, a few night frogs and the barking of the family dog.

"Oh, my God!" Mrs. Chris cried to her friend, "If I wasn't sitting here with you seeing this, I'd swear I was dreaming."

But the women were not dreaming. The neighbor woman's father had been awakened by the agitated dog and looked out the window to see the same unearthly formation rolling by. He verified the women's account of the scene early the next morning. Other than those three people, no one else saw the phantom funeral.

Mrs. Chris and her friend decided to remain on the porch to see if anyone returned from the cortege's obvious destination, the old cemetery down the road. But no one came back—not one of the forty wagons or twenty-six horsemen!

What had the women witnessed? And who was being buried by the ghostly mourners?

An apparent answer came in a few days from a friend of Mrs. Chris's neighbor who was visiting from DuQuoin. The two women told her about the strange events of a few nights before, and the visitor recalled that her daughter had just read an account of the early days at Fort De Chartres, built in 1756 by King Louis XV, in which a prominent man had been killed in an ambush by a disgruntled resident of the fort. The specific cause of the murder was unclear and the murderer was never apprehended, but the people at the fort were unsure what to do with the body. A delegation made a small trek to Kaskaskia, the seat of the regional government, to ask how the death should be handled. They were told to bury the dead man at midnight in an obscure cemetery with only the light of the full moon to lead the way.

Mrs. Chris and her neighbor realized that the procession they witnessed was the ghostly re-enactment of the original event, 100 years after it had taken place!

The current legend surrounding the ghostly funeral procession claims that only three people will be able to see the caravan in the hour before midnight on the evening of July 4. A full moon must be hanging in the night sky.

If you're curious, the Fourth of July will fall on Fridays in 1986, 1997, 2003, 2014, 2025, 2031, 2042, 2053 and 2059. And if you're brave, take along two friends, look for the full moon, and try to find that ancient cemetery. You may be the first people since 1889 to see the phantom funeral from old Fort De Chartres!

LAKEY'S GHOST

An early settler in McLeansboro, Illinois, Mr. Lakey had given his name to a small creek which meanders through that city. One spring he decided that he needed a more permanent abode, and he began construction of a cabin on the west side of Lakey's Creek, not far from the spot where a street now passes over the stream. In that long ago age, however, a ford passed through the water on the trail from Mt. Vernon to Carmi.

Lakey's house was soon completed, save for the clapboards he was fashioning from an oak tree that he had felled. On the evening before Lakey hoped to finish his work, several travelers reported seeing him near the site busily completing the cabin. Early the next morning, however, Lakey's torso was found propped against a tree stump; his bloody, severed head lay a few feet away.

Lakey's own broadaxe, now driven into the stump, had seemingly been used as the murder weapon.

Who would want to kill Lakey? That question burned in the minds of the community as soon as the crime was discovered. As far as everyone could tell, Lakey had no known enemies—his reputation was that of a kindly, simple man not known for extravagant ways. And he possessed no hidden wealth; indeed he was quite poor. Although the local authorities conducted a thorough investigation, no one ever discovered Lakey's murderer.

The townspeople buried Lakey adjacent to his never-completed cabin. But the corpse did not remain at rest!

On the night following the burial, two men were riding near the Lakey cabin on their way back from a trip to the Wabash River. They had nearly reached the creek when the horrible specter of a headless horseman mounted on a coal black steed joined them.

The riders spurred their horses to a gallop, but the ghost easily stayed abreast of the frightened men. As they all entered the stream, the phantom horseman turned downriver and disappeared into the mist below the crossing. The men eventually made it safely home, but they were reluctant to tell their story. However, a few nights later, two other men arriving from the east also encountered the ghostly horseman as they crossed Lakey's Creek.

The word quickly spread throughout the region that the ghost of old man Lakey would not stay in its grave. But while the ghost never communicated, it apparently never tried to harm any travelers. Always, however, it would appear immediately after sundown to riders approaching along the east side of the stream. The ghost was always mounted on a large, black horse which galloped along on the left, or downstream side, of the unlucky witnesses. And the specter invariably disappeared halfway across the creek.

The horrible figure was encountered off and on for decades, but lately its appearances have become infrequent.

A concrete bridge now crosses Lakey's Creek where the old ford used to be. Lakey's cabin has long since vanished. But, the legend of Lakey's ghost lives on in the minds of many of the residents of McLeansboro, Illinois.

BURIED ALIVE

Can you imagine the horror of being buried alive? Of waking up to find yourself encased in a solid wood box, buried beneath tons of tightly packed earth, and no hope to escape?

Irene Mache of Belleville, Illinois, told folklorist Charles Neely the story of one such woman who was spared that ghastly fate in a bizarre twist of luck.

The woman had been ill for several weeks. One morning her family found her "dead," and after a cursory examination the local doctor agreed. Modern embalming methods were unknown at that time, so after a brief wake, the woman was promptly buried in the local cemetery.

As it happened, grave robbers were at large in the southern Illinois region. On the night of the funeral, the robbers stealthily entered the graveyard in search of any jewelry that might have been buried with the woman. They quickly uncovered the coffin and pried off the lid. The woman lay just as her family had readied her. But, what attracted the attention of the robbers was her large ruby ring! They grabbed the woman's hand and pried at the beautiful jewel. Despite their best efforts, they could not dislodge the ring. In desperation they decided to cut off her entire finger.

As the knife split the woman's bony flesh, the woman's arm tremored slightly. Suddenly, she sat straight up and opened her eyes. The grave robbers fled the cemetery, their feet barely touching the earth.

The "dead" woman, who was quite alive, made her way home and told her startled family the tale. She said she had been aware of everything going on around her at the funeral and as she was buried, but was unable to speak or move. The pain of the knife cutting into her skin had caused her to recover her senses—and to retain her cherished ring!

Perhaps it is the association with the ever-mysterious Egypt of the Pharaohs which makes the "Little Egypt" area of southern Illinois so susceptible to the occult. Or perhaps it is as folklorist Richard Dawson says—"The ghost tale carries such conviction in southern Illinois that it is taken as fact." Whatever the case, that triangular shape of land and its inhabitants possess a very haunted legacy.

THE ROONEY COMBUSTIONS

Cases of spontaneous human combustion are rare and mysterious phenomena. Scientists have puzzled for years over just what causes a person to suddenly and inexplicably burst into flame and become a heap of ashes in a matter of minutes. Even more bizarre is the fact that highly flammable materials near the person may not burn at all.

Cases of human incineration have been recorded as early as the seventeenth century when an elderly woman in southeastern England burned to death in bed. Although the fire must have been intense, the undamaged bed coverings didn't even show scorch marks.

In more recent years, the English press reported the case of a man walking along an avenue who suddenly burst into flames. His hair burned off, his rubber-soled shoes melted and his clothes evaporated. One eyewitness said he appeared to have "exploded."

A particularly odd case occurred in the late 1950s at an English night club. A young woman and her date were on the dance floor when flames erupted from her back and chest. As her frantic boyfriend and horrified spectators tried to extinguish them, the young woman became a veritable human torch. She died of third-degree burns. Later testimony indicated no apparent cause for the woman's fiery death. No one nearby was smoking and her boyfriend did not see her pass near an open flame. The fire, he said, seemed to come from within her own body.

In this country, one of the strangest cases of death by human combustion came on Christmas Eve, 1885, in Seneca, Illinois.

Patrick Rooney and his wife, a large woman of over 200 pounds, were sharing a jug of whiskey with their hired man, John Larson. They sat around the kitchen table in their small farmhouse until Larson, only lightly inebriated, retired to his upstairs room, pleading drowsiness. Rooney and his wife continued drinking.

Early on Christmas Day, Larson awoke extremely ill. He stumbled down the stairs toward the kitchen for a drink of water and some fresh air.

Noticing a smoky haze as he made his way into the kitchen, he tried to strike a match on the kitchen range so he could light the kerosene lamp. The match just slid across the surface. A dark, soot-like grease coated the stove and everything else in the kitchen.

Larson groped his way to the first-floor bedroom shared by Rooney and his wife. Inside, he found Patrick dead on the floor, his coat and boots on a nearby chair.

The hired man shouted for Mrs. Rooney, but there was no reply. He quickly dressed and saddled a horse to ride for Rooney's son who lived on a nearby farm.

Larson, Rooney's son, Todd, and a neighbor returned to the house. The trio made their way back into the soot-encrusted kitchen where they discovered a hole in the floor near the table. The men peered into the opening. By the flickering lamp Todd held, the men saw, to their horror, on the exposed cellar floor below, a foot, part of a vertebra, a shrunken, burned skull and a heap of ashes.

The coroner identified the remains as those of the unfortunate Mrs. Rooney, but an inquest found only part of an answer to what happened.

Patrick Rooney had died of smoke inhalation, of that there was little doubt. John Larson escaped death by sleeping behind a closed door on the second floor.

But Dr. Floyd Clendens, the coroner, was stumped to explain the cause of Mrs. Rooney's grotesque demise. He determined that a fire strong enough to have left so few remains must have burned for several minutes at over 2500 degrees Fahrenheit. Yet the only signs of the fire were the hole in the floor, some scorch marks on the kitchen table and the sooty substance covering the kitchen furnishings.

Dr. Clendens read some accounts of spontaneous human combustion to the jury at the inquest, but they adjourned, bewildered by the case. In fact, a satisfactory answer to these peculiar deaths has not been found. However, research into accounts of sudden death by fire has established many similarities:

- Victims are more frequently women.
- Alcohol is often present.
- The victim is usually incinerated by the fire, although partial combustion has been reported in rare instances.
- The head, feet and hands often escape complete immolation.
- The combustion is rapid, usually taking place in a matter of seconds or at the most a very few minutes.

- Many of the victims are overweight.
- Few other nearby objects are scorched, although furnishings in the room are usually covered by a sooty, greasy substance.
- Virtually all of the spontaneous combustions have occurred during the winter in the northern hemisphere.

A few scientists have ventured the theory that many mysterious fires may be caused by individuals with an abnormal amount of electrostatic charge within their bodies. Almost everyone can build up electrostatic energy, particularly in dry winter months, by walking on carpets. Usually the charges are released harmlessly through the ends of the hair. Sometimes we feel that charge when we touch a metal doorknob or desk. Perhaps in rare instances persons can accumulate enough energy to be a danger to themselves and others around them.

But that theory doesn't help explain the cases that seem to be in defiance of natural law, such as the Rooney deaths. The mystery remains: Why wasn't anything else burned? How could such a fire flare and die within a few minutes? And what did Mrs. Rooney do to cause such a horrible conflagration? Mrs. Rooney's death and similar cases have never been solved. The matter is ruled, in the words of many coroners' reports, "death by misadventure."

SPIRIT OF THE SOBER DUCK

Was it the "restless soul" of Albert Cranor that was finally exorcised from a nightclub in Springfield? Did the ghost of Cranor, called Rudy by his friends, blow an invisible trumpet? Was he the source of the bone-numbing cold that permeated areas of the night spot?

Tom Blasko, proprietor of the Sober Duck Disco and Rock Club, told reporters that indeed Rudy's ghost had caused all the mischief.

The story began at the club on June 27, 1968, when Cranor, a bartender, shot himself in the head and died the next morning. Over the next few years, patrons and those who worked at the club had many eerie experiences.

While temperatures of ninety-five degrees baked the city, portions of the Sober Duck felt like a deep freeze— and there was no air conditioning. Bar glasses would sail across the room, pitched from unseen hands. On one occasion, Barbara Lard, a waitress, saw a disembodied head floating in midair. She told the Associated Press that an inhuman voice issuing from the skull warned of an impending death—the club owner's.

Sure enough, a few weeks after the mysterious visitation, the owner of the building, who had leased it to Tom Blasko, died. Although he was sixty-nine, his death was unexpected. Except perhaps to Lard and Rudy. Blasko had thought *he* was the one marked for death.

Still apprehensive at a high school class reunion in 1979, he asked two of his former classmates, now priests, for help with the bizarre incidents.

The Rev. Gary Dilley and the Rev. John Corredato agreed to perform the ancient Catholic rite of exorcism. Blasko reasoned that since Catholics consider suicide one of the worst sins, and Rudy Cranor had been a Catholic, his ghost would not rest until he was forgiven by the Church.

In August, 1979, the two priests, along with another cleric, visited the nightclub, said the prayers associated with exorcism and, according to the Rev. Corredato, "had a 7-Up and went home."

Apparently it worked. Blasko said Rudy has not been seen, heard nor felt since the exorcism rite.

And what did the Catholic Diocese of Springfield think of an exorcism in their midst?

According to published reports, an aide to Bishop Joseph McNicholas said church doctrine was not necessarily contradicted by a belief that until a person's sins are atoned, the soul of the departed may roam the earth.

Certainly the mysterious haunting of the Sober Duck convinced Tom Blasko that spirits of the dead walk among us.

THE REINCARNATION OF MARY ROFF

On the afternoon of July 5, 1865, eighteen-year-old Mary Roff died in the Peoria, Illinois insane asylum. Mary had been committed after a ghastly incident when she tried to slash her arms with a razor. It was but the last tragedy in the girl's harrowing descent into madness.

First came the voices, then long periods of unconsciousness followed by a hypnotic state during which she took on other identities. At the end, before the asylum, the need to rid her body of blood obsessed her. She used leeches, turning herself into a pincushion. She made "friends" of the creatures, giving them names much like family pets.

After the slashing, her parents found her on the floor with the razor still in her hand. They took her, unconscious, to Peoria.

Unfortunately, the "cure" for mental illness in the middle of the nineteenth century was nearly as bad as its symptoms. A favored "treatment" was the "water cure," a practice originated in the Middle Ages and still used in the 1860s in America. The patient, in this case Mary Roff, was first immersed naked in a tub of icy water, and then in scalding hot water.

But that wasn't the end of the horror. Female patients received a cold water douche administered with a hose. By that time, though victims were nearly senseless from the "cure," it continued with water-soaked sheets tightly bound around the body to literally squeeze shut the blood vessels. Finally, the patient's skin was vigorously rubbed to "improve" the circulation, if there was any circulation left.

The treatments were repeated several times a week, despite their noticeable lack of success in bringing anyone back to a healthy mental state.

It is little wonder that after Mary Roff's death, her father, Asa B. Roff, a spiritualist, declared that his daughter had been "in a condition terrible to behold, among maniacs, ruled and cared for by ignorant and bigoted strangers."

Lurancy Vennum was not yet fourteen months old on that steamy July day when Mary Roff died mad and alone. But their lives would become forever intertwined twelve years later in one of the strangest cases of possession ever recorded in the United States.

Lurancy was, from all accounts, a normal, healthy child raised in a loving and religious home. Born on April 16, 1864, she and her family moved to Watseka, Illinois when she was seven. Although Asa Roff, his wife and several children also lived in Watseka, and still grieved for their dead daughter, the Vennums did not know the Roff family beyond the casual acquaintanceship typical in small towns. On July 11, 1877, shortly after the twelfth anniversary of Mary Roff's death, a series of events began to unfold that would plummet Lurancy into the netherworld of the supernatural.

On that morning, Lurancy, sewing with her mother, complained of feeling ill. Before her mother could react, the child fell to the floor, unconscious. For the next five hours, Lurancy was held in a deep, almost catatonic sleep, oblivious to her surroundings. She later recovered without any visible adverse effects.

The next day, however, Lurancy again fell into the same deep swoon. This time, while apparently still unconscious, she began talking. She was in heaven, the child told her bewildered parents, and could see and speak with spirits, including her brother who had died in 1874.

After that, Lurancy's lapses into unconsciousness become more and more frequent. Furthermore, her visions took on a nightmarish tinge. She would sometimes shout at her parents, calling her father "Old Black Dick" and her mother "Old Granny." After one particularly long siege, she told her mother that "persons are in my room and calling 'Rancy! Rancy!' and I can feel their breath upon my face." Rancy, of course, was her nickname.

Continuing attacks lasted for periods of up to eight hours and occurred three to twelve times per day. While Lurancy could speak, her words seemed to be directed by someone, or something, the Vennums could not understand. Once her spells had passed, Lurancy remembered nothing of her strange jabberings.

The story of Lurancy Vennum's peculiar visions spread quickly through Watseka. Even the local newspaper published articles about the child and her dialogue with the spirit world. Among the townsfolk who closely followed the case was Asa Roff. His interest was more than casual. In the early stages of his daughter's sickness, she too had said she could communicate with spirits. Lurancy's symptoms sounded disturbingly like those of his deceased Mary. Roff was determined not to let another young girl die at the hands of "ignorant and bigoted strangers" whose ideas of medicine were more akin to medieval torture. He said nothing, however, until Lurancy's family had exhausted every known cure for their daughter's illness without success and the doctors and minister were advising them to commit the girl to the state institution for the insane in Peoria.

That was too much for Roff. On January 31, 1878, he intervened, persuading the skeptical Vennum family to let him bring Dr. E. Winchester Stevens, a physician originally from Janesville, Wisconsin and, more importantly, a dedicated spiritualist like himself, into the case. Stories both men had heard convinced them that Lurancy was not insane or catatonic, but rather the vessel through which the souls of the dead were communicating with the living.

Lurancy was sitting near a parlor stove when Roff and Dr. Stevens entered the house. Her unblinking gaze seemed riveted to the wall. Her legs were pulled up beneath her on the chair and she rested her elbows on her knees, with her hands clasped under her chin. Roff said later she looked every inch a mean old woman not to be trifled with. Even her voice had the raspy sound of age. She growled that she didn't want to talk to anyone.

After a few minutes, however, her mood changed. She announced that since she knew Dr. Stevens was a spiritualist, she would answer any question he might pose.

Dr. Stevens quizzed the strange girl: "What is your name?"

"Katrina Hogan."

"And how old are you?"

"Sixty-three years."

"Where are you from?"

"Germany."

"How long have you been here?"

"Three days."

"How did you come?"

"Through the air."

"How long can you stay?"

"Three weeks."

Then Lurancy's mood changed again. She had been lying, she admitted. She wasn't Katrina Hogan, but rather Willie Canning, a young man now in the spirit world "because I want to be here." Lurancy, speaking as Willie, said he had led a wild life and implied that he may have committed suicide.

For over an hour, Lurancy spoke to Dr. Stevens in the guise of Willie until she suddenly flung up her arms and fell backwards upon the floor, rigid as a plank.

Dr. Stevens grasped her hands in his, talking quietly but firmly in an attempt to "magnetize" her, as he later wrote. Gradually, she regained the use of her body. Now she was in heaven, she said, with spirits of a far gentler persuasion than Katrina or Willie.

Wouldn't she like to be controlled by a happier, more pleasant spirit than Willie? Dr. Stevens asked. Lurancy agreed that would be nice. A spirit was nearby, she added, the spirit of a girl named Mary Roff.

Asa Roff, who had been silently but intently watching the proceedings, sat bolt upright. "That is my daughter! Mary Roff is my girl! She has been in heaven these twelve years. Yes, let her come. We'll be glad to have her here."

The trance continued into the next day, February 1. Lurancy Vennum now *was* Mary Roff, desirous only of leaving the Vennum house, which she said was unfamiliar, and returning to her real home with the Roffs.

When Mrs. Roff heard of the reincarnation of her beloved child, she hurried to the Vennum home with her married daughter, Minerva Alter. As the two women turned up the walk, they saw Lurancy sitting by the window.

"Here comes Ma and Nervie," the girl cried. She rushed to the door and showered the startled women with embraces. No one had called Mrs. Alter "Nervie," Mary's pet name for her, since the girl's death thirteen years before.

It was now evident Mary Roff had taken complete control of the body and mind of Lurancy Vennum. Although her physical appearance remained the same, she seemed to know everything about the Roff family, treating them as her own. To the Vennums, her real parents, she remained polite and courteous as one would with friends.

Dr. Stevens later wrote of the girl's dramatic change in behavior: "From the wild, angry, ungovernable girl, to be kept only by lock and key, or the more distressing watch-care of almost frantic parents; or the rigid, corpse-like cataleptic . . . the girl has now become mild . . . and timid . . . knowing none of the Vennum family, but constantly pleading to go home."

And "go home" she did on February 11. The Vennums, with the happy acquiescence of the Roffs, agreed that it was best. They hoped that in time Lurancy would regain her true identity. Having lived through hell during the past seven months, they viewed this new persona only as another phase of the insanity, but they were willing to go along with almost anything to keep their lovely daughter out of the insane asylum.

For the Roffs, on the other hand, it seemed a miracle. Their Mary had returned from the grave! And an incident on the way home only strengthened their belief in the reincarnation.

In 1865, the year Mary died, the family had been living in a house near the center of Watseka. As Lurancy, with her new family, passed the old place, she asked why they did not turn into the drive. When Mr. Roff told her that their home was now elsewhere, Lurancy insisted that they lived in *this* home. Only after strong persuasion did the girl agree to accompany them further.

Thus began, for Lurancy Vennum, a period of contentment as Mary Roff. Although Mary's personality occasionally vanished for short periods, Lurancy seemed to have completely forgotten her former life. Yet she seemed to sense also an impermanence in the arrangement. When Mrs. Roff once asked her how long she could stay, she replied, "The angels will let me stay until sometime in May."

As the days and weeks passed, Lurancy continued to display remarkable knowledge about Roff family matters. She recognized most of the family possessions that had been part of Mary's world, welcomed "old friends" when they visited, and on one occasion even recited the entire itinerary of a long trip the Roffs had made to Texas in 1857. Of course, her "parents" were ecstatic. "Truly," they said, "our daughter has been restored to us."

Likewise, Mrs. Alter, Mary's sister, with whom Lurancy spent several weeks during the spring of 1878, was convinced that Mary had indeed returned from the dead. She later told interviewers that on at least two occasions, Lurancy had shocked her with specific remembrances, once pointing to a spot beneath a currant bush and accurately describing how her little cousin Allie had "greased the chicken's eye." On another occasion, the girl correctly identified an area in Mrs. Alter's yard where they had buried a pet dog. Both incidents had occurred several years before Lurancy was born.

Later, as an experiment, Asa Roff asked his wife to place a velvet bonnet Mary had often worn on a hat stand in the parlor. When she saw it, Lurancy ran to it and, mentioning the store where it had been purchased, talked about some of the things that had happened while she was wearing it. She then asked the Roffs if they had kept her box of letters from friends and relatives. When they produced the box, Lurancy exclaimed, "Oh, Ma! Here is the collar I tatted! Why didn't you show me my letters and things before?"

Not everyone in Watseka believed that Mary Roff had taken possession of Lurancy Vennum's body. Several of the doctors who had treated Lurancy before the arrival of Dr. Stevens ridiculed his diagnosis of "spirit possession." A "friend" of the Vennum family echoed the sentiment of many when she lashed out at the role spiritualism appeared to be playing in Lurancy's treatment. "I would sooner follow a girl of mine to the grave than have her go to the Roffs and be made a spiritualist!" she declared.

The local minister, who had tried to persuade the Vennums to have Lurancy committed, told Mrs. Vennum, "I think you will see the time when you will wish you had sent her to the asylum."

Meanwhile, Lurancy Vennum's life as Mary Roff continued. Any new test designed by Dr. Stevens to gauge her ability to recall distant events in that other life met with complete success. Still, the girl knew that physically she was not Mary Roff. When Dr. Stevens asked her if she remembered a cut she had received as a child, she replied, "Yes, indeed, I can show you the scar."

She rolled up her sleeve, pointing to the place on her arm where the real Mary had, indeed, scarred herself in a childhood accident, and said matter-of-factly, "Oh, this isn't the mark. That arm is in the ground."

Lurancy-as-Mary also had the power of clairvoyance. Early one day, she told the Roffs that her "brother," Frank, would become sick that night. He did. The girl then instructed her parents to take him to Dr. Stevens' home. Mr. Roff protested that Dr. Stevens was in another part of the city and wasn't expected home. An insistent Lurancy disagreed. They did, indeed, find Dr. Stevens at home and he treated the boy for "spasms and congestive chill" from which he soon recovered.

In early May, Lurancy took Asa Roff aside and said it was nearly time for her to go. She choked back sobs at the thought of leaving her "family" and forcing the Roffs again to say goodbye to their daughter. Over the next days, Lurancy's true personality occasionally returned, not understanding where she was or what had happened.

During the battle to control the physical body, Lurancy would hold sway one moment, Mary the next. On May 21, Lurancy announced it was now time to return to her real home. Next, Mary would address Mr. Roff as "Sir" and weep bitterly at the thought of leaving.

But leave she did. Once back with the Vennums, Lurancy displayed none of the alarming symptoms of the past year. Her parents were convinced that their daughter had been cured by the intervention of the spirit of Mary Roff. Lurancy became a happy, healthy fourteen-year-old girl, having survived with few ill effects one of the most bizarre experiences anyone had ever endured.

Lurancy remained in touch with the Roffs for the rest of her life. During her occasional visits, she would sometimes allow Mary to take control so the Roffs could communicate with their dead daughter. But Mary never wanted to stay long and allowed Lurancy to regain her identity whenever she wished.

Eight years later, in 1896, Lurancy Vennum married a farmer, a devout nonbeliever in anything spiritual, and moved with him to Rollins County, Kansas, where she lived the rest of her life and died an old woman. Never again did the spirit of Mary Roff possess her.

Can this case of spirit possession be explained?

Lurancy had the memories, emotions, recognitions, physical nuances and personality of a person dead for twelve years. In most cases of multiple personality, the individual does not have this knowledge of the early life of another, sometimes fictitious, personality. It seems irrefutable that the spirit of a real person who had actually been born, grown, loved and died upon this earth had taken over the body of Lurancy Vennum.

The idea that Lurancy had somehow acquired her knowledge of the Roff family and used it for a purpose of her own seems farfetched. Yet some claimed that was exactly what happened. Shortly after Lurancy's possession became common gossip, rumors spread that she had a crush on one of the Roff sons and wanted, for that reason, to be close to the family. The charge was never substantiated and it seems highly unlikely the boy could have coached Lurancy so convincingly. Such a deception also presumes an unusual sophistication for a teenage girl.

Did Lurancy, on her own, have the ability to see into the minds of those around her, as she had demonstrated with young Frank's illness? Had she thus "read" the memories of the Roffs? No evidence suggested that Lurancy ever possessed ESP.

We are left then with the possibility, and it's only a possibility since any trace of "proof" has long since vanished, that in 1878 in a small Illinois town, Lurancy Vennum was indeed possessed by the psyche of Mary Roff, a young woman twelve years dead.

THE TWO-HOUSE HAUNTING

Gertrude Meyers decided against telling her husband about that strange night. He would probably think her silly and emotional. But the man had returned—she thought it must be a man for the steps were heavy—again stopping just outside her locked bedroom door.

At last the torment became too much. She determined to confront the nightly walker, whatever or whoever he was. She sat up in bed waiting, the coverlet pulled to her chin. The clock chimed: ten o'clock ... ten-thirty. Then the footsteps began, as always, from the front door, across the front hall, up the stairs to the very threshold of her bedroom. She jumped out of bed and threw open the door.

Nothing was there.

The year was 1935. An end to the Great Depression was not in sight. For a young, newly-married couple in their late twenties, Gertrude and Raymond Meyers considered themselves fortunate to have a comfortable, though modest home in Springfield in a development where all the houses looked alike. In fact, their dwelling exactly mirrored the one next door.

Gertrude was an educated woman, a high school teacher with ambitions as a writer. She didn't want to admit to herself, let alone her husband, that she was bothered by the nights she spent alone while he worked the late shift as a printer. During the summer they had first moved in as newlyweds, she had been able to open the windows. Bird songs and traffic noises enlivened the empty evenings.

But now it was late fall. And she felt another presence in the house: the unseen tenant lurking just beyond the shadows whose footsteps punctuated the night.

At first, even as the footsteps continued, she had been able to convince herself that her imagination had the upper hand. Night after night, Gertrude Meyers bravely flung open her bedroom door. At that moment, whatever was out there vanished, the footsteps moving away down the hallway.

As fall merged into winter, she had little relief from the night walker. Unnervingly, he didn't come every night, but when he did come it was always at 10:30 P.M.

Unbeknown to his wife, Raymond Meyers had also heard mysterious sounds as the weather grew colder. He assumed it was Gertrude. He usually returned home from work around three-thirty in the morning, and went to the basement to stoke the coal furnace before going to bed. Often he heard someone moving around on the first floor. After several days, he finally asked his wife what she was doing prowling around in the middle of the night. That was when they discovered their similar experiences. Raymond also heard footsteps during the day, after Gertrude left for her teaching job.

But neither one of them ever *saw* anything. And they couldn't decide what the intruder was after. The nightly strolls seemed almost ritualistic, seldom varying in routine or duration. Always from the front door, up the stairs and to the bedroom door. But never did anything come through the door.

Who could the intruder be?

A possible answer came in the spring when Gertrude could again be comforted by human and animal noises drifting through the opened windows. The couple decided to plant a garden and, in the process, first met their neighbors from the identical house next door, a grandmother and her young grandson.

As neighbors often do, they chatted about their families and houses. That's when the Meyers mentioned their nocturnal rambler. Their neighbor revealed that she too had heard mysterious footsteps. Furthermore she explained that the two houses had originally been a single dwelling, a sort of duplex. For some reason, after the suicide of the original owner, the duplex had been divided into two separate dwellings moved some distance apart.

They decided the ghostly footsteps must belong to the former owner. Only he couldn't decide which half of the house he belonged in!

The haunting continued in both houses. Gertrude and Raymond Meyers grew used to it, although never enough to feel completely at ease.

THE MACOMB POLTERGEIST

Her name was Wanet and she was a disturbed child who lived with her father, uncle and aunt and their three children on a family farm near Macomb, Illinois in the year 1948. Max Willey, the uncle, owned the farm.

An only child, the little girl had been awarded to her father when her parents divorced. She hated the farm and wished desperately to live elsewhere. Other children might have run away, purposely failed their school studies or taken to petty mischief. But not Wanet. Through some mysterious psychic force, she started fires!

Investigators called it one of the most amazing stories of fire poltergeists ever recorded.

The attacks started with the sudden blooming of brown spots on the farmhouse's wallpaper. The size of a dime at first, they spread into ever-widening circles of heat. Witnesses claim they reached a temperature in excess of 400 degrees, never enough to burst into flame, though smoke curled up from smudges.

For days the brown spots polka-dotted the wallpaper, while neighbors stood guard with buckets and hoses to put out any fires. They would wet each spot as it appeared, until there were so many they couldn't keep up.

The local press reported the strange goings-on at the Willey farm and it didn't take long for "experts" to offer opinions on the cause.

An Air Force technician cited the presence of high-frequency radio waves or radioactivity. He explained that short radio waves had been known to trigger flash bulbs into going off. But no other farms reported the problem and it seems improbable that the radio waves would have been so concentrated as to affect only the Willeys.

Another expert suggested that combustible gases were accumulating in the house and causing the phenomena, but his theory failed to fit all the circumstances either.

The fires eventually spread to almost any combustible material in the house. The family found singe marks on curtains, bedsheets, clothing and various paper products. On occasion, things started smoldering before someone's disbelieving eyes.

Young Wanet became the focus of the investigation during the third week of the incendiary disturbances. The authorities eventually persuaded her to sign a confession stating she had started them. Witnesses who had observed fires starting in several parts of the house *simultaneously* did not see how Wanet could be guilty, unless she could be in two places at once, or had several co-conspirators.

But others cited "evidence" that children, especially unhappy children, may trigger poltergeist activities unconsciously. It is unusual, however, for a poltergeist, which more commonly manifests itself through the sudden movement of furniture, voices, noises or, in some cases, possession of a person, to resort to the setting of fires.

In fact, a fire poltergeist is extremely rare. One expert, Vincent Gaddis, suggested that some kind of psychological mechanism working through a frustrated or angry person can concentrate psycho-kinetic energy, normally stored in the human body, to control electrical forces in the atmosphere and thus produce small fires, such as those in the Willey household.

As unbelievable as this explanation may sound, there are dozens of recorded cases of objects or human beings bursting into flame for no apparent reason, often leaving unscorched normally combustible items near the consumed object. In the Willey case, the extraordinary number of fires over a relatively short span of time has never been satisfactorily explained.

Neither has the destructive power of human anger, so aptly mirrored in the fiery manifestations that scorched the Macomb farmhouse.

LINCOLN AND THE SUPERNATURAL

Abraham Lincoln hovered over the telegraph key in the U.S. War Department offices in Washington, D.C. on June 7, 1864, waiting for word from General Ulysses S. Grant, who was nearing Richmond. Oblivious to everything but the Civil War, he paid scant attention to the opening of the Republican Party Convention in Baltimore, Maryland. He left the office only to eat a hasty lunch in the White House.

It wasn't that the President didn't care about his own renomination taking place forty miles away. He didn't give it a thought because he *knew* he would be nominated and elected to a second term! He also knew, because of a vision four years before, that he would not survive that term.

Shortly after his election in 1860, on a day when the news of his victory over fellow Illinoisan Stephen A.

Douglas was still being transmitted to his private offices in Springfield, Illinois, Lincoln retreated to his quarters to rest. He sprawled his lanky frame on a settee near a bureau topped by a large mirror. As he caught his reflection in the glass, he saw the nearly full-length image of himself.

Hardly odd, except that Lincoln later confided to a friend: "My face, I noticed, had two separate and distinct images, the tip of the nose of one being about three inches from the tip of the other. I was a little bothered, perhaps startled, and got up and looked in the glass. The vision vanished. On lying down again, I saw it a second time, plainer, if possible, than before; and then I noticed that one of the faces was a little paler, about five shades, than the other. I got up and the thing melted away, and in the excitement of the hour I forgot all about it, nearly, but not quite, for the thing once in a while came up and gave me a little pang, as if something had happened.

"When I went home that night, I told my wife about it, and a few days afterward, I made the experiment again, when sure enough the thing came again."

Each time Lincoln tried to reproduce the image in his Springfield home he succeeded. His wife, Mary Todd Lincoln, never saw it, but was deeply troubled by the story. Claiming to have the gift of prophecy, she felt she knew the significance of the image. The healthy, vigorous face, she said, was her husband's "real" face, and indicated that the President would serve out his first term. The paler, ghost-like image, however, was a sign that he would be renominated for a second term, but he would not live to see its conclusion.

Lincoln apparently dismissed the entire episode as an optical illusion caused by an imperfection in the mirror or his own nervousness over the election.

Even so, he seemed preoccupied on that day of the 1864 Republican Convention and unmindful of the political events taking place.

An account of the day by one of his aides elaborates on his disinterest: "The President returned to the War Department after lunch in the White House. As he strode toward the offices where information from the front lines was being received, he was handed a telegram from Baltimore. It said that Andrew Johnson of Tennessee had been nominated as vice president. Johnson had been Lincoln's military governor in occupied Tennessee since 1862."

Lincoln looked perplexed. "This is strange," he commented. "I thought it was usual to nominate the candidate for president first."

"But Mr. President," his aide replied, "have you not heard of your own nomination? It was telegraphed to you at the White House two hours ago."

The President shook his head. He hadn't even paused in his private office to receive the information. Later he attached great meaning to that inattentiveness and recalled his strange encounter with the mirror four years before. Surely, he thought, a hand was guiding him toward a destiny over which he had no control.

Abraham Lincoln had always had a melancholy nature. The loss of his own mother as a child, constant hard, physical labor and the struggle to acquire an education combined to make him serious, even when cracking a joke.

The Civil War shadowed his countenance with almost constant sorrow. The heavy losses on both sides and the divided loyalties the war called up pained him deeply. His wife's brothers fought for the Confederacy and his own ancestry was Southern.

Lincoln paid fanatical attention to even the most minute details concerning the war. By the time of his reelection in 1864, deep lines etched his face and heavy black circles underlined his eyes. Typically, he slept little. During the five years he lived in the White House, he took less than a month's vacation. His only escape was an occasional theater outing or a late buggy ride. Shakespeare and the Bible gave him solace at night.

But there may have been more to his sadness than even he would admit. The disturbing mirror image in his Springfield home was only the first incident that seemed to predict doom. Lincoln is widely reported to have dreamed of his own death.

Ward Hill Lamon, a close friend of Lincoln's, wrote down what the President told him on an evening in 1865:

"About ten days ago I retired very late ... I soon began to dream. There seemed to be a deathlike stillness about me. Then I heard subdued sobs, as if a number of people were weeping. I thought I left my bed and wandered downstairs.

"There, the silence was broken by the same pitiful sobbing, but the mourners were invisible. I went from room to room. No living person was in sight, but the same mournful sounds of distress met me as I passed alone ... I was puzzled and alarmed.

"Determined to find the cause of a state of things so mysterious and shocking, I kept on until I arrived at the East Room. Before me was a catafalque, on which rested a corpse wrapped in funeral vestments. Around it were stationed soldiers who were acting as guards; and there was a throng of people, some gazing mournfully upon the corpse, whose face was covered, others weeping pitifully.

" 'Who is dead in the White House?' I demanded of one of the soldiers. 'The President,' was his answer. 'He was killed by an assassin.' "

Abraham Lincoln became even more depressed during April, 1865. Although Northern forces now firmly controlled the war, Lincoln rejoiced very little.

A few days after his horrifying dream, on April 14, 1865, President Lincoln called a meeting of his Cabinet. Secretary of War Edwin M. Stanton arrived twenty minutes late with apologies. The meeting proceeded as scheduled.

As Stanton and Attorney General James Speed later departed, the Secretary of War said he was pleased with the amount of work the men had accomplished.

"But you were not here at the beginning," Speed countered. "You do not know what passed. When we entered the Council Chamber, we found the President seated at the top of the table, with his face buried between his hands. Presently he raised it and we saw that he looked grave and worn."

The President spoke: "Gentlemen, before long you will have important news."

The Cabinet members were anxious to hear what news Lincoln might have. They pressed him, but he demurred.

"I have heard nothing; I have had no news, but you will hear tomorrow." He hesitated and then continued, "I have had a dream; I have dreamed that dream three times before, once before the battle of Bull Run, once on another occasion, and again last night. I am in a boat, alone on a boundless ocean. I have no oars—no rudder— I am helpless. I drift!"

Shortly after ten o'clock that evening, while the President and Mrs. Lincoln enjoyed a rare outing at the performance of "Our American Cousin" at Ford's Theater, a Southern sympathizer named John Wilkes Booth shot Lincoln in the back of the head. The President died at 7:22 the next morning, April 15, 1865. It was the anniversary of the Southern assault on Fort Sumter ... the opening salvo of the Civil War.

A train bore Lincoln's body home to Springfield. The legend tells that ever afterwards, on the anniversary of that sad journey, two ghost trains steam along the rails. The first engine pulls several cars, all draped in black. In one car a military band plays a funeral dirge. Before the belching black smoke of the locomotive can drift away, a second steam engine heaves into sight. Its only attachment is a flatcar upon which rests the coffin bearing the remains of President Lincoln. Each April, the ghost trains travel the route between Washington and Illinois. They never reach Springfield.

The curious events connected with Abraham Lincoln did not end with his death. Little Willie Lincoln, the President's favorite son, died while his father occupied the White House. Mary Todd Lincoln never again set foot in his bedroom. But others say they have seen the ghost of a little boy in there.

Lincoln's oldest son, Robert Todd Lincoln, died fewer than sixty years ago, in 1926. His life, too, was touched with a perplexing psychic cast. Robert was with his father when he died of the wound inflicted by John Wilkes Booth.

Sixteen years later, in 1881, James A. Garfield, less than four months after taking office as the twentieth president of the United States, strode through a railroad station in Washington, D.C. Robert Lincoln, his Secretary of War, was at his side when a crazed Charles Guiteau leaped forward and killed the President.

In 1901, President William McKinley invited Robert, by then the president of the Pullman Company, to tour the Pan-American Exposition in Buffalo, New York. An anarchist named Leon F. Czolgosg fired a pistol at President McKinley . . . and Robert Lincoln witnessed the third death of an American president.

As a result, this prominent statesman and lawyer, a graduate of Harvard University, refused ever again to meet or associate with a president. Although he had many invitations, Robert refused them all. He said he was a curse.

In the years since then, several presidents and visiting dignitaries have encountered Lincoln's ghost in the White House.

During the thirteen years Franklin D. Roosevelt lived there, his wife, Eleanor, often felt the presence of the Great Emancipator. She used his former bedroom as a study. As she wrote, Mrs. Roosevelt said, she sometimes sensed someone watching her. Even when she turned and found no one, she believed Lincoln was with her in the room.

A young clerk who worked in the White House during Franklin Roosevelt's first term in office said she saw Lincoln's ghost sitting on his own bed, pulling on his boots!

Queen Wilhelmina of the Netherlands spent a night in the White House during Roosevelt's presidency. She reported that a knock brought her out of bed to answer the door. The ghost of Lincoln stood staring at her from the hallway.

Lincoln seems to prefer knocking on doors. Presidents from Theodore Roosevelt to Herbert Hoover and Harry Truman all said they heard mysterious rappings, often at their bedroom doors.

And then there is that certain window in the Oval Office. From that portal, Lincoln would gaze toward the distant Virginia battlefields. Mrs. Calvin Coolidge said she saw his ghost standing there on several occasions, his hands clasped tightly behind his back, his attention focused on the bloody fields across the Potomac.

Chapter II.
Indiana

"In the eerie, flickering glow of a kerosene lamp, Matthew Larch followed his son's footprints in the snow. They started at the kitchen door and extended some seventy-five feet from the house. There were no other marks on the freshly fallen flakes.

Young Oliver's tracks just stopped. The oak water bucket he had carried lay on its side several yards to the left.

Matthew Larch huddled under the dark sky with the small group of family and friends. Not a word passed among them. They listened intently, but could scarcely believe their senses.

Oliver was crying, his voice growing fainter and fainter as he screamed for help . . . screamed from somewhere above them . . . in the black, cold sky . . ."

"THE ABDUCTION OF OLIVER LARCH"

DIANA OF THE DUNES

The naked young woman walked nimbly across the sand dunes, sheltered by a grove of black oak trees that shut out the sun. Emerging on the beach, she stopped to watch the shore birds tottering on long, spindly legs as they searched for breakfast at the water's edge. The woman plunged into the frigid water. She swam as gracefully as a dolphin, her strong, swift strokes carrying her body effortlessly through the water.

After swimming back to shore, she raced over the sand to get dry. Next she stood erect, raised her arms and tilted her face to the sky as if giving thanks for the glory of the day. Then she vanished across the dunes in the direction she had come.

Who was she? She was called Diana of the Dunes. From 1915 until her death in 1925, she lived in the then-wild and rugged Indiana dunes country that hugs the Lake Michigan shore. She might have lived and died in obscurity had someone not seen her bathing nude. Perhaps it was a fisherman casting a line, or a seaman far out on the water turning binoculars toward the shore. But word soon spread about the "nude, bronzed goddess" of the wilderness.

The press, sensing a story, sent reporters in search of the goddess. East of Gary, where there was virtually no habitation, they found her living in an abandoned fisherman's shack. She granted an interview, then another . . . and another. Always gracious, she was still a private person who pleaded to be left alone.

For nearly seventy years, the story of Diana of the Dunes has been printed and reprinted, with variations, in newspapers and magazines. It may be the best-known legend of the Hoosier state. Even today, visitors to what is now Indiana Dunes State Park report seeing the ghost of the mysterious Diana hurrying over the sands at twilight, or hearing sobs coming from the ruins of the old shanty that was once her home.

The line between myth and reality is finely drawn. And while legend and truth do share many aspects in common, they also decidedly differ in others. What follows is the "legend" of Diana of the Dunes:

Diana was born Alice Mable Gray, the daughter of a prominent Chicago physician. She was well-educated and well-traveled and had held a secretarial job. But a broken love affair shattered the young woman's world and sent her into the remote dunes country. Supposedly, she arrived in the dunes with only the clothes on her back, a glass, knife, spoon, blanket and two guns. After sleeping on the sand for several nights, she discovered a deserted fisherman's shack and moved in. Driftwood served as furniture.

At first Alice lived on fish she netted and wild fruits and berries. In time, she sold berries and fruit wine to earn money for essentials. Wearing stout boots and khaki clothing, she trudged many miles to Miller, Indiana, for food and library books. People who came to know her said she was shy, but always kind and courteous.

The same could not be said for some of Alice's neighbors. As she roamed the dunes, studied, read or wrote, voyeurs made her life a hell of dodging and hiding. Fishermen, knowing that the young woman swam nude year-round and ran on the beach to dry, found excuses to visit her beach. When one fisherman's wife learned of her husband's habit, she stormed to Alice's shack to protest. Alice, with gun in hand and a half-wild dog by her side, warned the wife away.

In 1920, a man joined Alice—a mysterious person named Paul Wilson. He was described variously in press accounts of the day as a Texas rattlesnake hunter who had read about the woman and came north to woo her, an ex-convict with a police record for armed robbery in Kansas or a Michigan City ne'er-do-well. He was tall, strong and resourceful. He improved the little shack immeasurably, peddled fish he caught and sold hand-crafted furniture. Their finances improved and Alice was content. She could not know that violence would destroy this promising new life.

In June, 1922, dunes hikers found the ghastly remains of a man near Alice's shack. He had been strangled to death and partially cremated on the beach.

Paul Wilson was the chief suspect. He was known for his hot temper, his great strength and his strong dislike of strangers. When Eugene Frank, a deputy hired to guard dunes cottages, confronted an angry Alice and Paul, a fight took place. Paul was shot in the foot and Alice's skull was fractured by the butt of a pistol.

Police arrested Paul and deputy Frank. Alice was transported to Mercy Hospital in Gary, where she hovered near death.

Someone vandalized the shack while the couple was gone, taking all of Alice's books and manuscripts.

Meanwhile, Wilson deepened the murder mystery by telling police that an insane, gun-toting hermit named Burke might be their man. Burke had a twisted foot, and Wilson claimed he'd seen Burke's tracks near the murder scene. But by then any telltale tracks had been trampled upon by police, reporters and morbid sightseers.

Burke couldn't be found. Was he the victim? If not, who was? And why was he slain? The body was never identified, the case never solved. Paul Wilson was exonerated.

Alice was discharged from the hospital, but never fully recovered from her injury. Harassed by sightseers, she and Paul moved a few miles farther east. But progress closed in on them. A new housing development known as Ogden Dunes was being built around their makeshift shack. Alice and Paul, dispossessed again, went to Texas, but returned within a year. Alice had contracted uremic poisoning.

On February 11, 1925, Alice Mable Gray died in Paul Wilson's arms. Knowing she was dying, she asked to be cremated, with her ashes scattered over the sands she loved. But no facilities were available, and the authorities refused to let Paul make a funeral pyre on the beach. Alice was buried in Gary's Oak Lawn Cemetery, but a reporter who searched for the grave forty years later never found it. Not even cemetery workers were certain of its location. In death, this sensitive and gentle woman found, at last, the privacy she sought so desperately in life.

Five years after Alice's death, a Paul Wilson was convicted of robbery and taken to the state prison at Michigan City. Was it Alice's Paul? No one knew.

That's the legend of Diana of the Dunes. However, the real story of Alice Mable Gray differs in a number of respects.

Alice Gray was no legendary beauty romping naked in the sand dunes. She did bathe in the lake, of course, for she had no other facilities. But a ravishing young lady? Hardly. She was thirty-four years old when she first went to live in the dunes, and was described as exceedingly plain and tiny.

Alice had graduated from the University of Chicago, a member of the Phi Beta Kappa Honor Society, an unusual accomplishment in an era when few women sought higher education and no value was placed on a woman's intellectual achievements. After graduation, Alice took the only job she could find—editorial secretary of an astronomy magazine. But it wasn't a broken love affair that caused her to leave Chicago. In an early interview, she told a reporter that her eyesight had begun to fail and a physician had given her the wrong medicine which made it impossible for her to continue the close work her magazine job required. She chose to live in the Indiana dunes because it was a familiar place. She'd been there many times and had, in fact, written a naturalist's dissertation on the area while a student. Hardly the stuff of legend.

And Paul Wilson? He was actually a skilled boat-builder and handyman. He and Alice shared an uncomplicated life of simple pleasures, saddened by her untimely death. That was the the *real* story . . . until 1981.

In that year, a researcher who had spent years pursuing the story of Alice Mable Gray and Paul Wilson turned up well-documented information. His findings are, in a sense, even more lurid than the legend:

- While Alice died of uremic poisoning, she also died of massive blows to her abdomen.
- Alice was buried in a cemetery plot with other bodies. (No wonder the reporter couldn't locate her grave!) The graveskeeper was convicted of burying several persons in the same grave.

- Alice's manuscripts had actually been taken from her shack and preserved by her relatives.
- Paul Wilson was never married to Alice; he was married to another woman.
- Paul Wilson was actually the illegitimate son of a distinguished La Porte County family; Wilson was not his real name.
- Wilson had a lengthy criminal record. After being released from prison in California, he was shot to death while stealing a car.

Later, an astonishing story from California seemed to support at least one of the researcher's findings. In the Winter 1982 issue of *Dunes Country Magazine*, Marguerite Bell Johansen wrote a detailed account of her association with Alice Mable Gray.

When Mrs. Johansen was twelve years old and growing up in Michigan City, Indiana, she said she babysat for Alice's *children*! She recalled that the house at 309 Finley Street was a shabby frame bungalow with sagging porch and dingy windows with cracked green shades. Inside, a barren room held two chairs and two small rustic pedestals; toys littered the floor.

Mrs. Johansen, who was known as Margaret, described her first meeting with Mrs. Willson (sic), whose real identity was unknown to her:

> "The faded smock did little to disguise the ungainliness of her body, yet she crossed the worn floor in old mocassins as quietly as if barefoot. Her hair was shapeless, untidy, long and dark, pinned back carelessly from features clean-cut as a coin. It was a proud, arresting face, the eyes deepset as if with a secret, a special knowledge.
>
> She had a naive delicacy that had nothing to do with social elegance. Dreamy, whimsical, absent-minded, she would start to do something,

see something else to be done, forget the first errand, finish nothing."

Margaret would earn ten cents an hour for looking after Alice's daughter, Bonita, two afternoons a week, after school. Margaret recalled that the child "looked perhaps seven years old." She had long, coarse black hair set in "an oval face with high cheekbones." Bonita said her father was an Indian who'd been shot and killed. Her mother had told her that, she said. Margaret was puzzled. She knew of no Indians closer than northern Michigan. Bonita also had five names, the last of which was Willson.

Alice and the child seemed nervous and frightened around "Mr. Willson," and little Margaret was nervous too. She wrote: "The breadth of his chest, the size of those hands was a little frightening. His hair, overlong and thickly blond, coiled and curled about his ears like the hair of gods in the mythology book at home. His small incurious eyes were china blue, devoid of warmth or even interest. No answering expression appeared on that sullen shut-in face."

The family lived mostly on stale bakery goods. Margaret understood that Mr. Willson was a woodcutter, yet she never saw any woodcutter's tools in the house, and it was unlawful to cut trees in the dunes area.

Because of Margaret's uneasiness in the presence of Mr. Willson, Alice promised never to leave the girl alone with him. Alice and Margaret soon became close friends in that rare and wonderful way in which sometimes a child and a woman relate to each other. The older woman enjoyed Margaret greatly and confided in her. She told Margaret about her years at a girls' school in Massachusetts, and complained about the way society treated women, keeping them ignorant and complacent in a world made for man's pleasure. Margaret didn't always understand what Alice meant and thought sometimes that the woman was crazy.

On a November day Alice told Margaret not to come for a while—she'd be going to Chicago to Michael Reese Lying-in Hospital to have her baby. Margaret and her mother thought it was odd for her to go so far. Poor people had their babies at home, and the Willsons were poor.

After the baby was born, Margaret returned to the Willsons. The new little girl was named Bluebell, her eyes the exact shade of the flower that colored the dunes in spring.

The family was now poorer than ever, and Margaret was often embarrassed to take money she knew they couldn't afford.

Then came the day Margaret would never forget. As she entered the Willson's house, fear tightened her throat. Bonita was nowhere to be seen. Alice, on the verge of tears, stood wringing her hands. The bedroom door crashed open and Paul Willson thundered out of the room. "By God! By God!" he yelled, his face red and blotchy, and stormed out the door. Margaret looked at Alice. Bruises were beginning to show on her arms and wrists.

"A gentleman would strike a lady where it didn't show, wouldn't he?" Alice said, her eyes wet.

Alice sat down and wrote a note for Margaret to take home to her mother. Margaret noted the fine, delicate handwriting. She would never have dared to unfold the sheet of paper, but she knew, somehow, that she would not be working for Mrs. Willson any longer.

Margaret's mother read the note and called on Mrs. Willson. Returning home, she drew her daughter aside. "She's the woman they called Diana of the Dunes," she began. "I'm sorry for her, but of course I can't let you go there any more." She paused. "She needs help. She has a family, but she'll never go back to her own people. Poor creature . . ."

The definitive story of Alice Mable Gray may never be known. And perhaps that's as it should be. All the woman ever wanted was the right to be left alone. Like Henry David Thoreau, Alice Gray lived her life moving to the tune of a different drummer. And some say that Alice has never left her beloved dunes, that by the light of a full moon her ghost stands silhouetted on *her* beach, giving thanks for the glory of the night.

THE LEGEND OF STIFFY GREEN

Have you ever heard a dog bark in a graveyard at night? Nothing so unusual about that, unless you're in Terre Haute, near the gates of the densely-wooded Highland Lawn Cemetery.

There is an ominous sign at the entrance. No one, it warns, is permitted in the cemetery after dark. The caretakers had good reason to mount that sign. Highland Lawn is the final resting place of John G. Heinl and his little bulldog, so faithful to his master that even now he stands watch in the family mausoleum.

The story begins nearly seven decades ago. John Heinl loved his dog, Stiffy Green. The kindly gentleman, and his bulldog, trotting obediently at his heels, were inseparable companions on the streets of Terre Haute. Stiffy returned his master's affection in countless ways; he rarely let Mr. Heinl out of his sight.

In 1920, John Heinl died. Stiffy Green was inconsolable. He refused to leave his master's side, even at the funeral and burial service. Whenever someone tried to pull Stiffy away, the little dog snapped and snarled.

Mr. Heinl's remains were sealed in the family mausoleum at Highland Lawn Cemetery. Stiffy positioned himself outside the bronze mausoleum doors, his bright green eyes set in a pugnacious countenance, daring anyone to interrupt his master's sleep.

There he stood vigil day and night, through rain and heat. He didn't eat, nor did he leave his guard post except on those few occasions when members of the Heinl family took him home. But Stiffy always found his way back to Highland Lawn Cemetery.

And that's were Stiffy Green died, his body beside a pillar at the entrance to the mausoleum.

Mrs. Heinl could not bear the thought of separating Stiffy from her husband. She asked a taxidermist to preserve Stiffy's body. Mrs. Heinl then placed the dog on the floor inside the mausoleum near the man he so faithfully followed.

Today, Stiffy Green still guards John Heinl. On sunny days you can peer through the filigreed bronze grillwork of the doors into the musty, dark interior and see the perfectly preserved body of Stiffy. It is disconcerting to see a dog inside such a place. At any moment you expect a tail to wag, or his head to tilt slightly as if to ask what the visitor wants in this place.

A legend persists in Terre Haute that the specters of Stiffy Green and his master still take their daily strolls together. Barking and whining often drift across the night from the vicinity of the Heinl mausoleum. A voice some say is that of John Heinl is heard hushing his little companion. People claim they've seen the mausoleum's doors standing open, while the figures of a man and a dog walk nearby.

No, a barking dog in a graveyard is not unusual. Unless you are at the Highland Lawn Cemetery in Terre Haute. Then it may be a ghostly bulldog barking at a shadow while following his master on one of their nightly walks.

BRIDGES OF ALARM

Old bridges are perfect settings for ghost tales, particularly in Indiana. Whether the structures are concrete or iron, wooden-planked or modern asphalt, still used or abandoned decades ago, hundreds of bridges spanning countless streams and rivers hold a bevy of prowling specters.

WHITE LICK CREEK

The railroad bridge over White Lick Creek near Danville, in Hendricks County, is today only a memory. But when Indiana was new, burgeoning with confident pioneer businessmen, the trestle was one of the first built by Irish laborers during the railroad boom of the 1850s.

Indiana was the site of a vast, track-laying network of beefy immigrant laborers, glistening steel and the staccato rhythm of ten-pound hammers slamming against heavy iron spikes. The story is told in Hendricks County that while one of the supports of the White Lick Creek bridge was being formed for the trestle, an Irishman lost his balance and fell to his death into the sucking concrete mixture.

The railroad company refused to retrieve the dead man's body unless his fellow workers would pay for the undertaking. But the men were too poor to do so; thus the body was sealed forever in the trestle support. As time passed, the railroad snaked westward toward the horizon. It wasn't long, however, before strange stories began to circulate about the bridge over White Lick Creek—weird, mysterious tales about the bridge and the ghost of a dead Irishman.

During the driest part of the Indiana summer, when the sun scorches the baked earth and little boys sit listlessly beneath towering buckeye trees watching heat waves rise from the bubbling asphalt, at that time of year the support in which the doomed Irishman saw the last rays of sunlight seemed to issue forth human tears. Some say it looked more like blood was dripping into White Lick Creek far below.

Local residents also reported that on the first night of a full moon, the Irishman's ghost would stand stiff and unmoving on the bridge span, a lighted lantern hanging from his bony right hand. If, in the distance, the echo of a train whistle reached down the track, the Irishman would swing his lantern to and fro, trying in vain to flag down the engineer. Sometimes he cried out in vain, "Stop, please. Take me aboard so that my soul may rest in peace." He never succeeded in stopping the train.

Now the railroad bridge is gone, but the legend, and the Irishman, still remain along White Lick Creek.

CRY-WOMAN'S BRIDGE

The town of Dublin straddles U.S. Highway 40 in east-central Indiana between Richmond and Indianapolis. It is a fairly typical, small midwestern city, dependent on a diversified industrial and agricultural industry and the trade a major highway can bring to city businesses.

There was also once a bridge which stood on Heacock Road, southeast of Dublin, a bridge known to local residents as "Cry-Woman's Bridge." The bridge is gone now, but its ghostly legend lingers.

The young woman who gave her name to the bridge was a stranger to the county, unfamiliar with the numerous twisting county roads. Late one rainy night, while returning home with her infant son, the woman approached the bridge far too quickly, lost control of her car at the sharp curve just before the bridge entrance, and plunged into the rain-swollen creek below.

The woman's body was later found by searchers. However, there was no sign of her baby. Only a little pink blanket and a baby's pacifier were recovered. The woman's relatives could not be located, and she was buried in a pauper's grave next to a coffin which held the infant's blanket and pacifier.

Following the incident, the ghost of a woman was said to be seen prowling the bridge, particularly on foggy, rainy nights. And the specter's infrequent appearances are accented by pitiful moans and sobs and a choking cry that seemingly pleads "Where is my baby?"

A young couple parked near the bridge one evening a few years ago. A short while later, they heard scratching sounds coming from the roof and trunk of their car. They were aware of the bridge's "ghostly" reputation and decided to leave. But their car wouldn't start! Suddenly, the scratching became louder and louder, accompanied now by heart-stopping wails. A voice drifted toward them crying, "Baby, where have you gone? Baby, where have you gone?"

The young couple finally got the car started. They examined it later and found scratches all over the hood, scraches that might have been caused by a woman's long fingernails!

Has the ghost ever found its offspring? Or is it still searching? No one really knows for sure.

THE ODON FIRES

Quite possibly the most terrifying fear of all may be that induced by the demon poltergeist which sets fires for no apparent reason. Hundreds of cases of mysterious fires have been recorded over the centuries, and while many have been attributed to the work of very human hands, still other cases ... and there are dozens ... remain unsolved—homes, automobiles and *people* reduced to smoldering embers.

What causes these spontaneous immolations? How can a fire erupt in one isolated place, consume only a few items, and leave the rest of the area unscorched? What *is* it that has given rise to the specter known as the fire poltergeist?

An investigator of this peculiar phenomenon can find many examples to study in the Middle West. One of the strangest ever recorded caused the peaceful countryside near Odon, Indiana to erupt in horror during April, 1941. The terrifying scene occurred at the William Hackler farm. Fires from no apparent source broke out all over the house. So disturbing were the events that Mr. Hackler actually destroyed his home and moved away rather than stay and face the terror of the flames!

The particular April morning began innocently enough. The Hackler family rose early and finished with breakfast a few minutes before eight. The weather had been unusually warm, and Mr. Hackler wanted to get an early start with his day's planting.

No one remembered just who smelled the first whiff of smoke. The heavy scent of smoldering wood was distinctive. Parents and children fanned out to search and soon found a small blaze in a second-floor bedroom under the window. The fire seemed to be coming from *within* the wall.

The Odon Fire Department was called and extinguished the fire.

What made this first fire, and all the rest, particularly unnerving was that the house had not been wired for electricity. Children and parents pleaded their innocence. No one had been seen going in or out of the bedroom all morning. It was usually unoccupied.

The long day had just begun.

No sooner had the Odon fire department returned to town than they were called back to the farm. Mrs. Hackler had discovered another fire smoldering in a mattress in another bedroom. Again the fire seemed to burn from *within* the feather mattress.

Within minutes all hell broke loose—fires began everywhere. In all, nine fires were discovered between eight and eleven a.m. that morning!

One firefighter noticed a thin wisp of smoke coming from a shelf in the living room. He walked over, picked up a book that seemed to be nearest the smoke, opened its covers and found it, too, *burning on the inside*!

A pair of Mr. Hackler's coveralls hanging behind a door went up in a quick flash of flame.

While neighbors stood staring, a bedspread turned to ashes. The calendar hanging on the kitchen wall ignited.

And on it went. No room in the house was spared. Yet nothing was seriously damaged. Only small items such as clothing and household items seemed to explode into flame. The house itself never caught fire!

What caused the Odon fires? There was no electricity in the Hackler house, nor was there a fire burning in the kitchen wood stove. In addition, no one was ever accused of deliberately setting the fires. Those who observed the events said it was as if an invisible hand had lit a thousand matches in the old farmhouse!

As the day finally ended, twenty-eight fires had been discovered and brought under control by volunteer firefighters from two adjoining communities. The Hacklers themselves were through. They had had enough. When the last fire had been extinguished, William Hackler gathered up his family, moved their beds outside and spent the night beneath the stars. Nothing could make him go back into that cursed house.

One week later, Hackler dismantled the house room by room, salvaged the lumber and built a new home several miles away. By all accounts the Hacklers were never again plagued with mysterious fires.

Several unusual explanations for the Odon fires were later offered to inquisitive reporters. One man claimed that the Hackler farm was situated in the center of a strong magnetic field which somehow had triggered the fires. Other observers believed that an old well may have produced gases that ignited sections of the house. Neither theory was ever validated. Officials eventually closed the case of the Odon fires by terming it a "most baffling mystery."

There was one ironic footnote to the Odon fires. The Traveler's Insurance Company later published a full-page advertisement in an April 19, 1941 edition of *Collier's Magazine* describing the Hackler fires. It seems that the company had insured the family against loss by fire—any kind of fire!

THE "UNOFFICIAL" LIBRARIAN

It would be every librarian's dream. A dedicated assistant who worked whenever necessary, often late in the evening, asked for no paycheck and was 100 percent effective in encouraging borrowers to return material filched from library shelves.

That "perfect" librarian did exist ... as a ghost, according to a legend at DePauw University in Greencastle, Indiana. The first report that a spectral being haunted old Whitcomb Library came in the early 1900s. A young man arrived on the DePauw campus. On his first visit to the library he discovered the rare book collection given to the school by the late Governor James Whitcomb, after whom the "Hoosier poet" James Whitcomb Riley was named. Whitcomb had been an avid collector of books most of his life, and he bequeathed his private library to DePauw on the stipulation they be used for research purposes *only* and *never* taken from the library building.

The student had read the rules. But he became so entranced with one volume in particular that he slipped it into his pocket to take home and read. He had every intention of returning it the next day.

The book was titled *The Poems of Oison*, a mysterious and exotic volume of verse written in India, published in Philadelphia in 1789 and given to the young James Whitcomb in 1813 as a gift.

It was late now, well past midnight. In his hands, the student held the yellowed, dusty volume; the vivid Indian poetry was alien to his mind. At last he snapped off the light, tucking the volume under his pillow. Sleep did not come easily, for the images contained in Oison's poetry floated through the student's brain.

He didn't know how long he had been asleep when suddenly he was awakened by what . . . a sound? Someone knocking at his door? His eyes slowly focused. At the foot of his bed hung a spectral body draped in dark, musty clothing. A skeletal arm reached toward the terrified boy, its bony finger pointed accusingly.

"Who stole Oison?" it intoned. "Oison! Oison!"

Over and over it moaned the title of the book hidden beneath the student's pillow. The ghost lashed out toward the quivering figure on the bed, its bony hand actually touching the boy's face.

"Oison! Oison!" came the wail. An eternity later, or so it seemed to the young victim, the figure faded away.

The student shivered in a protective crouch at the head of the bed. For the rest of the night he did not move, fearful the specter might return. At first light the boy quickly dressed and snatched up the pilfered volume of poetry.

The woman at the library's main desk was startled by the breathless student who raced up to her as the doors were unlocked.

"Here it is! Here is Oison!" he blurted out, confessing that he had taken the book from the library. Further, he told the bewildered librarian, the ghost of Governor Whitcomb had spent most of the night in his room demanding the pilfered volume be returned.

A few days later, as the story of Governor Whitcomb's ghostly visit spread across campus, a coed who heard it raced to the library just a few minutes before closing. She, too, had "borrowed" a volume from the Whitcomb Collection.

DePauw University opened a new library in 1956. Although the collection given by Governor Whitcomb to the school is housed in the building, there have been no recent reports of a ghost haranguing recalcitrant students. But then, there haven't been any books taken from the Whitcomb Collection. They are kept behind locked doors now. And with a protector like the ghost of Governor Whitcomb, students leave them where they are!

THE HAUNTING OF HANNAH HOUSE

Are ghosts naturally attracted to empty houses where they are less likely to be disturbed in their nocturnal wanderings? Or do they prefer the company of living occupants?

The ghostly reputation of the Hannah House, a stately red brick mansion in Indianapolis, was acquired *after* it had sat empty for several years in the 1960s. Yet within the past twenty years unexplained eyewitness reports abound, telling of a mysterious man in a frock coat who wanders the hallways, of the sickening smell of decaying flesh, of crashing glassware that is never found, of pictures that fall off walls for no apparent reason and of numbing cold spots.

The house, built in 1858, is part of the legacy of Alexander M. Hannah, an Indiana state legislator, postmaster, sheriff and clerk of the circuit court. In pre-Civil War years, Hannah reportedly used the basement of the twenty-four-room mansion to hide fleeing Southern slaves on the mysterious "underground railroad." Legend says that one night a lantern tipped over in the basement and the fire killed many of the slaves. They were buried in rude caskets in the basement.

From all outward signs, Alexander and his wife, Elizabeth Jackson, whom he married in 1872 when he was fifty-one years old, lived a peaceful life in the lovely Italianate-style home on Madison Avenue. While the couple may have had a stillborn child, they did not lead the sort of tragic lives that often beget unhappy specters.

Alexander Hannah died in 1895 and four years later, Roman Oehler, a prosperous Indianapolis jeweler, bought the house. His daughter, Romena Oehler Elder, inherited the mansion upon her father's death. In 1962, with all of the children gone, Mrs. Elder moved out and left the care of the place to her youngest son, David. The house then remained empty for six years.

David Elder was the first to suspect that the vacant Hannah House was "occupied." He was working there alone one bleak and rainsoaked day in 1967 when the sound of breaking glass resounded from the basement. Had neighborhood children broken into the house and overturned a basket of fruit jars? Elder investigated, but found nothing disturbed. Interestingly, the jars were stored in the area of the basement where the slaves had been buried more than a century before, causing Elder to wonder whether the restless spirits of those helpless, frightened, runaway slaves were plaguing Hannah House.

From time to time, the stench of death permeates the house. The odor of rotting flesh seems to emanate from a second-floor bedroom, and the smell is so strong that it has sent more than one visitor reeling from the house. Attempts to eradicate the smell with cleaning solutions, bleach, perfume and other potions have failed. However, at other times a scent of roses is emitted. But, of course, there are no flowers in the room which is normally locked up and used for storage.

In addition, the door which opens from the odoriferous room into the hallway seemingly possesses a will of its own—it swings open even when the handle is securely locked. And once it opens, an increase in other unexplained activity in the house occurs—strange noises, footsteps, cold drafts where there are no open windows, voices mumbling in shadowy passages and additional doors opening and closing.

Lynn Dohrenwend, an Indianapolis psychic, told writers Richard Winer and Nancy Osborn Ishmael (authors of *More Haunted Houses*) that she "saw" a pregnant woman in the haunted bedroom, one who was obviously in severe pain as a result of abdominal cramps apparently caused by the child she was carrying. The child was stillborn, Dohrenwend said. The birth was forced because the woman's system had become poisoned, putrefactive, from the child.

There is no official record of any child having been born in the haunted bedroom. However, Dohrenwend was so insistent that a child *had* been born in that room that a later investigation of the Crown Hill Cemetery uncovered a third, small tombstone next to the graves of Elizabeth and Alexander. No name was on the marker, only a single date. It may be the grave of an unknown Hannah infant.

Gladys O'Brien and her husband, John Francis O'Brien, operated an antique business in the house from 1968 until 1978 and lived there part of that time. During their stay, the couple was subjected to an array of strange incidents.

Early one evening, Mrs. O'Brien caught a glimpse of a man in a black suit walking across the upstairs hallway. She thought a customer had somehow ventured onto the second floor which had been closed to visitors. But by the time she reached the top of the stairs, the mysterious visitor was gone. Mrs. O'Brien called her husband. Together they searched the house thoroughly, but they could find no sign of any intruder.

On another occasion, a painter who had been hired to spruce up the interior became the unwitting target of whatever it was that haunted the house. Doors would swing open as he walked by, and pictures slid from their moorings. In the most bizarre event, a spoon Mrs. O'Brien had placed on a tray unexpectedly flew across the room! The painter fled.

Mrs. O'Brien's son volunteered to finish the house painting, but an uneasy feeling of being watched made him very uncomfortable on his first night on the job. So, the next night the young man's wife and two daughters accompanied him to the house. His daughter, Cheryl, played on the stairs while her father, mother and sister worked in an adjoining room. Soon, O'Brien heard Cheryl talking to someone.

"Hi, Dad," the girl said, employing the affectionate name the children used for their grandfather, John O'Brien.

But the elder O'Brien was *not* in the house! Cheryl continued to talk to her "grandfather," while the rest of the family looked on, dumbfounded. In a few minutes, Cheryl's father asked what "Dad" was doing now. She replied that "grandfather" was climbing the stairs. Cheryl's parents and sister quickly ran into the hallway. They didn't see anyone. The family then hurriedly left the house.

Mr. O'Brien also encountered the Hannah House mystery man. The transparent specter was standing in an archway on the stairs, sporting mutton-chop whiskers and wearing a black, old-fashioned suit of clothes. The ghost evaporated before Mr. O'Brien could reach him.

Quite often, the rustling of clothing and the sound of footsteps of varying loudness were heard on the staircase; some steps were light, others heavier. Oddly, the stairway was carpeted! When either one of the O'Briens would go to check on the source of the sound, the footsteps always ceased.

The door to a staircase leading to an attic from the second floor also had a mind of its own. Mr. O'Brien heard something upstairs as he was working on the lower floor, rushed up the staircase and ran down the hallway looking into each room. His eagerness waned, however, once he reached the attic door and saw the handle turning slowly. The door then swung open, emitting a cool draft from the unused loft.

There was *no way* the handle could have turned of its own accord, Mr. O'Brien believed.

The O'Briens often watched television in a room on the second floor. While he was alone in the house one night, Mr. O'Brien heard some loud groaning from somewhere down the hallway. He turned down the television to listen more closely, but the moans stopped. A few minutes later, however, they began again, louder than before. Mr. O'Brien yelled to the ghost to stop its "bellyaching" and leave them in peace. Strangely, the groaning stopped for that night.

By 1972 the Hannah House hauntings appeared to have stopped altogether. Mr. O'Brien credits his own consternation with the upsetting events to helping rid the house of its ghosts . . . at least temporarily.

From 1980-82 the Indianapolis Jaycees used Hannah House for their annual Halloween "Haunted House" project. They sponsored tours of the old mansion for youngsters, replete with "rigged," spooky effects . . . except that some of the effects were *not* planned.

For example, in October 1980, Dick Raasch, coordinator of the project, was relaxing with fellow workers in the old summer kitchen, a part of the original house. Next to the kitchen an old stairway, originally used by servants, goes up to the second floor. On this occasion, scratching sounds suddenly arose from *inside* the staircase landing wall. David Elder dashed beneath the stairs after the sound started but could not locate a source for it.

In that same year, Raasch installed his own stereo unit to reproduce the chilling sounds that would be used during the Halloween tour. His unit had an ON/OFF button which has to be depressed either to start or to stop transmission. One evening when Raasch and a friend were alone together in the house, the stereo, which was playing, suddenly went off. Raasch and his friend checked the unit and found the button depressed. They re-started the stereo. Later, it was shut down a second time! No one else was in the house—all the doors and windows were locked.

"Somebody *had* to have pushed that button," Raasch said. "But there is no way someone else could have been inside the house."

In October of 1981, Indianapolis' version of the TV show "PM Magazine" visited Hannah House to film a Halloween segment. One of the cameramen stood in the dining room doorway in order to take a shot across the room. An old chandelier hung from the ceiling.

The cameraman remarked, "Wouldn't it be eerie if the chandelier moved?" At that instant, the chandelier started to swing in a six-inch arc!

"Our mouths were open," said Raasch who witnessed the movement along with six or seven other people.

Raasch swore that there was no physical construction going on in the house, nor was there any truck traffic. And there was no one upstairs who could have jumped on the floor to set the chandelier in motion. All the doors and windows were closed and locked, hence no air was moving. And no wires led to the chandelier.

On that very same day, the television crew brought psychic Allene Cunningham to the house. She sensed cold spots. The crew, Raasch and Cunningham then moved into a room where they were going to film some "exit" footage. The cameraman stood in one of two doorways to the room, and the program's host stood in front of a coffin which had been placed against a wall. Suddenly, a picture above the coffin fell to the floor. The two-penny nail attached to the picture did *not* break. In fact, it was nailed into a two-by-four and was still angled upward! Furthermore, the wire on the old picture remained firmly attached.

"There is no conceivable way the picture could have fallen of its own accord," Raasch observed. "It lifted up and fell. It just looked like somebody dropped it to the floor."

How to explain these incidents?

"I can't explain them," Raasch confided. "Something was in there (the house), but I just don't know *what* it was."

OLD JACOB COX

Martin Winding had known the old man who lived by the side of the muddy, rutted road for decades. Everyone in Martin County, Indiana, knew Jacob Cox. He was the local character.

Winding reined his saddle horse a short distance from the Cox farm. Odd, he thought, there didn't seem to be anyone about the place. On these warm spring days folks usually found the old man shambling around the building, his yard filled with chickens, an old milk cow grazing on any patch of grass and the mule rubbing its back against the rotting, split-rail fence. And right in the middle of it all would be Jacob Cox, singing some ancient tune at the top of his lungs to the bored livestock.

Winding peered through the gathering dusk at the deserted homestead. All Cox's animals were gone. In fact, there was no sound at all, save for the cricket chorus along the trail. Only two weeks prior, before Winding had set out on his trip to the southern part of the state, he had spent several minutes in idle conversation with Jacob Cox. Now there wasn't a trace of the old man or his holdings.

Winding nudged his horse. Quite unexpectedly, Cox walked out of the barn and crossed the road a few yards in front of the horseman.

Winding yelled out. Cox kept on moving toward a corn crib filled with the residue of winter feed.

Oh well, Martin reasoned, the old fellow was getting on in years and his hearing was not at all what it should be. As Winding rode by he peered off toward the direction in which Cox had walked. A sudden gust of wind tickled his neck. In the next instant, Winding was nearly thrown from his saddle as a pair of hands suddenly and forcefully gripped his shoulders.

Winding's horse sprang forward, but the faster it galloped, the tighter the hands became on Winding's shoulders. He hung on as best he could, flopping in the saddle like a sewing machine bobbin gone wild. But not once did he dare to look to see who, or what, had joined him for a ride.

Within a few moments, Winding's horse came to a stream at the edge of the Cox farm, and the hands on the rider's shoulders relaxed their grip. Winding risked a glance backward—all he could see was the gloomy roadway that stretched toward the log cabins of old Jacob Cox's farm.

Nary a word had passed between him and his mysterious passenger—only the vice-like grip around his shoulders and something terribly cold pressing against him.

The following morning, Martin Winding related his strange tale to a friend in town. After a long pause, the man nodded his head. Yes, he allowed at length, your story just might be true. Another fellow claims to have had the same experience not more than three days before.

Winding's friend speculated that the fellow who jumped on the horse was probably old Jacob Cox himself. Winding laughed at the idea. There just wasn't any way that Jacob Cox could jump on a moving horse, why, he could hardly climb into a wagon!

"Yes there was," his friend replied, "if it wasn't Jacob Cox *in the flesh* who was doing the jumping! Old Cox *died* ten days before, and your weird riding companion was probably the *ghost* of Jacob Cox!"

With that, Martin Winding gulped down the rest of his beer and headed toward the door. He was never quite the same again.

THE VIGIL

Deloris Hart opened her eyes and tried to focus on the unfamiliar surroundings. What was this place? The bed was very large, much bigger than the one at home. The sheets were pulled tight, a light blanket drawn over the top. She couldn't move very well. Both of her legs and an arm felt as if they were held down by rocks. Something white was around them. She couldn't move her head. And it hurt very much.

The child's eyes shifted slowly about the room, noticing the window with the curtain and shade closed, a door going somewhere and two simple chairs. Deloris knew this was not her home. But where was she then? She couldn't remember exactly what had happened, only that she had been in the car with her grandpa and great-grandpa. But it was something bad, she sensed that much.

Deloris then saw the nice-looking lady who was standing at the foot of her bed. The little girl tried to speak, but the woman raised her hand to her lips. There was something peculiar about her, Deloris thought. She looked a lot like one of the pretty ladies out of one of her storybooks. A kind of haze shimmered around her.

And she didn't move. But she had such a nice smile that Deloris wasn't a bit afraid—she felt very warm and comfortable in the nice lady's presence.

Deloris drifted in and out of consciousness over the next several days. Men and women in white coats often came into the room. But apparently they didn't see the nice lady who never moved or spoke. Deloris tried to ask the man who looked into her eyes and throat where her mama and papa were, but somehow she couldn't make the right sounds.

Herbert and Rose Hart, Deloris's parents, were not allowed into their daughter's room for the first few days after the accident. Her condition was too critical—Deloris was not expected to live. On that earlier 1932 afternoon, another automobile had swerved across the center line into the path of her grandpa's car. Now, her grandfather was lying close to death in another Terre Haute hospital room; her great-grandfather had been killed instantly. Deloris nearly had her scalp sliced off by flying glass. She sustained several additional serious injuries.

Miraculously, Deloris Hart recovered. The doctors actually termed her recovery "a miracle;" her parents were thankful that their prayers had been answered. Yet the young child didn't understand or recall everything that had happened, only that the kind lady was always there in her room. The other people who silently entered her room always walked around the lady. That was silly, Deloris thought, why didn't they say hello? Couldn't they see her?

The small woman with jet black hair, deep brown eyes and light complexion never touched Deloris. Later, after Deloris had told her parents about the nice lady, hospital doctors and nurses stated emphatically that *no one* of that description worked at the Terre Haute hospital nor had been allowed into the girl's room.

Who then was the visitor who had kept vigil over Deloris?

Following Deloris's release from the hospital, her father became obsessed with discovering the identity of the woman in the hospital. He later found some old photographs tucked away in a trunk and showed them to Deloris.

Deloris's eyes shone. That was the nice lady she said. It was she who had been with her in the hospital.

That was impossible, her father replied. It simply couldn't be.

Yes, the child insisted, that was the woman who made me want to live.

Deloris's father could only shake his head in disbelief. The photograph was one of his mother, Belle Hart, who had been dead for twenty years!

OSCAR

The kids in Oscar's Evansville neighborhood knew him as a friendly, outgoing nineteen-year-old who took delight in giving them rides in his shiny new car, circa 1922. They would pile in, eager to career over the dusty roads around the city. Late in the evening Oscar would bring them back to his house, and calling goodnight, they would scatter to their own respective dwellings.

The routine didn't vary on that one evening in the early 1920s when everyone waved as Oscar went into his house. They never saw him again. His parents found him dead in bed next morning. The cause of death is not known.

Oscar's ghost may still linger in Evansville, attached now to a family that moved into Oscar's old home years after his death. At least that's what Warren and Gladys Reynolds think. They have been the targets of Oscar's friendly antics for over forty years, if that is indeed the explanation for all the strange occurrences the Reynolds have witnessed.

The house where Oscar lived and died and where the Reynolds first met his spirit is gone now. The lot is occupied by part of the Doctor's Plaza, a medical clinic. But back in 1942, Gladys and Warren Reynolds, a young married couple, lived there.

"At first I thought they were ordinary noises," soft-spoken Gladys Reynolds remembers. "But my husband thought from the beginning that something peculiar was going on. He always seemed to have the most experiences. I worked during the days, and he was on the night shift as a deputy sheriff. Oscar seemed to be around more during the day when my husband was at home."

The Reynolds's first indication that Oscar was still in "his" house came during a thunderstorm. The family was in a downstairs room. Footsteps suddenly pounded across an upstairs hallway. What followed sounded like windows being shut in the bedrooms. Sure enough, when the family checked upstairs, each window that had been open was now firmly closed against the brewing storm.

On another day, the couple's twelve-year-old daughter was home alone finishing some homework in the dining room. She heard someone coming down the staircase. The little girl was so frightened she hid under the big round table. The descending footsteps stopped abruptly on the last step. Peering out, the child could see she was quite alone.

Oscar was very shy. On only two occasions did he allow himself to be glimpsed. The witness in both cases was Warren Reynolds's mother. She lived with her son and daughter-in-law for several years before her death.

The senior Mrs. Reynolds occupied the same bedroom in which Oscar was reputed to have died. The first time she saw Oscar was quite late at night, when a sharp sound forced her awake. She looked around the room. There was Oscar standing with his back to her, bending over a grate in the fireplace. Hoping the specter would disappear, the old woman pulled the blankets over her head. A few moments later she peeked out. The shadowy stranger was still there. Oscar finally melted into the darkness.

Oscar's second visit to his old bedroom was a bit shorter, and again at night. He was standing quite still next to a potted plant, with his back toward Mrs. Reynolds, who had again been awakened from a sound sleep. And as before, after a few seconds, he seemed to melt away.

Oscar frequented his bedroom often. He seemed to prefer the cane-bottomed rocker, for the family would hear its familiar creaking back and forth for minutes on end. Each time they investigated, however, the chair was absolutely still and no one was in the room.

Gladys Reynolds recalled that Oscar also liked to prowl about the partially-finished attic. "My husband heard someone up there one afternoon. He thought some kids had broken in through the window. Well, since he was a deputy sheriff he took out his revolver and headed up the stairs. But when he got there, he couldn't find anything. All the windows were locked and nothing had been disturbed. From what he heard, he was convinced someone had been walking around up there."

An incident in 1948 involved a woman friend of Mrs. Reynolds who came to visit for several days. Late the first evening, after her friend had retired, Mrs. Reynolds heard drawers opening and closing upstairs, footsteps moving across the floorboards and doors slamming. Surprised at the activity, she thought perhaps her friend was preparing to leave early in the morning. That notion was dispelled at breakfast when her friend assured her she was indeed staying and had slept soundly through the night. She emphatically denied being the source of the nocturnal activity.

The Reynolds family moved out of Oscar's house in 1965. It was subsequently torn down to make way for the medical facility.

Oscar, however, may have been so taken with the Reynolds family that he moved with them into their next home! Sometimes they hear faint footsteps or the creaking of the rocking chair Oscar fancied.

In the new house, Gladys Reynolds says there have been two occasions when objects have mysteriously disappeared, only to be found later in places the family had thoroughly searched.

"When I couldn't find my make-up compact in its usual drawer," Gladys Reynolds says, "I thought my granddaughter had taken it to play with. I didn't want to say anything to my daughter; I didn't want her to spank the child. I looked everywhere and after a few days I just gave up. My daughter and her family left and I still couldn't find the compact. Well, one day I opened a cabinet and there it was right in front of my eyes. I had looked there and would certainly have seen it if it had been there earlier."

Mrs. Reynolds attributes such incidents to pranks pulled by Oscar. After forty years of his antics, the Reynolds treat him like one of the family. They don't fear him and, indeed, respond to his now infrequent visits with a matter-of-factness characteristic of people who have accepted what is sometimes so hard for others to believe.

"I never did believe in ghosts either," Mrs. Reynolds emphasizes with a laugh. "But I know what I heard, what my husband believes and what my mother-in-law saw. I can't explain it, but all those things did happen."

Do they want Oscar to reveal his presence more often? Mrs. Reynolds thinks probably not. "We always have the *feeling* Oscar is in the house," she affirms. And that seems to be enough for the Reynolds family and their old friend.

A GHOST IN TIME

The most famous haunted house in La Porte once towered over spacious lawns at the corner of I and Tenth streets.

Many families lived there during its 100 years of existence. Nearly everyone reported weird manifestations.

The hauntings have not stopped. Witnesses say unusual things have happened at a medical clinic now occupying the spot where the haunted mansion once stood. They may continue indefinitely because their apparent cause is related to the land itself.

Before La Porte was a settlement, Potawatomi Indians camped on the prairie at I and Tenth streets. They particularly liked a small pond which they named "Came and Went." At times, after a torrential rain, the pond filled to a great depth; on other occasions it would be nearly dry. The water came and went.

In 1848, the pressures of settlement forced the Indians on that part of the frontier to move to land set aside in Kansas. On the long march westward, the native Americans crossed near "Came and Went" pond. Legend says that a young Potawatomi maiden became ill there and died.

It is her spirit that may haunt the site of that long-ago pond, now the corner of I and Tenth.

The modern history of the property begins when Dr. George L. Andrew finished his medical studies in Ohio and New York and came to Indiana in 1845. He married Catherine Piatt Andrew, a distant cousin and daughter of James Andrew, one of the founders of La Porte. Soon after, he started construction of a three-story Colonial mansion.

Andrew was a remarkable man, one of the first to use ether in surgery. Later, he served with distinction in the Army of the Potomac and the Army of the West during the Civil War. He retired from practice in 1885 and died in 1911. Catherine Piatt Andrew died at the age of 100 in 1926.

George Andrew's La Porte mansion was one of the most impressive structures anywhere in the Midwest. Four towering columns rose skyward from an open veranda stretching the width of the house. A second-floor sun porch overlooked the circular driveway. Shutters closed it against the winter winds. An airy sunroom was at the rear. The house had several dozen rooms, five set aside above the kitchen for servants' quarters.

The Andrews sold the mansion in 1885 to the Dunn family who remodeled the house and razed the servants' quarters.

Later, the Gwynne family purchased the house and lived there from 1904 until 1948. They were the first to notice the hauntings.

The story of their forty-four-year life with a live-in ghost comes mainly from the recollections of Mrs. Madeline Gwynne Kinney, a daughter, and the former curator of the La Porte County Historical Museum.

One oddity was the appearance of several old coins. Mrs. Kinney recalled that once while cleaning an empty downstairs closet, a sound like that of something being dropped to the floor came from behind her. She turned to see four coins: two pennies and two nickels, dated 1876, 1877, 1867 and 1869. Where they came from was a mystery. There were no holes or cracks in the walls.

The ghost first made itself known by tampering with the front doorbell. It was the old-fashioned type that had to be cranked to produce a ring. One winter night, during a particularly fierce blizzard, the bell rang. When Mr. Gwynne opened the door, the porch was empty. The fresh snow lay undisturbed.

Mrs. Kinney lost track of the number of times pounding footsteps rattled up and down the main staircase. Often, when they securely bolted the doors and windows before retiring, they awoke in the morning to find each and every portal standing wide open. Crashes not unlike sonic booms often shattered the stillness, but nothing was ever found broken.

Was she or her family ever afraid of their unseen tenant? No. According to Mrs. Kinney: "I will say we always rather admired the ghost because one never knew what it would do next!"

The Zimmerman family was the last to occupy the house. They suffered far more from the ghost's antics than any of the other tenants. At one point, the father, Robert Zimmerman, purchased a revolver to protect himself against the ghostly visitations.

The Zimmermans always felt some presence in the house. Nothing visible, only an uneasy feeling of prying eyes. The upstairs hallway seemed to be a focal point for mysterious happenings. Doors to various rooms closed quietly as someone walked by, even though the room was empty. A movement of air, the rush of breathing down someone's neck, would cause a family member to turn quickly, but futilely to catch sight of the visitor.

Mrs. Zimmerman, like Mrs. Kinney, also experienced the falling coins incident. She had removed all the wallpaper in that same closet, washed the walls and was picking up her supplies when she heard a faint tinkling noise. She opened the door and found a small collection of old silver coins in the center of the closet floor. She had no idea where they'd come from.

Another incident occurred late one evening when Mrs. Zimmerman was alone in the house. She heard footsteps ascending the staircase, moving across the landing toward the shuttered door and then . . . silence, almost as if someone had entered the vanished servants' rooms.

The ghost in the Andrew house also continued his particular affection for the front door. One of the Zimmerman girls was alone in the house when the crank-type doorbell rang. She ran downstairs to answer it, but found the porch empty. The girl shut the door; the bell rang again. She stared at the crank as it continued to turn and ring . . . ring . . . ring. Making sure the door was locked, she scurried back upstairs. When she ventured down later, the front door stood wide open, snow blowing into the chilled hallway.

The only reported appearance of the ghost occurred to another Zimmerman daughter, Ginna. As she picked spring flowers in the garden, Ginna felt a chill, as if she were being observed. She looked around the yard and glanced toward the house. The figure of a strange woman stood in the attic window staring down at her. Immediately, the woman moved away. There were no visitors in the house. When Ginna checked the garret, it was clear that no living being had been there for a very long time.

The Andrew mansion passed through other hands, but no one ever lived in the house after the Zimmermans moved away. Finally, it became the target of vandals attracted by its ghostly reputation. To call up the demons, they built fires on the beautiful floors, but it's not clear whether or not they raised any spirits. The city of La Porte condemned the house and eventually tore it down to make way for the medical center in the early 1970s.

The Indian heritage connected with that piece of property apparently continues in the gleaming, modern world of medicine. Doctors and nurses say an elevator in the building seems to move between floors on its own. The doors open and close even though no one is in the conveyance or pushing call buttons.

On several occasions, a nurse working late in the basement of the clinic near the elevator heard the doors open. When she left her desk to check, the doors closed again, as if some invisible passenger had stepped in ... or alighted.

Custodians on their early morning rounds have found doors of windowless bathrooms locked *from the inside*. None of the bathrooms has a second exit.

The George Andrew home is only a memory. It has vanished along with many other reminders of La Porte's early heritage. That corner at I and Tenth streets is now a busy intersection just like many others. But some *thing* seems to linger. An entity that doesn't want to let go? An Indian maiden trapped between earth and a spirit world? That is what the legendmakers will tell you. As will a few doctors and nurses in the medical center, or those people still alive who confronted the mysteries in the vanished Andrew mansion.

THE ABDUCTION OF OLIVER LARCH

In the eerie, flickering glow of a kerosene lamp, Matthew Larch followed his son's footprints in the snow. They started at the kitchen door and extended some seventy-five feet from the house. There were no other marks on the freshly-fallen flakes.

Young Oliver's tracks just stopped. The oak water bucket he had carried lay on its side several yards to the left.

Matthew Larch huddled under the dark sky with the small group of family and friends. Not a word passed among them. They listened intently, but could scarcely believe their senses.

Oliver was crying, his voice growing fainter and fainter as he screamed for help ... screamed *from somewhere above them ... in the black, cold sky.*

Then all was silent.

Eleven-year-old Oliver Larch and his family had been in a festive mood that Christmas Eve of 1889. Good friends, including a local minister and his wife from nearby South Bend, had gathered with the Larch family to celebrate the holiday. Even out-of-town guests—an attorney from Chicago and a circuit judge—had joined the party.

After a feast of roast duck and mince pudding, the guests moved into the parlor where Matthew sat down to play the pump organ. Carols drifted from the snug little farmhouse as the hour edged toward midnight.

Meanwhile, young Oliver had popped corn, which everyone ate eagerly. Outside, the snow fell steadily until a fluffy new white blanket lay upon the frozen earth.

Late in the evening, on a visit to the kitchen, Oliver's father noticed that the water in the cistern was low. The dutiful boy quickly volunteered to bring in fresh water. He slipped on a pair of overshoes and a warm jacket before going out to the pump.

A few seconds after he closed the door, a scream from the yard startled the happy gathering. Mr. Larch grabbed a lantern and raced outside. The rest of the group, including Oliver's frantic mother, followed.

Matthew Larch swung his lantern to and fro as he followed Oliver's footprints. Though he could not see his son, the boy's cries tore through him:

"Help! They've got me!" Matthew heard his son scream. "Help! Help me please!" Oliver's voice issued from the empty sky.

As everyone stared toward the leaden heavens, the terrified cries grew ever fainter. They could see nothing: not a light, not an object and definitely not Oliver. Nor could they hear anything other than the boy's cries, now almost inaudible. The child had been snatched from the face of the earth.

Not able to believe it, Matthew Larch and several other men frantically searched the farmstead while the women led a distraught Mrs. Larch into the house. They found not a trace of the boy that night . . . nor any other night.

A police investigation confirmed what the Larch family and their guests had seen and heard that cold winter evening. Oliver's voice must have come from the sky for there was no other evidence to indicate he had been kidnapped or run away.

Speculation abounded, but what investigators found most troubling was that there had been no sound, other than the boy's screams, nor any lights in the inky blackness.

It seemed as if Oliver had been carried upward into the endless night by some unseen, demonic being. Preposterous? No one ever came forth with a better explanation. Oliver Larch had disappeared forever.

LA LLORONA

Her legendary name is La Llorona. The "wailing woman." For nearly 450 years the pitiful cries of her spirit have rung through the streets in central Mexico City. In a torn, blood-soaked gown she cries, "Mis hijos, mis hijos—my children, my children." She wanders the earth searching for the souls of the two illegitimate babies she stabbed to death when their father rejected her.

Is it conceivable that the ghost of La Llorona has found her way to Gary, Indiana? It is, according to a widely-held tradition in the vanished community of Cudahey, now an industrial neighborhood in that city.

La Llorona's American hauntings are centered on Cline Avenue, near its intersection with Fifth. The dank Calumet River and a railroad track cross Cline just north of there. A perpetual, shroud-like smog hangs above the dismal scene, and clumps of weeds and trees bereft of foliage add grimness even in the full light of day.

Little is left of Cudahey. It was once a thriving neighborhood, populated by Mexican-Americans who worked the steel mills. Most of the old homes have long since been torn down, their owners moving to more desirable communities as they settled into their adopted homeland and advanced at their places of work.

Only La Llorona remains. Or does she? The tales of the "ghost woman of Cline Avenue" intertwine La Llorona with a phantom Woman in White who seeks rides from unsuspecting motorists. Are there two ghosts or one?

The legend of La Llorona does have a historical basis in Mexico City. She was Doña Luisa de Olveros, a beautiful Indian princess who fell in love with a Mexican nobleman, Don Nuño de Montesclaros. The year was 1550. So deep was Doña's love for Montesclaros that she bore him two children, some accounts say twins. Although he didn't promise marriage, Doña prayed for the day when they would wed.

While Doña prayed and waited, Montesclaros lost his passion for her. At length, she decided to confront him. Late one evening, she ventured to his family's palatial home. To her surprise, Montesclaros seemed to be the center of a gala party in his honor. It was his wedding day.

Montesclaros laughed when Doña fell to her knees to ask why he had forsaken her. Marriage had always been out of the question, he sneered. She was Indian. Beneath his station. She was rudely ejected from the sumptuous home.

Doña Luisa fled through the streets, choking and sobbing, half-mad with anger at her humiliation. When she reached home, she pulled out a small dagger—a gift from Montesclaros—and murdered her children.

She wandered the streets for more than a day, babbling incoherently, her clothes ripped and smeared with her children's blood.

They found her and charged her with infanticide. The court quickly judged her guilty of "sorcery." She was publicly hanged, her body left swinging from the gallows for nearly six hours. Ever since, the ghost of Doña Luisa de Olveros has walked the earth, condemned to search forever for the children she cruelly murdered.

Folklorist Philip B. George thinks the Cudahey Woman in White and La Llorona may be the same, even though the former is identified with an Anglo community and the latter with a Mexican one. He wrote: "It is possible that the Mexicans, settling in the Indiana harbor area and in Cudahey, heard the tale of the Woman in White from the Anglos . . . . Within the Mexican community the ghost became identified as La Llorona. As the economic situation of many of the Mexicans improved, they moved to newer communities where day-to-day contact with Anglos was more common. The Anglos could then have picked up the tale from the Chicanos in its new form as the White Lady."

While the Woman in White and La Llorona haunt the same area of Cline Avenue, there are differences in their habits. The Woman in White is known for hitchhiking. She usually hails taxis and requests rides to Calumet Harbor. She is often seen standing near the Cline Avenue overpass, under which flows the muddy Calumet River. After the cab has traveled less than half-a-mile, the driver finds that she has disappeared from the back seat.

Sometimes the ghost doesn't bother to hail a cab. She just appears mysteriously in a car as it speeds along the boulevard, only to vanish a few minutes later. Sometimes the Woman in White simply floats across Cline Avenue toward the area of old Cudahey.

Like La Llorona, the Woman in White is said to have killed her illegitimate children in Gary and drowned them in the Calumet River.

The media have also played a role in the legend. Some years ago, after the stories of La Llorona spread beyond the Cudahey neighborhood, television, radio and newspaper reporters converged one Halloween night to investigate and, along with hundreds of spectators, scoured the woods near Cline and Fifth. With cameras and microphones in hand, the press hoped to capture one or the other of the elusive spirits on film and tape. No doubt the milling throng was enough to dissuade any specter from showing its transparent face.

Whatever does walk the night on Gary's Cline Avenue, the spirit of a tragic Mexican Indian beauty or of a young girl who drowned her babies in the Calumet River, there are those who believe her ghost will never know peace. Not until she finds the souls of those innocent children.

Chapter III.
Iowa

"Early the next morning preparations began for the exorcism. No one knew how long the holy rite would last. In most cases it took several days for the power of Christ to drive the devils back into hell.

Emma was brought to the room set aside for the undertaking and placed on the mattress of the iron bed. The sleeves and the skirt of her dress were tightly bound and Father Theophilus instructed the nuns to hold Emma firmly upon the bed."

"THE POSSESSION OF EMMA SCHMIDT"

THE POSSESSION OF EMMA SCHMIDT

Emma Schmidt was possessed by the Devil. When she was a teenager her father died, but not before he had cursed her for refusing his incestuous demands. Emma had a clear recollection of the moment he had handed her over to Satan, but she was too ashamed to tell anyone.

After his death, evil spirits seized control of Emma's mind and body, and the pious, sensitive girl changed into a hideous creature with a chilling laugh and a brazen mouth which hurled obscenities.

After years of agony, Emma underwent the grueling rite of exorcism in the fall of 1928 at the convent of the Franciscan Sisters in Earling, Iowa. The exorcism rite lasted an incredible twenty-three days.

Her sufferings up until that time can only be imagined. Doctors who examined Emma thought she was either hysteric or prone to nervous spells and hallucinations. Though specialists who saw her over a number of years found her to be normal, Emma did not improve.

Finally, when medical sources were exhausted, her family appealed to the Catholic Church. The priests soon recognized that supernatural powers controlled the woman. Emma understood languages she had neither heard nor read. When a priest blessed her in Latin, she foamed at the mouth with rage. If handed an article sprinkled with holy water, she would scream "Damn relic!" followed by more curses and blasphemy, and throw it against the wall.

For some reason, the Church hierarchy moved slowly before officially commenting on Emma's case. Only long years of intensive study and observation convinced the Church fathers that she *was* possessed by the Devil and should be exorcised.

Father Theophilus Riesinger, a Capuchin monk and experienced exorcist from Marathon, Wisconsin, agreed to perform the ancient rite. He knew Emma well. To protect her privacy, he arranged for the exorcism to take place in the convent of the Franciscan Sisters in the little village of Earling. Joseph Steiger, the parish priest at Earling and a longtime friend of Father Theophilus, was not eager for the exorcism to take place in his country parish, but the convent's Mother Superior readily granted permission.

Emma Schmidt traveled to Earling by train. Alone. Although she desperately wanted her demons exorcised, she felt overwhelmed by that uncontrollable rage which had plagued her for twenty-six years! Disembarking at the station, she raised her arms in a threatening gesture and screamed at the nuns who met her, "Whores of Jesus!" before going limp. The startled and apprehensive nuns helped her into their car and they all rode in silence to the convent.

Later that evening, the reluctant Pastor Steiger set forth to meet Father Theophilus's train. On the way to the railroad station, his car—a brand-new one—kept stalling. The pastor tried everything he could think of, to no avail. The car bucked and lurched and it took two hours to go the short distance from the rectory to the station. Embarrassed, Paster Steiger apologized for the delay.

Father Theophilus shook his head. "I wasn't wrought up about it," he said. "The Devil will try to foil our plans. I just prayed that he wouldn't harm you personally."

He blessed the car with the sign of the cross and recited the rosary all the way to the rectory and they arrived safely. At the convent, however, trouble had already broken out—a well-meaning sister in the kitchen had sprinkled holy water on Emma's supper tray as she set it before her. The enraged woman threw the food to the floor.

"It stinks!" she hollered. When unblessed food was substituted, Emma devoured the food, though she was by nature a light eater.

Early the next morning preparations began for the exorcism. No one knew how long the holy rite would last. In most cases it took several days for the power of Christ to drive the devils back into hell.

Emma was brought to the room set aside for the undertaking and placed on the mattress of the iron bed. The sleeves and the skirt of her dress were tightly bound, and Father Theophilus instructed the nuns to hold Emma firmly upon the bed.

The exorcist, with Paster Steiger standing beside him, sought divine aid "in the name of the Father, the Son, and the Holy Ghost." Then he began the prescribed church prayers and, as she would during every day of the exorcism, Emma lapsed into unconsciousness.

Suddenly, she tore loose from her restrainers. Some mysterious energy hurled her body as if from a catapult through the air and crashed it against the wall above the door of the room, pinning her with a force so strong that neither priest could pull her free. The nuns, trembling with fright, stood on tiptoe, yanking and tugging at

Emma's feet until they were able to dislodge her and return her to the mattress.

The exorcism continued. Suddenly, a wild howling rent the air. Emma's mouth contorted, but remained closed. The devils that had taken possession of her body would not speak through the woman's lips; instead, the inhuman sounds issued from some place deep within her body. The howling grew louder and more intense.

Father Theophilus called out, "Quiet, Satan, you infamous reprobate!"

As news of the exorcism spread like a prairie fire, alarmed villagers came running from all directions to find out what was happening inside the convent. Crowds would assemble beneath the windows of the room where the stricken woman lay, but many persons could not bear listening to the excruciating sounds.

During the next few days, those inside the room endured an incredibly gruesome ordeal; the twelve nuns attending Emma took turns, afterwards leaving the building to recuperate in the fresh air. Only the priest was self-composed.

Seemingly helpless, the poor woman frothed at the mouth, then spewed forth torrents of stinking excrement that filled pitchers and pails. Though for weeks Emma had scarcely eaten, she was now vomiting as often as thirty times a day.

Gradually Father Theophilus distinguished a number of different voices issuing from Emma's body and, in the name of Jesus, he asked Satan how many spirits were involved in the possession. When Satan boasted that there were several, Emma foamed and howled.

On several occasions when the exorcist brought the Blessed Sacrament near Emma, he saw the Devil moving around, like a pea, beneath her skin.

Every day from early morning until late at night the exorcism continued, and every day, hour after hour, the bellowing and the howling, like the sounds of lions, hyenas, cattle and sometimes dogs and cats, defiled the convent's usual stillness. But Father Theophilus persisted, now questioning, now probing, now praying, pitting the forces of light against the forces of darkness. So grueling was the task that he often had to change his perspiration-soaked clothes three or four times a day. Much of the time he despaired, fearing Satan had beaten him.

Eventually, he determined that of the many evil spirits possessing Emma, Beelzebub was the leader. He spoke to all of them: the Devil himself, Beelzebub and all the others in English, German and Latin. Each devil answered in the language in which he was addressed.

Most shocking to all was the deep, rough voice that claimed to belong to Judas Iscariot, the traitorous Apostle.

When asked his business, Judas exclaimed: "Emma must hang herself and go to hell!"

Horror-stricken, Pastor Steiger and several of the nuns ran from the room.

Steadfastly, Father Theophilus, never taking his eyes off the afflicted woman, wiped his brow and repeated the prayer of exorcism:

"I exorcise thee, most evil spirit, direct embodiment of our enemy, the entire entity and its whole legion, in the name of Jesus Christ, to go hence and escape from this creature of God. He, himself, commands thee, who is master from the heights of heaven to the depth of the earth. He who commands the sea, the winds and the tempests, now commands thee . . ."

Suddenly, another voice spoke from deep inside the woman. "I am Jacob, the father of the possessed girl."

Under questioning Jacob admitted he had tried repeatedly to coerce his daughter into having sex with him, but she had resisted. In his anger he had cursed her and prayed that the devils would take her, entice her to commit every possible sex act and destroy her body and soul. For the crime of casting his daughter to the devils, he had gone to hell. Now, at Lucifer's urging, he schemed how to further torture her.

Though almost overcome by his own horror at Jacob's evil, the exorcist's voice never quavered as he warned: "The power of Christ and the Blessed Trinity will force you back to hell where you belong!"

Then, a shrill, high-pitched voice interrupted. It was Mina, Jacob's mistress, sentenced to hell for having murdered her own children. Her hatred caused Emma to vomit so forcefully that both of the churchmen used towels to wipe the vomitus from habit and cassock.

During all of the hours that these devils taunted the exorcist, Emma's emaciated body was so grossly disfigured that she scarcely resembled a human being. Her head swelled and took on a red color, like glowing embers. Her eyes protruded from their sockets and her colorless lips bulged to twice their normal size. So bloated was she, the nuns feared the woman would burst. At times her abdomen and extremities became as hard and heavy as stone; then the increased weight of her body caused the iron bedstead to bend to the floor.

Satan detested the holy water Father Theophilus regularly sprinkled. "Away with that shit!" he would scream. "It burns like fire!"

As the agonizing, exhausting days passed, a change came upon Pastor Steiger. He developed a strong hatred for the whole procedure and he could scarcely tolerate the presence of Father Theophilus, his longtime friend. He gruffly told Theophilus so. Patiently, the exorcist explained that the Devil was using the pastor as he tried to foil the attempts to dislodge him from the woman he possessed.

Next the Devil began to verbally assault the pastor. "Leave Pastor Steiger alone," Father Theophilus warned. "He's doing you no harm. I am your enemy."

Satan laughed and repeatedly threatened Pastor Steiger. One day, he sneered, "Just wait until Friday . . ."

Sick of the Devil's howlings, the pastor refused to take any threat seriously. But on Friday he nearly lost his life.

It happened when, after Mass, a farmer called Pastor Steiger to perform last rites for his dying mother. Could the Pastor come at once?

Pastor Steiger left immediately, but recalling the Devil's threats, he drove carefully, and prayed to his guardian angel and to Saint Joseph, his patron saint, for a safe journey.

On his return to Earling, he approached a bridge flung across a deep ravine. A dense black cloud descended from the sky. Unable to see, the pastor yanked the car into low gear. He never heard the crash. The car disintegrated, leaving its dazed occupant sitting in a pile of twisted metal and broken glass, tilting precariously on the iron trellis of the bridge. A rock-filled chasm yawned far below.

A farmer plowing a field some distance away heard the crash and came running as Pastor Steiger crawled slowly from the wreckage. Although numb with shock, he seemed unhurt. The farmer took Pastor Steiger to a doctor, who found no sign of internal or external injury.

Determined to press on, Pastor Steiger went directly to the exorcism room from the doctor's office. He was met by the Devil's roar of laughter. "Your dandy new car all smashed to smithereens!" he taunted. "Serves you right!"

The priest and nuns stared. Did the Devil speak the truth?

The pastor nodded. "My car is a total wreck. But he didn't have the power to hurt me personally."

"No!" yelled the Devil. "Your goddamn patron saint prevented it!"

But Satan wasn't finished with the pastor. On another occasion Steiger awakened in the middle of the night to the sounds of scurrying noises inside the wall. Rats? Of course. What else could it be? Yet, during his fourteen years in the rectory he had never been bothered by rodents.

The pastor sat up and pounded on the wall. The noises increased, as if hundreds of rats were running up and down. The priest hit the wall with a cane and then a shoe.

Then, remembering Satan's threat, he draped his stole over his shoulders, lit two candles before a crucifix and recited a short exorcism. The noises stopped immediately.

A few nights later Pastor Steiger awakened again. The whole house seemed to be rocking, as if an express train clattered through the village. The noise ceased, then started again above the bedroom door, which the pastor found tightly shut. Satan was after him again. Pastor Steiger sprinkled the room with holy water and recited the exorcism he had used earlier, and again, all was quiet.

But such annoyances could scarcely match the suffering endured by Emma Schmidt.

She continued to lose consciousness each day after the exorcism began and only awoke late at night once it was over. She remembered nothing of what transpired. More frail than ever now from the daily ordeal, Emma had to be carried back and forth between her private quarters and the exorcism room.

Pastor Steiger feared that at any moment she would die. Father Theophilus knew better.

"Emma will not die," he promised. "Satan will not be permitted to kill her."

The exorcism continued for more than two weeks before there was any indication that the Devil might be forced to abandon Emma's body. At that point, Father Theophilus redoubled his efforts. For three days and three nights he worked with no rest whatsoever. Fortunately, his rigorous life of self-denial had endowed him with nerves of steel and nearly superhuman powers of endurance. But toward the end of the third night he became so weak that he pleaded with God to spare his life.

When not working with Father Theophilus, Pastor Steiger urged his parishioners to keep regular hours of adoration before the Blessed Sacrament, to pray for Satan's destruction and to fast and do penance so that their prayers might strengthen the prayers of the exorcism. From early morning until late at night, faithful villagers crowded into the church.

One miraculous day the Little Flower of Jesus appeared to Emma and spoke. "Do not lose courage! The pastor must not give up hope. The end is near."

The nuns saw a cluster of white roses on the ceiling of the room, but it disappeared before Pastor Steiger could be brought.

Nevertheless, the encouraging words from the Little Flower quickened the hopes of both religious men. They knew that victory was not far off.

Father Theophilus intensified his insistence that the Devil depart and return to hell. "You can't send *me* to hell," he growled. "I come to prepare the way for the Antichrist. This is the last century."

But Father Theophilus felt Satan's power waning. In a ringing voice he ordered him to depart:

"For it is God who commands thee.

"The majesty of Christ commands thee.

"God the Father commands thee.

"God the Son commands thee.

"God the Holy Ghost commands thee.

"The sacred cross commands thee.

"The faith of the holy apostles Peter and Paul, and of all the other saints, commands thee."

As the end neared, the priest demanded that the devils give a sign of their departure by stating their respective names.

On September 23, 1928, at nine o'clock in the evening, Emma Schmidt jerked free from the nuns' grip and stood upon the bed with only her heels touching the mattress. Fearful that she would be hurled to the ceiling again, Pastor Steiger shouted, "Pull her down! Pull her down!"

Father Theophilus blessed her with the relic of the cross determinedly, intoning, "Depart ye fiends of hell! Begone, Satan! The Lion of Juda reigns!"

At that moment Emma collapsed. Piercing voices shook the walls of the room, screaming, "Beelzebub, Judas, Jacob, Mina." The names were repeated over and over until they faded away, followed by the ever-fainter words, "Hell, hell, hell, hell!"

Everyone in the room froze. Then the miracle was made manifest. Emma opened her eyes and smiled. Looking from one face into another, she cried, "My Jesus Mercy! Praised be Jesus Christ!" Her eyes filled.

The exorcism that had begun on September first was finished at last. Rejoicing, the witnesses were not at first aware of the nauseating odor of human excrement that filled the room—the final indignity from the devils forced to abandon their victim. The nuns opened all the windows and a cool, fresh breeze blew across the sills.

Word of Father Theophilus's success spread quickly and the entire parish joined in giving thanks.

Is there really such a thing as demonic possession? Saint Mark tells of the seven devils that Christ cast out of Mary Magdalene, and of the devil cast out of a young man who had foamed at the mouth and gnashed his teeth since he was a child.

Similarly, Saint Luke tells of the devils that inhabited a nameless, wretched creature who lived in a tomb in the mountainside. The devils were successfully cast out and entered a herd of swine.

Some people believe that the Middle Ages were filled with cases of diabolical possession similar to those in biblical times, while others insist that the stricken individuals were probably either insane or epileptic. In recent years doctors have described a condition known as Tourette's syndrome. In its victims, it causes involuntary swearing, uncontrollable movements, grunting, the shouting of obscenities and strange tics and twitches.

The line between the physical and the metaphysical worlds is often blurred, and the Earling case aroused heated controversy among both Catholics and Protestants. Whether Father Theophilus, the Capuchin monk, was actually the nemesis of evil spirits can never be proved beyond a doubt. Perhaps Emma Schmidt suffered from a disease that today's sophisticated medical teams could diagnose and treat.

At any rate, it was said that after the exorcism, Emma lived a calm and holy life, her heart and soul at peace.

The Franciscan Sisters still occupy the brick convent in the little prairie town of Earling, Iowa.

THE GUTTENBERG POLTERGEIST

In 1959, the William Meyer house near Guttenberg, Iowa, was the most exciting place in Clayton County. In fact, it was so exciting that on December 17 the family fled— a poltergeist had taken over the premises!

As the Meyers were sitting in their living room late one evening, a crash shook the house. The couple hurried into the kitchen to find their refrigerator tipped over. In the next instant, a flower stand flew across the room and splintered against the stove; then an egg rose from a basket on the windowsill, soared through the air and bounced off a door.

Mrs. Meyer was frightened speechless; her husband was bewildered. How could these things happen? Had pranksters gotten into the kitchen? A thorough search revealed no hidden wires or any other devices that could have propelled the objects into space.

Too upset to stay in the kitchen to prepare dinner that night, Mrs. Meyer insisted that the couple eat out. She felt more relaxed away from home and out among people. In fact, while she was gone she almost forgot about the destruction in her home.

Later that night Mrs. Meyer decided to read herself to sleep. She placed a glass of water on the night stand and climbed into bed with her book. The glass rose from the table, hung in midair and exploded upon her head, showering her with water and shards of glass.

Her husband, who had witnessed the incident, was as frightened as his wife. He suggested that they move into another bedroom, which they did. But no sooner were the Meyers in bed than soot began falling on them from what was supposedly a solid ceiling!

In the morning, Bill Meyer called the sheriff. The constable tramped through the house, but nothing moved in his presence. He was called home suddenly, but promised to check back later. When he returned to the Meyer place, he found the couple in their front yard. They claimed that several chairs had scooted across the floor and that every window in the house had cracked. The Meyers couldn't explain the movement of the chairs or the broken windows. To their knowledge, no one had been lurking about the house, and they had heard no noises to indicate the breaking of glass. The sheriff examined the windows and shook his head. He confessed that he could not help them; the problem was beyond the long arm of the law.

Word soon spread of the strange goings-on at Bill Meyer's house, and visitors from Guttenberg and neighboring communities besieged the family. A towboat captain on the Mississippi River arrived one night with some friends.

"I was just wondering, ma'am," he began, "if I could spend the night. You see, I don't believe in ghosts."

Mrs. Meyer courteously offered the captain a bedroom. Shortly after he had gone to bed, his friends and the Meyers were drinking coffee at the kitchen table. Then they heard a loud commotion in the bedroom. They rushed into the room. There the river pilot lay—on the mattress which was now on the floor *eight feet away from the bed frame!* The perplexed captain had no idea how he had gotten there.

Sometime later, a Northwestern University psychologist visited the Meyer home to study the unexplained phenomena. He said that the activity was a result of "some intelligent motivation." He explained that the work of a poltergeist is usually set in motion by a young person who, unconsciously, transfers his suppressed rage and energy force to inanimate objects.

By that time, however, the Meyers didn't care much for theories. Weary of visitors, of assaults by unseen tormentors and of too many sleepless nights, they moved out. The house, however, had become so notorious that curiosity seekers could not stay away; they arrived regularly, uninvited, tramping through the place and spreading stories about the antics of the ghost.

Eventually the Meyers sold the house to their former neighbors, the Wallace Finnegans. Vandals then began attacking the house, smashing windows and breaking down doors. Young people came from near and far to hold all-night beer busts in the place. Mr. Finnegan, in desperation, filled the house with hay and turned it into a barn.

The Guttenberg poltergeist was never heard from again.

THE TELLTALE TOMBSTONE

At the turn of the century, Heinrich Schultz and his wife, Olga, were murdered. In cold blood. In their home in the middle of the night. The people of Washta couldn't recall a more heinous crime in all of Cherokee County; they spoke of it with outrage . . . and fear.

The Schultzes were a kind, elderly couple who farmed a short distance from town. They were well-respected by all who knew them. And they had no known enemies. In fact, they had lots of admirers among both neighbors and townspeople. The Schultzes were honest, God-fearing people who tithed both money and time to their church. At every congregational dinner, Olga could be found in the kitchen turning out her prized strudel and dumplings. Heinrich cared for the church grounds and donated a number of flowering shrubs to beautify the little rustic building.

The couple had been in Iowa for only five years. Heinrich's lifelong dream was to own a fine farm in America, and he and Olga had saved for years in order to finance their emigration from Germany to the Iowa farm with its rich, black soil. The couple had no children, so Heinrich would hire young men from the neighborhood to help with the chores. All of them preferred working for "old man Schultz," as they fondly called him, because he paid well. He also demanded an honest day's work.

A few days before his death, Heinrich had withdrawn a considerable sum of money from the bank. There had been rumors (later proved false) of impending bank failures, and the cautious farmer feared the loss of his life savings. He and Olga decided the money would be safer at home.

The couple were found three days later—their heads split open with an ax! There were signs of a struggle. The Schultz money was gone, and so was Will Florence, a hired hand employed by the Schultzes. He had first appeared in the area three months earlier, during haying season. A number of farmers, suspicious of a stranger with no visible means of support, told Florence they had no work and turned him away. But Heinrich hired the fellow and provided him with board and room in addition to a small salary. Although the neighbors were uneasy, Heinrich defended his decision.

"The man's down and out," he explained. "I'm pleasured to give him a chance."

Florence proved to be inexperienced and inept at farm work, but Heinrich instructed him with patience and understanding. Florence revealed little of himself, except to say that he'd had some medical problems and had been recuperating from surgery at the home of his sister in Texas. Now, he wanted to make his own way. Olga liked his determination and his quiet manner and treated him like the son she never had. Every Sunday at church Florence sat between Heinrich and Olga.

Although locating Will Florence after the murders seemed an impossibility, he was eventually found in Nebraska and brought back to Iowa for questioning. A grand jury examined him, but discharged him for lack of evidence. Florence then vanished for good. He was never seen again, at least not in the flesh.

A curious story, however, soon circulated through Washta. An old woman, one of the first to suspect Florence of the slayings, told her closest friends that the murderer's face had begun to appear on the headstone over the Schultzes' grave. She claimed that the face was unmistakably that of Will Florence! Her friends ridiculed her, of course, and even those who visited the grave to satisfy their curiosity saw nothing that resembled a man's face upon the stone of plain marble. Yet the old lady insisted that she saw Florence's portrait on this unadorned stone; she went so far as to say that the picture was developing more fully each day, just as photographic film under chemical action develops a negative.

The woman's bizarre story was told and retold in farm kitchens, in the village blacksmith shop and along the dusty roads of Cherokee County. Eventually, a few more townspeople came forward and agreed that they too saw the features of a man on the tombstone.

Was the power of suggestion working on unconscious minds? Or were heat waves weaving patterns on polished stone? Eyewitnesses reported that the face was becoming increasingly distinct, the lines deeply etched.

Someone suggested that a marble dealer be asked to explain the phenomenon. The expert came and trudged up to the little hillside burial ground. After studying the stone with great care, he explained that the features were being developed as a result of exposure to atmospheric influences of the rust and veins in the marble. He predicted that the portrait would continue to grow plainer.

It did.

At last law enforcement officials visited the graveyard, and even the most skeptical detective admitted that he could indeed see the features of a man's face in the shining marble. Soon, people from miles away began visiting the grave, and everyone who had ever seen Will Florence declared that the face bore a startling resemblance to him.

While these pilgrimages to the graveyard were taking place, new evidence implicating Florence in the Schultz murders reached the office of the prosecuting attorney of Cherokee County. The prosecutor, confident that he could now prove the guilt of the suspected man, ordered a vigorous search for him.

Florence was never found. But his guilt remained stamped upon the marble tombstone atop the graves of Heinrich and Olga Schultz.

OLD CHAPEL

Church-steeple evergreens crowd the huge brick building encircled in vines. Ribbons of old paint curl from the rotted window castings, and an ancient silver maple casts long shadows near the entrance doors that are locked, chained and bolted.

This is Old Chapel on the campus of Simpson College in Indianola, Iowa. For years students, faculty, alumni and employees have both cherished and feared this 115-year-old building that has served also as a library and conservatory. Even before it was condemned in 1980 because of crumbling ceilings and unsafe stairs, no one loitered on the premises after dark.

Strange things happen here—mysterious lights bob around inside the building when it's empty; something climbs the creaking stairs; and shadowy forms pace the halls and peer, with sightless eyes, through third-floor windows.

The sinister legends date back to the late nineteenth century when a young man, distraught by a failed romance, hanged himself in the belfry of Old Chapel. After his death friends believed they saw him wandering the gloomy halls or gazing out a window. Skeptics, however, say the suicide tale was a myth handed down after a professor was hanged in effigy in the tower.

A woman student also supposedly hanged herself in the chapel's tower. The words "In memoriam" follow a student's name in a 1924 yearbook, yet alumni who were there in the 1920s recall only that "something happened."

The tower was later destroyed in a storm and never rebuilt.

At least two women are believed to have died horrifying deaths when they fell over the railing of the chapel's wooden staircase and plunged three flights down the open stairwell. A young man also was thought to have died after losing his footing on the rickety steps and tumbling down them. A woman supposedly hanged herself from the massive chandelier visible through the Palladian window on the second floor.

Yet dark deeds have sometimes been attributed unjustifiably to the building that has witnessed so many deaths. In at least one instance in the 1880s, a young student who fell to his death in another campus building was reported to have been killed in Old Chapel.

Through the years these legends have been told and retold, until fact and fiction are inseparable. Nevertheless, the presence of ghosts in the old building is generally *not* in dispute. Seven students tell of meeting the apparition of a young woman on the stairs, and one member of the group insists that the ghost talked to him. "She wants to be left alone," he reportedly said.

A security guard was badly frightened at meeting a translucent figure in the corridor one night. And a cleaning lady told a news reporter that she knew mysterious things went on "all the time." She claimed that she and her co-workers consistently saw things they couldn't explain—they found basement lights turned on when no one was in the building; and lights on the third floor would blink on and off. Electricians repeatedly checked the wiring and switches and could find no reason for the erratic behavior of the lights.

On a chilly night in November 1979, Connecticut ghost hunters Ed and Lorraine Warren visited the campus. The couple, students of occult phenomena for nearly forty years, had examined the allegedly possessed house on Long Island, New York, which was featured in the book and film, *The Amityville Horror*.

After lecturing on paranormal phenomena to more than 300 students and faculty members, the ghost hunters entered Old Chapel just before midnight. They were accompanied by fifty students, photographers and press reporters. The crowd waited on the main floor while the Warrens worked their way up the staircase, through the drafty corridors all the way to the third floor, gathering psychic vibrations and impressions.

The couple soon determined that the building was occupied by something not of flesh and blood.

"You definitely have an earthbound spirit in this building," Warren told an Associated Press reporter. "She died here, but she's convinced herself that she didn't. She might have been contemplating suicide. But she didn't want to die at the end."

Mrs. Warren entered a light trance in order to communicate with the spirit. "It's a dark-haired girl in her twenties," she said, her voice seeming to come from a distant place. "She was wearing a skirt well below her knees."

That description was close to the one obtained by Twyla Dillard in her research on the ghosts of Simpson College. She told the wire service reporter that "we've pretty well confirmed" that in 1935 a young woman either fell or jumped over the third-floor railing. She died later. "She had heels, and a long skirt and an armload of books," Dillard said. "Apparently she caught her heel and fell."

Mrs. Warren was pleased to have a description of the spirit that closely matched her own. She had been given no information on the coed before she made contact with the ghost. And college officials agree that this is the one legend which has some basis in fact.

Curiously, the same ghost may have been captured that evening on film. Later, when a student photographer in the group processed his film from that evening he saw that he had photographed what some say is the reflection of a female spirit.

A few nights after the Warrens' visit, Greg States, a hypnotist and psychic, led another group through the building. States knew nothing of its history.

"The spirit might be angry at the way he died. Or perhaps it was a foolish death, like if he fell in front of a carriage or tripped over a root on a cliff—deaths that could have been avoided," he said.

As the group moved silently through the cavernous building, their candles casting wavering shadows on the walls, States detailed the deaths of five students whom he felt had perished there. But he determined that there were no ghosts left in the building. "I believe they were here," he said, "but I don't feel there has been any entity here for maybe two years.

But States had some reactions he himself had not anticipated. He said he had a burning sensation in his arms and one side of his face all day. After spending several hours in Old Chapel, he was convinced that someone was burned there. "I feel they are still living," he said, "and carry the scars today."

Later the group learned that certain opera properties stored on the third floor of the building had been retrieved from a fire in Center House on the campus some months earlier, and taken to Old Chapel for safe keeping.

States also felt that someone had contracted food poisoning in the building and died elsewhere. Actually, there was a woman, in the 1920s, who died from an infection and whose body lay in state in Old Chapel. A college publicist didn't know exactly what the infection was, but recalled that "it had something to do with her mouth."

Long before dawn the students blew out their candles. They had not met a single ghost. Pushing open the heavy double doors, they shivered as the night air rushed in. States lingered for a moment, beaming his flashlight toward the deadly third-floor stairs where he had experienced an uneasy feeling earlier. Then he snapped off his light and left. As the building's doors swung shut behind him, he muttered,

"Thought I saw something. I guess not. It was nothing . . ."

THE MESSENGER

In 1949, Elaine Worrel and her husband, Hal, lived in a century-old house in Oskaloosa that had been remodeled into apartments. The Worrels lived at one end of the top floor. At the opposite end lived a young widow, Patricia Burns. The landlady told the Worrels that Patricia had lost her husband, Raymond, in an industrial accident several months before, and had moved to the city to rebuild her life.

Patricia was an accomplished pianist and Elaine often heard music coming from the woman's tiny apartment. When the two women met in the hall, they exchanged smiles, but that was all. Elaine respected her neighbor's privacy.

One Saturday while Hal was away at work, Elaine felt uneasy, but she didn't know why. Perhaps a warm bath would relax her. Slipping into a robe, she edged down the hall toward the bathroom. As she groped for the light cord in the dark room, pipe smoke filled the air.

Elaine spun around. A young man lingered in the bathroom doorway. Black hair curled all over his head and a faint horseshoe-shaped scar outlined his left cheekbone. Cupped in one of his hands was a briar pipe.

Elaine was unable to scream. Instead, she stared closely at the mysterious visitor. He was not a tenant, Elaine knew that. But how did he get into the house then? What did he want? While Elaine searched the man's gray eyes for answers, she was struck by the fact that he never blinked. It was as if he were not really seeing her. Elaine knew then that the figure was not real.

The apparition turned and moved toward Patricia Burns' apartment. Elaine, swept by an unaccountable compulsion, followed. At the door of Patricia's apartment, the ghost vanished.

Elaine found Patricia's door unlocked and hesitantly entered the apartment. In the bedroom the young woman lay with her wrists slashed; she was barely conscious. Elaine put tourniquets on Patricia's wrists, then phoned her husband Hal, at work. He arrived within a few minutes with a doctor who stitched the young woman's wounds.

The next day Patricia thanked Elaine for saving her life. She told Elaine that she had been drinking and, overcome by despair, had decided to join her husband in death. Elaine said nothing of her own mysterious encounter, but she quickly realized that Patricia had slashed her wrists at about the same time she had seen the ghost.

Later that evening Patricia showed Elaine a picture of her deceased husband. Elaine shuddered—it was the apparition she had seen in the bathroom! She had never seen a picture of Raymond Burns, nor heard him described until that moment. Yet somehow Raymond Burns had sensed his wife's moment of crisis, and returned to lead a stranger to the bedside of his stricken widow.

THE HAUNTING OF HAM HOUSE

Dubuque pioneer Mathias Ham built his home to last. The twenty-three room Victorian gothic mansion straddles a wind-wracked bluff on the city's north end, its native limestone walls as sound today as the day they were completed. This antebellum house has always been the pride of Dubuque, a symbol of wealth and a statement of the owner's faith in the future of this Mississippi River town.

Yet for many years, frightening tales have been told of strange lights moving through the vast, dark corridors of the mansion and cold, sudden breezes that seem to have no natural origin.

The energetic Ham prospered in lead mining, lumbering and agriculture and operated a fleet of vessels to ship his products up and down the river. The thriving Ham then married Zerelda Marklin, his childhood sweetheart, in 1837. Three years later, he built a small, two-story rock house containing five rooms. It was considered lavish for its time, as most of the surrounding homes were of log construction. In 1856, Zerelda died, leaving Ham with five children. He was devastated by her death and by a number of business reverses that followed.

In 1857, while the Dubuque Federal Customs House was under construction, several loads of stones shipped from southern Illinois were rejected because of inferior quality. Mathias Ham bought these and erected a three-story addition to his Lincoln Avenue home for himself and his family. Then in 1860, he married Margaret McLean, who bore him two more children. As Ham was recouping his losses, he completed his Dubuque mansion, furnishing it with taste and elegance.

Soon the Hams were once again socially prominent. Their parties became well-known and guests felt honored to be invited. Many party-goers, noting the exquisite plaster rosettes and moldings of the fourteen-foot ceilings, the beautifully decorated window casings and the burnished walnut staircases, remarked that Mathias Ham had thought of everything.

But there were things about the Ham house that fawning guests would never know. For instance, twenty-five creaky stairs led from the third floor up into a tall cupola that, like a giant crown, topped the building and afforded a splendid view of the river. Legend says that Ham had built it to observe the movement of his ships. Pirates still roamed the Mississippi River, plundering steamboats carrying lumber, foodstuffs and various supplies, and Ham's spying eventually led to the capture of a band of pirates. When the pirates vowed vengeance, the Ham children seemed more excited than frightened.

Margaret Ham died in the house in 1874, and in 1889, just short of his eighty-fourth birthday, Mathias died. Of the children, all but May and Sarah had already scattered. May died first, in the 1890s, leaving Sarah alone in the mansion.

Late one night, while reading in her third-floor bedroom, Sarah thought she heard a prowler. The pirates' threat of years ago crossed her mind, but she didn't get up to investigate. In the morning, Sarah told a neighbor that if she heard the prowler again she would put a light in the window as a call for help.

Several nights later Sarah was again reading in her room. Distinct sounds came from somewhere deep within the house, probably the first floor. She put aside her book and called out, "Who's there?" No answer. Sarah locked her door, lit the lamp and put it in the window. Then, taking up a gun, she sat, waiting. Heavy footsteps crossed the front hall, and climbed the long flight of stairs. They stopped outside the bedroom. Sarah Ham fired two shots through the door.

Later, neighbors found a trail of blood leading from Sarah's door, through the house and out into the night. The intruder, an old river pirate, died at the water's edge from the gunshot wounds inflicted by Sarah. Some say that the mysterious light now seen moving through the Ham mansion at night is the lamp carried by the murdered outlaw searching for his assailant.

Since 1964 the Mathias Ham House has been operated as a museum by the Dubuque County Historical Society. And society employees regularly report a number of strange, inexplicable incidents. For example, a window in an upper hall will be found open from time to time after being securely locked the night before—a strong spring holds the lock in place and workers believe the window couldn't open accidentally, even if buffeted by gusts of wind.

In that same upper hallway a repaired light works only part of the time. An electrician came to fix the light, but after he left, it behaved as erratically as before. Called back again, the electrician told curator Debbie Griesinger there was no way the light could *not* work. But it has never been dependable.

Lights in the front rooms of the Ham House are usually turned on and off by screwing and unscrewing a fuse. One summer night an assistant curator who was closing the museum for the night heard the sound of a pump organ when she unscrewed the fuse! When she screwed the fuse tightly back in place, the organ sound ceased. The curator became badly frightened and fled. Ironically, there *is* a pump organ in the house, but it is closed and cannot be played!

On still another occasion, Dubuque police officers, conducting a routine check of the premises, noticed a light burning in the hallway of the house's older section. They called Griesinger who went to turn off the light, alone. She later told a news reporter that it was "one of the most frightening experiences of my life!"

"I entered the front door and went to the end of the hall to turn off the burglar alarm. Once you open the front door you only have a few seconds to throw the switch or the alarm will go off. Then I groped for the fuse so I could turn on the lights. It was dark and it was the first time I was in the house alone at night. I seemed to feel a presence."

John Schublin, a tour guide, also feels that someone, or something, is in the house. He spent an evening there in the fall of 1978, and sometime after three o'clock in the morning, heard womens' voices in the yard outside. Schublin checked, but could find no one. Returning to the house, he then heard footsteps on the second floor of the original part of the house. He investigated, but again found nothing. Later he heard soft, shuffling noises in the basement, as if someone were entering or leaving through some sort of tunnel. Schublin didn't go down, although there is a tunnel which has caved in twenty feet beyond the basement wall. Local legend says that there is buried treasure at the other end of the tunnel.

Many Dubuque County Historical Society employees have felt ill-at-ease in certain parts of the mansion. On the third floor, for instance, one can feel icy winds and strange chills as well as hear, quite clearly, noises from other parts of the house, especially when standing near the stairway to the tower. Supposedly, a man hanged himself in that tower sometime before 1900, but no verification of the incident could be made.

Thus, for over a century, this dark and brooding mansion, once housing the cream of Iowa gentility, has sheltered the living and the dying, making it difficult, if not impossible, to identify who roams the premises. Could it be the nameless pirate who searches for his killer? Or is it possibly Mathias Ham himself guarding his home forever from some vengeful plunderer?

THE PUNCTUAL GHOST

Emil Vogel slept. Beside him, his wife, Anna, stirred uneasily. The parlor clock downstairs had just struck two o'clock when the hinges on the back cellar door whined. Anna heard the bottom of the door scrape the sill as the door was forced open. Someone was in the cellar! Heavy footsteps crossed the cellar floor and started up the stairs into the kitchen.

Anna nudged her husband awake and he held her tightly in his arms. They heard the intruder tramp across the kitchen floor, then into the parlor. The front door clicked open and slammed shut. The footsteps were gone.

Emil got up and went downstairs. The front door was still bolted from the inside! The windows were closed and locked. Emil went to the cellar and found that door secure also. Yet someone had walked through the house; both he and Anna had heard the footfalls. It was no dream.

The next night the incident recurred. And the next night. And the next. Always at the same hour. Anna became tense and frightened. She and Emil had scrimped and saved for so long to buy the frame house in Fort Madison in March of 1897. Now it was May. In just two months Anna's dream house had turned into a nightmare.

On a number of occasions, Anna and Emil sat up late to watch for whatever was getting into their house. Sometimes they could hear footsteps near the house. Parting the lace curtains, they peered through the darkened windows, but never saw a living thing.

Night after night Emil checked the house after the ghost had left. Front and back doors were always solidly bolted. There was no sign of forced entry. Who was it that entered their home and walked in the night?

One evening Emil was called to the bedside of a dying relative who lived nearby. He kissed his wife goodbye and assured her he'd be back soon. Anna, tossing in bed, heard the clock strike once . . . twice. The cellar door opened. Anna knew she must confront the thing herself, find out what it was and what it wanted. With trembling fingers, she tucked her hair into her night cap and went to the head of the cellar stairway.

A heavy-set man was climbing the rough wooden stairs. He came steadily toward her as if unaware of her presence. He sported a full, gray beard and a red shirt open at the neck. When he was three steps from the top of the stairway where Anna stood, she fainted.

When she came to, Emil was at her side. He listened attentively to her story. Neither he nor Anna knew anyone fitting Anna's description. Emil checked the house and then the yard. Nothing was amiss.

Emil knew there was only one way to rid his house of whatever was getting into it. He loaded his gun, and the next night he crouched in the basement by the outside door waiting for the intruder. When he heard footsteps outside at the cellar entry, he fired two shots through the door. A moment later he flung it open. Only the smoke from his weapon rose in the night air.

In the morning Emil and Anna moved out of the house.

But others came. Curious visitors from all parts of the city thronged to the house, some bringing bedrolls to camp for the night in hopes of seeing the ghost. A policeman seemed shaken by his visit, but was unwilling to talk of his experience.

Eventually, the windows and doors of the house were boarded up. It was finally sold, then resold a number of times. No one stayed long.

On Wednesday evening, August 16, 1899, the old house at 2426 Des Moines Street burned to the ground. It was then owned and rented out by Charles Walker, a grocer living on the corner of Occidental and Division streets. His last tenants, the Sallady family and a widow named Rebb, had moved only that morning.

Some people claimed that a group of boys had set fire to the house. Others said that the ghost himself had destroyed it. The time of the calamitous blaze? Somewhere in the vicinity of two o'clock . . .

MRS. WEAVER'S PECULIAR TABLE

It was the kind of table you would expect to find in a used furniture store—heavy oak, stained dark brown. With its oval top and two shelves, it was a sturdy, utilitarian piece of furniture.

But the James Weaver family, of 1942 Francis Avenue, Des Moines, wished the table weren't in their living room. They found it far from ordinary. Rappings from inside the table were heard all over the house. It sounded as if someone's knuckles were knocking on the table top.

At first the Weavers ignored the strange sounds, then they laughed at them. But when the noises persisted, Mr. Weaver took the table apart. Finding nothing to account for the rapping, he reassembled the table and applied a coat of fresh varnish. The table still rapped. The family moved it to other parts of the room, but the noise was as loud and persistent as ever.

Mrs. Roy Clearwater, a married daughter of the Weavers, had originally bought the table in 1935 from a secondhand furniture auctioneer for fifty cents. She kept it for two years and heard no rappings.

Then she sold the table to a friend who likewise heard no noises. In late 1937 Mrs. Weaver bought it from her daughter's friend for seventy-five cents. She had always admired the table and knew it would be a perfect place for her pictures and plants. Shortly after Mrs. Weaver brought the table into the house it began to rap. Since it happened only occasionally, however, no one but the family was aware of the phenomenon. They never talked about it with friends and relatives. Mrs. Weaver didn't think it proper.

But the noisy table soon became an embarrassment. Friends who dropped in for the evening would be startled by its strange sounds. Leta, the Weavers' thirty-three-year-old unmarried daughter who lived at home, would say offhandedly, "Oh, don't pay any attention. It's just our spooky table."

The table made Mrs. Weaver increasingly nervous, and finally she persuaded her husband to contact a minister. Wilbur and Madelene Cornman, co-pastors of the McDivitt Grove Open Bible Church, soon visited the Weaver home.

The table made no sounds while the Cornmans were there, but Mrs. Cornman opined that it was possessed by "evil spirits." Placing her hands on the table, she read from the Bible and led the family in prayer. The table was quiet that night and the next day. And the next.

A week passed. Mrs. Weaver was clearly relieved. She didn't understand how evil spirits came to be lodged in her table; she was only happy that they were gone. But her joy was premature. Two weeks after the ministers' visit, the table resumed its rapping. The Cornmans advised the Weavers to destroy the table.

Instead, Mrs. Weaver got in touch with a spiritualist, a Mrs. E. A. Hanke, of 1524 Center Street. Mrs. Hanke thought the table might have been used by a spiritualist medium at one time and the raps were the cries of a bewildered spirit. She advised the Weavers to talk to the table.

"But the Cornmans are against that," Mrs. Weaver told a news reporter, "and now I don't know what to do." Neither did anyone else in the family.

Leta was entertaining a young woman friend one afternoon and telling her about the table and Mrs. Hanke's theory. The girl laughed. The table rapped.

But when the Weavers' twenty-nine-year-old son Floyd, who also lived at home and worked as an iceman, brought his girl friend home one night to hear the table rap, it was silent.

That was the most exasperating thing, said Mrs. Weaver. "The table is so unpredictable. You can never tell when it's going to rap."

One day in the middle of September, 1940, the Weavers' daughter, Mrs. Clearwater, and her sons, Kenneth, thirteen, and James, ten, were visiting. The table set a record by rapping six times. Everyone heard the rappings, and the last time they occurred Mrs. Clearwater and Kenneth saw the table jump.

Kenneth said he wasn't afraid, but his brother was. So was their mother. She was not well and the incident greatly upset her. Mr. Weaver and Floyd remained calm, at least outwardly, but Mrs. Weaver and Leta were worried by what they took to be an ominous event. The table had never moved before. What did it mean? And what did the increase in the frequency of the rappings mean? In the beginning the table had rapped only once a week, or maybe twice.

Remembering the Cornmans' visit, Mrs. Weaver placed a Bible on the table and hung above it a wall motto: "The Lord is my Shepherd."

But the evil spirits remain undeterred by the religious articles. The next day the table rapped louder than ever. As incredible as it sounds, Mrs. Weaver refused to get rid of the table.

Parapsychologists classify knocks as "physical" if everyone present hears them. This was true in the case of the Weavers' table. The fact that the table also performed for strangers, as well as for family and friends, suggests the antics of a genuine poltergeist.

In so far as is known, experts did not study this case. But among many cases of rappings in furniture that have been thoroughly investigated, a *normal* cause is rarely found.

GEORGE, THE MISCHIEVOUS GHOST

In 1968, Jim and Sue Anderson moved into a rambling clapboard house in Des Moines. It had an upstairs sleeping porch, narrow double-hung windows and gingerbread trim. The house was once owned by Jim's grandparents, and the young couple was delighted to be raising their family in such spacious, comfortable quarters.

But one night shortly after they had moved in, their delight turned to horror. Jim was visiting a friend. At ten o'clock he phoned his wife to tell her he'd be staying a while longer. Sue was tired and, although she usually waited up for her husband, she went on to bed. The children were already in bed and asleep. Sue was drifting off when she heard her husband come in the back door, walk through the downstairs hall and into the pantry.

Then the phone rang. Sue lifted the receiver from the bedside phone.

"Hi, honey," said Jim, "I'm just leaving. See you soon."

"Wise guy," cracked Sue. "I already heard you come in."

"But honey, I'm not in the house."

Not in the house.

But someone was! Sue gripped the phone in both hands; she could hear the hum of the dial tone. Her husband had hung up! She eased the receiver into its cradle, went to the bedroom door and cracked it open. Footsteps squeaked on the freshly-waxed kitchen floor. Sue tiptoed across the upstairs hallway to the childrens' room and gathered her young son and daughter in her arms. Back in the master bedroom, she locked the door and tucked the children into bed with her.

Moments later, footsteps raced up the staircase, shaking the walls of the old house. Sue saw the glass knob turn. Then the pounding began.

"Sue, open up! It's me!" The voice was unmistakable. She flung open the door and collapsed in her husband's arms.

When the front doorbell rang, Jim ran downstairs.

"It's Crime Alert," he shouted over his shoulder. "I phoned them before I left Bill's place."

Sue wrapped herself in a bathrobe and followed her husband downstairs. The officers listened to her account of the intruder, then fanned out through the house. They searched from basement to attic, shifting furniture, trunks and boxes, poking into dark corners with their flashlights. They found nothing. Windows and doors in the basement and on the first floor were all locked, and there was *no* indication of any tampering. No one could have entered the house.

After the officers left, Sue felt foolish; yet she knew that she had not imagined the incident. Someone had walked through the house.

Late one evening, a few months later, Sue was ironing in the upstairs sleeping porch when she heard a knock at the window. She put down the iron and looked out, but the inside light prevented her from seeing beyond the dark window glass. Then it came again—knuckle-sharp rat-a-tat-tats on the glass.

Sue snapped off the light and walked to the wall of windows. Cupping her hands to her face, she peered out. Moonlight washed the high limbs of the old cottonwood and the grove of walnut trees at the far property line. No leaf stirred in the night air. Besides, there were no close tree limbs that could have scraped against the windows. No outside stairway led to the porch. What had made the noise? Sue went to bed, but didn't sleep well.

On another evening, Sue finished washing the dinner dishes and set bags of garbage in the adjacent mud room. In the morning she'd take them out to the garbage can. But the next morning the bags were gone. Jim checked the trash cans; they were empty. The couple searched the house, but never found the bags.

Several times during that year the couple would come downstairs early in the morning to find lights blazing in the hallway and den, and front and back doors standing open. The double locks on the doors were not broken— just unlocked from the inside. The children were not sleepwalkers and their parents, not wishing to alarm the youngsters, said nothing to them about the burning lights and the open doors.

Sue wondered if a ghost was inhabiting the house, but scoffed at the idea. "It's silly," she said. "Who'd believe stuff like that? I don't."

Jim shared her feelings; he figured there was a logical explanation for everything. But he had failed to find one.

During the couple's second year in the house, their small daughter reported at breakfast one morning that a man had come into her room during the night. She woke up suddenly and saw him standing beside her bed, smiling down at her. Since the girl wasn't upset by the incident, her parents asked no questions.

Sue explained to her that Daddy had been in her room. "Oh no, it wasn't," said the child.

Sue was greatly distressed. Perhaps her daughter had seen some kind of reflection? Sometime later, Sue invited her friend, Kathy, to spend the evening. The two women sat in the living room and, during the course of the conversation, Sue mentioned the odd events of the past year.

Kathy, who was interested in the occult and had some psychic abilities, interrupted. "There's a spirit standing in the corner of the room."

Sue saw nothing. Kathy said the ghost had a gentle smile on its face and would not harm the family. Sue glanced nervously at her watch. It was ten o'clock. The conversation drifted to other topics and, toward midnight, the friend left. Sue carried the coffee cups to the kitchen and when she returned to the living room she noticed the wall clock. It had stopped at ten.

The same clock stopped at ten o'clock for three nights; then it quit running altogether!

For a year, to Sue's relief, nothing more happened. She had spent many sleepless nights worrying about whether the mischievous ghost would return or harm her daughter.

The next fall the ghost came back. The Andersons were entertaining dinner guests Linda and Al Peters. Linda and Sue lingered over coffee at the dining room table. Suddenly Linda stared into the adjoining living room and shouted, "Look! There's a white, misty figure pacing back and forth."

Sue saw nothing.

Then Linda leaned back in her chair and laughed. "Of course, it's one of the guys clowning around."

Sue didn't laugh. She knew Jim and Al were in the kitchen. Her fears returned.

Three nights later, Linda, Kathy and another young woman were at the Anderson house to work on a craft project for a bazaar. Midway in the evening's work, Sue served coffee and cookies and the room buzzed with friendly small talk. Linda mentioned that her white cat had been missing for four months. The animal had never strayed from home, and Linda and her husband couldn't understand the cat's sudden disappearance. They had asked neighbors and ran advertisements in the newspaper, but no clues were forthcoming. No one had seen the cat.

When the women finished their evening's work and prepared to leave, Sue turned on the porch light. A white cat was curled up on the steps. Linda was astonished— it was her cat. She cradled it in her arms and it purred and blinked its green eyes. Where had the cat been? And why did it appear just then on the Anderson's porch?

The Andersons were as mystified as Linda. However, they sensed that their mischievous ghost was somehow involved.

By now, Sue was desperate for answers. She suggested getting a Ouija Board. Her husband agreed. Perhaps they could learn the identity of their visitor and find out what he wanted.

The couple sat face to face in the living room, the board across their knees. When Sue asked about the ghost, the marker spun around on the board, spelling out G-E-O-R-G-E. It said that George had lived on this land in the early 1800s, that he didn't want to be here, but that he would not harm them.

Sue then checked records at the Polk County Court House. But deed transfers prior to 1866 were not available, and she failed to locate any information on anyone named George who had lived on the tract of land on which the house stands. The Ouija Board yielded no further information.

In the fall of 1972, the ghost became unusually active. One afternoon Sue and a friend were in the basement when the television set suddenly blared forth from an upstairs room. Both women raced up the stairs. No one else was in the house. Who had turned on the set?

A couple of days later, Sue was alone, working in the kitchen, when she heard a crash in the basement. She ran downstairs to find a large mirror smashed to bits on the floor. The nail remained in the wall and the wire was still firmly attached to the back of the frame. The mirror had hung in the same place since the day they'd moved into the house.

In November of that year, Jim often awakened in the middle of the night. He'd see a man standing beside the bed, staring down at him; he would awaken Sue and they'd both get up and turn on the lights. But no one was ever in the room, at least no one they could see.

One night, Jim got up and went to the bathroom. As he started back to the bedroom, he saw a man standing against the back wall of the hallway, staring at him. Jim edged past the figure. For some unexplainable reason, Jim, like his daughter, was not afraid of the dark specter.

That winter, Sue and her friends decided to hold a multi-family garage sale. Lacking table space to display small household items, the women made shelves by putting boards across the rungs of two upright ladders. Everything was stored in the Anderson's locked garage.

On the morning of the sale, Sue unlocked the garage. All the items that had been placed on the makeshift shelves lay broken and strewn about on the concrete floor. The ladders and boards remained solidly in place. The only access to the garage was through the door.

And that's the last that has been heard from George. Or is it?

Chapter IV. Kansas

"For years after Elizabeth Polly's death, local residents referred to her burial spot as the 'Lonely Grave.' Nearly inaccessible by car, the grave was rarely visited . . . in the 1960s a group of citizens erected an obelisk on Elizabeth's Hill, a fitting memorial to this selfless pioneer woman who rested there.

Or does she?

Fifty years after Elizabeth Polly's death, a. sequence of strange events seemed to indicate that she may have left her 'Lonely Grave' . . ."

"THE LONELY GRAVE"

GHOST OF THE PURPLE MASQUE

Carl Hinrichs, a speech and drama professor at Kansas State University in Manhattan, was working late one night in the campus theater, the Purple Masque.

"My Fair Lady" was well into rehearsal and Hinrichs, as scene designer, still had a great deal of work to do. He was alone in the building.

At two o'clock in the morning Hinrichs went into the scene shop. He poured paint from a five-gallon container into a smaller bucket which he carried back to the stage where he was working. Then he heard a tremendous crash.

"Who's there?" the professor called out.

When no one answered, Hinrichs walked back to the scene shop. The five-gallon bucket of paint was turned upside down in the middle of the floor and at least ten feet from where he had left it.

That incident occurred in 1964. Hinrichs had just had his first encounter with Nick, the mischievous ghost of the Purple Masque.

The theater occupies a portion of the main floor of East Stadium, a cafeteria during the 1950s. The building also served as an athletic dormitory at that time, with the men billeted on the second floor. The story goes that a football player named Nick was injured in a game, carried into the cafeteria and placed on a table where he died. But Nick's disembodied spirit returned as a poltergeist, one who is heard but not seen.

During Nick's most active period (1964-1969) he supposedly talked on tape machines, clomped through hallways and up and down stairs and played various tricks to get attention. He became one of the crowd and generally shared the stage with students and faculty. But Nick often ran the show *his* way, sometimes frustrating the cast and stage crews.

After a rehearsal of "American Yard," the theater doors and the building were locked. In the morning a stage hand found all the chairs from the set piled in the hallway. The theater doors were still locked. The worker put the chairs back on stage.

That night at rehearsal, after the house lights dimmed, the actors found their entrance blocked by the same chairs. No logical explanation was ever found.

At that same rehearsal, when the stage manager ordered the stage lights brought up, the student running the light board could not comply. "I can't," he admitted. "I gave them power. I can hear them, but they're not coming on."

Seconds later, the lights came up slowly. The student was amazed. He said he had nothing to do with it. Others agreed. It was just Nick, they said, up to more pranks.

Kay Coles, a former theater major at Kansas State, told a reporter that a crew once unloaded chairs in the Masque to be set up later. The men then went outside. Hearing a commotion in the theater, they rushed back in. All the chairs were set up and programs were neatly placed on all the seats!

"There was nobody around," recalled Coles. "It happened in five minutes, and it usually takes at least half an hour to do the job."

Coles herself had a baffling experience at the Purple Masque in the spring of 1971. She and another student had just finished working with the sound system; they turned off the equipment and locked the theater.

"Suddenly, music started playing," said Coles. Her companion unlocked the theater and found the tape running. He turned off the machine and again locked the theater.

The music started again. "It (the machine) came on four more times," Coles explained. "We looked for someone playing a joke, but there wasn't a soul around."

Hers was not an isolated instance. David Laughland was alone in the Masque taping sound cues late one night. In playing back the tape, he heard a voice call out on the tape, "Hi Dave!"

Laughland rewound the tape and played it again. There was no voice.

Nick's pranks always startled, and sometimes frightened, younger players. One night an actress was alone in a dressing room waiting to go on stage. The room held a desk and several wooden cubes. The actress made a quick costume change and sat down on the desk to rest.

One of the cubes in the room raised up, turned over and set itself gently down on the floor in front of the student.

The frightened girl stammered, "Not nice, Nick."

She got up and moved to the doorway to await her cue. Just before going on stage, she looked back over her shoulder. The cube was no longer by the desk—it had moved back to its original position atop another cube!

The actress, keyed up and alert to her role in the play, did not think she had hallucinated.

The next night, the actress took a cigarette lighter into the same room with her, but it would not stay lit. The following night she carried a flashlight and it wouldn't stay on either.

Another inexplicable Purple Masque incident involved two technicians working together on a set that included a bed and a couch. In the early morning hours they decided to take naps. One took the bed, the other the couch.

They hadn't slept long before the fellow on the couch struggled awake. He seemed to be choking to death. Squinting through one eye, he saw the fire extinguisher discharging in midair. But no one held it! The apparatus, like a torpedo, zeroed in on him, the nozzle spraying a malevolent chemical into his face. The student leaped from the couch and ran.

When Nick wasn't taking a hand in productions, he was clomping through the theater.

Once, when he was alone, Mark Grimes, a former president of the K-State Players, heard footsteps in the theater's hallway. He and a friend later stood at opposite ends of the hall and heard footsteps tread the entire length of the corridor between them. The pressure of invisible feet caused a number of the floorboards to creak.

One fall evening three students were working at the theater. During a break they all heard tromping upstairs— "like a two-hundred-pound person walking," according to one of them. The doors to the second floor were locked. Although the students had keys to the upstairs quarters, no one dared to go up and check.

Next the heating pipes started to clang as they always did when the boilers were fired up at the heating plant.

The heat came on and the theater became pleasantly warm.

The students learned later that the campus boilers had not been turned on for the season until three weeks after this incident!

It is not only students, however, who believe that an unseen presence lurks in and around the theater. A woman visitor, touring the campus, told her guide that she felt a presence in the Purple Masque. She knew nothing of the supernatural history of the place. Her guide simply smiled and nodded.

When they entered the room where platforms were stored, the woman froze for a moment, then fled, screaming. After she calmed down she said there was a dangerous element in that room; no one should ever enter it alone.

One student who did enter the room alone said she always felt presences around her that made her uneasy.

Others felt icy hands on their shoulders in that same storeroom. What was the "dangerous element" in that place? No one knew, but few believed it to be Nick. Mischievous, but friendly, he was never known to have knowingly harmed anyone.

Was there really a Kansas State football player named Nick? Records show that there was. And legend has it that he died in the cafeteria which is now the Purple Masque theater.

Eventually, during a séance a medium made contact with Nick's spirit. When she asked him what they should do to put his soul at rest and relieve him of his need to haunt, he reportedly told them to run a Dalmation through the theater at midnight!

To date, no one has complied with Nick's wishes. But to this day, Nick remains the best documented spirit in Manhattan. William E. Koch, Professor of English and

Folklore, Emeritus, at Kansas State University, calls Nick's story "one of the classics" in Kansas ghost lore.

MÉNAGE À TROIS

Billy Plummer was restless. He tossed and turned in bed on that frigid December night in 1939. Suddenly, he felt his wife, Gert, tickling his feet.

Jerking his knees up to his chin, he screamed, "No, Gert, no! Quit that!" But when Billy glanced across the bed, he saw that his wife was sound asleep. In the next instant, she jumped. "Billy, cut it out!"

"What d'ya mean, cut it out?"

Gert propped herself up on an elbow. "You've got a sick sense of humor. You know I *hate* being tickled."

"But I never touched you."

Gert sat bolt upright in bed. "You didn't?"

Billy threw off the covers and snapped on the light.

"Look," he began, "if you weren't tickling me and I wasn't tickling you, then we've got bedbugs."

Gert was horrified. She leaped up and helped her husband strip the bed. They shook out blankets, sheets and mattress pad . . . and found nothing.

Back in bed, the Plummers were attacked again. They squirmed, they laughed and they cried, and eventually they fell asleep. At four o'clock in the morning, taps and thumps from the bed frame awakened them. Billy reached for the light switch. The couple saw no one in the room, but the thumpings continued. They seemed to be coming from the headboard, the siderails, the springs, indeed, from all over the bed. The couple lay rigid, bedclothes pulled up under their chins.

Every night from then on the Plummers' sleep was interrupted by the strange sounds. One night in February, a deep voice came from somewhere beneath the bed.

"Is the baby asleep?" it asked.

Gert Plummer, wild with fright, dashed into the baby's room. Their infant son was sleeping soundly. After that incident, Billy Plummer took the bed apart. Finding nothing unusual he put it back together.

One night in mid-March Billy decided to try to snare whatever it was that was in the bedroom. He strung a copper wire from the bedspring to a gas pipe in the kitchen. Not a tap, a thump or a tickle disturbed the couple all night. Gert rose happy and refreshed. Her joy was short-lived. The next night "the thing" was back in the bedroom tapping, thumping and tickling.

Amateur ghost hunters from Wichita and the surrounding area, as well as the police, were consulted. They all found the ghost accommodating as well as agile in producing noises anywhere on the bed, yet they were unable to learn its identity or to discover what it wanted.

At the end of March, Dr. William H. Mikesell, a psychologist and author, was invited to the Plummers' Wichita home. Seven witnesses, including a detective, had already gathered. When the professor asked the ghost to thump the bed, it obeyed. Dr. Mikesell then ordered it to rap on one side of the bed and it likewise obliged. He asked it to rap a certain number of times in another place on the bed and it did so promptly.

"I could feel several raps near my hand on the bed," Dr. Mikesell told a news reporter. But when he asked the ghost to tap on the chest in the room, it refused. It would touch no piece of furniture other than the bed.

Dr. Mikesell's rendezvous with the entity lasted for two hours. By then the professor was tired and ill at ease because of the large number of spectators. He promised to return at some other time when fewer persons were present.

But the professor never had a chance. On the first warm spring day, Billy Plummer carted the bed to the Wichita dump. Both he and Gert were tired of sharing their bed—especially with something they couldn't see!

THE LEGEND OF WHITE WOMAN CREEK

Today, the stream bed is dry and pocked with gravel. But once—many years ago—the clear water ran swiftly through the sweeping prairie of Greeley, Wichita and Scott counties in western Kansas. The creek's meager remnants would not receive a passing glance today, although the origin of its most peculiar name is one of the most enduring legends of Kansas—White Woman Creek is haunted by the ghost of a lovely young woman captured by the Cheyenne people over a century ago.

The Cheyenne nation once roamed the vast grasslands of Kansas, hunting the bison and the antelope. Their quarry was numerous, their lives relatively untouched by the approaching white settlers.

Cheyenne Chief Tee-Wah-Nee led a small party of hunters during one foray for game. They camped near the bank of a stream they called "River-that-runs-between-the-hills-that-are-always-covered-with-smoke." The bison had been plentiful, and the men spent many days in this camp curing the meat and preparing the hide for clothing and blankets.

One night, a band of white men raided the camp. They stole the meat and hides and many horses. Chief Tee-Wah-Nee and his brother, Tan-Ka-Wah, were wounded; many of their brothers were killed.

At dawn, the Cheyenne rode after the enemy and seized ten men and two women from a white settlement where the raiders had retreated. The braves also recovered the meat and hides.

The prisoners were forced to return to the Cheyenne camp with the horses they had stolen. The women, two sisters, Anna and May, were given the job of nursing the injured Cheyenne men back to health.

The months passed. Autumn came. Chief Tee-Wah-Nee and his brother were fully recovered . . . and deeply in love with the sisters. Anna and May returned their affection.

On the day set for the Indians' return to their village, Tee-Wah-Nee convened a council and proclaimed himself the husband of Anna. Tan-Ka-Wah stood next to him and repeated the phrase, asking May to be his wife.

Anna then sought permission to address the group, although women rarely spoke before councils. The men listened intently as she spoke to them in their own language:

> "My heart is swollen with love for you, my people. To Tee-Wah-Nee I promise my love until the rain no longer falls from the sky.
>
> "At first we were afraid. But no longer do we fear. The names by which you call my sister and me—Anna-Wee and May-O-Wee—are signs of our acceptance.
>
> "I have only one request. We are now going home—a home I have never seen. When five suns have gone, release the white men who are still with us. In return, they must promise never to steal the Cheyenne's horses or take my sister and me away from our husbands. Our only brother is among those you hold and we are thinking of him and his future happiness."

The council discussed Anna's request. It was granted.

Then Anna-Wee's brother, Daniel, rose to speak. None of the prisoners wanted to return, he said. None had families in the settlement, nor could they promise that other white men would honor a promise not to attack the Cheyenne. He asked that he and the other white men be accepted as brothers. The Cheyenne, who had long since stopped guarding the white men as prisoners, granted their request.

Camp was struck and the party set out for the main Cheyenne village. Scouts rode ahead to announce the arrival of Chief Tee-Wah-Nee, his brother and their wives. A ceremonial feast of thanksgiving was prepared.

In time Anna-Wee bore a son. The happiest lodge in the whole village was that of Tee-Wah Nee and Anna-Wee.

The child was just learning to crawl when word came that Henrich, one of the adopted white men, had left the village. He had stolen one of Tee-Wah-Nee's finest ponies, but no attempt was made to stop him.

Henrich eventually reached Fort Wallace. He told the Army Commander that the white men and women held by Tee-Wah-Nee were still prisoners and were being mistreated.

Tee-Wah-Nee heard of Henrich's lies. Before he could send a delegation to correct the story, cavalry troops lay seige to the Cheyenne village.

The traitor Henrich rode at the front of the first charge. The troops fell back many times after being repulsed by the well-fortified Cheyenne village. Eventually, Henrich and Tee-Wah-Nee found one another at nightfall, realizing full well that one of them must die. Henrich fell upon Tee-Wah-Nee with his bayonet; the Cheyenne chief lay mortally wounded.

Henrich ran to the lodge of Anna-Wee. There he murdered her infant son, grabbed the weeping and terrified woman into his arms, mounted his horse and sped away with her down the streambed.

A short distance from the smoldering village, Anna-Wee spotted the body of Tee-Wah-Nee. She feigned illness, sat on the ground and asked Henrich to allow her to take some beads and bracelets from her husband's body. Henrich sneered his assent. Anna-Wee knelt close, gathered Tee-Wah-Nee's bow and quiver of arrows and hid them in the folds of her skirt. As Henrich turned to watch the fighting, she picked up the bow, slid an arrow against the curved wood and shot Henrich in the back.

"You are a traitor to both your own people and my adopted people," she cried as Henrich fell to the ground. Anna-Wee took his rifle and ammunition, along with the bow and arrow, and returned to the battleground.

At dusk, the body of Tee-Wah-Nee was carried to the ruins of his lodge. Anna-Wee kept vigil beside the remains of her husband and son, singing the Cheyenne death song and imploring Manitou, the great spirit, to take their souls.

The Cheyenne village was attacked again the next day by the cavalry and Anna-Wee bravely fought against the troops. She was killed late that afternoon.

On fall evenings, in those brief minutes between sunset and darkness, mists arise from the sandy banks of that Kansas stream bed now known as White Woman Creek. And supposedly out of that mist comes the ghost of Anna-Wee, wandering the prairie of her earthly happiness. The song she sang long ago for Tee-Wah-Nee still drifts across the tall grasses like a single white cloud in the endlessly blue Kansas sky. Many have heard her song but few remember the story of the "white woman" and the Cheyenne chief.

THE ELLINWOOD CAPERS

Fred Koett quit his farm near Ellinwood, Kansas. He sold most of his household goods and moved his wife and infant son out of the state. Nothing unusual in that. Except in Koett's case—he claimed he was driven out of his home by ghosts!

"I couldn't stand it any longer," he told a news reporter. "I don't know what it is that has caused so many mysterious happenings, but I've experienced things that are hardly believable and I have withstood it longer than any other man would."

The trouble became public knowledge in June, 1926, when Koett, his four hired hands, and his brother-in-law, Samuel Waddell, spotted a wraith-like form one night near the orchard. All six men fired at it; Waddell, an expert marksman, got off several shots. But the figure vaulted leisurely over the orchard fence.

The next day Koett sought protection from the Barton County attorney's office. That night several sheriff's deputies stood vigil on the grounds of the farm. They saw nothing unusual.

Later the family's pet dog was found dead, stabbed in the back with a pitchfork.

Meanwhile, inside the house, pictures were discovered turned to the wall, and a small statue of the Virgin Mary apparently moved by itself from its usual place. The officers couldn't explain these events and Koett let them go three nights later.

Neighbors were quick to offer opinions. Many thought that Waddell, his wife, and his mother, Mrs. S. Waddell, were creating the disturbances to drive Koett off the farm so they could manage it for themselves. Waddell's eighteen-year-old sister was Koett's second wife. After she married the middle-aged farmer, her brother, her sister-in-law and her mother moved with her to her husband's farm.

Waddell was hurt by the gossip. "I came here from Fort Smith, Arkansas," he explained, "where I have a respectable name, and folks there can vouch for my veracity. The neighbors may say that we're trying to scare Mr. Koett off the place so that we can get it, but that's a lie. He has a life interest in the farm and cannot dispose of it. When he does it will go to the children of his first wife. None of us will get any part of it."

Koett's life interest in the farm was undisputed. His father had broken the land and Fred was born there. For as long as anyone could remember it was known as the "Koett place."

The elder Koett had died several years earlier. And it wasn't long before the trouble began. Mrs. S. Waddell blamed it on the ghost of Fred's father whom she claimed had come back to tell Fred something important about the management of the property. She believed that until the ghost could deliver a message strange things would continue to happen.

They did. Over a period of many months.

Manifestations occurred first upstairs in the southwest bedroom where old man Koett had died. Pictures were found hanging sideways and strange thumping noises were heard at night. Then the same phenomena were repeated downstairs, in the northwest room where the corpse had lain.

On one occasion a hired man heard a noise in a closet. When he opened the door he was punched in the nose. The family searched the closet, but found no evidence that anyone had been in there.

Once, when the family was leaving the house for the evening, a voice whispered the warning, "Get out! Get out!"

And on a Sunday when the family returned home, they found a strong odor filling the house. "Like medicine," recalled Mrs. S. Waddell. "I think maybe it was tear gas."

Koett crated the furniture and other household effects that he and his family planned to take with them. Then he watched as the large, bulky crates moved around the room under their own power. Koett still had business to tend to before leaving the area, but he did not wish to spend another night in the haunted house. He quickly arranged for the family to sleep in a granary half a mile down the road.

Although Koett suffered ill health caused, in part, by the unearthly torments, he was confident that the ghost would not follow him to his new home. Just before leaving on that spring morning in 1927, he rented the farm to Dave Meier, a neighbor.

The Koett farmhouse was eventually razed and the story of the Ellinwood capers faded from memory. To this day no one knows if the ghost disappeared with the farm's passing or followed the Koett family from Ellinwood. No one living, that is ...

PHANTOM RIDERS OF THE PONY EXPRESS

Near the town of Hanover, in northern Kansas, stands a frail wooden building. It is known as the Hollenberg Station, the largest relief stop on the famous Pony Express trail that stretched from Missouri to California. Believed to be the only unaltered station in its original location, it has another distinction too. Some say the rambling, weathered building holds the spirits of both men and beasts who pounded across the prairie, carrying the mails a century and more ago.

In 1860 the rail and the telegraph ended at St. Joseph, Missouri. From there the mail was carried by stagecoach to California, a trip that took three weeks or longer. Nearly half a million Americans were then living west of the Rocky Mountains. Many had gone to prospect for gold or to take up lands, and all hungered for news from family and friends in the East. It was frustrating to wait for the slow and sometimes unpredictable stage. Besides, the rapid expansion of the young country required a faster means of communication between the federal government and the western settlements. To fill this need, the Pony Express was born.

The hope was that horsemen, riding fast ponies in relays, could carry the mail across 2,000 miles of prairie and mountain in half the time it took the stagecoach. It was a grand and daring scheme fraught with every imaginable danger, from Indian attack to natural catastrophe. Even the Pony Express Company recognized the risks. Its advertisement of March, 1860, read: "WANTED—Young, skinny, wiry fellows not over eighteen. Must be expert riders, willing to risk death daily. Orphans preferred."

Orphans or not, 100 to 120 riders were quickly hired, and eighty were in the saddle at all times. One at a time, several hours apart, forty riders headed westward from St. Joseph and forty others started eastward from Sacramento.

The route followed the Oregon-California trail across northern Kansas, then along the Platte River in Nebraska, and on west by way of Fort Kearney, Scotts Bluff, Fort Laramie, South Pass, Fort Bridger and Salt Lake City. The trail crossed Nevada and the Sierra Nevada Mountains and ended at Sacramento, California. River steamers on the Sacramento River then carried the mail on to San Francisco.

At relay stations, set up ten to fifteen miles apart along the route, the rider would give a whoop as he galloped in on clouds of dust and switched to the fresh pony waiting. At every third station a new rider took over. The men rode day and night, through searing heat and deepest snow, for the mail had to go through.

The Pony Express lasted only eighteen months, but in that short time it changed boys into men and created instant heroes.

William F. Cody, later known as Buffalo Bill, was only fifteen years old when he signed on as a rider. Galloping into his home station once at the end of his ride, he learned there was no one to take his place. Without a second thought, young Cody rode on, finishing the trip for a total of 322 miles! His sister Julia later wrote, "They sayed (sic) he was . . . the lightest and swiftest rider, and he seemed to understand the Country."

Another of Cody's rides is notable for a different reason. He was entrusted with a large sum of money destined for California. Cash was rarely transported, but in this case it was unavoidable. At any rate, rumors flew that bandits knew there'd be cash for the taking and planned to ambush the rider. Cody, realizing he would be helpless in the face of a gang of armed, desperate men, devised a simple plan. He placed the money *under* the saddle, hidden in the blanket which lay between the leather and the horse's skin. The saddlebag, which he stuffed with blank paper, was in plain sight.

In changing mounts at relay stations, Cody carefully placed the blanketful of money under the new saddle. On the last lap of his trip the bandits waylaid him. Cody handed over the saddlebag and galloped off, arriving in Sacramento with the cash safely intact, and leaving behind some startled robbers.

Thomas Owen King's enemy was the weather. The twenty-year-old rider lost his way in blinding snow. Coaxing his pony through drifts that reached the stirrups, he eventually found the trail and reached his next station.

Nick Wilson, at eighteen, was caught in the Indian war that blazed across Utah Territory early in May of 1860. In that bloody conflict with the Paiutes who were bent on driving the white man from the West, Wilson was nearly killed—a barbed arrow pierced his skull above his left eye. Although he survived, Wilson carried the ugly scar for the rest of his life and usually wore a hat to hide it.

One of the youngest riders may have been the bravest. Billy Tate was an orphan and only fourteen years old when the Paiute war broke out. A dozen braves charged after him, driving him behind a rock. Friends found the youngster's body pierced by a number of arrows. Seven of his attackers lay dead before him.

While these courageous riders dared the dangers of the long trail westward, the telegraph and the railroad were pushing back the frontier. By October, 1861, the thin wires of the telegraph began flashing messages to the

West Coast, and the need for the horsemen on their spirited ponies was gone.

With the demise of the Pony Express, many of the old stations fell to ruin. But the Hollenberg Station survived the caprices of weather and time. Located 123 miles west of St. Joseph, it occupied part of a ranch owned by Gerat Henry Hollenberg. The building, a long, frame, two-story structure, housed the store, tavern, post office and living quarters for the station keeper and his family on the ground floor and accommodated Pony Express horsemen and overland stage drivers in a second-floor sleeping loft.

Fresh mounts for the riders were kept in a stable that could house a hundred head of horse or oxen. Countless wagon trains stopped at the Hollenberg Station for food and clothing, feed for the animals, and various supplies for the long westward journey.

In 1869 the nearby town of Hanover was founded and its residents were to assume a leading role in preserving the Hollenberg Station. Then, in 1941, the Kansas legislature appropriated funds for the purchase of the structure and seven acres of land. The building, now a state historical park, has been restored and operates as a museum.

Some visitors claim that the Pony Express riders and their mounts still travel the worn, familiar trails. Near quiet stretches of highway late at night, people tell of hearing pounding hoofs and a faint "Hallooo!" as something passes them with the speed of wind.

The ghost of a young rider spurring his phantom horse on to the next station?

A DOG'S TALE

Franc Shor, former associate editor of *National Geographic Magazine*, never had any interest in psychic phenomena. But a compelling and evidential incident in the summer of 1964 left him with many questions.

Shor's mother and other relatives lived in Dodge City, Kansas, while he himself was raised by his grandmother, Mrs. Frank Luther, in Cimarron, Kansas. Mrs. Luther, an antiques buff, was especially fond of the Meissen porcelains she had collected over the years. And little Frankie, as Shor's relatives called him, was fascinated by the delicate figurines. His favorite was of a small child dressed in a smock, patting a dog that stood on its hind legs. Whenever his Aunt Ethel came from Dodge City to visit, she would tease her nephew by insisting that the figure in the smock was a girl. "There's little Frankie wearing a dress," she'd say, and Shor would vigorously protest.

When Mrs. Luther died, she left her porcelain collection to Ethel. Sometime later, Ethel died and Shor inherited the porcelains. After attending Ethel's funeral, he went back to her house. Her husband Dick had set out the china, and Shor packed it for shipment to his home in Washington, D.C.

While inventorying the pieces, Shor discovered his favorite one missing. He searched the house and in a corner of the basement found the figurine. Unfortunately, however, the dog's tail had been broken off. Sentimentally attached to the little statue, Shor took it to his mother's home not far from Dick's. Later he would arrange to have a ceramist make a new tail.

Back in Washington, Shor became immersed in his work and forgot all about the porcelain figure until his mother died in June, 1964. He flew to Dodge City again, and this time brought the figurine home with him.

A week after his return, he awoke suddenly at three o'clock in the morning. There in the center of his bedroom stood Aunt Ethel, warm and lifelike in a loose-fitting, silk dress that he had often seen her wearing. Shor was amazed. He was wide awake, certain that he was not dreaming.

The ghost looked directly at him, smiled and said, "Why don't you look under the piano?"

Puzzled by the remark, Shor asked the specter to repeat it. It did, then added, "Frankie's little statue." Then the ghost began chanting in singsong manner, "Look under the piano! Look under the piano!"

With the refrain ringing in his ears, Shor watched the apparition. "She gradually disintegrated," he later recalled, "and I decided that I needed some strong coffee. In fact, I consumed two potfuls before dressing and going to the office."

All day Shor pondered the bizarre episode. Why hadn't Aunt Ethel retrieved the dog's tail herself if she knew where it was? Had she died before she could reveal the location to anyone and now, after death, wanted to get that information to her nephew? Preposterous, Shor thought. He had no answers, but he had a plan.

That night Shor telephoned his sister, Camilla Haviland, a probate judge in Dodge City, and asked her if there was a piano in Dick's house. Having been in the place only a few times, he was not familiar with all the furnishings.

Judge Haviland said that Dick did have an old player piano in the basement. After Shor related the night's incident, his sister offered to make a search.

Two weeks later Judge Haviland telephoned her brother. A servant had found the dog's tail intact under the piano, just where Shor's Aunt Ethel had told him it was!

THE MAD WOMAN OF TOPEKA

Everybody said the lady was odd. Of course she was different, an albino with colorless hair, stark white skin, and small pink eyes. And her habits were unusual too, reinforced perhaps by her physical aberration. She roamed the streets of Topeka at all hours of the night. And during the day she would stand in her yard staring at the children as they walked to school.

The lady sought no friendships, nor did she welcome any.

Mrs. Cook, a resident of Lower Silver Lake Road, told a news reporter that the albino lady lived next door to her once and that everyone avoided her because of her icy stares. Mrs. Cook recalled that children taunted the bony, willowy creature even though they were scared to death of her. So far as anyone knew, the old woman lived alone and had no relatives.

She died in 1963. And that's when the trouble began. People in the Seaman district began seeing "walking ghosts." The sightings were along a route from Seaman to the Rockingham Cemetery where the albino lady was rumored to be buried.

On April 11, 1966, Paul Bribbens saw a pulsating white form in the front yard of his home on Rockingham Road.

"It kept talking in a woman's low monotone," Bribbens said. "I couldn't make out a word of it. Like she was stark raving mad or something."

The homeowner's dogs, at sight of the ghost, dived under the porch and could not be enticed out. Bribbens called the sheriff's department, but by the time the officers arrived the thing had vanished.

Reports continued to come in from residents, passers-by and people who worked in the area that a "glowing-white woman" was walking the streets and woods at night. The ghost's terrain was bordered by Soldier Creek, the Goodyear Tire Factory, the Boys Industrial School and Lower Silver Lake Road. Several employees of the factory and the school saw the apparition regularly as it skirted the Soldier Creek dike basin.

An elderly man and longtime resident of Topeka who lives west of the Boys Industrial School on U.S.

Highway 24 near Soldier Creek always knew when the ghost was about. "Everything will become very quiet," he explained. "Dogs will back up under houses, and cats will band together in the trees."

The old gentleman warned against being out alone on foot "when you hear that Godawful silence."

Predictably, the ghost was often sighted in Rockingham Cemetery. George Sanderson, Jr. was the caretaker in 1968. One late night in the fall of that year he and his wife, Carol, arrived home from a dinner at the Elks Club. As they turned into the driveway of the caretaker's house at the edge of the cemetery, Carol shouted and pointed through the windshield. In the wash of headlights, the couple saw a thin, white figure hurrying among the gravestones. A kid up to another prank, Sanderson thought. He drove on and positioned the car so that the lights illuminated the graveyard more fully. Then he saw a woman kneeling at one of the graves.

The caretaker leaped out of the car. "And when I did," said Sanderson, "this 'woman' got up and turned around and glared at me like I had no business being there, and then walked farther into the cemetery."

Sanderson admitted that he and his wife were badly shaken by the incident. He called the police, but they never found anything. "Not even tracks," added the caretaker, shaking his head. "Maybe there was nothing to find."

The Sandersons weren't the only ones to be upset by a close encounter with the ghost. Youngsters parked in Lovers Lane were often terrified by a rat-a-tat-tat on the car window and a red-eyed face on the other side of the glass. Oftentimes motors stalled and headlights failed when the ghost was lurking nearby.

Most Topeka residents argued that the lady's ghost never became violent. But Marvin Richstatter wasn't so sure. The albino lady appeared in Richstatter's backyard at least once a week, usually on warm, clear nights. His house, on the corner of Rockingham Road and Soldier Creek, was on the route of the apparition's nocturnal travels.

Richstatter, a widower whose wife was killed in an automobile accident several years earlier, said he felt a kind of mystical affinity with the ghost following his wife's death. Watching for the apparition helped him pass the long, lonely hours after his two young children were tucked into bed. The father found a certain comfort in sitting in the window of the darkened house, waiting for the ghost to come strolling across the grass.

But then Richstatter's backyard drama took a chilling turn. The albino lady paused one evening in her journey across his lawn and looked up briefly at the house. At first the man thought the ghost was aware of him and wished to communicate.

Every week after that the specter came closer to the house. Then one night it stood at the window of the children's bedroom. Richstatter saw it studying his children, Tammy and Ginger, as they slept. His face filled with fear.

"I think she's lost someone or something," he observed "and now she wants my kids."

But evidently the ghost was only curious about the children for she never harmed them in any way.

No one ever learned the identity of Topeka's albino apparition, nor discovered what she wanted. Lately, reports of sightings have decreased considerably, possibly because fewer young people park their cars in Lovers Lane and few people stroll aimlessly outdoors after dark. But those who encountered the woman's ghostly image will not soon forget her.

HAUNTED FRATERNITY HOUSES

The fraternity houses of Kansas State University in Manhattan have sheltered thousands of men through the years. Here, friendships are formed that last a lifetime. Good times, replete with joy and laughter and the warmth of camaraderie, brighten the weekend hours.

But the Greek life possesses its dark side too. In the history of many fraternities there lurks the story of the student who "died" under mysterious circumstances, either accidentally or by his own hand. Supposedly, the events took place years ago and details are usually sketchy. But one day, in this or that particular fraternity house, lights will go on and off and doors will open and close on their own! The witnesses to these unexplained pranks soon begin to speculate that the disturbances are somehow associated with the earlier tragedy—the deceased student's ghost has returned to haunt the fraternity!

This kind of speculation is especially abundant in Manhattan. Here are the legends associated with three haunted fraternity houses at Kansas State University.

THE TURNING DOORKNOBS

On a crisp October evening in 1976, Don Clancy hunched over his desk at the Phi Gamma Delta house. It was late and most of his frat brothers were in bed. Clancy wished he were too, but he hadn't finished studying. He stood up to stretch and his teeth chattered. The room had chilled. Funny. He hadn't felt it growing colder.

Beyond the closed window, footsteps crackled through the drifts of leaves on the outside stairway. Every fall the large elm tree in the back yard spilled its leaves onto these steps, making it easy to hear people coming and going. But who was leaving the house at this hour? Or coming in? Clancy's clock read half past one in the morning.

Clancy opened his door and checked the hall. No one in sight. Then he went downstairs, out the front door and around to the outside stairway, washed in moonlight. Someone, or something, was coming down those stairs.

Audible, but invisible. Boot prints crushed the leaves on every step!

Clancy ran back to his room and slammed the door. He was shivering again, and it wasn't that cold. Either his Phi Gamma Delta brothers were playing a joke on him or a ghost stalked the fraternity house!

A moment later Clancy cracked open the door and squinted into the hall. He felt, rather than observed, the unearthly being that swept down the corridor. But he did see quite distinctly that the knob of every door was being turned! Don Clancy had just encountered Duncan, the live-in ghost. But he was not the only one to encounter the specter.

Duncan was a former student who had died in the house some years before, when it was occupied by the Theta Xi fraternity. Apparently, his death occurred during an initiation ceremony, but details vary.

One story says the pledges were bending over to be paddled, and when Duncan's turn came he straightened up suddenly and was struck fatally in the head. A second story attributed Duncan's death to a heart attack after the young man had been placed in a coffin. And the third account noted that Duncan died after falling, or being pushed, down the stairs.

"You have to take these stories with a grain of salt," said fraternity president Dave Dawdy. "But . . . it's pretty unnerving to stay by yourself in this house."

The first indication of Duncan's presence occurred shortly after Phi Gamma Delta bought the house in 1965. The room in which Theta Xi stored its pledge paddles was to be converted into a library. Two paddles had been left hanging on the wall. One of them had Duncan's name on it.

"We threw the paddles away," noted fraternity member Rick Lawrence, "but when we started painting the wall the image of Duncan's paddle kept reappearing. We finally had to panel the wall."

In the fall of 1974, some of the brothers held a séance in the library. After they asked for a sign of Duncan's presence, one fellow started screaming. His fingernails had turned a luminous green color. The men, all of whom witnessed the phenomenon, believed that their brother was possessed by the dead man's spirit.

But Rod Smith may have had the most chilling encounter with the ghost. Smith occupied a basement room in the house, and one night he heard a noise outside the door and flung it open. Standing before him was a lifeless figure whose ghastly face stared vacantly at him. In horror Smith slammed the door. He would never forget that horrible face for as long as he lived!

GEORGE AND THE NIGHT NURSE

When the Delta Sigma Phi fraternity moved into the old St. Mary's Hospital building at 1100 Fremont Street, they inherited more than bricks and mortar. Two resident ghosts came with the building—the spirited poltergeist of a former patient and the taciturn countenance of a long-forgotten night nurse.

The patient, George Segal, was said to be the last person to die in St. Mary's, and his death was caused by a tragic sequence of events. While elderly patients were being moved into the new hospital, George rolled off his bed and was trapped between the bed frame and the wall. When an attendant checked that third-floor room, he could not find George on the bed, and he assumed that George had already been moved. Unfortunately, the elderly gentleman died there during the night.

The Delta Sigma Phi brothers have never seen George, but they've heard him, even loudly at times. They credit him with turning lights on and off, opening locked doors and locked windows, and using the third-floor hallway as his own private bowling alley. But for all his irksome pranks, George has been helpful on occasion, once repairing broken clocks that he had found lying around the premises.

In addition, George was apparently an ardent fan of the popular television show, "Star Trek." Scott Cummins, a fraternity member, explained:

"In 1973 there was an ice storm. The electricity was off all along our street, but every day at four in the afternoon the electricity would come back on in our house and stay on until 'Star Trek' was over. No other house around us had electricity. We figured that George wanted to watch the show."

And the ghostly nurse? Unlike George, she has been seen, but not heard.

Up until the last few years, the specter used to walk the first floor halls of the old hospital late at night, carrying her medicine tray in one hand, a candle in the other, a nameless Florence Nightingale making her appointed rounds. The woman eventually learned that the new owners were not in the business of providing health care. She has not been seen since the late 1960s.

THE HANGING

At the Kappa Sigma fraternity house, a hanging led to the building's haunting. Or so it is believed. House brother Mike Dahl recalled that years ago one of their pledges supposedly hanged himself in the file room. Since then the residents have heard all sorts of strange sounds, particularly those of someone who is apparently jumping on the roof!

One night a brave Kappa Sigma member, hearing the sounds, went out of his window and onto the roof. He found no one. Nor did he find anything that could have accounted for the noises.

On another night several brothers were playing cards in the housemother's room which was situated to one side of the front door, adjacent to the stairway that led to the second floor. Suddenly, the men heard a noise upstairs. Since it was a vacation period and the house was generally empty, they threw down their cards and raced up the staircase to see what the commotion was. At the top of the stairs fraternity member Tom Vera saw a white haze that he presumed was a ghost. His companions saw nothing. But a thorough search uncovered *no* living person on the upper floors of the Kappa Sigma house.

Perhaps these stories, and others like them, are merely a part of collegiate folklore, making the rounds of many campuses with minor changes to suit the time, place and circumstance. It is true that the macabre legend of the "fatal fraternity initiation" has turned up in various forms across the country. And the other tales also bear striking similarities to those told elsewhere.

Yet, if these events never really occurred, then who or what was turning the doorknobs in the Phi Gamma Delta house? Who was standing at Rod Smith's basement door? And who or what was the white haze beheld by Tom Vera upstairs in the Kappa Sigma house?

THE CURSED KNIFE

Jane Armbruster was uneasy. Her husband, Peter, locked the bowie knife in a strongbox in the bedroom closet, and hid the key in the false bottom of a bureau drawer. But somehow that didn't seem enough. The antique knife was a rare find, yet the circumstances by which the couple had bought the weapon were frightening.

The two years which had elapsed since the knife first came into their house had not erased the memory of that afternoon in 1929.

The auction took place not far from their Topeka home. The bidding had been intense. Many persons admired the long, silver blade and the exquisitely carved handle inlaid with semi-precious stones. The knife gleamed in the afternoon sun, an almost electrical glow glancing off the blade. It looked as if it had never been used, but with a bowie knife nearly 100 years old that seemed impossible.

The Armbrusters' bid was highest of the six persons seeking the knife. As they left with their treasure, a swarthy young man with ebony hair and eyes came up to Peter.

"Mister," he began, "I'd like to buy that knife from you. I'll offer you a fair price."

Peter shook his head. "If you really wanted the knife, you should have kept bidding."

"I'm short of money just now," the insistent man said as he walked beside them. "If you give me the knife today, I promise I'll pay you ... double ... what you just paid. That seems fair to me."

Peter had never seen the man before. The couple knew most of the regular auction goers around Topeka, and this nervous young man was not among them.

"But if I give you the knife," Peter countered, "how do I know I'll ever see you again?"

"I'll give you what money I have." He dug into his pocket and pulled out a fifty-dollar bill. "I'll get the rest of the money from, er, my parents." He sounded desperate. "Mister, that knife is special to my family!"

And then the young man added the words Jane Armbruster would never forget: "That knife can bring riches and pleasure ... or misery and death!"

Peter laughed. "So that's it! A bowie knife with an authentic curse! I suppose you'll tell me next that you're its immortal guardian. No sir! You can't buy it at any price!"

Peter took Jane by the arm and climbed into their car.

"You'll regret this day!" the young man shouted, waving his fist at the departing car. "I'll get that knife one day! It will bring you only death!"

Jane Armbruster shrank against the seat as those last words pounded through the window. Peter didn't appear shaken by the stranger's threats, but he did worry that the man might follow them and steal the knife. He locked it in the strongbox that night along with several other valuable possessions.

It was now 1931, almost two years after the auction and the knife's entrance into the lives of the Armbrusters. On occasion Peter would remind his wife that nothing terrible had happened to them.

"That nonsense about a curse was just that creep's way of trying to get the knife at half what I paid," Peter was fond of saying.

Jane almost believed her husband—and almost forgot the curse—until a night during that second year. She awoke early in the morning. Her husband lay gasping and shaking beside her. She reached out to him, and his trembling stopped. Peter was dead of a heart attack.

A month later, Jane's doctor was discussing Peter's sudden death with her. He thought a moment, and then said that Peter's death was so sudden it was as if someone *had plunged a knife into his heart.*

Jane shuddered at the words. A *knife—the bowie knife!*

She felt sick. She rushed home, anxious and agitated, haunted by the words spoken by that demented young man two years before—"I'll come get that knife. It will bring you only *death . . .*"

Jane hadn't been near the strongbox since before Peter's death. She located the key in its usual hiding place and opened the box. Inside she found a gold pocket watch, her pearl necklace, Peter's old silver money clip and other small objects. She lifted them all out and stared into the emptiness inside the box. Her heart seemed to stop—the cursed bowie knife was gone!

THE HAUNTING AT POTWIN PLACE

Potwin Place, in Topeka, is a picture-postcard neighborhood of Victorian homes reminiscent of an age both gentler and more genteel. Even the casual visitor to this historic district can imagine the leisurely graces of an earlier time when residents sipped tea behind lace-curtained windows and dined at a rosewood table with Aubusson carpeting underfoot.

But even the most imaginative sightseer would not know that behind the walls of the handsome house at 424 Greenwood Avenue cavorts an unearthly being. The owners, retired Gen. J. E. "Speck" Gardner, and his wife, Dorothy, believe the ghost moved into their house in the spring of 1972 once they began remodeling the kitchen and an upstairs bathroom.

Dorothy's sisters, Madge and Fay Smith, had come to visit. According to a news account, both women went to bed fairly early, sharing a guest room. At quarter past ten that night they heard a loud noise in the unoccupied bedroom next to theirs. It sounded as if a yardstick were being slapped on the bare wooden floor.

Both leaped out of bed. "What the hell was that?" Fay asked.

The women checked the next door bedroom. It was empty. Returning to bed, Madge and Fay heard the sound again. This time they were too frightened to make another check.

In the morning the guests mentioned the incident to their hosts. Gardner explained to them that the noise was probably caused by the settling of the house.

It wasn't.

A month later at exactly quarter past ten at night he and his wife heard a noise—a loud ringing that reverberated throughout the house. It sounded as if someone were beating the floor with a one-by-four.

The noise continued intermittently for exactly one year, then stopped as suddenly as it had begun.

"It could have been caused by the settling of the house," observed Gardner, "but why it happened at exactly the same time is not easy to explain."

But the unexplained noise was only the beginning of a series of odd manifestations that occurred at Potwin Place during 1972 and 1973.

On one occasion, Dorothy noticed her silver ice cream dipper missing. She searched everywhere for it. Weeks later, while cleaning the basement, she discovered a small, green box she'd never seen before. Opening it, she found the dipper inside, wrapped in white tissue paper.

"When I saw the dipper, the hair on my arms bristled," she said. "That really frightened me."

Sometime later, when Gardner was away on a trip, Dorothy had just gone to bed when she felt something pushing down the mattress on both sides of her.

"I could hear heavy breathing," she recalled, "and then it felt like someone was trying to pull my legs off the bed. I jumped up and turned on the light, but no one was there."

When Dorothy told her husband about the incident, he claimed that it was her imagination. Months later, however, her sister Fay had the same experience.

"The heavy breathing was loud," Fay explained, "like a horse after it has been running for a long time. I threw back the covers and sat up in bed, but I still heard it."

Fay leaped out of bed and ran to Dorothy's room where she spent the rest of the night.

In 1973, after the kitchen and bathroom remodeling was completed, the Gardners decided to redecorate the west bedroom, the one in which the slapping noises had originated. The house had been built in 1888 and, although basically in good repair, little redecorating had been done through the years.

Dorothy selected new wallpaper and began hanging it one afternoon on the walls of the west bedroom. She was working alone. Suddenly she heard a man's voice say, "You're doing a nice job."

"I looked around, but there was no one in the room," Dorothy said. "The voice was as clear as any normal voice."

And familiar. Dorothy recognized it as the voice of the former owner who had sold them the house. But the old gentleman had been dead for years!

One evening in 1973 when the Gardners were not at home, Gen. Gardner's niece, Kay Church, telephoned from San Juan Capistrano, California. She heard the phone ring, then stop. Someone had lifted the receiver, but no one spoke! She dialed again and got a busy signal.

When the couple returned home later, Gardner went to his bedroom to change clothes. He noticed the telephone receiver lying next to the phone on the bedside table and replaced it. Half an hour later Kay called and told her uncle what had happened.

"Someone had to pick up the receiver and place it next to the phone," stated Gardner. On another occasion, he found the same phone on the bedroom floor with the receiver next to it.

Sometime later, the Gardners took a trip to New York for a convention. When they returned they discovered a gold watch (which had been suspended from a hook in a bell jar) lying on the base of the jar. The watch crystal had been unscrewed and placed next to the watch. Nothing else in the house had been disturbed and all the windows and doors were locked.

Another perplexing incident occurred in the winter of 1973. The family ran a humidifier in the basement. It had worked well for several weeks, but one day Dorothy told her husband that it didn't seem to be operating. Upon investigation, Gardner discovered that the spigot at the cold water line near the basement ceiling had been turned off. The spigot was always very difficult to turn, and Gardner knew that it couldn't have been jarred into the "off" position by any kind of vibration.

The Gardners' son, Dennis, and his wife, Vickie, witnessed another unusual incident in the spring of 1973. While relaxing in the sitting room of the house one afternoon, they saw a lazy Susan start spinning on a table—by itself!

Although the Gardners were convinced that the ghost of the previous owner was responsible for all of these pranks, no one ever actually saw him. In true poltergeist fashion, the ghost remained invisible, announcing its presence only by mischievous antics.

But Dorothy thinks that she may have startled the ghost once. Upon entering the kitchen one night, she saw, from the corner of her eye, a formless apparition disappearing through the far doorway into the sitting room.

The ghostly visits at Potwin Place ended in 1973 when work on the house was completed.

In 1980, however, three sink stoppers inexplicably vanished. The Gardners realized then that their unseen visitor had returned. Or had he ever left? Some ghosts, like some people, like to putter around a house . . . forever.

THE LONELY GRAVE

A merciless sun flattened the land from horizon to horizon as Ephriam Polly pushed his team westward. His hard, brown hands held the reins loosely, and half moons of sweat darkened the armpits of his shirt.

Beside him on the wagon seat sat his wife, Elizabeth, her back as straight as a newly-driven fence post. Her wide blue bonnet scarcely shielded her face from the sun and the wind that whirlpooled dust under the wagon wheels.

But Elizabeth never complained. She loved Ephriam deeply. She also understood him. He was a thoughtful man, but not shrewd. He wanted to give his wife the better things in life, but did not know how to seize an opportunity. In her heart, Elizabeth knew she would always be the wife of a "drummer," peddling wagonloads of candies, tobacco, sewing kits and other necessities to soldiers in lonely outposts along the Smoky Hill River trail, and bringing news along with the wares. For Elizabeth Polly, it was enough.

At sunset, on a scorching day in 1867, the Pollys reached Fort Hays, in western Kansas. Elizabeth did not know that her travels with Ephriam were over. She would never leave the Fort.

While the couple were at Fort Hays, a horrible cholera epidemic struck the post. Neither history nor legend recounts whatever happened to Ephriam Polly, but his wife, Elizabeth, volunteered to help the one doctor at the Fort.

Elizabeth Polly was not a trained nurse, but she brought hope to the sick and comfort to the dying. Through the long, hot days she worked in the sick ward, doing what she could to ease the suffering around her. She packed flannel cloths and hot bottles around the mens' bodies to help them retain body heat; she offered sips of barley water and beef tea to those able to drink. And she held the hand of more than one frightened youngster.

Sometimes for an hour or two in the early evening, Elizabeth would leave the wardroom and walk to a hilltop a couple of miles southwest of the Fort. There, alone under the vast sky, she would welcome the wind combing her hair and billowing her long skirts as she listened to the meadowlarks singing in the bluestem grasses far below. These peaceful moments renewed her strength. Then, in the fading light, she would return to the stench of sickness and the sounds of death.

Elizabeth Polly ministered to the men for many weeks. No one ever knew anything about her, not even where she had come from. It didn't matter. To the soldiers of Fort Hays, she was an angel of mercy.

Then Elizabeth too contracted the dread disease. As she lay dying, she asked those attending her to please bury her on top of her beloved hill. When assured that her wish would be granted, she died peacefully.

A full-dress military funeral was given Elizabeth Polly in the fall of 1867, her body transported to the hilltop by horse-drawn ambulance. Major Gibbs, Commandant of Fort Hays, assisted in the burial service.

For years after Elizabeth Polly's death, local residents referred to her burial spot as the "Lonely Grave." Nearly inaccessible by car, the grave was rarely visited. From time to time a wooden cross would appear on the site, put up by a Boy Scout troop from Hays City. Then, in the 1960s, a group of citizens erected an obelisk on Elizabeth's hill. It would be a fitting memorial to this selfless pioneer woman who rested there.

Or does she?

Fifty years after Elizabeth Polly's death, a sequence of strange events seemed to indicate that she may have left her "Lonely Grave" on at least one occasion . . . and perhaps two.

Dawn was just breaking over the prairie on an April day in 1917 when John Schmidt, a western Kansas farmer, rode out to the pasture. It was his custom to go each morning to drive the cows back to the barn for milking. His dog trotted along at his side. Schmidt had ridden about halfway across the pasture when he noticed a woman crossing fifty yards in front of him.

He saw her old-fashioned bonnet first, and then, as the sky brightened, her long blue dress. She was quite tall. Schmidt couldn't see her face well, hidden as it was by the bonnet, but he observed her walk; it was the steady stride of a purposeful woman.

Schmidt had never seen her before; of that he was certain. She would have to be one of the women from the Fort Hays Normal School, or from town, but her route perplexed the farmer. She had come from the direction of the old Fort Hays and was headed southwest. In that direction lay nothing but an abandoned one-room shack about a quarter of a mile from the "Lonely Grave."

Why was the woman walking in the pasture? And why was she dressed in such a peculiar fashion? Schmidt cupped his hand to his mouth and called to her. There was no response. The woman never turned her head, nor broke her stride.

Schmidt put the whip to his pony, but the beast fought him. The dog yelped and took off for home, tail between its legs. Schmidt yelled at the dog and at the same time lashed the horse who was snorting and trembling with fright.

The dog kept running, but Schmidt, fighting the beast all the way, was able to drive the pony close to the lady in blue. Had he reached out with his whip he could have touched her. But he didn't. Irked by her indifference, Schmidt circled widely around her and went on after the cows.

After Schmidt returned to the barn, his whole family was waiting. His wife and children had witnessed the entire episode. Mrs. Schmidt told her' husband she had never taken her eyes off the strange woman and had seen her enter the old shack near the top of the Lonely Grave Hill. The shack was in full view of Schmidt's place.

Schmidt asked his family to watch the shack, even though they would be busy doing morning milking and chores. They promised to take turns.

Schmidt hitched his team to the wagon and headed down to the Smoky Hill River bottoms where each day he dug and hauled sand for various construction projects in the area. The job provided a needed supplement to the farm income.

His brother-in-law, Anton Rupp, was working with him and it didn't take Rupp long to notice that Schmidt was upset about something. Schmidt finally told Rupp about the morning's incident and asked if he would come with him after work to investigate the shack. Rupp readily agreed.

At supper, Mrs. Schmidt said she and the children had taken turns watching the shack and the woman had not come out.

Their meal finished, the two men rode up to the old cabin, now silvered by moonlight. They called out. They banged on the weathered door. They called out again. But only the wind answered. Schmidt told Rupp he was going in.

The old latch was rusted in place, so Schmidt gave the door a violent kick and it snapped inward, whining on its hinges. He stepped cautiously into the room. Cobwebs embroidered the corners of the decrepit hut and dust lay thick everywhere. Obviously the place hadn't been occupied for some time. There was no sign of the lady in blue.

Years later (in the 1940s), John Schmidt told a young friend, Robert Maxwell, the story that had perplexed the Schmidt family for nearly thirty years.

It was several days after hearing the tale before Maxwell got up the courage to ask the question that plagued him. "John, do you reckon that gal could have been Elizabeth Polly? Or her ghost?"

Schmidt took a long time answering. "Bobby," he said softly, "I just don't know."

But he told Maxwell that after he saw the woman that day in 1917 he went to see George Brown, a night watchman at the Coliseum on the college campus.

Brown was a youngster when the old Fort Hays still stood, and he used to herd cattle for the officers there. Perhaps he would remember Elizabeth Polly.

Brown was eager to talk about those long-ago days, and he told Schmidt that indeed he *had* known Elizabeth Polly and remembered her husband also. He described her funeral and recalled that she was buried in a big bonnet and a long, flowing blue gown. It was the outfit she had worn most of the time at the Fort.

That was the outfit John Schmidt and his family had seen the ghost wearing that morning in 1917, fifty years after her death!

In 1967, on the hundredth anniversary of Elizabeth Polly's death, Hays City celebrated its Centennial. Men and women, dressed in nineteenth-century attire, gathered downtown for the festivities. Those who were there recall the many bonnets and long blue gowns in evidence.

Some say that at the edge of the crowd there *may* have been a lady in blue, a stranger watching the activities, a wistful smile on her face. A lady who, at the coming of the night, set off alone, walking silently toward the "Lonely Grave."

Chapter V. Michigan

" 'I apologize for what must seem to you peculiar behavior on my part,' Strand began. 'But you see, I have good
reason to fear the storm. I, that is the person you hear speaking, am Stephen Strand. But the body you see is that of
another.'

Harper Allyn rose in his chair. He was not going to spend
the night with an insane man.

'Please!' Strand pleaded, reaching out to grasp Allyn's
arm. 'Please, I am not mad, despite that rather odd statement.
If you will allow me, I shall explain. But, I must warn you,
it is a story you will find difficult to believe.' "

"THE SOUL OF STEPHEN STRAND"

THE PHANTOM SHIPS

The ghost ships of the Great Lakes are legion. From their
home ports—Chicago, Superior-Duluth, Detroit,
Cleveland—they have sailed into oblivion and legend. The
W. H. Gilcher, a coal steamer lost in the torturous Straits
of Mackinac in 1892; the *Nashua*, vanished in Lake
Huron; the *L. R. Doty*, slipped into eternity on her way
to Ontario from Chicago. And what of the *Edmund
Fitzgerald*? Does her broken hull still float vaporous-like
on the lake called "Gitche Gumee," her condemned crew
reaching out for salvation?

Honest sailors will tell you that the Great Lakes are
more dangerous than any of the world's oceans. A fast-
rising storm tosses the waves about as if some awesome
hand were tipping a half-filled pitcher bowl. Ships caught
unawares have been known to vanish in minutes beneath
the whitecaps.

But the danger comes not just from nature ... if one confronts the spectral ships that legend says continue to cruise the Great Lakes ...

THE LOST GRIFFON

She was the first sailing vessel on the Great Lakes. Sixty feet in length and forty-five tons, her mainmast and mizzenmast carried more than a dozen square sails. She was built from a single white oak, her lines faithfully followed the natural shape of the living tree. Crouched upon her stern was the "Griffon," the mythical animal of the ancients with the head and wings of an eagle and the body of a lion. The Greeks believed it inhabited Scythia to guard its gold; the creature supposedly devoured any man or beast who dared to stand in its path.

On the ship's bowsprit perched the same talisman, its eagle ears pointed heavenward, as if beseeching God to give those beneath its wings swiftness, strength and wariness.

But it was not to be for the gunboat *Griffon*, the ill-fated dream of Rene Robert Cavalier, Sieur de La Salle, the great French explorer. Lost on its maiden voyage somewhere on the Great Lakes, the barque *Griffon* has sailed on as a ghost ship ... for the past 300 years!

During the long winter of 1678-79, La Salle and his band of loyal followers built a ship that would transport them across the great inland lakes into the wilderness that is now Wisconsin. He brought from France the master shipbuilder Moyse Hillaret, and under the watchful eye of La Salle, Father Louis Hennepin and Luc, La Salle's pilot, the vessel took shape on the banks of the Niagara River, five miles above the Falls, near Cayuga Creek.

The nearby Iroquois tribes gave the men fresh fish and game, but more often jeered the men and their "beast," which they believed would never float upon the water. They even planned to burn the ship, but their attempts failed.

The Iroquois prophet Metiomek, converted to Christianity by the Jesuits, cursed the ship, its builder La Salle and its blasphemous talisman.

"Great Chief La Salle, you are too proud," spoke Metiomek. "You have shown contempt for the Great Spirit who rules all things, and you have set up an evil spirit on His throne. You seek the tribes of the West to trade with. But you will destroy them with your fire-water. Metiomek bids you beware; darkness, like a cloud, is ready to envelop you—the Christian Indian's curse rests upon you and your great canoe. She will sink beneath the deep waters and your blood shall stain the hands of those in whom you trusted!"

Metiomek's prediction proved all too accurate. After the *Griffon* slipped easily into the water on August 7, 1679, her journey west was fraught with problems. A dense fog becalmed her on Lake Erie, a violent squall nearly tore the little ship apart as it entered Lake Huron and, on August 25, another calm settled on the ship. The *Griffon* finally reached Detroit Harbor at Washington Island, off Door Peninsula, Wisconsin. There, La Salle loaded 600 tons of fur into the ship, but a four-day storm forced it to remain anchored.

La Salle decided not to return with the *Griffon* to Fort Niagara, preferring to set out for the lands to the south, perhaps even as far south as the Gulf of Mexico.

As La Salle watched the ship set sail on September 18, 1679, his would be the last verified sighting of the ship. The *Griffon* simply vanished!

No one knows precisely how or where the *Griffon* sank. Yet there is some evidence that the *Griffon* made its way across Lake Huron and then turned northward toward the French River. In 1955, a Canadian named Orrie Vail and Harrison John MacLean, a *Toronto Telegram* reporter, claimed to have found the wreckage of the *Griffon* in an inner island bay of Cove Island near the tip of the Bruce Peninsula. Vail, who lived in the tiny village of Tobermory on the peninsula, was a near-legendary figure on Lake Huron and Georgian Bay. He claimed to know every island and inlet in the region, and few people disputed his word. Vail had first found the ship's remains in 1900, but it wasn't until he and MacLean found historical evidence that he was sure he had discovered the great explorer's ship.

Upon scrutiny, a drawing of the ship made by Father Hennepin as it was being constructed, plus an analysis showing that the wood was 300-year-old white oak and that there were primitive forging and hand-threads on the wreck's iron spikes all helped to confirm the ship's identity as the *Griffon*.

But there are still doubters, including one underwater archeologist who claimed that the wreck was actually that of a nineteenth century Canadian gunboat. Since carbon-14 dating and controlled scientific excavations have yet to be performed on the wreck, proof cannot be absolute.

And what of the crew? A group of Potawatomi Indians later told La Salle they had seen the ship tossing violently in a storm on northern Lake Michigan. Perhaps it sank. Another theory holds that the crew was murdered and the ship burned.

Metiomek believed that his prophecy was fulfilled— the angry Lakes swallowed the devil ship. La Salle, too, felt the curse. After leaving the *Griffon*, he got only as far south as Starved Rock, on the Illinois River, before winter forced his return to Canada. Eight years later, in 1687, La Salle again tried to find the source of the Mississippi, but his expedition was plagued with illness and mutiny. La Salle was later murdered at the hands of his own men on a small Texas river he mistakenly believed was the Mississippi.

We are left then with superstition, namely the curse of Metiomek. And there is also the legend of the Ottawa drum, a peculiar, booming sound, not unlike that of sonorous male chanting, which is heard whenever a ship is lost on the Great Lakes. Some say that the rhythmic chant was heard as the *Griffon* glided away from Washington Island in a fair wind ... to become another phantom ship still sailing the Great Lakes.

THE SCHOONER ERIE BOARD OF TRADE

One of the strangest, and least known, ghost tales of the Great Lakes unfolded over 100 years ago during a moonlight night in Lake Huron's Saginaw Bay. It is the tale of the blandly titled, but cursed, schooner, *Erie Board of Trade*.

The ship's story is taken from an account published in 1883, and vouched for by all who knew the case. The story was first related on South Street, in Saginaw, Michigan, in much the same way as it is repeated here.

An old sailor was seated on an anchor stock in front of a ship-chandler's store along the lower part of Saginaw's South Street. Other men were seated on a bale of oakum, a wide-mouth pump without a plunger and on the single stone step of the store. The ship-chandler and a young friend were seated across in chairs just inside the door. The group was exchanging ghost stories. One of the men had just finished telling of his experience.

"You're a sorry dog," spoke the ship-chandler to him. "You were drunk, and the spirits you'd taken made you *see* the other spirits!"

Everyone laughed, except for the oldest sailor who had been listening in silence. He threw one leg over the anchor stock and addressed the group solemnly.

"Well, I saw a ghost once," he began. "I saw it as plain as ever. The captain of the schooner I was on and the man in the waist both saw it too. And there wasn't a drop of liquor on board."

His audience quieted; they knew the old man always spoke the truth.

"It was a little over ten years ago. I was before the mast then. It was the opening of the season, and I was in Chicago. I heard at the boardinghouse that some men were wanted on a three-masted schooner called *Erie Board of Trade*. The boys gave her a pretty hard name, but they said the grub was good and that the old man paid top wages every time, so I went down and asked him if he'd got all the hands aboard. He looked at me a minute, and asked me where my dunnage was. When I told him, he said I should get it on board right away.

"The *Board of Trade* was as handsome a craft as ever floated on the lakes. As I came down the dock with my bag under my arm, I had to stop and have a look at her. The old man saw me. He was proud of her, and I thought afterward that he rather took a fancy to me because I couldn't help showing I liked her looks.

"I was in her two round trips. The last trip up was the last on the lakes. Not but what times were pretty good up there. We were getting $2.50 a day for the first trip out and $2.00 the last. We messed with the old man, and, with fresh meat and vegetables, and coffee and milk, it was first-cabin passage all around. But the old man made it hot for most of us. There wasn't any watch below in the day and we were kept painting her on the down trip and scrubbing the paint off again on the passage up.

"The first trip around to Chicago, every man but me got his dunnage onto the dock as soon as he was paid off. When I got my money I asked the old man if he'd want anyone to help with the lines when the schooner was towed from the coal yard to the elevator. He said he reckoned he could keep me if I wanted to stay, so I signed articles for the next trip there.

"When we were getting the wheat into her at the elevator, we got the crew aboard. One of them was a red-haired Scotchman. The captain took a dislike to him from the first. I don't know why. It was a tough time for Scotty all the way down. We were in Buffalo just twelve hours, and then we cleared for Cleveland to take on soft coal for Milwaukee. The tug gave us a short pull outside the breakwater, and we had no more than got the canvas up before the wind died out completely. We dropped anchor, for the current, settling to the Niagara River, was carrying us down to Black Rock at three knots.

"When we'd got things shipshape about docks, the old man called Scotty and two others aft and told them to scrape down the topmasts. Then he handed the boatswain's chair to them. Scotty gave the chair a look and then turned around, and touching his forehead respectfully, said, 'If you please, sir, the rope's been chafed off, and I'll bend on a bit of ratlin' stuff.' The captain was mighty touchy because the jug had left him so, and he just jumped up and down and swore. He told Scotty that, by God, he'd better get up there damn fast or he'd see to it that he never worked on the Lakes again.

"Scotty climbed the main rigging pretty quick. He got the halyards bent on the the chair and sung out to hoist away. I and a youngster, the captain's nephew, were standing by. We handled that rope carefully, for I'd seen how tender the chair was. When we'd got him up, the young fellow took a turn around the pin, and I looked aloft to see what Scotty was doing. As I did so he reached for his knife with one hand and put out the other for the backstay.

"Just then the chair gave way. He fell all bunched up till he struck the crosstrees, and then he spread out and fell flat on the deck, just forward of the cabin, on the starboard side. I was kneeling beside him in a minute, and so was the old man.

"I was feeling pretty well choked up to see a shipmate killed. I said to the captain: 'This is pretty bad business, sir; this man's been murdered.'

"When I said that, Scotty opened his eyes and looked at us. Then in a whisper, he cursed the captain and his wife and children, and the ship and her owners. While he was still talking, the blood bubbled over his lips, and his head lurched over to one side. He was dead.

"It was three days before the schooner got to Cleveland. Some of the boys were for leaving her there, but most of us stayed because wages were down again.

"Going through the rivers, there were four other schooners in the tow. We were next to the tug. Just at the big end below Port Huron a squall struck us. It was too much for the tug, and some lubber cast off the tow line without singing out first.

"We dropped our bower as quick as we could, but it was not before we drifted astern, carrying away the headgear of the schooner next to us and smashing our own dinghy. We were a shaky lot going up Lake Huron and no lifeboat under the stern.

"There was a fair easterly wind on the lake, and as we got out of the river in the morning we were standing across Saginaw Bay during the first watch that night. I had the second trick at the wheel. The stars were shining bright and clear and not a cloud was in sight. Every stitch of canvas was set and drawing, though the booms sagged and creaked as the vessel rolled lazily in the varying breeze.

"I had just sung out to the mate to strike eight bells when the captain climbed up the companionway and out on deck. He stepped over to the starboard rail and had a look around, then the lookout began striking the bell. The last stroke of the bell seemed to die away with a swish.

"A bit of spray or something struck me in the face. I wiped it away, and then I saw something rise up slowly across the mainsail from the starboard side of the deck forward of the cabin. It was white and all bunched up. I glanced at the captain, and saw he was staring at it too. It hovered straight up and then struck the crosstrees. There it spread out and rolled over toward us. It was Scotty. His lips were working just as they were when he cursed the captain. As he straightened out, he seemed to stretch himself until he grasped the maintop mast with one hand and the mizzen with the other. Both were carried away like pipe stems. The next I knew the squaresail yard was hanging in two pieces, the top hamper was swinging and the booms were jibing over.

"The old man fell in a dead faint on the quarter deck, and the man in the waist dived down from the forecastle so fast that he knocked over the last man of the other watch. If it had not been for the watch coming on deck just then, she'd rolled altogether. They got the head sails over and I put the wheel up without knowing what I was doing. In a minute it seemed we were laying our course again."

The young man sitting next to the ship-chandler had listened with intense interest.

"The old sailor's story is true," he said. "I was there. I'm the captain's nephew he spoke about. I was reading in the cabin that night. As the bell began to strike, I felt a sudden draft through the cabin, and my papers were taken out of my hands and blown out the window. I hurried out of the cabin, but as I got my head through the companionway I heard a crash of the falling masts. When the schooner began to go off the other tack I saw a bit of a waterspout two miles away to leeward."

"Well," finished the old sailor, "the main facts in the story can easily be verified. The next voyage the schooner was sunk. The insurance companies resisted payment on the ground that she had been scuttled by her captain. During the trial of the case the story of the death of Scotty and the loss of her top-masts under a clear sky was all told under oath."

THE MAN ON THE BEACH

Captain Truedell was a dreamer. Throughout his decades-long career in the Great Lakes Life Saving Service, including twenty years commanding the station at Grand Marais, Michigan, the Captain always dreamed of the important things in his life *before* they happened. His mother had the gift, and passed it on to him.

The most chilling example of the captain's foresight occurred during his second year in the Life Saving Service while he was stationed at Deer Park, Michigan. Once a busy lumber port, Deer Park was little more than a "ghost town" in 1892.

Truedell usually slept from eight in the evening until shortly before he was called for his watch at midnight. On the night of April 30, 1892, however, Truedell had a particularly fitful sleep. In fact, a dream was playing in his brain which was so lifelike that when he eventually awoke he was soaked with perspiration.

In his dream, Truedell was standing on the beach near the Station. Out of the mist walked a man, well-dressed and obviously cultivated. As the man passed Truedell, he reached out, as if to shake the captain's hand. But his grasp felt cold and wet to the touch. Truedell could not keep the hand in his own grasp, and the stranger turned and walked into the surf, dissolving in the turbulent waters.

Truedell's watch that night was quiet and uneventful. Although a gale was blowing in from the northwest, the men at the Life Saving Station had received no calls for help.

At breakfast the next morning, the men joked about Truedell's "dream," claiming that his quiet duty was evidence that this time his precognition was wrong.

But early in the afternoon, a dazed sailor straggled into the Station. His ship had gone down in the gale, and only he survived as far as he knew. His name was Harry Stewart, the wheelman.

His ship belonged to a millionaire shipowner, Peter Minch. Minch was proud of his flagship, the *Western Reserve*. At that time it was the biggest ship on the lakes, a sturdy 300-feet long. Minch was so confident of the *Western Reserve* that he took his family aboard for a pleasure trip from the Soo Locks to Two Harbors, Minnesota, where the ship was to take on a load of iron ore.

Once the storm had hit, Minch ordered Stewart to continue sailing around Whitefish Point and Point Iroquois against the captain's advice. The pounding gale buckled the decks; the ship snapped in two, sending the crew, Minch and his family into a steel lifeboat and yawl. The lifeboat sank, but its occupants were able to scramble aboard the yawl.

Early on the morning of May 1, however, the yawl capsized in the surf, fifteen miles west of Deer Point. Only wheelman Harry Stewart lived.

True to Captain Truedell's dream, the *Western Reserve* had sunk at about nine o'clock the previous evening ... just at the time the psychic captain was beginning to "see" the disaster in his sleep.

After listening to Stewart's story, Captain Truedell was assigned to patrol the beach in a westerly direction, searching for any other possible survivors. He soon found the body of a well-dressed man lying face down in the sand. Truedell hesitated. He then approached the body and rolled it over. As Truedell did so, the man's finely-manicured fingers brushed against his own.

Truedell was taken aback—it was the man in his dream! The tragic sinking of the *Western Reserve* and its owner, Peter Minch, had been witnessed by a man miles away from the incident—and in his sleep!

The sunken hulls of these and other ghost ships may now be resting against the cold, muddy bottom of a great lake. But to many old hands the ships still ply the trade routes of the great inland seas, their rotted sails fluttering against a summer wind. These ships and their crews journey forever as Great Lakes *Flying Dutchmen*, unaffected by ice flows or the gales of November. They are, in a sense, beyond all of that, for their voyages now occur in a different dimension, in a world apart from our own.

THE LADY AND THE SOLDIER

The French, the British and, finally, the Americans all played critical roles in the development of early Detroit. As far back as 1648 French explorers had visited the area, but it was not until 1701 that Antoine de la Mothe Cadillac founded the first permanent settlement, Fort Pontchartrain, also called Fort Detroit. British troops led by Captain Robert Rogers seized the location in 1760 and held it until 1796 when the Americans took possession under commander "Mad Anthony" Wayne.

The British name for the settlement, Fort Lernoult, was kept as the Americans set about building the community, first incorporating it as a village in 1802 and then naming it the seat of government for the new Michigan territory in 1805. In that same year, a fire destroyed all that remained of the early French quarter; its old houses of square logs and steep roofs speckled with dormers and its wide streets and foot-wide sidewalks of hewn logs were all swept away.

The "Detroit" community began its reconstruction with streets laid out in a fashion suggested by the "modern" city of Washington, D.C., and the settlement grew steadily until the winds of a new conflict between Great Britain and America roared into flames with the War of 1812.

The war was especially difficult for the residents of Detroit. The people were a mixture of French, British and newly-arrived eastern Americans, and the hostility affected many families in the region, often pitting one branch of a family against another. The majority French were reconciled to American rule, and were unwilling to give up the city to their old British adversaries.

Oftentimes the memorable stories associated with any life and death struggle emerge from the experiences of those everyday people who are touched by the unfolding tragedy. During the War of 1812, in Detroit, there arose the legend of Marie McIntosh ...

Across the Detroit River, in the Canadian village of Windsor, Marie McIntosh lived with her doting father Angus, a Scotchman transplanted to the rugged North American wilderness. The British were solidly in control of the Canadian territory and had begun to make threatening noises in the direction of Detroit, a few hundred yards away.

Young Marie was sought after and admired by all the eligible young men in Windsor. With her red hair, fair complexion and emerald green eyes, she was always the first to be asked to any social gathering.

Marie was the passionate love of one British officer in particular, a Lieutenant William Muir. While Marie consented to be escorted by the lieutenant to dances, she was reserved as befitted the courting style of that era. Lieutenant Muir, for his part, professed his love for Marie to anyone who would listen.

Muir was attached to a regiment that was selected to attack an American force at a place called Mongaugon on the morning of August 9, 1812. Muir's troops would be in the first wave thrown against the Americans. Plus, the British would be aided by their Wyandot Indian allies under their famous chief, Walk-In-The-Water.

The lieutenant hoped that he could receive Marie's pledge of love to carry with him into battle. Perhaps now, he hoped, with the prospect of never seeing him again, Marie would give him that simple declaration.

On the night before the scheduled attack, Lieutenant Muir found Marie alone in the McIntosh mansion. He asked for her love—and loyalty—to him only. But Marie was irritated—even though she had heard from others that Muir loved her deeply, he had always acted shy and hesitant in his courting. Now, suddenly, he was all forthrightness and bravery!

Marie turned her head.

"I do not know Lieutenant if I shall be yours or not," she replied. "It remains to be seen whether I might not find another more to my liking. After all, the life of a soldier's wife is not the best for a respectable young woman."

The naive young lieutenant did not understand. Was his beloved playing the coquette, testing his willingness to continue the pursuit? He stammered a reply, turned on his heel and left.

Marie was startled. She quickly followed the disappointed lieutenant but could only capture the sound of the pounding hooves of his retreating horse.

"Men are so foolish," she called out after him. "If a woman does not immediately say yes, they feel wounded."

That night, as her lieutenant rode off to battle, Marie slept fitfully. A dread pervaded her thoughts until she was startled awake by the sound of footsteps moving across her bedroom floor. She drew aside the drapes on her canopied bed. The figure of Lieutenant Muir stared down at her, his ghastly white face stained by the blood from a terrible wound in his forehead.

"Do not fear, Marie," the specter spoke. "I died honorably in battle. But I beg of you only one favor . . . my body lies in a thicket. Rescue it from the forest and bury it in a respectable place."

Marie numbly nodded, drawing back into the pillows as the ghost leaned forward.

"Our blood has not been shed in vain. England's flag will float again over Detroit." He reached out and touched her right hand . . . and was gone.

Marie collapsed and did not awake until late the next morning.

Had the ghost of Lieutenant Muir actually visited her or was she dreaming? She recalled his parting touch. As she lifted her hand, she noted with horror a deep, red impression, like a brand, embedded in her palm!

Marie dressed quickly, saddled a horse and rode to the British lines at Malden, Ontario. She related her dream to the commander, an old friend of her father. She was later escorted across the river to the battlefield.

Marie found Lieutenant Muir's body in a thicket . . . with a bullet hole through his head. She and her escorts carried his body back to the British camp. Lieutenant William Muir was buried at Sandwich with full military honors.

However, the specter of Lieutenant Muir was not so easily stilled. For decades after the War of 1812, his ghost was seen trodding silently through the forest near Mongaugon, still moving toward the American forces. His arm was raised, a sabre held firmly in his grip . . .

And what of Marie McIntosh? She eventually fell in love again, this time with a British nobleman. But she never forgot her lieutenant, nor did she ever forgive herself for her rash behavior on the night he died. On the anniversary of the battle, each August 9, Marie dressed in sack cloth and sandals and begged for money to feed the poor of Detroit, an act of contrition for her foolishness in rejecting her first love.

Marie had another curious habit . . . she kept her right hand covered with a black glove. Only a few knew why it always remained hidden.

REDEMPTION

The old woman named Marie Louise Kennette lived on the river road to Springwells. She was rude, unkempt, loved only her money and violin and lived alone in a little house. A shoemaker by trade, she was so miserly that she spent her evenings wandering the streets lest she spend money on fuel, and begged food from neighbors so as not to fritter away her hoarded sums.

No one mourned the death of old Marie in 1868. But in her last year, those who knew her noticed a change—she took some care in her appearance, often stayed home at night reading by the kerosene lamp and spoke pleasantly to those whom she met on the roadway. The reason for Marie's "redemption" constitutes one of the oldest ghost stories in Detroit.

A number of years before her death, Marie had decided to make a little extra money by taking in a boarder, Clarissa Jordan, an old lady who regularly attended church and prayed several times a day.

Marie laughed at such piousness, since she herself had been ostracized by her church brethren for her eccentricities.

Yet the woman tried to reform Marie. She attempted to persuade her to attend church more regularly and, after that failed, sought to scare Marie with ghost stories that illustrated the interdiction of supernatural forces in human lives.

There was, for example, old Grandmere Duchen, argued Clarissa, who sat at her spinning wheel for weeks *after* she had died. The droning of the wheel nearly drove her son insane until he had bought fifty masses for the repose of her soul.

She spoke also of the *feu follet*, the will-o'-the-wisp, sent to the door of a girl at Grosse Isle while her lover was trapped in a swamp. The mysterious light led her to him, and he was rescued.

And there is the French hunter Sebastian's ghost boat, Clarissa solemnly added, which ascends the Straits of Mackinac once every seven years to keep Sebastian's promise to his betrothed that he would always return to her—dead or alive.

Marie hooted at all of Clarissa's tales. The old woman would have nothing to do with superstitious nonsense!

"Bah!" she sputtered. "I don't believe in your silly stories, or your purgatory or hell! But I will make a bargain with you—if you die first, come back to me here. Should I die before you then I will return. Then we will know if there is any other world but our own!"

And so it remained until the women fell to arguing. The subject of the dispute, Clarissa's alleged using of too much water in her bath, was of little consequence, but Marie declared her intention *never* to speak to the lodger again. But, she added, their agreement to return from the dead was still to be upheld.

For the rest of their time together in the house, the two women never spoke to each other. Instructions or messages were written on scraps of paper and left for the other to find. The pair ate at separate tables, in different rooms. If by chance one saw the other coming down the hallway, she would duck through the nearest door. To the outsider, it appeared as if each woman existed in a different dimension, unable to see, hear or communicate with the other.

Clarissa Jordan was the first to die. One evening not long after, Marie was out visiting, so as to spare the expense of heat and light. A young neighbor boy spotted her and asked why she had left the lights on in her house. He knew of her miserliness and was surprised. Marie left at once, but when she got to the house, the lights were off.

Marie's lights were reported blazing over several evenings, but she never quite returned in time to catch the "culprit." The stout cane she held in her hand was always poised, ready to strike down the intruder.

Determined to put an end to the problem, Marie sneaked into the house one night well before her usual time to return, quietly climbed the stairs and hid in her bed. Moments later, a light blinked on downstairs in the sitting room. But, instead of remaining where it was, the glowing orb began to ascend the staircase. It was phosphorescent, and seemed to shimmer as it moved down the hall, through the door and into her room. The glow gradually changed into the shape of a human being ... the form of her old, pious lodger Clarissa Jordan!

"I know you!" Marie cried out. "Come no nearer!"

Until her death in 1868, Marie grew softer, kinder and more neighborly. She even stopped her miserly walks at night. But, she also aged very rapidly. The sight of the ghost of her old lodger, it is said, had a most profound effect on Detroit's Marie Louise Kennette.

THE DEATH CAR

Michigan has a unique place in the history of American folklore. The origin of one of the most enduring legends of our time—The Death Car—was tracked down and verified as having begun in a small Michigan community during the late 1930s. The tale still makes the rounds of American cities.

A typical version goes like this: "My brother in Chicago had a friend who bought a 1980 Porsche for $1000. He had to take it back to the dealer because it had an awful smell. He didn't know that a man had killed himself in the car and his body hadn't been discovered for months. The dealer had washed out the car and changed the mats, but the smell was still there. That's why he had sold it at such a low price."

In the telling, the date, geographic location and how the car owner died vary, as does the model. Buicks seem to be favored, while Chevrolets, Fords and sports cars are mentioned occasionally. Suicide leads as the cause of death, although one version relates that the owner was shot to death as he sat in the car. In nearly all variations, the death smell resulted from the tardy discovery of the body. One of the tales even circulated in England around 1951.

Unlike many legends, this one seems to be based on a real event. The researcher who established its authenticity was folklorist Richard Dorson. He traced the tale to a version featuring a Lansing, Michigan, Buick dealer who had supposedly obtained the car in 1944. When he advertised it for fifty dollars, he had been overwhelmed with phone calls. Since auto plants weren't producing cars that year, the story goes, the Buick sounded like an incredible bargain. Some of the callers said they knew a man had died in the vehicle but didn't care.

In 1953, Dorson, by then collecting black folktales, visited the small village of Mecosta, Michigan, founded by black settlers following the Civil War. Invited to speak before the townsfolk, he recounted numerous legends, including his version of the Death Car. After his speech, several Mecosta citizens took Dorson aside and said the story of the Death Car was not a legend, but an actual happening, and the triggering event had occurred in Mecosta!

The facts were not quite as Dorson had them. The car was a 1929 Model A Ford owned by one of the few white settlers in the community, a man named Demings. After his girl friend, Nellie Boyers, jilted him, he drove the car into the country, blocked all the cracks with concrete, and ran a hose from the exhaust through the window, poisoning himself with a lethal dose of carbon monoxide.

Demings died in August, but his body wasn't discovered until October when a hunter noticed it had been parked in the same place for several weeks. Investigating, he found the decaying corpse inside.

The Model A with the smell of death came into the possession of a car dealer in Remus who sold it to a Clifford Cross. Cross tried every means imaginable to get rid of the stench, but all failed. Even in winter, he drove it around town with the windows wide open. Eventually, he gave up and sold it for scrap.

The Death Car continues to be a popular story among young people and many adults. Although its origins are known and even prosaic, the story illustrating the ineradicable odor of death holds a lingering fascination for us all.

GHOSTS OF THE BIG PINEY

The Big Woods rolled across the heartland like an undulating green ocean. For hundreds of miles, only crystal lakes and swift-flowing streams broke the vastness of cedar, spruce, oak and king pine. Its depths stretched deep and dark as any sea bottom.

Its secrets, however, were plumbed more easily, beginning with the earliest French and English explorers. They saw its wealth in the rich pelts of beaver, muskrat and fox; and they coveted the seemingly endless virgin timber, enough, they thought, to last forever.

Until the early twentieth century, waves of lumberjacks swept across the forests of Michigan, Wisconsin and Minnesota, leaving stump fields in their wake. Too late they realized that what seemed everlasting to the earliest loggers was depleted in the blink of a geologic eye. Although their conservation techniques were rudimentary, the rugged men who cleared the northern wilderness left a wondrous legacy of folktales. Every school child knows about Paul Bunyan, that mystical lumberjack who was actually the modern creation of a lumber company. But the loggers also told great ghost stories, many of them based on real tales of eerie events. In the days before electricity and modern transportation, when the lumbermen spent the winter months isolated in the wilderness, it was easy to stare at the flickering lamps and imagine . . .

THE HAUNTED LUMBER CAMP

Six men were making their way to a lumber camp in the north central region of Michigan's Lower Peninsula. The year was 1888, the season early fall when the camps began to fill with men anxious to earn top wages by giving up civilization for the winter. The snow made it easier to haul the logs out of the forest on giant sledges.

The men changed trains at Bay City and, while waiting for the cars to the lumber camp, amused themselves telling stories of their exploits. Each had escaped death a dozen times, fought a hundred black bears and generally had enough adventures for ten men. All except one. He was the oldest, slightly stooped, gray haired and silent, who sat puffing his pipe at the fringe of the group. The evening wore away, and at last he was persuaded, with great reluctance, to tell his story.

This was the eerie tale the Old Man spun: Three years ago that fall he had made his regular trip north as an agent for a hospital in Bay City. Every autumn he traveled a lumber camp circuit selling hospital "tickets" entitling the holder to medical treatment for the next year.

He left the train at Otsego Lake, a small village on the Michigan Central Railroad about sixty miles south of Mackinaw City, and started for the camps of Sage and McGraw, about thirty-five miles from Otsego Lake. A tote teamster headed for the same camp joined him. The teams and wagons made slow progress as the road lay through heavy timber untouched by the lumberman's axe. Its impenetrable depths loomed silent and grand.

Just before dusk the two men reached a small deserted shanty on the banks of a narrow, swiftly running stream. The horses faltered and stopped. The Old Man himself was weary, having walked nearly all the way. Since they were still some miles from camp, he suggested they stop at the shanty for the night. As they debated, the lead horse on one of the teams collapsed in violent spasms, settling the question. They unhitched the teams and tied the three healthy horses to nearby trees. The sick horse refused to get up, and they left him lying in the road.

The shanty stood in the middle of a small clearing, surrounded on three sides by giant pines. In front ran a stream, a small tributary of the Au Sable River, its banks fringed with cedar and spruce. The Old Man seated himself on the trunk of a fallen pine, a cigar in his mouth. The teamster, a jolly man on the journey but now a bit sullen, joined him. They smoked and talked till the gathering darkness warned them it was time to be making preparations for the night. Gathering armfuls of wood they went into the shanty.

The low-ceilinged interior did not seem very inviting. Some of the moss filling the cracks between the logs had fallen out, or hung down in strips, giving the room a ragged and unkempt appearance. On each side of the single large room, a row of bunks three deep had been put up against the walls. Together with a few benches, they comprised the only furniture. In the center was an open fireplace. A roof aperture directly overhead let out smoke. The men soon had a roaring fire, and as the cheerful blaze filled the place with light, the atmosphere lost some of its gloom.

The Old Man went to the wagon for the lunch basket, and the teamster accompanied him, he said, to see after the down horse, which had recovered considerably. But the Old Man more than half-suspected that his companion was unwilling to remain alone in the shanty. The Old Man paused a moment in the doorway taking in the calm night. A whippoorwill in a thicket set up its strident cry and the rising moon's rays turned the river's dark waters to molten silver.

After the men had done ample justice to the good things contained in the lunch basket, they drew their benches close to the fireplace and resumed their cigars and conversation. The Old Man noticed that several times his companion cast quick furtive glances toward the dusky corners, which the flickering fire left in shadows.

"Old Man," the teamster said abruptly, "are you in any ways superstitious?"

Though an Irishman subject to plenty of superstitions, the Old Man evaded the question: "This place reminds me of tales I have heard about the haunted shanty. I suppose you are thinking the same thing."

The teamster eyed him warily. "Yes, partner," he replied. "I see you've heard of it: the celebrated haunted lumber camp of Northern Michigan! If it had been possible, I would have gone the other ten miles tonight rather than put up here. It's altogether different now that dusk has fallen. I don't know how you feel about it, sir, but for me I would have given twenty-five dollars if that horse had held out till we got to camp."

On his side, the Old Man, despite a few tremors, rather looked forward to seeing for himself if any truth existed in the stories. Perhaps Providence had directed him here for the purpose of unraveling the mystery. He tried to recall exactly what he had heard about the shanty. All the tales had agreed on one point, the description of the apparition: an ordinary-looking man, rather below medium height, dressed in shantymen's clothes, restless and ill at ease and with a distressed look upon his face, who moved about mechanically as though in great mental anguish. He seemed compelled to return to the pine forest and the shanty and always used the door, disappearing at the threshold.

The Old Man had also heard about the two young men, when the camp was first built, who were killed hauling logs to the banking ground. Such tragedies were not rare in the woods, and nothing was thought of it until a party of sportsmen took possession of the camp during the hunting season. They had reckoned without a host.

About two o'clock in the morning, one of them, feeling something cold brushing his face, struggled awake. Through slitted eyes he saw by the dying firelight the figure of a strange man standing by his bunk. The apparition was just withdrawing his hand. As the hunter raised himself to get a better view, the figure turned slowly, walked to the securely bolted door, opened it and gently closed it behind him.

The now wide-awake hunter followed. Opening the door, he saw nothing, although the moon lit up the little clearing with almost midday brightness. He refastened the door and sought sleep, but in vain. When he related his experience next morning, his companions laughed at him. They told him to eat less venison steak for supper!

The next night, the same visitation again awakened the hunter. His howls brought his friends out of their bunks in time to see the mysterious apparition reach the door and pass through. They all ran outside, but there was nothing to be seen or heard, save the hoot of an owl on the edge of the clearing and the distant howl of a hungry wolf.

The next day the hunters sought a less inhabited hunting shack and the cabin, referred to now as the haunted lumber camp, stood untenanted. The toughest lumberjack spoke of it with awe.

It had grown late. The Old Man and his companion securely fastened the door and lay down on a wide mattress of cedar and pine boughs.

After what must have been several hours, the Old Man awoke with a start. The fire smoldered in the fireplace, throwing off fitful flashes that momentarily lightened the shadowed room. He had the feeling something was about to happen, although he knew not what. He glanced at the teamster snoring soundly and then raised himself on an elbow to survey the room.

The next instant produced a shock like a dash of cold water. Seated on one of the benches directly opposite his bunk was a figure of a man he readily recognized as the ghost of the lumber camp. He was young and rather small, with a smooth round face and dark hair, and he wore a wide, white hat like a Mexican sombrero. He was without coat or vest, but wore a red sash around his waist. High-top boots neatly covered his small feet. He leaned forward, gazing into the fire with the saddest expression the Old Man had ever seen.

Gently, the Old Man awakened his sleeping companion and pointed toward their nocturnal visitor. Abject terror spread over the teamster's face. His eyes bulged to twice their natural size and he seized the Old Man's arm with a bone-crushing grip.

The Old Man remained calm. He sat up in bed and in a voice he tried to keep steady, he greeted their unwelcome visitor:

"Hello, Chummy!"

No answer came, but the figure slowly rose and made a circuit of the fireplace. He passed by their bunk within arm's length. The horrified teamster saw him coming, loosened his hold on the Old Man's arm, let out a blood-curdling scream and dove under the blankets, his teeth chattering like castanets.

The figure looked neither to the right nor to the left, and with a slow measured tread reached the door, opened it, passed through and closed it behind him. As he did, the Old Man jumped out of bed and ran after the specter.

He threw open the door to the silence of the empty clearing, and felt the cool air on his face. The wind was beginning to sigh through the pine tops with its peculiarly mournful sound and the moon was just disappearing behind the trees. The Old Man judged morning could not be far distant. He returned indoors and, after convincing the teamster that it was not the ghost that had returned, persuaded him to come out from under the covers. Together they watched the night out.

With the morning, the Old Man and the teamster gladly left the haunted camp and resumed their journey, reaching the Sage and McGraw camp about noon. They duly related their adventure. Instead of making fun of them, as might have been expected, the lumberjacks congratulated the two men on their courage.

As for the teamster, he could never again be persuaded to put up at the haunted shanty. "I am no hog," he would say. "And I know when I have had enough." He would drive all day and part of the night to reach his destination, always taking care to pass the shanty in the daytime.

The Old Man leaned back against a barrel on the railroad platform. His audience had barely moved during the telling of his tale. "As for myself," he concluded, "I have no settled opinion on the subject. I've simply stated what I saw with my own eyes. Now you'll soon have a chance to see for yourself. We'll pass the haunted shanty on our way to camp. It's still standing on the banks of the stream."

"But has no one an explanation for the supernatural visitations?" asked one of the men gathered around the storyteller. "Did no one try to investigate the matter?

Might someone be trying to scare people to lower the value of the property?"

"No," the Old Man replied. "The land is worth nothing, as it was lumbered off years ago. In fact, the owners have let it go back to the government for the taxes owed. Besides the absence of any reason for the haunting adds to the charm of the story."

"But didn't you tell us two young men had been killed there?" the listener insisted. "Might it not be that they were murdered and their spirits were haunting the scene?"

The Old Man took a long time to reply. "Aye. That's the idea that poor old McElroy had. He declared he was not afraid of all the ghosts that were ever created and he swore to find out what the matter was." There was a long pause. "Well, he took himself to the old camp, but one night in the place turned his hair completely gray. He not only refused to tell anyone what he had seen but he left the country. No one knows to this day where he went."

In the distance, a long, low whistle signalled the arrival of the Michigan Central coaches. The men piled aboard, but the story had left an impression. It was a silent group who left the cars at Otsego Lake station and made their way to the lumber camp . . . by way of the haunted shanty.

THE LYNCHING

One of the most gruesome legends in all of American history was spawned in the Michigan lumber town of Menominee, on the shore of Green Bay a few miles north of the Wisconsin border.

On September 26, 1881, a pair of thugs known as the McDonald boys stabbed to death a young half-breed named Billy Kittson. The next day, a crazed mob broke into the jail holding the killers and subjected them to "timber justice" so grotesque that it almost strains credulity, were it not so well-documented.

The sadistic carnage also gave rise to a grimly accurate superstition that each member of the "necktie party" would die with his boots on.

The McDonald boys were actually two cousins, although they were closer than most brothers. Their surnames were different, but everyone called them the McDonalds. The tall slim one, called Big Mac, was born a McDougall. His small cousin was known, naturally enough, as Little Mac.

They had reputations as mean, deadly knife fighters, especially when they had been drinking, which was most of the time. It was the wise citizen who gave them a wide berth.

By most accounts, the trouble began after the 1881 spring lumber drive. The McDonalds got into a fight in Pine River and stabbed Sheriff Ruprecht. The sheriff deputized the 200-pound George Kittson, Billy's half-brother, to track down and arrest the pair. He did, and the McDonalds spent the next several months in jail.

They were released on September 24 and drifted down to Menominee, swearing vengeance on George Kittson. They both found work at the Bay Shore Lumber Company.

The Kittson family was fairly prominent, if not highly respectable, in the pioneer lumber town. There were three boys, all sons of an Englishman who had fled the catastrophic Peshtigo fire in 1871. He moved to Menominee shortly thereafter to become its second permanent settler. George's brother Billy, the youngest boy, was a rough character known to like whiskey and women. The older brother was called Norman.

On the afternoon of September 26, the McDonalds left work at the Bay Shore Company and headed for the Montreal House, a seedy saloon in the west side neighborhood known as Frenchtown. Norm Kittson bartended there.

The more the McDonalds drank, the more belligerent they became. They warned Norm that his brother, George, was a dead man. To back up the threat, they drew knives. Eventually they staggered out of the bar and headed for the Frenchtown whorehouse ensconced behind the jackpine near Bellevue Street.

Inside, Billy Kittson was drinking whiskey out of a jug with the girls of the house. When the McDonalds barged in, a fight ensued. Billy hit one of the McDonalds over the head with an empty bottle, then headed for the relative safety of the Montreal House. The McDonalds caught up with him in the street outside. Norm Kittson saw the pair closing in on Billy and shouted a warning.

"I'm not afraid of those s.o.b's!" Billy yelled back.

Big Mac smashed Billy across the head with a heavy club, then plunged a knife deep into his rib cage as he lay sprawled on the ground. Norm ran to Billy's aid, but Little Mac knocked him away. Billy struggled to his feet, only to be stabbed again by Big Mac, this time in the side of the head.

Nearly unconscious, Norm managed to draw a revolver from his coat pocket. He fired twice. Little Mac clutched his leg as he and his cousin fled.

By all rights, Billy Kittson should have fallen. But he had drunk so much whiskey that he was oblivious to his mortal wounds. He limped inside the Montreal House, ordered drinks for everyone . . . and prompty keeled over dead.

Norm's wounds were not serious.

The McDonalds were captured a few hours later at the train depot and promptly locked up. Word spread like a fire through the pinery that young Billy Kittson had been killed by the notorious McDonald boys. At every tavern and hotel, on each street corner in Menominee, lumbermen talked of little else. Their voices were loud and angry, especially the next day, September 27, when it became clear that a hearing on the murder would be postponed. The prosecutor had trouble finding witnesses, for even though the McDonalds were in custody, the thought of testifying against them didn't sit well with some men.

As the liquor flowed, the talk turned to inflicting rough justice on the pair. They had knifed a sheriff, killed the son of a well-known family and generally created a reign of terror in the city.

Six men were ringleaders, seeking immediate "necktie justice" for the McDonalds. Frank Saucier, a drayman, offered the use of a large timber to batter down the jailhouse door. Bob Stephenson, the superintendent of the Ludington, Wells and Van Schaick Lumber Company, supplied the rope. Max Forvilly, owner of the Forvilly House on Ludington Street, the gathering place for the mob, constantly replenished the whiskey.

At the head of the mob were Stephenson; Louis Porter and Tom Parent, both timber bosses; and Robert Barclay, an ex-sheriff who ran a livery stable.

Late on the afternoon of September 27, the half-dozen men, followed by a group of hangers-on, grabbed a timber from Saucier's wagon and marched on the courthouse. Only two deputy sheriffs guarded the McDonalds. One of them, Jack Fryer, challenged the mob, but Louis Porter immediately disarmed him and shoved him aside.

The mob ransacked the jail and found the two McDonalds cowering in a cell. Big Mac pleaded to be allowed to argue against his imminent fate. They ignored his whimpers and threw a rope around his neck.

Louis Porter grabbed Little Mac, but the outlaw pulled a small knife from his boot and stabbed him in the hand. Enraged, Porter grabbed an axe from a man named Laramie and whacked Little Mac over the head, killing him instantly.

The mob drew ropes tightly around the McDonalds' necks and dragged them from the jail. Big Mac was still conscious even as he was pulled over an iron fence. Witnesses say his neck stretched several inches when his head got caught on the fence rail.

Down Main Street the jubilant mob hauled the McDonalds, taking turns jumping on and riding the bodies, stomping out pieces of their flesh with their heavy boots. The macabre procession took on the appearance of a parade as men, women and even children joined in. Church bells peeled and whistles blew. Everyone cheered the spectacle of the McDonald boys getting "just what they deserved."

Near a railroad crossing, the mob strung up the McDonald boys on a tall pole. Big Mac twitched, moaned once or twice and then was silent.

The sight of the boys swaying in the breeze at such a prominent location wasn't appreciated by everyone. Some thought the bodies might scare the horses and frighten the women and children. After some arguing the mob came up with a solution. Why not take the boys back to where the trouble had begun—the Frenchtown whorehouse?

And that's just what they did. They lowered the corpses and dragged them up Bellevue Street. As they passed the church of Father Menard, he tried to stop them, but they brushed him aside. Father Menard glared after them and declared that each man there present would "die with his boots on."

Undeterred, the men dragged their prizes through the front door of the whorehouse and into one of the bedrooms, dumping the bloodied, mangled remains on a bed. They rounded up the girls and one by one, forced the dozen ladies to climb into bed with the corpses.

When the mob tired of their entertainment, they ran the girls out of the house and burned it to the ground. They left the McDonald boys tied to two small pine trees outside the burning building. Their mangled remains bore little resemblance to anything that had been human.

Had the leaders of that mob known what strange fates awaited them, they might have thought more seriously about their actions. Every man among them died a violent or unusual death. Some say it was Father Menard's curse coming true.

The curse first struck Bob Stephenson, who supplied the rope. A few months after the lynching, Stephenson's lumber yard caught fire. His men refused to run between two piles of lumber and tip them over to save them. Cursing them, Stephenson himself ran between the piles, trying to douse the flames with a water hose. The fire caught him, however, and when he cried out, his whiskey-sodden breath ignited. His body exploded in flames, from the inside out. He lingered in excruciating pain for three days before he died.

Frank Saucier, who had supplied the battering ram to break down the jail door, died without apparent cause on a train trip from Iron River to Menominee.

Louis Porter, who recovered from the knife wound Little Mac had inflicted on him, came to his end when he went with his men on a log drive. Porter sent them on ahead, saying he was tired and wanted to rest. When the crew returned at the end of the day, they found his body propped against a tree, his arms folded across his chest. No one knows why he died. Some say a poisonous snake bit him.

The list goes on: A man named Dunn was accidentally sliced in half by a head saw in a Green Bay sawmill ... Albert Lemieux, a timber cruiser, slashed his own throat midway through a poker game in a lumber camp ... Alfred Beach drowned when his boat capsized.

Some of the men learned of the bizarre deaths of their comrades and vowed they wouldn't die in a similar manner. But the curse was too strong. The ex-sheriff, Robert Barclay, on his way to a family reunion, pulled up at the gathering, jumped out of the wagon, waved and dropped dead.

Max Forvilly lost his hotel, his money and his family. He died on a small farm at Peshtigo Sugar Bush, crazy and penniless.

The grisly events of September, 1881 are still told in hushed tones among the old-timers around Menominee. They know that Father Menard's curse was strong, with the power of the supernatural. The hanging of the McDonald boys, an act of unspeakable depravity, was avenged in a way that defied logic and reason.

THE CORPSE IN THE CLOSET

The new house, Bill Adams thought, would solve his problems. His change to the midnight to eight shift at the Cadillac assembly plant had been hard on him. His body hadn't adjusted to the new hours and he had difficulty sleeping during the day. So when he, his wife, Lillian, and their three children found the gray frame home on Martin Street in Detroit, with the cozy little bedroom tucked away at the back, he hoped its isolation would enable him to get his needed rest, despite the children's noisy games.

The room was barely large enough for a single bed and a closet. Reached by a door off the kitchen, it seemed to have been added to the house as an afterthought.

On a morning shortly after they had settled in, Bill climbed into bed. He had just finished his shift and promptly fell asleep. But within minutes, he was reeling from the most chilling, lifelike dream he had ever had. He awoke gagging, the sweat pouring from his body. He glanced nervously at the closet door. In his dream, he had opened that door. Propped against the wall inside was a mutilated, blood-soaked corpse.

Bill tried to dismiss that first nightmare as an aberration, the product of his new work schedule and the confusion of moving. But the bad dreams continued night after night, each one worse than the one before, jolting him awake with the sound of his own throat-aching screams. When he couldn't stand it any longer he decided to resume sleeping in the master bedroom. No nightmares plagued him there. He wondered why a mere room should make such a horrible difference in his slumbers.

As the weeks passed, Bill grew accustomed to sleeping in the master bedroom, even as his children whooped and hollered outside. The horrible dreams from his brief stay in the tiny back bedroom receded from his mind. Nothing else about the house was unusual. He figured the nightmares must simply have been a product of his own overactive imagination. So, when Bill's grandmother visited the family in August, 1962, they didn't hesitate to put her in the back bedroom.

The immediate reaction of Grandmother Adams, however, showed that something indeed was wrong with that room. After one night there, she complained about the "strange sounds" that had kept her awake. Like someone hammering at the door to get into the room— or get out of the closet. She was too terrified to scream for fear that whatever lurked outside the door—or in the closet—would "get her." Each night brought the same sounds and Grandmother Adams soon decided to return home to Georgia.

It dawned on Bill and Lillian that their terrier would not go near the room and neither would their children. And it was clear that whatever inhabited the back bedroom terrorized anyone who spent the night there. To solve the problem, they locked the door and hid the key.

But the room's evil would be tested one more time when an old friend of the family visited for a few days in October. Dick Patterson was a sensible man and not at all superstitious. If he survived a night in the room undisturbed, Bill and Lillian reasoned, they could assume the noises and nightmares were caused by something else.

They decided not to tell Patterson about the room's reputation. He had no reason to suspect anything unusual as he drifted off to sleep that first night. Shortly after midnight, he awakened when he felt someone turn him over. Opening his eyes, he saw a woman he thought was Lillian standing in the doorway, staring into the kitchen. But this figure had long hair, and was dressed in a blue dress with a short fur coat.

Patterson sprang from the bed and ran toward the apparition. At that instant all the lights in the house went off. A few seconds later, they blinked on and Patterson found himself in the kitchen. Bill had left for his midnight shift and Lillian was washing her hair in the sink.

Neither Patterson nor Lillian understood what happened next. A horrid stench, so strong it made both of them sick, wafted from the room. Then an awful wailing, like that of a wounded animal or a half-mad human, rang out. Reeling from that double assault on their senses, they watched in horror as a trapdoor in the floor of the utility room next to the kitchen rose slowly and then slammed down with a thud.

That was too much for them. Frantically they telephoned the police. The officers who responded searched the house from the attic to the earthen cellar beneath the trapdoor, but could find nothing to explain what Dick and Lillian had seen and heard that night.

Patterson and Lillian were still awake when Bill got home shortly after eight o'clock that morning. They told him about the frightening series of events. Instead of accepting the vague explanation of a ghost, Bill Adams vowed to get to the bottom of the trouble. He decided to spend another night in the back bedroom.

Shortly after supper, he turned the lights out and got into bed. After awhile, he heard a rustling near the door to the kitchen. Thinking it was Lillian, he told her loudly to leave, as her presence might scare off the ghost. As he spoke he found himself staring into the most hideous face he could ever imagine. Only inches away, its eyes gaped vacantly and the mouth moved as if forming words, but only a hissing noise came forth. A sewer-like stench oozed from the figure's twisted body.

Bill leaped from the bed and ran screaming into the kitchen. Patterson and Lillian caught him, but could quiet him only by throwing a blanket around him and dragging him to the floor. All around them the awful smell spread like some malignant tumor: the odor of decomposing flesh.

Within twenty-four hours, the Adamses had packed up their children and household furnishings and moved into Lillian's parents' home in the suburbs of Detroit.

Bill Adams had finally given in to the reality of the demon in the back room. As far as he was concerned, the house belonged to it.

The Lake Odessa Mystery

The old house at the corner of Tupper Lake Street and Sixth Avenue in the small town of Lake Odessa was haunted, of that there is little doubt. But just *what* or *who* flitted through its darkened rooms and tromped across the front porch remains as much a question today as it did three-quarters of a century ago.

Lake Odessa, a quiet village at the turn of the century, slumbered midway between Lansing and Grand Rapids, a few miles south of State Highway 16. No one really knows how the place came to be called Lake Odessa. No nearby body of water bears that name. Tupper Lake forms the village's eastern boundary, while Jordan Lake lies at the southern end of the town. There was no Odessa family, nor do records indicate any connection between the town and the Russian city of Odessa.

In 1903 the villagers still used kerosene lamps and wood stoves, drew their water from wells and used the outdoor facilities in the little backyard shed with a half-moon cut into its door.

To this town came Daniel and Cora Shopbell, a couple disillusioned with life on their farm a few miles distant. They decided to build a house on a vacant lot across the street from Cora's parents, George and Delilah Kepner. Uncle Dan, as everyone called him, built the house himself, right down to the cabinetry in the kitchen. As the foundation he used the old cellar that remained after the previous house burned many years before.

Uncle Dan first put up a barn where he and his wife camped out until the house was finished. He took great pride in the dwelling, pouring several inches of concrete into the walls so rodents couldn't enter, and installing one of the first indoor bathrooms in Lake Odessa. He also made most of the furniture.

But there was one detail he could not control. Soon after Daniel and Cora moved in, they realized something was very wrong. They rarely talked about it with her parents, or her sister and brother-in-law, the Gardiners, who lived with the Kepners across Sixth Avenue. The Shopbells were devout churchgoers—practical, hard-working people not given to flights of imagination. They found it uncomfortable to discuss these strange experiences they could not understand.

It is through the recollections of Leona Gardiner, Cora's niece, who lived with her parents in the Kepner house, that most of the story of the mystery house has been revealed. Four years old at the time, she was a teenager before she found out why her aunt and uncle had fled the house after only a year. Later she investigated the hauntings.

The Shopbells had just settled into the house when odd noises began. If the couple was in the sitting room, a banging would come from the back of the house. Daniel ruled out rodents since the concrete prevented their getting into the walls, and there were no tall trees near the house to scrape against it. At other times, a sound like that of a big pumpkin rolling across the porch and then slamming into the front door would bring the couple out of their chairs. No pumpkin. No nothing.

In the sitting room stood an old-fashioned, wood-burning stove. As Cora and Daniel watched, the stove door would sometimes gently swing open and then slam shut. Just as if someone were checking the fire.

They made their decision to move one evening when Daniel, who was sitting in his favorite chair, was picked up, chair and all, held aloft for a few seconds and then set back down. There was absolutely nothing to explain what caused the bizarre levitation.

The Shopbells sold the house for a small sum and moved back to the farm.

The young couple who bought the house were Gottlieb and Anna Kussmaul. He was a first-generation American who spoke with a heavy accent. Stocky in build, with a profane vocabulary, Gottlieb was described as a generous man, always ready to come to the assistance of neighbors. He worked at a local elevator, hoisting 100-pound bags of grain for hours at a time.

His wife, Anna, contrasted sharply with her husband. She was a small refined woman, educated through the twelfth grade, who had studied music. She taught piano lessons for many years in Lake Odessa. At one time, she and her brother, Byron, a violinist, formed a dance orchestra, which played at local events and practiced in the Kussmaul's sitting room.

The couple had one daughter, Hattie, a pale, thin child who was the delight of her parents. She was to marry young, but died in her midtwenties in the severe flu epidemic following World War I.

The family also had a big gray tomcat, Tiger, who was Hattie's special playmate, and seemed to have a mysterious way of walking through solid walls.

During the day, the family let the cat into the house, but at night, Tiger slept in the barn on a pile of straw. Nevertheless, the parents were often awakened in the early morning hours when the cat walked across the foot of their bed. But when Gottlieb, Anna or Hattie would finally struggle up to put the cat outside, they would never be able to find him. Yet next morning there he would be as usual, *outside* the back door, meowing to come in.

Little Hattie was the unwilling witness to another strange episode in the old house. Her mother often gave music lessons in nearby towns. She would take the morning Pere Marquette Railroad to her pupils' homes and return late in the afternoon. Hattie stayed with the Mosey family after school, across Tupper Lake Street, until her mother returned.

One day after school, Hattie decided instead to go on home. She was soon back at the Mosey house, crying that a man was in their bathroom with his foot up on the tub shining his boots. Mrs. Mosey sent her two sons to investigate and waited on her porch, holding Hattie by the hand. A search through the house turned up no sign of an intruder. Mrs. Mosey tried to convince Hattie it must have been her imagination, but the little girl refused to go home until her mother came for her.

A later episode seemed to vindicate Hattie. One summer night in 1911, pounding on the front door awakened the nearby Kepner household. Crying out that her husband was ill, Anna Kussmaul had come to fetch Mrs. Gardiner, a nurse who often stayed with families. Mrs. Gardiner remembered what happened:

"I threw on my clothes and ran over with the kerosene lamp in my hand, for the street lights in those days went out at midnight. As soon as I looked at Gottlieb and heard his breathing, I knew what was wrong and called Dr. McLaughlin . . . . We worked over him the rest of the night before the doctor felt it was safe to leave him. He left strict orders not to let Gottleib sleep more than twenty minutes at a time, for fear he might slip into a coma. He was to be roused enough each time to answer a question rationally.

"I worked there ten days or maybe two weeks, and I will never forget those nights. It seemed that as soon as Hattie and Anna were asleep, the noises would begin. At first I was scared; then I got mad and would try to find what caused them.

"The only way I can describe the noises is that they sounded like men fighting, or anyway how I imagine it would sound if men were fighting. There were dull, heavy sounds like people wrestling on the floor; dull thumps like blows and grunting sounds. I can't describe it any different. It always came from the back of the house, from the dining room or kitchen, and the minute I would get out of my chair to go and see what it was, it would stop short . . . I never heard a sound while I was up and moving around, taking care of Gottlieb. I always said I wouldn't spend a night alone in that house for a million dollars!"

It wasn't until much later—when Mrs. Kussmaul described the harrowing night in an interview—that Mrs. Gardiner found out *everything* that happened the night Gottlieb became sick.

As Mrs. Kussmaul told the reporter: "It was a stifling hot day in August. Gottlieb came home from work drenched with sweat and simply exhausted. He said he was too tired to eat supper, but I coaxed him to eat a bowl of bread and milk, then bathe and go to bed. It had been a terribly muggy day, and it didn't cool off after sunset, as it sometimes does. However, he had fallen asleep almost at once and I could hear him snoring while I washed the supper dishes.

"Hattie and I sat on the porch a little while, but it was no cooler out there, so I cleaned Hattie up and put her to bed soon after eight. I was so miserably hot I took off my corset—what horrid, heavy things those old corsets were!—and decided to go to bed myself although it was not yet nine o'clock ...

"Gottlieb was still snoring and I got into bed facing him and lay that way for a few minutes, but soon turned with my face toward the window in hopes I'd get at least a breath of air.

"As I turned, I was paralyzed with fear for I could clearly see the figure of a man silhouetted in the doorway. He was advancing toward the bed. I was too frightened to make a sound or move until he was right beside the bed, when I jerked the sheet over my head and called, 'Gottlieb!' I got no answer and tried to kick him and awaken him, but he just kept snoring. I don't know how long it was before I got up the nerve to uncover my head and reach out and pull the string that led from the light bulb down to the head of the bed, where one end of it was tied. When the light came on, I was afraid to look around the room. But there was no sign of anyone there, nothing was disturbed, and there was no sound except for my husband's snoring.

"I fell asleep at last, but not for long. I awakened to realize that something was wrong. The snoring that I had heard so long did not sound right, it was more than just snoring. I tried to awaken him, but it was impossible to rouse him. I knew then that something was terribly wrong, and that was when I went running for (Mrs. Gardiner)."

Gottlieb Kussmaul recovered from his seizure. Anna always believed that the "man" she saw had been there as a warning that her husband was ill.

The Kussmauls stayed in the house until 1946. During all those years they were plagued with odd noises, thumps, groans and footsteps. The house was searched after a particularly disturbing sequence of events, but there were apparently no natural explanations.

What, then, might have caused the disturbances? Was the house haunted?

Could the mysterious events be connected with the previous home that had burned in the late nineteenth century, leaving only the excavated cellar upon which Daniel Shopbell built his home?

There are two versions of what transpired in that first house, either of which might have produced a few ghosts. The owner was a cattle buyer or real estate agent, depending upon the story one hears. In both versions, a stranger appears one day with a good deal of money. In one story he wants to buy cattle, and in the other he is a land speculator from out-of-state who wants to settle in Lake Odessa. He is murdered, apparently for his money, and shortly thereafter, the house burns.

The scenario makes sense. Mrs. Gardiner claims she heard the sound of men fighting and a body falling to the floor. A reenactment of the fight that preceded the murder? And perhaps that man in Anna Kussmaul's bedroom and the mysterious intruder Hattie saw were both the same person . . . the victim of that killing whose name has been long forgotten.

"Beware . . . Jack!"

Automatic writing. The supposed ability of spirits to communicate with the world through a living person's handwriting. Without any conscious intent, the person loses control and the spirit takes over, using as the instruments of communication the human subject's hand and pen to form words on paper.

In St. Louis, Mrs. Pearl Curran wrote entire novels and sonnets while a spirit named Patience Worth guided her hand. Mrs. Curran claimed to know nothing of how the writing came to take place and, indeed, was shown to be ignorant of many of the names, places and events included in the poetry and stories. More recently, a British woman, who had never studied musical composition in her life, claimed that long-dead composers, including Beethoven, were using her to write symphonies. She would sit before blank sheets of music notepaper, her hand flying across the pages, jotting down musical phrases. When played, the pieces sounded much like the music of the composer with whose spirit the woman said she was communicating.

But there are even more bizarre incidents of what has been called automatic writing, including one in Michigan in the early 1960s in which a spirit message probably saved a woman and her infant daughter from the murderous intentions of her berserk, estranged husband.

The city of Pentwater lies north of Grand Rapids on the rocky shore of Lake Michigan. It comes to life each summer as hundreds of families from Detroit, Chicago and other large, industrial cities of the Middle West trek northward to the sunny beaches and clear air of the lakeshore. Near Pentwater lived Celeste McVoy Holden, recently separated from her husband, in an isolated residence of many rooms and several wings, typical of the bygone era when summer homes were as grand as permanent residences. Aside from a chauffeur and a maid who lived in Pentwater and came to the house during the day, Mrs. Holden and her four-month-old daughter lived alone in the rambling mansion.

The summer after she separated from her husband, Mrs. Holden invited one of her closest friends, a well-known artist, Mrs. Buell Mullen, to spend a few weeks at the Pentwater house. Mrs. Mullen, famous for her etchings and paintings on stainless steel, lived in New York City and exhibited her work in galleries from Brazil to Detroit. President Eisenhower once commissioned her to etch his likeness as a gift to a military regiment.

Mrs. Mullen agreed to come and arranged with her husband to meet her later at the house. He had some business to finish before he could get away.

Shortly after her arrival, alone in her room, Mrs. Mullen sat down at the desk to write a letter. She wanted to give her husband the rather complicated directions to the Holden house. Suddenly, her hand was jerked away from the paper, as if it had been grabbed by some unseen intruder. She fought unsuccessfully for control. Then, she watched her hand, as if it belonged to someone else, move across the paper writing without any conscious effort on her part. The handwriting was different from her own and the words: "Beware! Beware! Beware!" made no sense to her. Beware of what? Then her hand scrawled the word "Jack" across the stationery.

Buell Mullen ran to Celeste Holden's room, told her what had happened and showed her the paper. Mrs. Holden blanched. "Jack," she said, her voice trembling, "is my former husband's name." His violent temperament was part of the reason they had separated. Were the women being warned that he might do them harm?

Hoping to find the source of the mysterious message, Celeste and Buell searched the house for a Ouija board. When they found none, they went to Pentwater to buy one. Back home, they sat the board across their knees, with their hands resting on the teardrop-shaped marker.

When Mrs. Holden asked what was going to happen, the words spelled out in response terrified them: "Murder, you and your child." Then: "Prepare!"

But how? She had no weapon. Celeste telephoned her chauffeur and, without revealing the cause of her concern, asked if he could come to the house at a moment's notice in case of trouble. He said he could.

As it was getting late, Celeste and Buell locked each door and window, picked up the sleeping baby and retreated to the most secure wing. Here they piled furniture against the doors, blocked the windows and . . . waited. Unable to sleep, they played cards through the long night, stopping and listening hard each time they heard the slightest sound. Eventually morning came and nothing had happened.

The women felt silly to have taken seriously such an absurd notion as spirit communication. Until two days later. A friend named John Malloy phoned to ask Celeste if she had seen Jack. The startled woman said no, she assumed he was in the city.

Then Malloy told her that two nights before he had seen Jack in Pentwater. Jack had staggered into a party at nearby Harbor Point, drunk, waving a gun and boasting to the stunned gathering that he was going to kill his wife and baby. Malloy had wrestled the gun away and calmed Jack down. Holden had left the party about three o'clock in the morning. Malloy assured Celeste that was the last they had seen of him.

Celeste thanked Malloy and put down the phone. Had Jack left town at three a.m. as Malloy had said? Or had he left the party and come to kill them as he had sworn to do? Perhaps they would never know whether the action they took to barricade themselves into the most inaccessible part of the house had saved their lives. And all because of a most timely warning from . . . the other side.

THE SOUL OF STEPHEN STRAND

A decade before the American Civil War, there unfolded near Battle Creek, Michigan, a story so strange, so

unbelievable as to be immediately categorized as fiction.
Yet an Indian spiritualist, Mrinal Kanti Ghosh, included
the case in his 1934 book *Life Beyond Death*, in a chapter
entitled "A Case of Reincarnation From America." The
story originally appeared in an 1851 issue of the New
York *Mercury*, again in a 1911 edition of the *Progressive
Thinker*, and finally in the Philadelphia *Morning Inquirer*
in the early 1930s. No less a publication than the *Journal
of the American Society for Psychical Research* discussed
the case's circumstances.

What was the story? An instance of long-term
possession, the transference of a soul from someone dead
to someone who lived for years. Is it possible for a
wandering spirit to drive the soul from a living person?
As incredible as it sounds, this is what happened:

Harper Allyn, a bachelor, worked as a wool-carder
at the mills of Captain William Wallace between the years
1850 and 1851. He was a quiet man, given to long evenings
alone by the fire, or to pursuing solitary sport such as
hunting and fishing the shores of Goguac Lake, a few
miles from Battle Creek. Little is known of him. His age
was never reported, nor his personal history. The only
characteristic of note seems to be his curiosity about the
"hermit of Goguac Lake."

It was on a hunting trip that Allyn first noticed the
tidy small cabin nestled among the pine trees on an island
in the lake. The hermit who lived there was Stephen
Strand, an unusual character who shunned human
companionship. An old dog and spooky black cat lived
with him. As far as anyone knew, he never ventured into
Battle Creek, and appeared to live through trapping,
hunting and fishing the abundant waters of Goguac Lake.

The quiet bachelor and the mysterious hermit were
thrown together when a rattlesnake trapped Strand's black
cat against a rock ledge. Allyn, who was hunting at the
time, happened along and killed the serpent. He returned
the cat to Strand, who showered Allyn with gratitude.

After that, the men often hunted and fished together. And although they spoke of many things, Allyn learned little about Strand's life and even less about the circumstances that brought him to such an isolated existence.

Their friendship might have continued uneventfully had it not been for a thunderstorm. Allyn and Strand had been fishing on the lake. They just made it back to Strand's cabin as the first wave of dark clouds, belching lightning, erupted. Allyn was forced to spend the night with the hermit.

He had always sensed that something lay hidden within Strand, a black secret that would provide the key to understanding the man. On this wild night, Allyn would learn the truth.

Never had Harper Allyn seen a grown man react with such abject terror to a thunderstorm. While it raged, Strand paced the cabin. From time to time he nervously glanced out the shuttered windows, as if waiting for someone. He noticed Allyn's curiosity, but said nothing. At last the storm abated and the hermit seemed to visibly relax. He beckoned Allyn to join him and together they sat near the fire.

"I apologize for what must seem to you peculiar behavior on my part," Strand began. "But you see, I have good reason to fear the storm. I, that is the person you hear speaking, am Stephen Strand. But the body you see is that of another."

Harper Allyn rose from his chair. He was not going to spend the night with an insane man.

"Please!" Strand pleaded, reaching out to grasp Allyn's arm. "Please, I am *not* mad, despite that rather odd statement. If you will allow me, I shall explain. But I must warn you, it is a story you will find difficult to believe."

Allyn hesitated. Was he close to finding that hidden secret? Or were Strand's words the ravings of a lunatic?

"Very well," Allyn said at last. "Continue. How can you speak as one man and be another?"

"That, sir, is why I fear the storm. I shall begin at the beginning. I was born nearly six decades ago in the village of Becket Corner, Massachusetts. As Stephen Strand. At the age of sixteen years, I signed on with a whaler out of New Bedford. I rose steadily in rank until, at the age of twenty, I felt assured enough in my status to return home and marry."

Stephen Strand's eyes clouded. He turned to gaze into the deep, red embers of the blazing fire.

"Her name was Molly ... Molly Lawton. We had known each other since childhood. After we married, I worked ashore for five years, first as a storekeeper and then at a livery. We had a good life together ... but for me that wasn't enough. I knew I belonged at sea. Molly accepted that as a good wife must.

"I shipped out on a merchantman bound for France. The trip was uneventful. I stayed with the ship, even though it was to be delayed several months before its return to America.

"At last we left France, bound for Ireland where we were to take on cargo. Late one night, as we neared Cornwall, a violent storm descended upon us. We couldn't hold the course in the channel and smashed against the English cliffs.

"I was below decks when we hit. I was thrown across the sleeping compartment and must have struck my head for I remember nothing until ... until I ... woke up ..."

He was struggling with the recollection. Allyn sensed it was the first time in a long while that he had told the tale.

"Go on," Allyn gently urged. "You struck your head, but obviously you lived."

"Ah, but that's just it," Strand continued. "I did *not* live! I awoke, yes, but as I did I realized at once that I was, in fact, dead. I had the sensation of floating above the cabin deck, looking down upon the scene. I could not find my body. My soul, for that is what I presume I had become, had traveled some distance. I was in a different part of the ship.

"I did not want to stay in that ... limbo! I wanted to see my family again, to rejoin the world of the living. All around me, my shipmates lay dead. Suddenly, I noticed that one of the Frenchmen who had joined us as passengers was stirring.

"I then realized that his body could become mine! I tried to enter him, but his soul prevented me. We fought. I remember little, except that after what seemed like hours I succeeded. His soul fled. But not far. It still ... lingers. Always has."

Strand was breathing heavily, the sweat visible on his forehead, as if reliving the nauseous fear which must have gripped him on the English coast. "Whenever there is a storm, as tonight, the soul of that man tries to repossess what once was his—the body you see before you. I am the soul and mind of Stephen Strand, but the body belongs to the Frenchman I conquered that night so very long ago."

Allyn sat back in his chair, not quite knowing what to say, or even whether to believe such a preposterous story.

"Did that Frenchman, er, did *you* find any possessions on the body you entered?" Allyn asked at last.

"A few," Strand replied. "Some letters that I destroyed and a knife and purse I lost years ago." He reached into his pocket. "But this match-safe I have kept since that night. You may have it. For saving my cat. Please, take it. And for it, perhaps you would be kind enough to give me that daguerreotype of yourself you told me about. A fair trade? I want to remember you ... and your many kindnesses."

Allyn took the proffered gift. It was an exquisitely designed gold box. The workmanship was of the finest quality. Engraved upon the outside was the name "Jacques Beaumont."

"I shall certainly give you that picture. I fear this is far more valuable, however. But are you ... is that the body of Beaumont?" Allyn asked.

"Yes," replied Strand, "although I know little of him. He is a vessel within which lives the soul of Stephen Strand. It is a stranger's name."

"What then? How did you reach this country? And end up here?" The questions crowded Allyn's mind.

"I ... or Beaumont, whichever, was the only survivor. The ship broke apart, but I was able to ride a large piece of wood, like a raft, to shore. I made my way to Liverpool and thence to Boston. I must say, it was a peculiar experience. This body ... I was not used to it! Silly things happened." Strand began to chuckle. "I began to crave French cooking! Of course I was out of luck in Britain on that score."

He grew serious again. "It was as if I had suddenly been transported as a blind man into a new house, one in which I was expected to live and work, and yet I knew nothing of its rooms or furnishings. Each time I glanced into a looking glass, I expected to see Stephen Strand. Instead, this stranger stared back at me. I can tell you I was frightened more than once by the ordeal. And yet ... I *was* alive!

"Well, once in Boston, I prepared to reacquaint myself with my wife. I made my way to Becket Center and ..."

"Go on," Allyn urged, for Strand had suddenly covered his eyes and begun to sob.

"I'm ... I'm sorry," Strand cried. "It's just so very painful for me. But I must tell you. I hadn't reckoned with the shock my new ... self ... would have on those whom I loved. I poured out my story to Molly, my wife. She shrank from me. She said her husband had been drowned off the English coast. I tried to convince her it was I, her Stephen, but it was of no use. She took me for a madman. My friends shunned me. I was forced to flee for my life. I was afraid they would lock me up. I wandered for several years and finally settled here on this island where you found me."

His peculiar narrative at an end, Strand stared intently at his friend.

Allyn met his gaze but said nothing. The first light of dawn was knifing through the cabin, casting the men and the cabin's furnishings in an eerie, amber-colored glow.

"I must take my leave," Allyn replied at last. "I have to think about what you have told me. It is so ... so unbelievable. But it has the sense of truth about it. I don't fully understand why, myself, but I think I believe you."

Allyn saw little of Stephen Strand over the next few months, occasionally stopping by the cabin to check on his welfare, but never staying more than a few minutes at a time.

He did not forget the story, however. Nor did he fail to try and find proof to support Strand's bizarre assertions. He wrote a letter to the editor of a newspaper near Becket Corner asking for information regarding Stephen Strand. Was there ever such a man in Becket Corner? Did he go off to sea? Marry? And, most importantly, was he still living?

In reply, the editor said that a man named Stephen Strand had lived in that village. But, he continued, Strand was lost at sea. Many years ago, a stranger had arrived in Becket Corner claiming to be Strand, but nobody believed him, as he looked nothing like the man he was "impersonating." He was driven from town.

Molly Strand and her children had left Becket Corner to live with her wealthy brother in the West and hadn't been heard from since, the editor concluded.

Allyn realized the letter confirmed many of the details of Strand's impossible story!

About a year after that, Stephen Strand vanished. A severe thunderstorm struck the Goguac Lake area, and when Allyn visited the cabin a few days later, he found only Strand's starving dog cowering in a corner. The black cat was missing.

Had Jacques Beaumont's soul finally regained possession of its body? Allyn found the normally tidy cabin in disarray; there had been a tremendous struggle there, of that he was sure. The lake was dragged but nothing was ever found of the mortal remains of Stephen Strand, nee Jacques Beaumont.

Harper Allyn didn't stay in Battle Creek. He inherited a small fortune, allowing him the prospect of spending his remaining life traveling and living in modest luxury.

A childhood friend of Allyn's, Charley Bushnell, had taken up residence in France, studying at the Academy of Art in Paris. Allyn decided to visit him. The saga of Stephen Strand had remained with him, and the thought of visiting Beaumont's native country intrigued him.

Bushnell was well-connected in Paris society and soon had Allyn attending numerous social functions. At one such gathering of artists and literary figures, Allyn was introduced to an attractive woman. When she saw him and heard his name, she nearly collapsed.

Allyn was at her side when she regained her composure.

"I am so sorry," she said. "It's just that your face and name are familiar to me."

Allyn was dumbfounded. "How can that possibly be? I have only recently arrived in Paris, and, to the best of my knowledge, I have never seen you before."

"But I have seen you. In a picture only last week," she replied.

"Please explain all this to me," Allyn requested. "I am quite confused."

"My name is Lily Beaumont," the woman said. Allyn paled. *Beaumont*. That name again. Could it be . . . ?

"My name means something to you?" she asked, noting Allyn's discomfort. "Last week a very old man came to my mother in the village where she has lived since my father died. He was a sailor, lost at sea near the English coast. Anyway, this man, whoever he was, claimed to be *my father*. My mother didn't recognize him, nor did I. How could we? It's been over forty years. He told this preposterous story about being possessed by another man and said he was only recently able to regain his own identity. The prefect of police came and took him away to an asylum. I . . . we . . . thought he was quite insane. But now I see that the photo he had in his pocket was a picture of you! And your name, Harper Allyn, was written on the back."

"My God!" Allyn exclaimed. He then told Mlle. Beaumont the story of Goguac Lake. When he finished, she was even more upset than when she had first seen Allyn in the flesh.

Allyn left immediately for the asylum. He found Jacques Beaumont in a tiny cell: he was older, quite thin and sickly, but the same man Allyn had known as Stephen Strand. The man didn't recognize Allyn, nor did he seem to understand English. Since he was in such ill health, Allyn stayed only a short time.

Later, he showed Madame Beaumont, Lily's mother, the match-safe Strand had given him. She collapsed at the sight of it. It was the same one she had given her husband before he vanished at sea.

The incredible story quickly circulated through the small village. Was the old man, indeed, the long-lost Jacques Beaumont? Some people claimed he looked like the man they had known decades earlier. Others were convinced he was an imposter preying upon the kindness of a respected family.

Meanwhile, the old man grew sicker and was taken to the hospital. Doctors said they could do little for him except to make his final hours as comfortable as possible.

Harper Allyn was notified, as was a Catholic priest who administered the last rites of the Church.

Strange, Allyn thought. The Strand he knew professed to be an atheist.

Allyn sat at the old man's bedside, not knowing what to say or even where to begin. But he had to know.

"Will you now tell the truth? Are you Stephen Strand or Jacques Beaumont?" Allyn asked the dying man.

"In the presence of the Almighty and by the Sign of the Cross, I swear . . . ," the priest translated. Strand-Beaumont sank back against his pillow, opened his mouth to speak again and collapsed. He was dead.

The tale that Harper Allyn heard on that island in stormy Goguac Lake would forever remain in dispute. Who was this man? An imposter, claiming one of the most fanciful cases of possession in history? Or had he, for most of his life, been two men, the body of one and the soul of another? The answer went with him to the grave.

Chapter VI.
Minnesota

"The Milford mine collapse was the worst disaster on Minnesota's iron range. Yet, when the mine reopened, many miners signed up to go underground again ...

But not a miner on the entire Cuyuna Range was prepared for the horror that lay in the bowels of the Milford mine on opening day .... At the base of the shaft at the 200-foot level, the men's carbide lamps shone upon the translucent form of Clinton Harris! The ghost's bony fingers clutched the side rail of the ladder, its vacant eyes staring upward. The whistle cord was still knotted around the ghost's waist.

The miners staggered back.

Suddenly, the phantom whistle screamed through the dark, winding tunnels. The terrified men scrambled up the ladder. They never looked back as they climbed toward the surface ..."

"THE PHANTOM MINER"

THE HORRORS OF HEFFRON HALL

August 27, 1915. Patrick R. Heffron, bishop of the Winona diocese, was celebrating Mass in the empty chapel of St. Mary's College in Winona, Minnesota. Motes of dust danced in a shaft of gray light from a high window. Dawn was the bishop's favorite hour—the day was new and fresh and full of promise. Yet on this day the bishop felt apprehensive. Perhaps it was the heat, already oppressive; his vestments hung heavy upon his shoulders and sweat beaded his forehead.

Bishop Heffron had just raised the chalice when he heard a door latch click behind him. No one ever entered the chapel at this hour. Had a restless student or nun come to join him? He listened for footsteps. There were none. Strange. He spun around, and saw Father Lesches, one of the college tutors, dressed in a Prince Albert suit, standing against the back wall. Lesches raised a revolver.

The first shot struck the bishop in the left thigh. The second tore into the right side of his chest and penetrated the lung. A third bullet shattered the top of the altar.

Bishop Heffron slumped against the altar, a pool of blood spreading beneath his feet. A blood-stained Mass card lay near by.

The assailant fled, the bishop staggering after him until he collapsed in the chapel doorway. Father Thomas Narmoyle, who was crossing the lawn, rushed to the bishop's side.

Ten minutes later, the Winona police arrested Father Laurence Michael Lesches for assault in the first degree. The priest, located in his room, did not resist arrest. He said he shot Bishop Heffron because the bishop had called him unfit for the religious life and better suited to work on a farm. The revolver lay in an open suitcase and a shotgun was found in the priest's trunk.

At the hospital, officers questioned Bishop Heffron. It was common knowledge that although the bishop and the priest had known each other for seventeen years they had never gotten along. Bishop Heffron, a visionary committed to education, had single-handedly raised the funds to establish St. Mary's College. He was respected and generally well-liked, but dealt ruthlessly with associates who flouted his orders or failed, in some way, to meet his standards.

Father Laurence Michael Lesches never met those standards. An arrogant, abrasive man in whom the arts of diplomacy and negotiation were wholly lacking, he had few friends.

Bishop Heffron, in recounting his last meeting with Father Lesches, told the investigators that the priest had pleaded again for a parish of his own, saying that at age fifty-five he should have the security of settling in one place instead of being transferred from one parish to another.

"But I told him that he was too emotionally unstable to handle such an assignment," explained the bishop. "I have believed that for years and again I suggested that he consider farm work which would not require close, personal relationships."

On December 1, 1915, Winona Court judge George W. Granger called his court to order. The proceedings of the "State of Minnesota vs. L. M. Lesches" had begun.

The trial lasted two days.

Bishop Heffron, recovered from his wounds, was the state's chief witness. He testified that Father Lesches was mentally disturbed, unable to distinguish between right and wrong at the moment of the shooting and unable to judge the effect of his act.

Other witnesses supported the bishop's testimony. Father Thomas Narmoyle testified that he saw Father Lesches running from the chapel on the morning of August 27 with Bishop Heffron staggering after him. The pistol was entered as evidence in the case.

Court-appointed defense attorneys also pleaded their client's disturbed mental condition. And Dr. Arthur Sweeny, the priest's personal physician and final witness for the defense, stated that Father Lesches was a paranoiac and a potentially dangerous man to be at large.

The jury returned its verdict in less than an hour: acquittal on grounds of insanity, with the recommendation that the defendant be committed to a mental institution.

Father Lesches was transported to the State Hospital for the Dangerously Insane in St. Peter, Minnesota. Embittered by his confinement, he nevertheless began to trust his physicians and to cooperate with them in his care.

Several years later, the doctors pronounced the priest in sound mental and physical health and recommended his release. But Bishop Francis W. Kelley, successor to Bishop Heffron, refused to sign the necessary papers.

Father Lesches languished in the state hospital and died there of a heart condition on January 10, 1943. He was eighty-four years old and had been hospitalized for twenty-nine years. His remains were returned to Winona and buried in St. Mary's Cemetery, two-and-a-half miles from the campus.

Yet twelve years before Father Lesches's death, his presence on the campus was recalled by a strange event . . .

On May 15, 1931, a nun entered the room of Father Edward W. Lynch in order to clean it. She found the priest sprawled across the bed—dead! The bed and the body simulated a cross, the bed forming the vertical part and the body the horizontal beam. The corpse, lying face upward, was charred all over. The priest's Bible was also burned. Nothing else in the room had caught fire, not even the bed sheets.

The Winona coroner determined that the priest had died early that morning. Father Lynch had been lying in bed reading. Apparently he reached up to turn off his faulty bed light and ten volts of electricity in the light killed him instantly. But experts said the voltage was not enough to completely char the body!

Father Lynch was a close friend of Bishop Heffron and an enemy of Father Lesches. The two priests had lived together in St. Mary's Hall. They had had numerous arguments, and on one occasion, Father Lesches predicted Father Lynch would go to hell because of his interest in athletics.

Father Lesches often quoted the Bible and had once repeated to Father Lynch the Biblical passage: "And the Lord shall come again to the sounding of trumpets."

Close examination of Father Lynch's charred Bible revealed a single passage that was not burned: "And the Lord shall come again to the sounding of trumpets."

Had Father Lesches put a curse upon his enemy because he was the bishop's friend? The priest's death remains mysterious and unexplained.

In that same year, a priest living on the campus died in a fire. And three other priests were killed in an airplane crash.

In 1921 a new dormitory on St. Mary's campus was named Heffron Hall to honor Bishop Patrick R. Heffron. The Bishop died of cancer six years later.

Since shortly after Father Lesches's death in 1943, students living in Heffron Hall have reported strange late night footsteps and tappings and unusual drafts and cold spots on the third floor. Papers lift from the hall bulletin board when no breeze is stirring, and women students sometimes suffer identical nightmares on the same night.

One night in 1945, Mike O'Malley, a third-floor resident, was walking along the dimly-lit corridor to his room. Hearing footsteps behind him, he turned around. No one was there. He hurried to his room, pushed open the door and slammed it shut. The footsteps stopped outside the door. Someone knocked.

Mike opened the door. A dark-cloaked figure stood there, his face hidden by shadows.

The student thought it was a resident priest. "What do you want, Father?"

The only response was a deep groan. And then three words. "I want *you*."

Mike slugged the figure in the jaw. He broke every bone in his hand. His roommate, who claimed to have seen the visitor's face, said it was made of clay.

School disciplinary records noted that a student had broken his hand in a fight in the cafeteria. But no one on campus was known to have suffered a broken jaw!

More than twenty years later, a student on the fourth floor of Heffron Hall started to walk down the staircase to the third floor, but was restrained by an invisible force!

In 1969, staff members of *Nexus*, a weekly student publication at St. Mary's, launched an investigation into the perplexing incidents at Heffron Hall. Photographers, researchers and witnesses were brought in to work under the direction of Robert Kairis, instructor of history and advisor to the *Nexus* staff.

The team spent two nights on the third floor of the hall, using high-speed cameras with infrared film to record changes in temperature, equipment to measure changes in heat and pressure and tape recorders, in the company of Kairis and other faculty members.

Just before two o'clock each morning, the instruments showed a drop of ten to fifteen degrees in the 700-foot-long corridor; the temperature dropped perceptibly every 100 feet. Natural causes, such as open doors and windows, were ruled out.

Cold spots are known to occur in structures supposedly occupied or visited by ghosts. Does this prove Heffron Hall is haunted? If so, who is the ghost? Bishop Heffron? Father Lesches? Father Lynch?

Experts say the spirits of persons who have led troubled lives cannot rest. Of the three holy men, only Father Lesches suffered a life of bitter frustration. Also, the footsteps were not heard until after Father Lesches's death.

Father Lesches died between one-thirty and two o'clock in the morning, about the time the temperature in Heffron Hall had started to drop. And the priest had always walked with a black, gold-headed cane, possibly accounting for the tapping sounds heard up and down the corridor.

But why would Father Lesches' ghost haunt Heffron Hall? To exact revenge upon his old enemy in the building which bears his name?

No one knows for sure. But to date no "earthly" explanation has been applied to the strange happenings at Heffron Hall.

GIBBONS'S GHOST

Dick Gibbons leaned back in the comfortable armchair of the library in his St. Paul home. He was already accustomed to the pleasure of having his own special hideaway in which he could spend time with his hundreds of books. An English teacher, he reflected as he picked up the novel he was reading, needs to spend time with the fictional characters he tries to bring to life in the classroom. This room, his private place, was one of the unique features which first persuaded him and his wife, Valjean, to buy the two-story brick house a few months earlier.

During the evening, when Valjean was away, Dick liked to settle into his favorite chair and read, as on this particular May night in the mid-1960s. His yellow labrador was snoring on the floor beside him. Unexpectedly, since there was no sound save for the occasional car passing on Goodrich Avenue, the dog raised her head and whined. Dick glanced down and saw the animal stare at something in the adjoining living room. When she growled again, Dick put down the book. He patted her, got up from the chair and led the dog into the next room.

Dick remembers well what he saw there. "The rocking chair was going back and forth as if someone were having a good time. I suddenly felt clammy and very nervous. It seemed like all the blood was rushing to my head."

Dick didn't trust his eyes, at least not at first. The light from his reading lamp in the library barely penetrated the living room. He reached around the corner and turned on the bright overhead chandelier. The chair still rocked. For some reason, he looked at his watch and *timed* the chair's movements. It rocked for exactly one minute, fifteen seconds . . . and then abruptly stopped.

Dick had no idea how long it had been moving before he noticed it. He took his dog by the collar and tried to lead her to the chair, but she dug her claws into the carpeting, stiffened her legs and stayed right where she was. But she never took her eyes from the rocker.

A few seconds later, the animal abruptly turned her head toward the dining room as if following something with her eyes. Then she bolted from Dick's grasp, trotted into the dining room and on toward the kitchen. At the foot of a stairway leading to the second floor, she stopped, sniffed and looked up. Dick followed her gaze up the stairs but could make out nothing unusual.

That eerie experience marked Dick Gibbons's first brush with the supernatural. He later confided that "the rocking chair episode changed me from a mocking skeptic to a believer" in the paranormal.

Dick's wife, Valjean, would also change her views. One afternoon six weeks after her husband's strange night, Valjean was home alone, finishing a painting project. She went down into the cellar to fetch her can of paint. The lid was stuck fast. She pried all the way around the lid, but could not loosen it.

Finally, she decided to get a bigger screwdriver from a toolbox in the kitchen. When she got back to the cellar, however, the lid from the paint can was gone. The can itself had not been moved. She searched the cellar ... the lid was *never* found.

Valjean later told her husband that some*thing* had taken that paint can lid. But there was no one else in the house!

In the late summer of that same year, Valjean again found herself alone when the crash of breaking glass sent her running to the cellar. Two stacks of storm windows were piled on the floor. Dick had propped the windows against a wall at the beginning of the summer. Now they had fallen ... in the opposite direction from the way they were stacked! The glass was cracked in only two of the windows.

Dick and Valjean were not the only ones in the neighborhood who knew there was something odd about the house. They had a very difficult time finding babysitters. None of the young girls on the block ever seemed to be available. Dick suspected it was because they knew the Gibbons's house was haunted.

The couple started to research the home's history, hoping to find a clue to the mysterious events. A family named Moriarity had built the house during World War I and it had remained in the family until the Gibbonses bought it. Neighbors said old Mrs. Moriarity lived alone for some time before moving to a nursing home. They also told the couple that Mrs. Moriarity claimed to have awakened one night to find a man crouching near her bed, staring down at her. She thought it was a ghost. Skeptics claimed the elderly woman had either dreamed or imagined the incident. A few people said a burglar had broken in.

The Gibbonses never found out just *who* their uninvited guest was. They concluded it was a member of the Moriarity family who resented "outsiders" in the house. Or perhaps Mrs. Moriarity just wanted to see what kind of people had bought her house.

In any event, if the ghost was indeed a member of the Moriarity family, it must have been satisfied with Dick and Valjean Gibbons—the couple has not seen, nor heard, from the specter in over seventeen years!

THE TALKING CORPSE

The blizzard of 1873 swept across southwestern Minnesota, rattling the skeletons of trees and burying those cabins that stood unprotected on the prairie.

Inside a small cabin in northern Nobles County, Mary Weston fed the last chunk of wood to the stove and pinned another shawl around the shoulders of her three-year-old daughter, Margaret. The blizzard had raged for three days and there was no sign of her husband John. His parting words still echoed in the woman's mind: *"Don't worry, honey. I'll be back soon."*

Mary recalled the leaden February sky and the rising wind on that day when her husband trudged off to gather more firewood. She had begged him not to leave her and the child, but he had insisted that they would need more wood, especially if the thermometer plunged below zero as it often did following a blizzard.

The Weston cabin was sturdy and well-chinked, but there were, nevertheless, little air pockets through which the brutal winds blew. Mary had tried to use the wood sparingly. At night she and Margaret slept in their clothes with all of the bed quilts and coats piled upon them. Now, the terrified woman watched the glow from the last stick of wood and spread her hands to the warmth.

As Mary did so, she had the strange feeling that something was different. She listened intently. The wind was no longer howling about the chimney. Mary scraped a film of ice from the small window and peered out. Through the condensate of her warm breath on the cold glass, she gazed upon a white world pierced by bare, black tree branches. The storm was over.

The air was still. No sound of man or beast broke the silence. Yet, there *was* something. A faint whisper in the snow? No, she thought, it must be her imagination. Pulling her robe tighter around her, she turned to comfort her child.

In the next instant, Mary Weston knew she had not imagined the sound. The distinct crunch of footsteps drew closer. John was back! Of course. He always kept his promise. Why had she worried so? He would make the fire and she would prepare a hearty meal. She bustled around setting the table and pulling plates from the shelf.

A knock shook the door and a neighbor's voice rang out, "Mrs. Weston, John is froze to death!"

The startled woman rushed to the door and threw it open. No one was there. The quilt of snow lay unbroken as far as she could see, all the way to the dark row of pines at the edge of the grove. She slumped into a chair and remained there until friends, not knowing if John had returned, arrived with firewood and a basket of hot food. Only later did Mary learn that the man whose voice she had heard at the door had *not* left his home that day and knew nothing about her husband's absence!

A neighbor woman offered to stay with Mary, but she said no. She would manage. Although the neighbors presumed John Weston to be dead, his wife did not. She wanted absolute proof and there was none.

Six days after the storm ended, Elmer Cosper, who lived a mile and a half from the Weston place, called on Mary Weston. She was excited to see him. Perhaps he had brought word of John.

"Mrs. Weston," he began, twisting his cap in his hands, "I seen John early this morning."

Mary's face brightened. Those were the words she had longed to hear. "Where? When is he coming home?"

Mary motioned Elmer to sit down and she poured coffee for both of them. Elmer did not look at her.

"I don't know how to tell it, ma'am. I was pitching hay to my cattle. I was standing inside the barn door." He stirred his coffee hard. "When I looked up, I seen John standing in the doorway no more'n fifteen feet away."

Mary interrupted. "You must be mistaken. Why would John go to your place?"

Elmer shook his head. "I don't rightly know. But, it was John all right. He had on his old Union soldier's overcoat."

There was no mistake. Mary knew that John was the only man in the county who still wore his wartime coat.

"Well, ma'am," Elmer continued, "John stepped into the barn and said, 'Mornin' to ya, neighbor.' I was pretty startled 'cause I heard that John was dead. But ... I returned his greeting."

Mary's knuckles turned white as she gripped her cup with both hands.

"I held tight to my pitchfork. And I said, 'But, John, why are you here? We thought you was froze to death.' Then ... then your husband said, 'That I am. My body lies a mile and a half northwest of Hersey.' "

Mary Weston's eyes filled. She knew Elmer Cosper to be the most highly respected man of the neighborhood. His word was good. He never made up stories.

Margaret, who had been playing on the floor at her mother's feet, began to cry and Mary picked her up and held her close.

"After your husband spoke to me, ma'am, I seen the wind shake his coat about his knees. Then ... well ... he vanished ... just like a mark wiped from a slate. I searched all around, but there weren't no footprints. No sign of anyone."

Mary Weston and her neighbors undertook a thorough search of the Hersey area, but the body of John Weston was never found. His widow remained in the little cabin until her death, anticipating her husband's arrival at the close of every raging blizzard.

THE INVISIBLE HOMESTEADER

On a storm-filled night when the wind is high, Bob Jameson roams the darkened rooms of his Monticello farmhouse, shouting, "C'mon, Tobias, scare the hell out of me!"

But Tobias takes no orders from the living. He's a ghost.

That's what Bob and his wife, Marion, believe. And so do the townspeople. Tobias Gilmore Mealey, familiarly known as "T.G.," built the house in 1855 and some say he's never left the premises.

The Jamesons haven't seen Tobias, but they've heard him. And they believe he has a right to be there. "He's a pleasant old fellow," observed Marion, "and besides, he was here first."

Bob and Marion Jameson bought the house in 1965 and for ten years witnessed a number of odd incidents—footsteps paced the upstairs rooms when they were empty; beds jiggled by themselves; lights were turned on by unseen hands; knocks and raps shook doors and windows when no one was there.

The white frame house straddles a hilltop at the end of a winding, rutted dirt road off East Broadway in the little Mississippi River town. Here, Tobias, a founder of Monticello, and his wife, Catherine, raised their five children.

But the old Mealey place was in shambles when the Jamesons first saw it. Vacant for several years, it was ravaged by vandals and neglect. Ice stood on the basement floor, skunks had taken up residence indoors and poison ivy vines grew profusely everywhere. Yet beneath the dilapidation, Bob and Marion sensed the charm of a comfortable old house and began its restoration.

The couple, longtime antique dealers in Minneapolis, eventually moved to Monticello after losing their Twin Cities' home to an urban renewal project. Bob accepted a position as librarian at the Veterans Adminstration Hospital in nearby St. Cloud, and Marion became Wright County historian. The Jamesons moved their antique business with them and dubbed their new home "Chaos Castle."

However, Bob was soon to discover that there was something "wrong" with the house. He went upstairs one evening to begin repair work on the bedroom at the top of the stairs accompanied by his two pups, Homer and Roy. Once inside the room, the pups whimpered and dived under the bed. Bob was perplexed. He didn't see or hear anything.

A moment later, the dogs yelped and crawled out; with tails between their legs, they plunged downstairs. Bob brought the animals back, but they refused to enter the room. Later, another family dog, Freckles, dashed out of that same bedroom and never stopped running until he scooted under a parked car several blocks away.

On another occasion Bob was sitting in a downstairs room taping jazz recordings. The microphones were turned on when, suddenly, footsteps reverberated across the bare floor of the mysterious bedroom overhead. Bob figured Marion was working up there, and called to her to be more quiet. But the footfalls got louder and the sound marred Bob's recording. Shutting off his equipment, Bob went into the hallway and yelled:

"Hey, Marion, either quiet down or put on some slippers!"

There was no response. He started up the staircase and the footfalls ceased. A short time later Marion came into the room where Bob was working. She said she'd been out back all evening working in another building. Bob had been alone in the house! But who or what was walking in that bedroom?

That's what the Jameson's son David also wanted to know. The owner of a construction business in Minneapolis, David visited his parents one night and slept in the bedroom at the top of the stairs. At three o'clock in the morning, he flew out of the room, screaming.

Marion was returning to bed after a trip to the downstairs bathroom when she saw David standing at the top of the stairs, swinging his Navy lantern in great arcs to illuminate the walls, the stairs and the doorway to his room. She thought he was walking in his sleep and feared he might tumble down the stairs.

But David was far from asleep. "There's *something* in that room, Mom," he shouted. "Somebody shook my bed and woke me up. I thought I dreamed it, but then after I got back to sleep someone knocked twice at the window. I got up and couldn't see anything. I went back to sleep, but then the bed shook again and raps hit the window."

Marion and David examined the room that night and the next morning and could find nothing to explain the incident. Plus, there were no trees or anything else outside that could have swayed or brushed against the window.

Meanwhile, various lights in the Jameson house developed a will of their own. Marion would often remain downstairs to read after Bob had gone to bed. On one particular evening she asked Bob to leave the light on for her at the foot of the stairs. She couldn't recall how long she'd been reading before she heard Bob walk back downstairs, flip off the light and walk up again. She thought that he was trying to tell her it was time to go to bed, and she resented this gesture. She stormed up the stairs and confronted Bob. "Why did you turn the light off on me?"

But Bob was sound asleep. He rolled over and opened his eyes. He assured his wife that he had never been out of bed.

Similarly, the living room lights often went off for no apparent reason. At first, Marion accused Bob of turning them off. But after he vehemently denied it, they called in an electrician. The worker spent an entire morning checking every light and could find nothing wrong. But as the man walked toward the door to leave, all the lights came on!

"How'd you do that?" asked Bob.

"I wish I knew," said the electrician shaking his head.

Bob smelled frankincense from time to time in the formal parlor. The odor filled the room and drifted into the hallway. Bob later learned that Tobias Mealey had died in 1905 and that his wake was held in that very room! Bob was smelling the lingering odor of incense that had perfumed the room where the corpse had lain over sixty years ago!

But not all the phenomena occurred inside the house.

One late fall evening when Bob was alone in the house, he heard a creaking noise like that of an ox cart. The rumbling drew nearer, and Bob wondered if something was coming along the old dirt road, a faint trail through the pasture that was once a section of the old Territorial Road from St. Anthony (Minneapolis) to North Dakota.

Bob went to the window and peered out, but could see nothing. Then he heard sleigh bells, "like brass bells on horses." The bells were clear and distinct, fading away gradually. In the morning, Bob went out to check the grounds, but found no tracks of any kind.

On another evening when Bob was alone, he saw a ball of light several feet in diameter go by the front door, turn a corner and float past a first-floor window. At first he thought it was St. Elmo's fire (a bluish glow seen sometimes before and during electrical storms), but decided it was too large for that. He was never able to determine what it was.

Although the Jamesons were never frightened by these experiences, they were eager to discuss them with the previous residents of the house. Thus, Marion contacted Jeanette Sebey who, with her husband, Carl, had owned the house in 1947 and lived in it until Carl's death. The two women corresponded at length and were intrigued by similarities in the manifestations witnessed by the two families.

Six weeks after the Sebeys had moved into the house in 1947, Jeanette claimed that she was ready to move out. The unnatural noises had begun.

On a sunny May morning, Jeanette and her mother were waiting for a crew from Northern States Power Company to install the poles and make the electrical connections. Suddenly, loud thumpings and bangings shook the house.

Jeanette suspected the men had come and were putting up their ladders, but when she went outside, she found no one in sight!

After Jeanette got back inside, she and her mother heard heavy pieces of furniture being dragged across the floor of the bedroom at the top of the stairs. The commotion shook the walls, vibrating pictures and bric-a-brac in the living room.

The noises continued for half an hour. When they stopped, the bewildered women went upstairs to look around. Nothing was out of place. When Jeanette told her husband the story he remarked, facetiously, that probably old Tobias was cavorting around. According to local gossip, "T.G." was a "lecherous old goat" who chased the chambermaids all over the house.

When friends of the Sebeys arrived from Minneapolis to spend the night, they were assigned the haunted bedroom at the top of the stairs. The two couples stayed up late visiting around the fireplace. Suddenly, they heard the scraping of furniture overhead as if heavy chests were being pushed across the bare floor. The guests laughed and congratulated Carl on his skill in rigging a room to sound "exactly like a haunted house." They went to bed and slept well despite the footsteps that paced their room all night.

On another occasion, the Sebeys were working in their front yard, burning the stump of a large elm tree which had blown down the previous year. With a hot fire going, they decided to toast wieners and enjoy a picnic supper. As the couple sat down on the grass to eat, someone banged on the kitchen door. The Sebeys' dog raised her hackles, barked and ran toward the rear gate.

Carl started for the rear of the house and met the dog racing back with her tail between her legs. She dived over a grassy bank and hid. Carl saw no one.

The couple had just settled down again to eat when the rappings repeated. As a joke, Carl hollered, "T.G., you old goat, if it's you, knock twice!"

Two knocks shook the door!

Marion Jameson also corresponded with relatives of Tobias Mealey, sharing with them some of the strange incidents in the house. Up until then, the Jamesons always thought that Mr. Mealey's middle name was Godfrey. But in 1975, a granddaughter of Mealey's wrote and told them that his middle name was Gilmore. She suggested that if the Jamesons would call the old gentleman by his correct name, then he might then be at peace and stop bothering them.

At about the same time, the Jamesons jacked up the center of the house and replaced the old horsehair and plaster ceiling in the living room.

"The ceiling we tore out is right underneath that room where we had the problems," Marion observed. "After that we had no more manifestations of any kind."

Whether it was the relative's letter or the repairs on the house that eventually drove Tobias away will never be known. The ghost may have appreciated the dignity of being called by his correct name. But it appears more likely that the invisible homesteader lingered on earth to warn the Jamesons about the unsafe conditions in the house. Ghosts usually have a reason for haunting a place, and after their mission is accomplished they oftentimes leave.

"Something was definitely here," Marion argued. "And now it's gone."

"You can't prove it one way or another," added her husband. "It's like proving the existence of God—by the time you get absolute proof, it'll be too late."

TUNIS PARKIN'S GHOST TALE

Tunis Parkin was the first person to see the ghost in the Goodhue churchyard. It was a dubious honor; Parkin just happened to be in the right place at the right time. Or perhaps the wrong place at the wrong time.

Parkin was the Goodhue house painter whose artistry showed itself in the homes, barns and windmills of the area. But on that pleasant fall evening in 1922, Parkin laid aside his brushes to court the girl who would become Mrs. Parkin. It was after midnight when he started home, whistling as he walked.

As Parkin approached the apple orchard beside Holy Trinity Church, the whistle died on his lips and his feet turned to stone. Someone was following him. From the corner of his eye Parkin caught sight of the figure—silent, shrouded in mist—right beside him. Maybe if he appeared unconcerned it would go away. Hands in his pockets and eyes on the heavens, the painter began walking faster. So did the ghost. Parkin slowed down. The ghost did too. It stuck to him like a shadow.

At last Parkin broke into a run and never stopped until he reached the home of the town marshal, T. W. Taylor. He stammered out his frightening tale. The marshal, brave and conscientious in the discharge of his duties, hurried to the orchard and made a diligent search. He found nothing of a supernatural nature.

In the morning every resident of the little community knew about Parkin's ghost. Most were skeptical of the story, saying that Parkin had probably seen his shadow in the moonlight. There had never been a murder or a suicide in Goodhue, and everybody knew that only violent and unnatural deaths precipitated a ghost. If there really was a ghost, it must be a stranger to the community.

But the timid ladies of the town were taking no chances. If they had to be out after dark in the vicinity of the churchyard they arranged to be escorted by a fearless male.

Thomas McNamara was not among the ranks of the brave. Two weeks after Parkin's ghost sighting, McNamara had his own frightening encounter with the specter. He was returning home from a dance late at night. When he passed the orchard, a ghostly figure sidled up to him and began behaving exactly as it had with Parkin. He panicked.

"I turned around to talk to him," said McNamara, "but I didn't like his appearance so I left."

Tom Riley also met the ghost late one night at the edge of the graveyard, a few blocks from the church. There, among the dark and silent tombstones, marched a pale form. Riley ran all the way to the main street of town, shouting that he'd seen Tunis Parkin's ghost. Had he? Some folks claimed it was only Fred Frederickson's white cow.

One night Harriet "Pete" Hintz, Florence Taylor and Margaret Clever were passing the orchard when a blood-curdling scream issued from the trees. Harriet fainted. But since she was given to frequent fainting spells, the townspeople disputed the women's report.

At eleven o'clock on a different night someone saw the ghost bobbing up and down and gyrating among the trees. Investigators later found Joyce Shelstad, a delivery boy from the grocery store, contorted over the parish clothesline. He had a lug of peaches to deliver and, finding no one at home at the parish house, was simply killing time in the fidgety ways peculiar to the young.

And so it went. Wherever people gathered during the long Indian summer days and nights, they spoke of the ghost. And nearly every day brought reports of new and terrifying encounters.

Finally the marshal decided to act. As chief official responsible for the maintenance of law and order, T. W. Taylor knew it was up to him to rid the town of the bothersome being. The plan was simple—he and Tunis Parkin would hide in a thicket near the orchard and nab the ghost as it passed.

Parkin wasn't enthused. But on the appointed night he and the marshal scrunched low in the bushes, watching, waiting. Unbeknown to Marshal Taylor, the armed forces of Goodhue also were deployed in the shrubbery directly opposite the ghost hunters. Parkin had alerted his friends to the ambush, and they had gathered up all the small artillery in the town.

The evening was dark and quiet and time itself seemed to stand still. For the first couple of hours Parkin and Marshal Taylor sat side by side, the latter fixing his gaze upon the dark orchard. Suddenly, a howl split the silence, an agonized cry like that of a wounded animal in pain.

Marshal Taylor was ready. He jumped up, groped his way through the maze of trees. He found the culprit. Two gnarled limbs of a prized apple tree, scraping against each other, produced the wild wailings when the wind stirred them. The musketeers, hearing the marshal, thought he was the ghost, but caution prevailed and no shots were fired.

In the gray dawn, Tunis Parkin and Marshal Taylor emerged from the bushes. The marshal, on cramped legs, limped down the street, muttering and wheezing as he went. Parkin, beside him, peered anxiously around every street corner for a glimpse of his friends. Finding them nowhere in sight, he decided they had crept away in the darkness.

The ghost evidently melted away too, frightened by the threat of fire power or the presence of the marshal in the bushes. Although Tunis Parkin whistled his way home from his girl's house every evening that fall, he never again met the specter.

THE PHANTOM MINER

Fourteen-year-old Frank Hrvatin, Jr., would never forget the date—February 5, 1924. On that blustery morning he shivered in the dry house of the Milford manganese mine as he removed his street clothes and climbed into his slicker and waterproof boots. Because of a high water table in the area, the mines were wet most of the time. But young Frank didn't mind; he was glad to be working instead of going to school. He toiled at the 175-foot level, shoveling dirt that remained after timbermen had erected cribbing in newly-opened drifts.

At the bottom of the 200-foot shaft, Clinton Harris, the skip-tender, operated the electric hoist which dumped ore from the ore cars into the bucket, or skip, which was then raised to the surface, emptied and sent back down. Two skips were in use, each counterbalancing the other. Harris was substituting that day for Harvey Rice, the regular skip-tender, who had called in sick.

That February afternoon, just after three o'clock, a crew of miners blasted a cut near Foley's Pond which abutted a portion of the mine. A terrific wind rushed through the mine, knocking down many of the men. Suddenly, the electric lights went out. Someone tripped the circuit breaker, the lights came on briefly, then they went off again. And again. And a third time as well.

Then young Frank heard the roar of water and saw it spilling down a tunnel. "The lake is coming in! The lake is coming in!" he cried, running for safety.

On his race for the shaft, Frank met old Matt Kangas, a veteran miner. Kangas ran as hard as he could, but by the time he reached the ladder, the elderly miner could barely climb. Hrvatin got behind Kangas on the ladder, jumped between the old man's legs and boosted him up rung by rung.

The last man up the ladder was soaked to the waist and encased in mud when he staggered to safety. Some of the miners were slammed against the walls of the mine tunnels and crushed to death by the terrific impact of rushing air; others, caught by the wall of water, drowned. In fifteen minutes it was all over. Of the fifty men on the shift, only seven lived.

Clinton Harris, the skip-tender, died at the foot of the shaft. He apparently could have escaped, but chose to remain at his post. Standing next to the ladder, Harris pulled on the whistle cord in order to warn miners on the upper levels. For four and a half hours, after silt had closed the shaft, the bell he tended rang incessantly. Whether Harris's body had caught in the rope or whether he had tied it to himself was never known. Workmen from the engine room finally disconnected the bell, silencing the last voice from the mine.

The Milford survivors fell exhausted and gasping on the frozen ground where they were rescued by men rushing from the mine office. Young Frank Hrvatin stood by the shaft for three hours, staring down into the black, churning water. His father, Frank Sr., was entombed below.

Within minutes word of the disaster was out. The village siren in nearby Crosby blew for hours, as did locomotive whistles, summoning families to the mine. Some residents stood on the shore of Foley's Pond and watched with horror as the water level went down, the ice on the surface sinking further still as the water beneath poured into the mine. Others gathered silently by the entrance to the shaft, aware that those miners who had not escaped would *never* come out of the mine alive. Clusters of new widows eased their pain by linking arms and walking all night, their bright shawls shielding their heads and faces from the biting wind and thin, sharp flakes of snow.

By midnight, mine-clearing operations were under way. In the sub-zero temperature, men took turns operating the giant pumps that sucked out 12,000 gallons of water and slime each minute. Yet, water continued to pour into the mine, filling the small drifts and cross-workings. The Crow Wing County mine inspector said he doubted that most of the bodies would ever be found.

For a while it seemed he might be right. Pumping crews worked for twelve days to drain Foley's Pond; it took three months to drain the mine. Then mud had to be shoveled by hand from the clogged mine drifts before the bodies of the victims could be retrieved. Nine months later the bodies were brought out. The Milford mine collapse was the worst disaster on Minnesota's iron range.

Yet, when the mine reopened, many miners signed up to go underground again. Manganese was in great demand by the steel industry and mine owners were guaranteeing steady work to every man who wanted it. Most did. And, of course, in almost every case, mining was the only job the men of Milford knew.

But not a miner on the entire Cuyuna Range was prepared for the horror that lay in the bowels of the Milford mine on opening day. Not only was there the lingering stench of decomposed flesh, but there was also something even more repulsive. At the base of the shaft at the 200-foot level, the men's carbide lamps shone upon the translucent form of Clinton Harris! The ghost's bony fingers clutched the side rail of the ladder, its vacant eyes gazing upward. The whistle cord was still knotted around the ghost's waist.

The miners staggered back.

Suddenly, the phantom whistle screamed through the dark, winding tunnels.

The terrified men scrambled up the ladder. They never looked back as they climbed toward the surface.

And not a single one of them ever re-entered the Milford mine.

The survivors of the Milford mine disaster are all deceased, but their story lives on. And so may the ghost of their dead comrade.

THE HOUSE ON SUMMIT AVENUE

Howling shattered the midnight air, trembled in the frozen treetops, then subsided. Again. And again. A man parted the velvet drapes at his window and peered out. The house next door hulked in darkness, the bone-chilling cries coming from somewhere within. The neighbor called the St. Paul Police Department.

Patrolman Jerry Dolan and his partner sped to the address given: 476 Summit Avenue, a Romanesque-style mansion on a boulevard of grand old Victorian homes in St. Paul, Minnesota.

The officers parked their squad car and turned on the spotlight. The light traveled slowly over the red sandstone walls of the darkened house, but revealed nothing out of the ordinary. No person or animal seemed to be on the premises. The patrolmen left their car, went to the back door of the house and pushed it open. Standing on the threshold, they swept the room with their lights. Two steps led down into a combination utility-laundry room whose ceiling was webbed with clotheslines.

In a far corner of the room crouched a young man, black hair disheveled, eyes wild with fright. He wore only undershorts. He crossed his arms over his bare chest and shivered uncontrollably.

The officers leaped toward him. Just then the howling rose again. Officer Dolan, recalling that February night of 1965, said, "I could feel my hair stand on end."

A quick search revealed no other occupant in the house, but there was no time for a thorough investigation. The young man must be taken care of immediately.

What had happened?

"I have seen death!" he cried over and over again, staring at a pentagram (a five-pointed star used in Devil worship) painted on the floor. The patrolmen wrapped him in blankets and rushed him to the nearest hospital. The examining physician found no evidence of physical trauma, but told the officers the man was in deep shock. The officers learned later that he was a university student caring for the house in the absence of the owner, Carl L. Weschke.

Chauncey W. Griggs, a wholesale grocery tycoon, built the mansion in 1883. Its twenty-four rooms are high-ceilinged and cavernous, the dark woodwork casting an aura of gloom on the sunniest day. Griggs, however, didn't stay long. He soon grew restless in his business and sought greater challenges. After four years, he sold his home and moved to the west coast where he established lumber and transportation companies.

During its 100-year existence, the house has been used variously as a private residence and as an apartment house. It once housed an art school. It's reputed to be the most notoriously haunted house in St. Paul, and changes hands so often that one observer remarked, "It's like a hot potato."

Over the years, each family would move in, spend thousands of dollars on furnishings and the hiring of servants, and leave within a year or two. Records, of course, do not disclose the reasons for the rapid turnover.

But the tales of the hauntings in the house can be traced to its early years. In 1915 a young maid, despondent over a love affair, supposedly hanged herself near the fourth-floor landing. Since her death, her presence has been strongly felt by many people, including those who know nothing of the history of the house. Visitors have sometimes fallen on the stairs near that top landing, or felt an uneasy sense of foreboding while climbing the staircase. The ghostly maid, however, is not alone. Apparently she shares the house with other apparitions.

The ghost of a gardener named Charles Wade is believed to return to the house to consult books in the library. When he lived, he kept the grounds in beautiful and immaculate condition.

Roma Harris, a St. Paul spiritualist-medium, once visited the house and saw, clairvoyantly, a general in a blue uniform with gold trim. Griggs was an officer during the Civil War. Had he returned to check up on his home?

Roma also felt the shadowy presence of a teenage girl named Amy who had often played the piano in the house. It is unclear whether Amy lived in the house at one time or was a frequent visitor. The psychic said the girl died young.

"There has been much sorrow here, a lot of suffering," Roma said.

No documentation of these stories is available, but the tales persist. Footsteps resound on empty staircases. Doors open and close by themselves. Rasping coughs come from behind closed doors of unoccupied rooms. Light bulbs shatter. And heavy drapes swing when no one is near them.

In 1939, the mansion was donated to the St. Paul Gallery and School of Art by the Roger B. Shephard family. A skylight was installed on the upper floor and painting classes were offered to the public. But teachers and students felt nervous in the house. They sensed presences walking among them or stopping to peer over their shoulders as if to study the half-completed works on their easels.

Malcolm Lein, who directed the gallery from 1947 to 1964, told a newsman that he personally never saw or heard anything unusual in the mansion, but he could not discount the reports of others.

"These people were sound, educated and well-read," Lein said. "Yet many had the feeling of some kind of supernatural or unknown thing in the building."

In the early 1950s, Dr. Delmar Kolb, a military intelligence officer in World War II, joined the teaching staff. He was a lawyer as well as an artist. At first he lived in the quiet and comfortable carriage house behind the mansion. Sometime later he moved into a front basement apartment in the house. It was far from comfortable.

"One night I felt two dead fingers on my forehead," Dr. Kolb said. "I was in a cold sweat. I reached for the light, but when I turned it on there was a blue flash and then the room was dark." He did not sleep the rest of the night.

Two nights later, Dr. Kolb opened a kitchen cupboard door to get a paper bag. The bag leaped off the shelf. "It took three hops across the floor and stopped," he said. "I thought there was a mouse inside the bag. But there was no mouse—and no draft." Dr. Kolb went on to bed. He was awakened shortly by the presence of a thin man in a black suit and top hat standing at the foot of the bed. At first Dr. Kolb thought it was a costumed intruder. It wasn't. As he watched, the figure evaporated through a solid brick wall.

Dr. Kolb left St. Paul in 1959 and two college students moved into his apartment. In the middle of the first night, one young man awoke. Usually a sound sleeper, he had no idea of what had roused him. He neither saw nor heard anything in the room. But then he looked up. The head of a child floated in the air above his bed.

In the morning, the student asked the staff if anyone had noticed anything peculiar about that apartment. He had no way of knowing about Dr. Kolb's experiences in that bedroom.

Meanwhile, another student had moved into an apartment in the rear of the building. He too was shaken out of a deep sleep one night. The head of a man floated back and forth across the ceiling of the room! Was it perhaps a reflection? The student didn't think so; he claimed that the apparition moved in controlled fashion, staring down at him. The student was never able to describe the features of the disembodied head, but he was quite certain of the reality of his experience. He knew it was *not* imagination.

Was Chauncey Griggs making another check of his old homestead? Had Charles Wade, the gardener, returned? Or was something else in that room?

The St. Paul Gallery and School of Art occupied the mansion for twenty-five years. Then the new Arts and Sciences Center was built in St. Paul and the mansion was put up for sale. In 1964 Carl L. Weschke, a publisher of occult books, bought the house to use as both his office and home.

Weschke ordered painting and repair work done before he moved in, and often stopped by the house to check on progress. One day he found a window open on an upper floor and closed it. The next day it was open. Again he closed it. The workmen said they hadn't touched it. After repeatedly finding the window open, Weschke had it nailed shut. On his next visit it was open!

A workman once told Weschke that he'd seen a shadowy figure upstairs. The only other person in the house at that time was a workman one floor below.

On a number of occasions after Weschke moved into the house, he heard odd noises at night—footsteps padding through the hallways and up and down the staircases and doors slamming shut. He always sensed a restless presence, he told an interviewer, but was not afraid because he believed in some kind of world beyond the one we live in.

One fall afternoon in 1967, he was working in his library. Needing a break, he pushed his chair away from his desk and got up. There in the doorway stood the figure of a man. He wore a dark suit. His face was long and thin and his hair bushy white. Weschke recalled that the figure waited about thirty seconds before fading away. Could this have been the thin man in a black suit seen a decade earlier by Dr. Kolb?

A lady once called Weschke to tell him she had worked in the house as a girl and had seen the ghost of a young woman in the fourth-floor hallway. The butler, she said, had also seen the apparition.

Weschke wasn't surprised. He feels that any traumatic event, such as a suicide, releases a great deal of energy that can last for years. Weschke himself once fell on the back staircase after feeling himself being picked up by some force and tossed into the air.

During the last week of February, 1969, veteran reporters from the *St. Paul Pioneer Press* arranged to spend a night in the house to gather material for a series of articles they were producing on ghosts. Weschke welcomed staff writers Don Giese and Bill Farmer and photographer Flynn Ell and briefed them on the legal history of the house. As the visitors sat with their host in his study, they noticed one of the owner's three cats, a Siamese, crouched on its master's desk and stared up at the ceiling. The men heard no sounds, but the cat kept looking up.

After a tour, the newsmen decided to stay in the large top-floor room with its vast skylight, just off the back landing where the maid had hanged herself fifty-four years earlier, and where most of the supernatural activity seemed to be centered.

Weschke retired to his second-floor bedroom with its private bath, and said he would not be leaving his quarters. He was unusually tired after an eighteen-hour work day.

Photographer Ell set up two cameras. One was loaded with regular film and fitted with a wide-angle lens; the other held infra-red film that would record heat changes if anything invisible to the human eye appeared. Giese and Farmer turned on their tape recorder. Then the three men sat in a circle beneath the one shaded light in the room. Beyond the doorway a bright light burned, illuminating the hall and the top of the staircase.

Within a short time, all three men were overcome by feelings of distress. Giese and Farmer wrote later: "As newsmen we have each been in hundreds of situations that held far greater risks of possible physical danger. There was no sign of danger in that room. We had no reason to feel apprehensive.

"Yet each of us soon reported feelings of general uneasiness—a definite sense of discomfort we couldn't define. Each was especially anxious about the hall—brightly illuminated—and the staircase leading to the floors below."

They never heard anything approach, but suddenly one of Weschke's cats appeared in the room and went directly to reporter Giese. He stroked her back. Then she walked to the doorway, twitched her tail and looked back into the room. Giese walked toward her.

She moved to the top of the stairs and again looked back, as if urging Giese to follow. He did. But when the cat went on down to the first landing, Giese could not follow. Standing under the bright light of the hallway and peering over the railing at the top of the staircase, he was overcome by fear. He stepped back into the room.

Ell went out into the hallway. He returned.

Farmer went into the hallway. He returned.

All three men agreed that *nothing* could induce them to go down the staircase alone.

At twenty minutes past one in the morning, five distinct thumps were heard just beyond the doorway to the room. They sounded like heavy footsteps. The men sat listening, waiting, eyes fixed on the lighted hall. They saw nothing. They heard nothing more.

At three-thirty-five, the stairs creaked. Something was coming up. But then the noise stopped. Giese went alone into the hallway and stared down over the railing to the landings below. He saw nothing, but when he returned to the room he told Farmer and Ell that he knew *something* was on those stairs.

Five minutes later the stairs creaked again. Then silence.

At four o'clock the men packed up their equipment, descended the stairs together and left by the back door.

Giese and Farmer wrote: "We all agreed on one thing. There is no prize on earth that could get us to spend a single night in that great stone house that seems to speak in sounds we cannot explain or understand."

For nearly three-quarters of a century those sounds have signalled the wanderings of unreal presences: the maid who climbs to her invisible hanging rope on the fourth-floor landing, the gardener who riffles the pages of books in the library, the thin man in the black suit who slips in and out of rooms by day and by night.

What do they want? Why are they here? A psychic hints they may all be victims of past tragedies, trapped forever in this place of sorrow.

The house still changes hands regularly, but the present owners do not believe in ghosts or in psychic phenomena of any kind and refuse to speak of their experiences.

Meanwhile, the mansion remains cast in shadow by great trees moaning in the wind and by rumors of things unknown, unknowable behind the silent sandstone walls.

MARY SHARPE

Fourteen-year-old Mary Sharpe was floating in the air. Beautiful blue clouds drifted past her in a limitless expanse of sky.

The clouds turned lavender and pink, then golden. And out of this dazzling light came a stranger. His face was framed by brown hair flecked with gold, and although he didn't speak he somehow impressed upon Mary that his name was Edwin Emeny. Stretching out his arms, he placed them gently beneath the child. Mary had never seen him before and she had no idea what he was doing there in this place of ineffable peace and loveliness.

Then she turned to look back at the room she had left. It was so far below that everything appeared in miniature, yet each detail was amazingly clear. Mary quickly saw that something was different. Her head was now at the foot of the bed near the window. Her mother and two other people stood beside the bed. The concern in their faces, especially the look of resignation and despair on her mother's face, drew Mary back to her body.

Seconds later, Mary wriggled her shoulders, opened her eyes, and asked for a drink of water. A breeze blowing through the open window cooled her face and she seemed to understand, without asking, that her mother had placed her in that position to benefit from the moving air. Mary sipped the water, then drifted into a natural sleep.

The doctors attending her—Dr. Cora Emeny and Dr. Henry Fullerton—were relieved. They felt that the crisis had passed for the little child from Stillwater, Minnesota, who had lapsed into a coma and come close to death on that hot July afternoon in 1903.

During her convalescence Mary often described her out-of-body flight, but no one paid any attention. Then one day she asked Dr. Cora Emeny who Edwin Emeny was.

The doctor asked Mary where she had learned that name. Mary described the man and her meeting with him. She said he resembled Dr. Emeny.

The doctor was shaken. Turning to Mary's mother, she said, "My brother Edwin has been dead for fifteen years. I've never mentioned him in this house. How could the child have known even his name?

How indeed?

Mary had no answer. Her "trip" had been sudden. One moment she was tossing feverishly on her bed; the next moment she was traveling through a strange place far removed from the world she knew.

"You were dreaming, dear," said Mrs. Sharpe, soothing her daughter's forehead with a cool cloth.

"No, Mother," Mary insisted, "it was *not* a dream."

Although Mrs. Sharpe refused to believe in the reality of the child's experience, she could not explain how Mary was able to describe a man whose previous existence was unknown to her. Can the mind function consciously outside the physical body, even for a limited time? Experts say it can under certain conditions.

Mary's unique and profound experience changed her life. Inspired by the intimation that something within her might at death be able to escape the body and soar away, she wanted to share it with everyone. At first, one or two listened, but then they turned away, as though she were daft. Nevertheless she lived her life comforted by what she had learned from her out-of-body excursion.

THE RETURN OF GRANDMA JENSEN

Jimmy Jensen knew something was wrong with the house. While building it in 1893, he had felt uneasy in the upstairs southwest bedroom. A presence shadowed him, seeming to peer over his shoulder as he worked. He would turn around, but find no one there. When he completed the house, his family was too frightened to use that bedroom. It stood empty during the fifty-three years they lived there!

The rambling farmhouse, graced by peaks and porches whose angular lines were softened by ancient trees, straddles a hilltop outside Albert Lea, Minnesota.

It occupies the site of a log cabin, the original land grant having been signed by President Abraham Lincoln in 1862.

The Jensens moved out of the house in 1946, and during the next eighteen years it had a procession of fourteen owners, perplexing the neighbors. They offered friendship and hospitality to each new family, but for some reason none of the newcomers stayed long. A few local farmers wondered aloud if something was wrong with the house.

By the time Dick and Anita Borland toured the house there was a lot wrong with it, but nothing that could not be remedied. Or so they thought. The house had been vacant from 1960 to 1963, and broken windows, peeling paint and sagging porches signaled its forlorn condition. But the dilapidation failed to deter the Borlands, and they tackled the renovation enthusiastically. The house would provide welcome spaciousness for their nine children. In 1964 the family moved in.

Shortly before the move, Anita and her sisters-in-law, Kay Arnold and Mavis Pearson, were cleaning up the yard.

Suddenly, Kay shouted, "Look! Your mother's upstairs!"

Anita looked up and waved to the figure standing on the upstairs porch outside the southwest bedroom. It certainly did resemble her mother, and Anita was pleased she had come by.

The three women hurried into the house. They found the southwest bedroom empty. No one was on the porch. Or in the entire house!

"It raised the hair on our necks," Anita recalled.

Anita and Mavis finally decided they must have been seeing things. But Kay was so upset she never went upstairs again.

Seven months after the Borlands moved in, Rebecca Borland and her brother Richard met a woman one morning in the upstairs hallway. She was tall and thin and wore a flowered print dress with an apron; she seemed to be searching for something. In the dim light the children thought it was their mother.

"Help me!" cried the lady. "Please help me."

Her sepulchral voice chilled them. The frightened youngsters plunged downstairs. Their mother stood in the kitchen. She was *not* wearing a flowered dress. She was *not* wearing an apron. And she had *not* been upstairs!

Anita thought the children had imagined the figure in the hall. But the mysterious lady returned, hovering near the closet in the upstairs southwest bedroom. A number of the Borland children saw her there or felt her presence. They described her as a tall, thin woman, thirty-eight or forty years of age.

One August night young Elizabeth Borland was sleeping in that bedroom when she was awakened by a sawing noise close to her bed. Thinking that her father was working in the adjoining room, she tapped on the wall. Then, as a cold breeze blew across her neck, the covers lifted off the bed. Elizabeth grabbed the sheet. Peering over its edge, she saw a woman enter the closet and dissolve. Elizabeth fled downstairs and slept on a couch in the family room for the rest of the night.

But the ghost returned. Elizabeth was sharing the bedroom one night with her sister, Rebecca, when both awakened to see the ghost standing in the closet beneath a glowing lamp, in spite of the fact that there was no light fixture in that closet! The ghost walked out of the closet and shook the bed. Rebecca described her as the same tall, thin woman, wearing a flowered print house dress and apron.

As a teenager, another daughter, Theresa, occasionally liked to read in the southwest bedroom. Stretched out with her book, completely alone, she often felt a cold hand on her foot. Invisible fingers would close around her instep, then jerk her foot back and forth. Theresa told her mother that if she continued reading she was all right, but if she pulled her foot away, the jerking became more insistent. Theresa learned to ignore the sensation, but she never liked to be alone in the house.

The ghost who came out of the closet also moved into other rooms of the house and, curiously, most of the phenomena occurred with a number of people present. The most frightening incident happened in 1981 in the upstairs southeast bedroom. Seventeen-year-old Christopher Borland had gone to bed early. But every time he dropped off to sleep, someone would bounce on his bed and jar him awake. He thought it was his kid sister, fifteen-year-old Nancy.

"Hey, cut it out!" he yelled.

He straightened out his six-foot, six-inch frame and pushed with his foot. Something pushed back. Chris leaped out of bed and ran screaming from the room.

He never again slept in that bedroom.

The Borland children, however, were not the first young people to live with an upstairs closet ghost. Anita once met a cousin of the Jimmy Jensen family who had worked on the place during the Depression years for room, board and $1.25 a week.

The man told Anita that one night a woman came into the upstairs southwest bedroom where he was sleeping and pulled the covers up over him. In the morning he asked his aunt about it, but she said she hadn't gone upstairs during the night. After the figure appeared in his bedroom on three more occasions, he refused to sleep in the house. He preferred to walk the six-mile round trip each day to do the chores.

Renters who lived in the house before the Borlands bought it wouldn't sleep upstairs either, except for an unusually brave sixteen-year-old boy who also claimed a woman came in and covered him at night and walked up and down the hallway.

The ghostly lady was never seen downstairs.

Something *else* was. One morning Anita went into the kitchen and saw an old woman standing in the place where a pantry had once been. Anita thought it was a neighbor soliciting for a charity and offered her a cup of coffee. Suddenly, Anita realized the woman was not of flesh and blood. Watching the apparition fade away, she thought it resembled the one that had appeared on the upstairs porch.

During the next eighteen months, Anita saw the old woman on three more occasions.

"She's so nondescript you don't even notice how she looks," Anita said, "and she doesn't frighten you."

Yet one time Anita *was* frightened. While she napped in a downstairs bedroom, alone in the house, something she couldn't see pinned her to the bed. After she broke free, she was so shaken that she got dressed and went to town.

Three other family members had similar experiences in that downstairs room. "If I'd been the only one to experience the incident," said Anita, "I would think I was hallucinating."

In spite of all these reported encounters, Anita's husband, Dick, was skeptical of the supernatural. But one morning as he sat in the kitchen watching his wife prepare breakfast, he heard footsteps in the southwest bedroom and the rattling of the light fixture. He thought they were alone in the house. Anita heard the footsteps too and figured it was one of the children's friends, brought home late at night. She never knew how many youngsters would show up for breakfast.

The footsteps continued, but no one appeared.

"Who's up there?" Anita called.

Silence.

She and Dick went up to check, searching every bedroom, and found no one. Still, Dick refused to believe in ghosts. "Maybe the noise was caused by somebody drilling some place," he suggested. Anita said that during their twenty years in the house something unexplainable had occurred in every room except the master bedroom.

In an attempt to identify the ghosts, Anita talked to Jimmy Jensen's daughter, Alpha, a retired teacher, who was born in the house in 1906. She remembered it as a happy place. The only discordant note was Grandma Jensen who later died in the house. Alpha remembered her grandmother as a loving person, but a harsh disciplinarian. When Alpha's parents were gone and the children wandered into the off-limits pantry, the older woman would shut the door so they couldn't get out.

At other times, Grandma Jensen punished the children by sending them to a back room to sit on a narrow ledge around a water-filled cistern. This room later became the downstairs bedroom in which Anita was held down by a mysterious force. From descriptions that Alpha provided, Anita suspected the downstairs ghost was old Mrs. Jensen. She has not been around in recent years.

But who is the upstairs closet ghost who lingers in that southwest bedroom? Is it the same presence that frightened Jimmy Jensen nearly a hundred years ago? No one knows for sure, but some say the site itself is haunted. In that case, the ghost may be a revenant from pioneer days when a log cabin occupied the land. Could a mother who died young be "caring" for the children she thinks are her own?

Experts believe that violent or untimely deaths generate energy, or psychic imprints, that can last for a long time. If that is so, the ghost who came out of the closet may be a permanent lodger in the Borland home.

WINDEGO OF THE NORTH

Today the legend of the windego is unknown to most residents of northern Minnesota. Yet for untold numbers of years, people believed the awesome being, with the star on its forehead, stalked the villages of Roseau County. Of those who saw it, some felt terror, others dread, for the windego *always* foreshadowed death.

In the early 1900s, people still respected the legend. It was the first day of spring in 1904—a day when anything might happen. That's what Jesse Nelson told his little sister, Edna, as they hopscotched over the patches of snow in the old logging road near Roseau. The jack-in-the-pulpit might be up in the maple grove where they grew thick and close. The catbird might be building its nest again in the shrubs behind the schoolhouse. And Miss Anderson just *might* dismiss school early.

Thinking of these delights, Jesse did not see the being until Edna screamed. Ahead of them, in the middle of the road, stood a giant. He wore dazzling white. A large, bright star shimmered in the middle of his forehead. And he cast a long shadow.

Jesse fell back, reaching for his sister's hand. "It's ... it's the ghost!" he stammered, his eyes widening. The *windego*. That's what the Chippewa called it.

The children scrambled into the woods, and never stopped running until they reached school. Edna told everyone what had happened. She and her brother were the envy of the young children; not everyone has met a real ghost. But the older children were fearful; they knew that the windego meant someone in the community would soon die.

Three days later, a young brave in the nearby Indian village of Ross dropped dead. He had never even been ill.

A month later, Jesse and Edna Nelson saw the ghost again, this time on their way home from school. It appeared in the same place on the road. Again, a sudden death followed.

The children's father, Jake, discussed the incident with Sam Mickinock, his next door neighbor and a

Mandan Indian. The two families visited back and forth regularly. Sam Mickinock enjoyed the company of white men and handled their stock and chores when they were ill or away from home. Mickinock recalled that six years earlier, in 1898, the windego had also appeared twice within a short time. In both instances, unexpected deaths followed. The Indian said the ghost had been seen for so long that his people had no tales of its first visit.

One day, Mrs. Mickinock's elderly mother, who lived with them, became ill. On the third day, she rose from her bed and, with the help of her granddaughter, Anna, managed to reach the yard. Anna had placed an easy chair in the shade of an apple tree and the old woman eased herself into it. Her eyes were heavy, her cheeks flushed. Jake Nelson's mother, his sister, Kate, and a Mrs. Warner were gathered in the yard and the sick woman, too weak to talk, raised a hand in greeting. Anna, who adored her grandmother and never tired of hearing the legends of her people, sat on the grass at her grandmother's feet.

Suddenly, the sky darkened and a cool breeze chilled the air. Anna stood up and scanned the horizon. With outstretched arm, she pointed south across the fields. "Grandma die soon," she said quietly. "See windego."

The guests fell silent and looked in the direction the girl pointed. Striding across the prairie was a tall being, dressed all in white. It skirted a grove of trees on a ridge and vanished.

Mrs. Mickinock's mother died the following morning.

The next year, Jake Nelson hired Mickinock to help him with the haying. The two men worked side by side through the long hot days, and when they were finished, Mickinock jumped on his pony and rode up into Canada to join his family's hunting party.

The next day, he killed a moose and his wife built a fire to dry the meat on a stifling hot, airless day. Becoming overheated, she felt faint, even when she moved away from the fire. Her skin felt dry, her lips parched. She recalled, from a previous visit, that a spring was not far away and set off on the trail.

At the spring, she knelt in the damp soil and splashed the icy water over her face, cupped her hands beneath the flow and drank greedily. It was pleasantly cool and she lay down on a mossy carpet beneath a canopy of tree leaves. She may have fallen asleep. But when she got up to return to camp, she felt chilled.

The next day the family packed up and returned home, camping for a time on the banks of the Roseau River above the village of Ross.

On the third afternoon following their return, Jake Nelson was alone in the yard of the Mickinock's house. Mickinock had been called indoors to tend to his ill wife. Nelson happened to be looking south when he saw the dreaded figure—striding along the edge of a swamp. It appeared to be fifteen feet tall and was clothed in white. Nelson shivered in the hot sun, and as he watched, the ghost turned toward the west. It stumbled several times, but each time recovered and ran on for about a quarter of a mile. Finally, it disappeared behind a grove of trees.

In the morning, Mrs. Mickinock died.

Nelson couldn't explain what he saw, but he never doubted the reality of his experience. "Whatever it may have been it was not a hallucination or superstitious fears in the dark, for I saw it in broad daylight."

Some say the windego still roams the farms and prairies of northern Minnesota. It's these same folks who steer clear of his path, lest the death of a loved one follow quickly on the heels of an encounter with the dreaded windego.

THE LEVITATION OF ARCHIE COLLINS

Police files in any community contain reports of missing persons, most of whom are only temporarily lost or delayed. They either return on their own or are eventually located by a search party.

But occasionally a person disappears for no accountable reason, and is never seen again. It's as if he or she had vanished into thin air. And that's exactly what Herman the Hypnotist and Archie Collins did. In front of several hundred persons, they vanished from the stage of a theater.

The year was 1872. Minneapolis was celebrating its incorporation as a city. Lampposts were decked with bunting, the streets reverberated with the sounds of marching bands and carnivals, and residents keen on revelry partied late into the night.

In a field south of the city, Copson's Traveling Theater pitched its tent for a week-long schedule of performances. Actors roamed the city streets, delivering handbills and hawking the delights of the repertory tent show.

The ballyhoo wasn't needed. This type of frontier theater was extremely popular throughout the Midwest, and Copson's well-known troupe had a loyal following. Ephraim T. Copson, Jr., whose grandfather had brought the company from New York to the Upper Midwest in 1847, ran the outfit. From early spring until late fall, it played villages in Minnesota, Wisconsin and the Lake Superior coast of Michigan.

On opening night, playgoers from all parts of Minneapolis began arriving early at the tent theater. Three one-act plays were to be presented, with specialty acts in between. During the first intermission, a fat lady would perform on a donkey. During the second, Herman the Hypnotist would entertain. Herman, a German actor whose surname was Aikmann, billed as a performer of amazing feats, had recently joined Copson's Theater.

The crowd, eager and expectant, jostled one another in line at the ticket office. Inside the tent, the canvas chairs in front and the rows of benches toward the rear filled quickly. Children sucked indolently on sticks of candy while their parents munched peanuts and popcorn. Heat from the oil lamps intensified the oppressive and pungent odors of food and damp trodden grass, but few people seemed uncomfortable. Then, minutes before curtain time, the show sold out and late arrivals were turned away.

On the raised platform at the front of the tent, the first play began. Spectators cheered their favorite performers and soon the unfolding drama absorbed everyone.

When it was over, the fat lady inspired raucous laughter; then the second play began. It was received with even more enthusiasm than the first, the thunderous applause perhaps based less on merit and execution than on the anticipation of seeing Herman the Hypnotist.

Earlier in the evening, however, Herman had been taken ill and in the-show-must-go-on style, the fat lady had agreed to repeat her act. She stood backstage, waiting to go on, when Herman suddenly appeared, rudely bumped her aside and swept past, never even acknowledging her presence. She felt both offended and startled. He was usually gracious. Yet she was glad the German felt well enough to do his act after all.

On stage a firecracker exploded and out of its acrid smoke Herman appeared. Tall and thin and clad in funereal black, he resembled an animated exclamation mark. Dark eyes flashed in a cavernous face powdered the color of chalk.

Fingering his string tie, the hypnotist strode to one side of the platform and called for a volunteer. Men nudged one another in the audience, but no one stepped forward.

"I must have a volunteer," repeated Herman, his words edged with contempt. "I cannot do my act until someone joins me. It is harmless. No one will get hurt."

He surveyed the audience and finally a girl seated in the third row got up and mounted the steps to the makeshift stage.

The hypnotist bowed and directed the girl to a chair in the center of the stage. "You will relax and go to sleep. Then you will do exactly what I tell you."

The girl had other things in mind. She leered up at the actor and made a crude remark.

He glared at her.

Suddenly a huge ball of sticky taffy soared through the air and landed on the girl's head. The performer spun on his heels. "Who did that?" he screamed in rage.

People stared at their shoe tops; silence enveloped the auditorium.

When the hypnotist stopped trembling, he waved the girl off. Facing the audience again, he sneered, "Maybe the clown who threw the candy would care to assist me."

All eyes riveted on Archie Collins, who sat in the center of the front row. Catching the cue, the hypnotist began taunting the young man.

Collins blushed and squirmed in his seat as the crowd chanted, "Archie! Archie!" The chanting grew louder and feet began stomping.

Finally Archie could stand it no longer. He leaped from his seat and jumped to the stage to sit in the chair vacated by the girl.

Murmurs of speculation rippled through the audience. Collins, while a likeable and well-meaning fellow, was a daredevil with a strong will. Surely a poor candidate to be hypnotized. Yet, in less than a minute the young man was nodding as the hypnotist droned, "You are now asleep. Sound asleep. You will do anything I say." He leaned close to Collins. "Remember that. Anything."

Collins sat rigid in the chair.

"Now, rise, rise like a puppet on a string!" The actor's voice trembled with excitement and he stood on tiptoe to emphasize his command.

The audience gasped as Archie Collins rose and hung in midair.

"Rise! Rise!" shouted the hypnotist.

Collins floated out over the front row of chairs.

"It's a trick! Cut him down!" called a guy in the rear of the tent. No one seconded the demand. Most of the playgoers sat numb, electrified, staring with open mouths as Collins floated higher and higher like a leaf carried by the wind.

Then someone shouted, "Hey! Look at the hypnotist!"

The actor had turned into a skeleton, a crazy, crooked smile on the skull and long white bones shining eerily. Was it a trick of the lighting?

Slowly the skeleton levitated itself a foot or two above the stage floor, then disappeared completely.

A man stood up and screamed, "Look!"

All faces turned upwards.

Overhead, Archie Collins's prone body smashed into the top of the tent. The impact spun him around, revealing his battered face. When he hit the roof a second time, the rotted canvas split and Archie Collins vanished into the night sky. He was never seen again.

The audience sat mute, the children wide-eyed with wonder. Finally shuffling feet broke the silence as the bewildered spectators streamed from the theater. The last play never went on.

One of the show's officials went directly to Archie Collins's home to report the young man's disappearance. The family was stunned, Mrs. Collins becoming nearly hysterical with grief. How could her son have been spirited away by some unseen force, in some unknown manner? Mr. Collins called the police who launched an immediate investigation of Copson's Theater.

At the theater site, all was confusion. Actors and actresses, some still in costume, milled around or stood talking quietly in small groups. Knots of spectators lingered in the shadows at the outer edges of the field.

Ephraim Copson, visibly shaken by the events of the evening, told the law enforcement officers that whoever had walked on stage as Herman the Hypnotist was *not* Aikmann. Earlier that evening, Copson said, Ulrich Aikmann, Herman's son, reported that his father had been bothered by food poisoning and would be unable to perform. He had spent the evening in bed, cared for by his wife and by Al Jones, Copson's personal assistant.

Copson stated further that he himself had summoned a doctor for Aikmann and that he had then asked the fat lady to take Aikmann's place.

Police officers questioned the fat lady at length about the man who bumped into her backstage. The poor woman felt somehow at fault. Choking back sobs, she mentioned the performer's unexpected rudeness, but said he had looked a lot like Aikmann.

Who was the imposter? And how did he vanish before the eyes of that Minneapolis audience? And where was Archie Collins? These questions were never answered.

While the truth may never be known in this particular case, a possible explanation of the disappearances can be set forth. They could have been faked by a magician skilled in the use of magic lanterns and limelight (a powerful light that could be directed and focused to create a vast array of optical illusions). Here's how the skeleton act was done in sideshows around that time:

A volunteer stepped into an upright casket placed behind a sheet of glass set at a forty-five degree angle to the stage. (The audience as well as the volunteer were usually unaware of this glass partition.) Bright lights, concealed from the audience, shone upon and in effect blinded the volunteer. At the side of the stage, in total darkness, stood a skeleton in an upright casket placed at right angles to the casket containing the volunteer and to one side of a panel that held a vertical strip of lights.

When, at the same moment, the lights were switched off the volunteer and onto the skeleton, the spectators saw the image of the skeleton in its casket reflected in the sheet of glass. It appeared to be exactly where they had seen the volunteer.

A magician, using similar aids with help from an assistant, could have created his own metamorphosis and disappearance from the stage.

A levitation such as that performed on Archie Collins could be achieved by smoke pictures from a magic lantern—a device consisting of a small metal box with a carbide lamp and colored glass slides—hidden at the rear of the stage. With the tent and most of the stage in darkness, fires were lit in braziers at the front of the stage and chemicals added to the fires to cause columns of smoke to rise.

An assistant to the magician projected onto the smoke a series of slides of a young man in various positions suggesting levitation. As the images flashed by, the movements of the smoke brought them eerily to life. It was to these images that the magician gave his commands, while the volunteer, in this case Archie, left the stage unobserved.

A stooge planted in the audience could have shouted that Archie was going through the roof while appropriate sound effects simulated the noise of ripping canvas. The audience, distracted by the sudden appearance of the skeleton and confused by the smoke images, believed it had actually seen Archie vanishing through the roof of the tent.

Records do not indicate that Archie Collins ever returned to Minneapolis. Perhaps his life was unhappy and he welcomed the opportunity to make an unforgettable departure from his hometown. But who had taken Herman the Hypnotist's place? Were he and Archie in the scheme together? Perhaps the hand is indeed quicker than the eye . . .

Chapter VII.
Missouri

"When St. Louis housewife Pearl Curran sat down to work the Ouija board, she thought it a silly, boring game. Beneath her fingertips the little three-legged pointer moved around the board, stopping at one letter after another, spelling nothing but gibberish. Until July 8, 1913. As Mrs. Curran and her neighbor worked the board, they got this message: 'Many moons ago I lived. Again I come—Patience Worth my name . . .'

For nearly twenty-five years Patience Worth dictated to Mrs. Curran a total of some 4,000,000 words! . . . Her works—5,000 poems, a play, numerous short pieces and several published novels of high literary acclaim—form perhaps the most remarkable case of automatic writing associated with the survival of bodily death . . ."

"PATIENCE WORTH"

PATIENCE WORTH

When St. Louis housewife, Pearl Curran, sat down to work the Ouija board, she thought it a silly, boring pastime. Beneath her fingertips, the little three-legged pointer moved around the board, stopping at one letter after another, spelling nothing but gibberish. Until July 8, 1913. As Mrs. Curran and her neighbor worked the board, they got this message: "Many moons ago I lived. Again I come—Patience Worth my name."

The startled women knew no one by that name. Who was she? Probably no one at all. Mrs. Curran had little interest in the occult and doubted that the dead could make contact with the living through the mechanism of a wooden board. Yet the letters *had* spelled out Patience Worth. At her neighbor's urging, Mrs. Curran asked the sender of the message to tell something about herself. Answers spun across the board and were recorded by Mrs. Curran's mother. Patience indicated that she had lived in Dorsetshire, England, in either 1649 or 1694. She had then moved to America where she was murdered by Indians.

Patience spoke in archaic fashion, using words such as "hast" and "doest," "thee" and "thou." Mrs. Curran was fascinated, and from that day on she spent increasing time with the Ouija board. When the messages started coming faster than anyone could write them down, the housewife realized she didn't need the board at all and weaned herself from it. The sentences were forming in her mind and could be taken down directly as she spoke. Later, a secretary and a stenographer would be employed, although Mrs. Curran would sometimes record the words herself, using first a pencil and then a typewriter.

For nearly twenty-five years Patience Worth dictated to Mrs. Curran a total of some 4,000,000 words! Her works—5,000 poems, a play, numerous short pieces and several published novels of high literary acclaim—form perhaps the most remarkable case of automatic writing associated with the survival of bodily death.

Was there really a discarnate entity speaking from the grave? Or was the writing produced by the unconscious mind of the Missouri housewife? No verification has ever been made of the existence of Patience Worth. Yet experts who studied Pearl Curran doubted that she could have produced the works herself for she was a woman of limited education, with no knowledge of the language used or the history and subject matter developed by Patience Worth.

As a child, Pearl Lenore Pollard seemed quite ordinary. She grew up in Texas, played outdoors a lot and rode a cow to explore the countryside. Her parents, George and Mary, were easy-going and demanded little of their daughter. The little girl's education was mediocre, at best, ending in the eighth grade. She went to Sunday School sporadically, but remembered little of the material presented. Her parents never went to church and Pearl never read the Bible.

Actually, the girl read very little at all. She liked *Black Beauty* and the books of Louisa May Alcott, and she recalled reading Grimm's and Anderson's fairy tales, but she never read more than a few minutes a day. Unlike many children, her imagination seemed undeveloped; she didn't name any of her dolls or pets. Her only real desire was to act on the stage, but she gave up the idea at age twenty-four when she married John Curran.

Pearl's marriage was as uneventful as her childhood, at least until the arrival of Patience Worth when Pearl was thirty-one. Not rich, but idle, Pearl kept a maid, smoked cigarettes and enjoyed the movies. In the evenings, she and her husband often played cards with neighbors. Mrs. Curran seldom read a book, and never bought any; her husband read the daily newspaper. The couple had no opportunity to associate with well-educated, well-traveled people, but appeared to be happy and content in their small, middle-class world.

Never could they have imagined that the fame of Patience Worth would spread far beyond their intimate neighborhood, bringing the larger world to them.

Shortly after Patience made known her presence, the Curran house overflowed with neighbors, all curious about the peculiar events taking place there. A marvelous phenomenon, they said, the likes of which had never been known. When word reached the press, Casper Yost, Sunday editor of the *St. Louis Post-Dispatch*, began publishing articles about Pearl Curran and the intelligent spirit who seemed to be dictating to her. With the publication of his book, *Patience Worth, A Psychic Mystery*, in 1915, the obscure housewife from St. Louis became a celebrity.

The Currans, always gracious and unpretentious people, warmly received all visitors who wished to witness the automatic writing sessions. Authorities in the field of parapsychology came, as well as persons from all over the country who had begun to read and admire the writings of Patience Worth. No one was ever charged a penny for admission to the house, and all writing periods were conducted with openness and candor.

Although Ouija board communications were not new, this marked the first instance when something of literary worth was being produced by such means. That a disembodied literary genius was using a semi-literate housewife as a channel of communication seemed preposterous.

In *The Sorry Tale*, a lengthy novel set in the time of Christ, Patience brought to vivid life Jews, Romans, Greeks and Arabians, revealing accurate knowledge of the political, social and religious conditions of the times. Some regarded the book as the greatest story since the gospels of the life and times of Christ.

A *New York Times* reviewer, aware of the author's identity, wrote:

> "The long, intimate tale is constructed with the precision and accuracy of a master hand. It is a wonderful, a beautiful, and noble book ... one vivid scene after another passes before the reader, pictures from the life of dissipated Rome, as Theia remembers and tells of their lewd horrors, of the shepherds upon the hills, of the men and women of the city, of Herod's palace, of the desert. And through it all goes a sense of life, of reality, of having been seen and lived until all its scenes are familiar."

When *Hope Trueblood*, a novel of Victorian England, was published, the *Athenaeum* reviewer did not realize he was praising a 'psychic' production. He wrote:

"This is a novel of decided promise, written by a new author; the story is noteworthy in more than ordinary measure .... The story is marked by strong individuality, and we should look with interest for further products of the author's pen."

W. T. Allison, a prominent Canadian writer and professor of English literature at the University of Manitoba, was equally impressed, believing the book to be one of the most powerful character novels he had ever read.

In *Telka*, a 70,000-word novel of medieval England, the language is that of Milton's time. There is not a single break into modern speech. Most of the words are of one or two syllables, and ninety percent are of Anglo-Saxon derivation. Mrs. Curran said she didn't know the meaning of many of the words, nor could she recall ever having heard anyone speak in the language she was receiving from Patience. The book was written in thirty-five hours.

Such phenomenal speed of composition was typical. Once, in a single evening, thirty-two short poems were delivered, along with seven witty aphorisms. Sometimes in the same evening, Patience dictated portions of four novels, always resuming the work in each of them at the place she had left off. Pearl took down the words as dictated, often before an assembly of critical guests. There were never any revisions.

Patience never delayed in responding to questions or tasks put to her. Asked to compose a poem upon a certain subject, she would deliver the words so quickly that they had to be taken down in shorthand. Weeks or months later, when asked to reproduce the poem, she recited it without change. Her literary stunts astounded those who witnessed them, for they seemed well beyond the normal limitations of writers.

One night Walter Franklin Prince, chief psychic investigator of the case and a regular visitor at the Curran house, posed a prodigious task. Could Patience deliver a poem on "The Folly of Atheism" while simultaneously producing a dialogue between a wench and a lout at a country fair? (Every two or three lines must alternate between poem and dialogue.) She could and did. Dictation began eight seconds after the request was made.

When she finished, Mrs. Curran said she felt as if her head were in a steel vise, and as if she weren't there, but under gas.

On another evening, Mrs. Curran wrote a letter to Mrs. A. B. Smith of Los Angeles, California, while dictating a poem coming from Patience. The first stanza read as follows:

Will O' The Wisp

"Oh you marshlight, flashing across the marshes,
    beckoning!
Is thy light that I see a beacon to tomorrow?
Give me a sign, oh, you banshee! Give me a sign!
Make tomorrow's question marked against the
    sky
Fitfully, as thy flash, oh you marshlight flashing,
Then shall I be more accustomed to the
    questioning that I live . . ."

"Dear Dotsie:

I am writing you while I write a poem. It is a new trick. Do you like it? See here, honey, my hands are full! I don't like it, honey. It's like baking bread and stirring soup! I am sick of the job. I wish you were here and that we could go over this together. This is a mess of a letter, honey bug. I'm nuts! This is some chase! Slinging slang and purring poetry! Jack is doing his best in this Marathon. This is fine business and I'm up against it.

'Finis' honey, and I call it going some!

Pearl"

Although distraction is evident in the letter, the experiment was considered a success.

Literary critics of the time agreed that Patience Worth was indeed producing remarkable literature, superior in plot, characterization and dialogue to anything else then being published. Reviewers unfailingly praised her splendid vocabulary and use of archaic words.

Curiously, the poems approached modern English, while the novels were written in the vernacular of earlier times. The poems of Patience Worth were as well regarded as her novels, receiving higher ratings that those of Edna St. Vincent Millay, Amy Lowell and Edgar Lee Masters in the 1918 *Anthology of Magazine Verse and Year Book of American Poetry*. Patience herself believed her poems were good. She said of them: "I shall play with words like castinets (sic) . . . I shall set them twinkling like stars . . ."

The following poem is generally considered one of the finest:

The Sounds Unheard By Man
"I have heard the moon's beams
Sweeping the waters, making a sound
Like threads of silver, wept upon.
I have heard the scratch of the
Pulsing stars, and the purring sound
Of the slow moon as she rolled across
The Night. I have heard the shadows
Slapping the waters, and the licking
Sound of the wave's edge as it sinks
Into the sand upon the shore.

I have heard the sunlight as it pierced
The gloom with a golden bar, which
Whirred in a voice of myriad colors.
I have heard the sound which lay
Between the atoms which danced in the
Golden bar. I have heard the sound

Of the leaves reclining upon their
Cushions of air, and the swish of the willow
Tassels as the wind whistled upon them.
And the sharp sound which the crawling
Mites proclaim upon the grasses' blades,
And the multitude of sounds which lie
At the root of things. Oh, I have heard
The song of resurrection which each seed
Makes as it spurts. I have heard the sound
Of the night's first shadow, when it
Intermingles with the day, and the
Rushing sound of Morning's wings as she
Flies o'er the Eastern gateway.

All of these I heard, yet man
Hath not an ear for them. Behold,
The miracle He hath writ within me;
Letting the chord of imagination strum!"

Pearl Curran was irrevocably changed by her relationship with Patience Worth, and she was open and candid in discussing that change. "Whatever may be the association which I describe as the presence of Patience Worth," she wrote, "it is one of the most beautiful that it can be the privilege of a human being to experience. Through this contact I have been educated to a deeper spiritual understanding and appreciation than I might have acquired in any study I can conceive of."

The alliance demanded a great deal from Mrs. Curran, both mentally and physically, but she never became obsessed by Patience. She respected her in the same way she respected other friends who had died. And there was never an attempt on the part of the Currans to exploit the partnership for material gain. Mrs. Curran continued to do all her own shopping and housework, with the help of her maid, and she prepared the family's meals as she had always done.

Two or three nights each week were set aside for writing sessions. No matter how many visitors were in the house on those evenings, Patience always dictated; she was deterred only by a sudden, sharp noise, or Mrs. Curran's need to converse with the guests.

Mrs. Curran explained that panoramic scenes appeared to her as the words issued forth. When the poems came, images of each successive symbol appeared before her eyes. If the stars were mentioned, she saw them in the sky. If wide, open spaces were mentioned, she got vast, frightening panoramas. Whenever the imagery began she felt pressure in the top of her head.

When Patience dictated stories, Mrs. Curran saw the details of each scene. If two characters were talking on a street corner, she saw portions of both streets with the buildings, dogs, horses, shopkeepers just as they would appear in a real scene. If the people spoke a foreign language, Mrs. Curran heard the talk, but also heard above it the voice of Patience either interpreting or indicating which part of the dialogue she wished to use in the story.

Oddly, the housewife often saw herself in the scenes, standing as an onlooker, or walking among the characters. And on occasion, she would take an active role, approaching a fruit vendor to taste his wares, or smelling flowers in a garden. The experience was as keen as if it had been an actual one. In this uncanny way she gained familiarity with things she had never known—with lamps and jugs and cooking utensils used in distant countries long ago, with types of jewelry and clothing worn by different peoples in older historical periods, with the sounds and scents of a thousand different places that were, to most people, mere pinpoints on a map.

On several occasions Mrs. Curran received premonitory flashes of pictures which she came to recognize as signals that the stories were about to be told. Yet often the stories did not start until a week or ten days later.

One story, *The Madrigal,* overwhelmed her. In a single flash, she received the entire framework, the characters, the plot, the central idea and the purpose. All of these components came to her as she and her mother walked to market on a warm June morning. In later years, Mrs. Curran noted: "The incident still remains upon me as the most startling and wonderful thing that Patience Worth has brought me."

The poems signalled their imminent arrival in the form of a sudden ecstasy that swept over Mrs. Curran. At other times Patience showed the housewife pictures without comment. Once Mrs. Curran was shown a lovely yellow bird sitting in a hedge. She did not recognize it. Finally Patience said, "He who knoweth the hedgerows knoweth the yellow-hammer."

As the Currans learned when they consulted an old encyclopedia, it was not the yellow-hammer seen in the United States, but rather the English yellow-hammer.

A peculiar aspect of the case was that Mrs. Curran never went into a trance, never immersed her consciousness with that of Patience. She understood the meaning of the writing as it came and often marveled at its beauty and strength. Yet, while calling out the words, she would twirl a cigarette between her fingers, take an occasional puff, and think about the midnight snack she would eat after the guests had gone. She seemed always to be aware of her surroundings and, while she spoke, read the expressions on the faces of her visitors.

Patience, however, went a step farther, evidencing knowledge of the inner life of those who came to the Curran house, and telling them things about themselves that no one else knew. This happened hundreds of times and even Mrs. Curran was amazed at the extra sense Patience seemed to possess.

If Patience Worth was really the spirit of a deceased person, she should be able to describe life on "the other side." One night a guest asked her to do so.

Patience said she couldn't make plain what man had not experienced. "This be not the will o' Him ... that thou shouldst see the Here," but she explained that Heaven was desirable. "I tell thee Heaven be all, and doth to clothe o'er all ... Each man enjoyeth his Heaven— I say *his* Heaven—for the thing he enjoyeth in that same Heaven shall not be thine." Heaven is also a place of continual progress. "This path leadeth on and on and on."

Was there an intermediate state?

"This be a busied land," she said, "and be thy building not afinished, thou shalt finish it afore thy setting unto His task. Yea, thou mayest build within this land, for building defileth not Him. He be the first builder."

Would one recognize his deceased friends there?

"Ah me," sighed Patience, "what a fogged land thou thinkest! He is a sire, not a monster."

As Patience Worth's literary reputation soared, Pearl Curran determined to take up writing herself. Except for bits of doggerel written as a child, she had never written a thing, nor had she ever had the urge. Perhaps now, she thought, writing would be easy. Or perhaps she needed a counterbalance to the spirit's prodigious output. Whatever the reason, she began to write and found the effort tiring and not at all exhilarating as it was when Patience was dictating. Two of her short stories, however, sold to *The Saturday Evening Post*.

Here is a passage from one of those stories, "Old Scotch":

> "You're going to wear something nifty. It's no go, kid, in your togs. Miss Peabody don't go in this burg as a modiste. Sister, I'm going to tog you out in some nifty cloth. I got a black velvet, one-piece, that will set you off to the nth degree ..."

Patience was tolerant of Mrs. Curran's efforts. " 'Tis but a babe's mixin' ..." she said. Meanwhile, her own words were being sent with no dilution of excellence.

Patience appears to have had a love-hate relationship with her copyist, scorning her at times, yet exhibiting forbearance and kindness at other times. Mrs. Curran often failed to grasp spellings and meanings of words. She had difficulty understanding the name Legia in *The Sorry Tale* until Patience finally explained, "Thou hast an eye, thou hast an arm, thou hast a Legia!"

How did it happen that an intellectually gifted spirit such as Patience chose to express herself through the limited mind of Pearl Curran? Mrs. Curran said Patience had searched a lot of "crannies" to slip into, but succeeded in slipping into hers only because she was very tired and inattentive that day at the Ouija board and her mind was in a vacuum state.

Patience put it this way, "I have said it be a trick o' throbbin.' The wench be atuned unto the throb o' me ... Follied un she be, but, I say me, pithed o' the thing that be like unto a siller (silver) string."

The world, however, tires of mysteries, expecially one with no solution. After the publication of several books and hundreds of poems, interest in Patience Worth flagged, and cynicism replaced it.

Detractors accused Mrs. Curran of hiding her literary talent in order to exploit it later in bizarre form to become famous. Yet, exhaustive studies of Pearl Curran showed it highly unlikely, if not impossible, for a woman of such limited education and interests to bring forth, with facility, works of rare literary quality.

Was Patience Worth, then, a secondary personality of Mrs. Curran, that is, a personality other than the normal one? Probably not, because secondary personalities supplant the customary personality for a time, and this was not true in Mrs. Curran's case. Her own personality co-existed with the personality of Patience Worth and Mrs. Curran was well aware of this fact.

Is it possible that Patience Worth is who she said she was—the surviving spirit of a seventeenth-century girl who found a way to communicate with the living? Many thought so.

Pearl Curran died in California on December 4, 1937. The *St. Louis Globe-Democrat* headlined her obituary: "PATIENCE WORTH IS DEAD."

To this day the case of Patience Worth remains unsolved. Experts agree that Patience is a remarkable enigma. A remarkable writer too.

THE HORNET SPOOK LIGHT

Twelve miles southwest of Joplin, near the Missouri-Oklahoma line, a gravel road arrows through a canyon of blackjack oak. This obscure east-west lane, not quite four miles long, lies in Oklahoma, just beyond the former border village of Hornet, Missouri. Known as Spook Light Road, or the Devil's Promenade, as it is called locally, it is similar to other lanes in the Ozark foothills. Except at night. When darkness falls, a mysterious light appears, bobbing along from west to east. It has been seen almost every night from dusk to dawn for nearly 100 years. Early pioneers called it the Indian Light, but it is now more commonly known as the Hornet Spook Light.

The ball of fire, varying from baseball-sized to larger than a bushel basket, spins down the center of the road at great speed, rises to treetop level and hovers, then retreats. At other times, it sways from side to side and up and down like a lantern being carried. But no one is ever there to carry it.

Observers say the light is silver, red or yellow. Sometimes blue or green. It is usually seen as a single glow, but one woman said she saw it "burst like a bubble, scattering sparks in all directions." If chased, the light seems to go out, only to reappear later. One man drove his car directly at the light till it vanished. Witnesses saw the light pulsating over the roof of the car.

Although the mystery light has never been known to harm anyone, some observers have reported frightening encounters with it. Gregory Briones, while driving his car one morning at three o'clock, happened to turn around and saw the Spook Light on the lid of his trunk. "It throwed off a good bit of light, like an electric bulb close up to you," he told a news reporter. "I took off in one big hurry."

A man walking along the Devil's Promenade said the light swung past him so closely that he felt its searing heat.

Another man swore that he saw the figure of a crone tottering down the road with the light on her shoulders where her head should have been.

When Bill Youngblood lived near the Devil's Promenade, he said the light bouncing around outside his bedroom window kept him awake.

Garland Middleton, operator of the Spook Light Museum at the east end of the Devil's Promenade, claimed the light had chased him home several times.

Other people reported seeing the light bob through open windows of automobiles; one car caught fire.

On at least two occasions, the light was observed six miles beyond the western end of the Devil's Promenade, near Quapaw, Oklahoma.

Chester McMinn, who farmed near Quapaw, was working his fields late one summer night when the Spook Light appeared overhead, illuminating his acreage with silvered brilliance.

Louise Graham was riding home in a school bus from a carnival at Quapaw when the light appeared at the rear window of the vehicle. The brilliant yellow fireball badly frightened her and her schoolmates, and forced the nearly blinded driver to pull over. Only then did the light drift away.

Generations of local people believe that the Hornet Spook Light is a ghost, or "ha'nt," in local parlance. There are many legends to account for the queer glow. Here are three of the most commonly told tales:

- The area was once the home of the Quapaw Indians. An Indian maiden and a young brave fell in love. The girl's father, a greedy chief, demanded a larger dowry than the young man could afford. Unable to marry with the tribe's blessing and unwilling to separate, the lovers eloped. Their absence was soon discovered and a party of warriors sent in pursuit. Overtaken on a bluff above the Spring River, the couple joined hands and leaped to their deaths.

  Shortly afterward, in 1886, the light first appeared; it was thought to be the spirits of the young lovers. It created such a panic in the village of Hornet that many people abandoned their farms and moved away. The light was a hoodoo, they said, that brought death.

- The Spook Light may be the ghost of an Osage chief who was decapitated on the Devil's Promenade. The chief came back to search for his lost head; the Spook Light is the torch held high in his hand.

- During Prohibition (1920-33), when alcoholic beverages were forbidden by law, stills operated in the Ozark hills. With some regularity, federal agents tramped the countryside, flushing out moonshiners.

  Eventually they caught old Uncle Dick Hunt, purveyor of the finest "corn likker" in the area. It was so fine, in fact, that Uncle Dick refused to pour it into bottles that had contained any blended stuff. He used bottles of only the best brands or the buyer's own stone jug. But after the "Feds" raided him and broke up his still several times, Uncle Dick got smart. He mounted the still on the rear of an old spring wagon. Then whenever the agents were around, Uncle Dick moved the still to the safety of a nearby cave. The Spook Light is Uncle Dick Hunt's still, jouncing around on the back of the wagon heading for cover . . . forever.

Over the years the light has been studied, photographed and even shot at with high-powered rifles in efforts to identify and explain it.

What is it?

Marsh gas? Probably not. Winds fail to disperse the fireball as they do conventional marsh gas.

A will-o'-the-wisp? The light is far more intense than the luminescence created by rotting organic matter.

Glowing minerals from the numerous piles of mine tailings in the area? Maybe.

A pocket of natural gas ignited by lightning and once worshipped as a fire-god by Indians of the area? Not likely. Natural gas flames and, in time, burns out.

Anomalous lights, such as the Hornet Spook Light, have been reported all over the world for thousands of years. Some experts believe that these lights are electrical atmospheric charges generated by the shifting and grinding of rocks deep below the earth's crust (although such lights are frequently associated with earthquakes, their presence does not necessarily predict quakes). The distorted electrical field that results from these charges can make the light appear to act in an "intelligent" way, changing direction and altitude and giving chase. And physical encounters with the electrical field can make a person fearful and apprehensive. Sleep difficulties, skin burns, nausea and temporary blindness may follow.

Joplin, Missouri, just north of the Spook Light area, lies on a great fault line running from east of New Madrid, Missouri, westward into Oklahoma. Four earthquakes during the eighteenth century were followed by a devastating series of quakes that convulsed this area in 1811-12. Strange lights may have accompanied these quakes, but it was not until 1886 that the Hornet Spook Light was first reported. Although the appearance of the light has not been accompanied by any major quake in this century, seismologists consider this region of Missouri one of the most unstable areas in the country, and the generation of an electrical atmospheric charge may possibly explain the Spook Light.

Yet some experts have a different opinion. Teams of investigators who have studied the lights conclude that they are those of automobiles driving east on U. S. Highway 66. This highway is about five miles away in a direct line with the Devil's Promenade, but at a slightly lower elevation. A high ridge lies between the two roads. The density and rarity of atmosphere as it rises over the ridge causes the light to bend, creating the eerie effects.

Old-timers smile and shake their heads. They know the mystery light was seen in the same spot in these woods long before the automobile was invented and the highway built.

"I was coming here in horse and buggy days," said L. W. Robertson, "and saw the light then."

Whatever the Hornet Spook Light may be, it attracts thousands of visitors each year. Cars park bumper to bumper on the narrow gravel road, while drivers wait and watch for that strange light that swings and sways and bobs along in the night sky. It is, as they say in that region, one of nature's unexplained mysteries.

AUNT ETERNITY'S CURSE

Boonville, on the crest of the Missouri River Bluffs, was founded by Kentucky and Virginia settlers in the early years of the nineteenth century. Many of the homes here were made of brick, replete with generous rooms and wide halls. But none was as fine as that built by Howard Thornton Muir. His mansion was said to have been one of the most magnificent private homes in all Missouri.

A wealthy Virginian, Muir spared no expense in the construction of his mansion. The walls were made of hand-patted plaster, highlighted with rosettes and mosaics; fine woodwork and wainscoting decorated every room; and a sweeping staircase of polished mahogany connected the upper and lower floors.

The Muir family held a prominent social position in the Boonville community for many years. An invitation to dine at their home or to join them for a country drive in their beautiful coach pulled by a span of high-stepping horses were both highly coveted.

But tragedy struck the Muir mansion without warning. Young Nancy Muir awakened one morning with a chill and a raging fever. She had never before been ill. Her father, much alarmed, summoned the finest physician in Boonville. He gave her quinine.

When Nancy did not improve, Muir called in a specialist from St. Louis who prescribed various medicines that he said "would cleanse the system and lower the fever." They did not. The young woman slipped into delirium. The desperate father then consulted a local herb doctor who offered a brew made of ginseng and wild berries. Still, Nancy did not respond. She languished in bed and grew weaker and more frail until she died.

Howard Muir was distraught. He loved his daughter more than life itself and, as the days passed, he sat in silence, brooding upon her death. It had seemed so senseless. The more he thought about it, the more he was convinced that someone had caused her death. Had someone, perhaps one of his slaves, placed a curse upon poor Nancy?

As the empty, endless days passed, Muir became obsessed with trying to find out who had bewitched his daughter. One night, while rocking in the darkened living room, he called to mind each of his slaves who lived in the row of huts, little more than mud shanties, at the rear of the estate.

It wasn't Charity, the mulatto, he thought, who beneath her playful sauciness was obedient and loving. Nor was it Tobiath, the gentle, crippled woman with a heart of gold. And it couldn't have been Jethro, her husband, who told the day's news to the horses as he curried them.

Suddenly, the baleful face of Aunt Eternity loomed before him—old Aunt Eternity, the ancient slave feared by all the rest. Aunt Eternity never spoke—she thundered, her voice alone frightening all who heard it. Some said she was that way because she'd lost all her kith and kin and was sour on life. She lived alone in the hut on one end of the row and, in so far as possible, ruled her peers with an iron hand.

With a start, Muir recalled the night a year ago when Aunt Eternity had stolen a guest's imported silk scarf from the foyer during a dinner party. Nancy had caught her leaving the house with it while the family and guests were dining. Later that night Muir had demoted the old slave from front parlor duty to scullery maid, putting her under the supervision of the trusted Hezekiah whose bright, watchful eyes missed nothing.

Howard Muir, his mind warped with grief, was now certain that Aunt Eternity was guilty of bewitching his daughter. He rose and walked to the rear of the house. Taking down a horse whip from a peg in the rear entry, he strode out into the night. Fog filled the swale between the main house and the slaves' huts, but Muir's steps never slowed. He knew exactly where he was going.

An oil lamp flickered through the dull-paned window of Aunt Eternity's hut, and by the lamp's light the old slave nodded in the single wooden chair, a Bible open in her lap.

Muir stepped to the door, pushed it open. It rasped on its rusty hinges. He raised the whip before the old woman could raise a hand. In the pain of dying, old Aunt Eternity screamed out a terrible curse upon the Muir family of the present generation and for all generations to come.

Within a few years Aunt Eternity's curse was fulfilled. The Muirs lost their large fortune, and every member of the family died a sudden death. The mansion, uncared for, soon decayed. The front veranda collapsed, torn from the house by a succession of storms; the window glass fell out as the wooden frames rotted; and loose shutters banged eerily in the wind. It was a gloomy, empty place.

But was it really empty? There were reports later from individuals who claimed that they observed strange lights burning in the dilapidated mansion, glowing through the broken windows of one room, then another. And on certain summer evenings when the air was warm and still, neighbors saw the airy figure of a maiden standing under the great oak tree and singing an old love song. They said that the solitary figure bore a striking resemblance to Nancy Muir, perhaps the only member of the family to elude the wrath of Aunt Eternity's curse.

SENTRIES IN THE NIGHT

The snow came, blanketing roofs and mortaring window frames. Inside the house on the hill, Dr. John J. O'Brien lit another lantern and set the dinner table. His wife, Elizabeth, added wood to the cookstove, then peered through the kitchen window now clouded by steam from the kettle of stew bubbling on the stove. John went to stand behind her, his full red beard barely touching the top of her head. Usually the gaslights of St. Louis shone like a jeweled carpet spread far below, but now, beyond the swirl of flakes, no lights were visible. Nor were there any human sounds—not the clatter of buggy wheels on the cobblestone street, nor the call of children at play. There was only the incessant howling of the wind.

"It's unreal, isn't it?" murmured Elizabeth, turning to look up into her husband's face. "It's as if we're suspended in time, cut off from all living things."

John detected a quiver of excitement in her voice. Like a child, she both loved and feared a blizzard.

"I'm glad you finished your rounds early today," she went on, ladeling the stew into bowls and setting out great slabs of freshly-baked bread.

Dr. John J. O'Brien nodded and sat down at the table, the chair creaking beneath his weight. He was truly a massive man with a deep, hearty laugh and a streak of Irish whimsy that some people said was his best medicine. But tonight no whimsy brightened the doctor's face.

"Elizabeth," he began, "I haven't seen Mrs. Kilpatrick for a long time." He knifed butter onto his bread. "I've had her on my mind all day. As you know, she has a weak heart."

Elizabeth's jaw tightened and her cheeks flushed, but John saw the shining in her eyes. It was the same gentle light that had first attracted him to her, when she was Elizabeth Fitzwilliam and he was the stranger passing through town—an Irish physician newly graduated from medical school in Dublin and traveling across America to see the world before settling down to a practice in Australia. But Elizabeth had charmed him; so had St. Louis. And the adventurous young visitor never did get to the South Pacific.

John had known from the beginning that Elizabeth was the only woman with whom he wished to share his life; he sensed that she was both proud and glad that his patients' needs came first, and he loved her deeply for it.

Now their eyes met across the table.

"But John, you wouldn't be going to see Mrs. Kilpatrick on a night like this."

He stared into his empty bowl. "If I thought . . ." His voice trailed off.

"She needed me," added Elizabeth quickly. She then murmured an understanding "of course."

The dinner table conversation became desultory. John's preoccupation distracted him and he fell silent. Finally he rose, went into the living room and laid another log on the crackling fire in the fireplace. Hands clasped before him, John O'Brien watched fingers of flame encircle the dry wood and bounce the light off the soot-blackened back wall of the firebox. From the corner of his eye, he saw Elizabeth clearing away the dinner dishes. She moved deftly, with that certain resilience that all adaptable women possess.

John went to the kitchen doorway. "I'm going to Mrs. Kilpatrick." Elizabeth nodded, having realized his decision long before he said it. He never knew how he had acquired the sixth sense about the condition of his patients, but his intuition often meant the difference between life and death. He suspected it was a gift given to all country doctors in that era before the telephone.

John O'Brien pulled on his boots, put on his heavy overcoat, cap and fur-lined gloves, then wrapped the long wool muffler Elizabeth had made for him around his neck. He kissed his wife goodbye and told her not to wait up.

Trudging to the stable behind the house, he kicked the drifts into snow showers.

Moments later, the horse was hitched to the buggy. The doctor sat high on the box spring cushion, his bag beside him. Glancing back, he barely saw Elizabeth's face framed in the window, hands cupped to her cheeks, nose pressed against the glass. He knew she would watch the rig until the buggy's twin oil lamps vanished in the storm-filled night. Little did Dr. John J. O'Brien know that he was setting forth on the most unusual trip of his life, one that he would never forget.

The wind had picked up, driving the snow, with stinging fury, against his cheeks. Dr. O'Brien tried to shield his face with one hand while guiding the horse with the other. Perhaps he should have put up the rubber side curtains, but he never liked to use them because they obstructed his vision.

He hunched forward now on the seat, trying to see where to make his first turn. The Kilpatricks lived several miles away down a maze of side roads. In daylight and in good weather the route wasn't difficult. But now, in the darkness and the swirling snow, familiar landmarks were obliterated, and Dr. O'Brien found it impossible to see a junction with another road.

Following a bend on the main road, the buggy and its passenger met the blizzard head-on. The nag slowed, and Dr. O'Brien could hardly see three feet in front of the buggy. The oil lamps were useless.

Then, in the wind's pause, came the faint sound of a barking dog. At first the doctor thought he had imagined the sound. But he heard it again, louder, more distinctly. He half rose, leaned over the leather dash and peered through the cloud of snow.

Then he saw them—two mastiffs, one on each side of the buggy and slightly ahead of the horse. Where had they come from? Why were they out on a night like this? Dr. O'Brien was puzzled. They must be the Kilpatricks' dogs, he thought. In all the times he'd been to the Kilpatricks' house he'd never noticed any dogs, but he wouldn't necessarily have seen them.

Now he had no choice but to follow where they led. When the dogs turned to the left, the horse and buggy turned with them. When the dogs turned right, the rig followed. The doctor lost track of all the turnings, the jigs and the jogs, but he never took his eyes off the barking four-footed guides as they plunged through the driving, drifting snow.

After a final turn to the right, Dr. O'Brien saw the Kilpatricks' little frame house hunched in the snow, its roof rimmed with ice. A lantern shone through a frosted window. The doctor grabbed his bag and eased himself down from the seat, after driving the rig beneath a shed at the side of the house. He banged the knocker and Mr. Kilpatrick opened the door immediately.

"Oh doctor, it's so fine you came. The missus is poorly today and has such trouble breathing. Here, let's dry your clothes at the fire. And warm yourself, please."

Mr. Kilpatrick took Dr. O'Brien's overcoat and spread it over the back of a chair by the hearth and put the boots close by. The traveler warmed his hands briefly by the fire, let the ice melt out of his beard, then went into the bedroom to check Mrs. Kilpatrick. Her pulse was slow and her breathing labored. Dr. O'Brien gave her medicine for her heart and something to put her to sleep. In a short time she breathed easier and drifted into sound slumber.

Mr. Kilpatrick insisted that Dr. O'Brien stay for hot coffee and food. Grateful for the chance to relax after the strain of his trip, the doctor pulled a rocking chair close to the fire. It was then he remembered the mastiffs.

"Tell me, Mr. Kilpatrick, where are your dogs?"

"Dogs?" echoed the host. "But I have no dogs, doctor."

As the two men ate and drank and talked quietly, Dr. O'Brien learned that none of Kilpatrick's neighbors owned mastiffs. Neither man could explain the presence of the dogs.

At four o'clock in the morning, the storm had passed and the moon was out. Dr. O'Brien drove home slowly. At each turn, he watched for the dogs, listened for their barking. But he met no living thing and he heard nothing save the occasional puff of a snowball slipping off a fence rail.

At the back door of his house, Dr. O'Brien stomped the snow from his boots and pulled them off. Then he went inside quietly and hung his outer clothes on the hooks by the stove. His shoulders ached and his head hurt. Perhaps he could coax the living room fire into life and relax a while before going to bed.

In stocking feet, he padded into the living room. Elizabeth, curled up in her sewing rocker, was nodding by the hearth; circles of sleep pinched her eyes.

Suddenly aware of her husband's presence, Elizabeth jerked awake.

"Coffee first, then tell me," she said.

John never knew how she sensed what he needed. Tonight, after the long, late trip, he wanted to relax his body and unravel his mind.

When Elizabeth stood, John took her into his arms and held her close. Then he added a log to the still hot embers and watched the fire flame up.

John and Elizabeth sat together, drinking and talking until dawn washed the windows with gray light.

During the next few days, the O'Briens asked everyone they knew about the mastiffs. But no one kept such dogs nor knew of anyone who did. Dr. O'Brien recalled that when he had pulled into the Kilpatricks' yard, the dogs had vanished. At the time he had given it little thought, believing that his eyes were overly strained from trying to focus through the blizzard.

But Dr. John J. O'Brien, the practical, down-to-earth country doctor, eventually concluded that the dogs had never existed. The mastiffs, he decided, must have been ghost dogs on emergency call, dogs who had materialized, somehow, for the single purpose of guiding him through the storm to the bedside of the ailing Mrs. Kilpatrick.

THE MIDNIGHT RIDER OF SAND SPRINGS

Before the Civil War, wagon trains rumbling westward often stopped for the night at Sand Springs, two miles west of Roubidoux Creek, between Rolla and Springfield, Missouri. Sand Springs was a campground that took its name from a spring of soft lime water that boiled up through sand and gravel. Near the spring stood a small, weathered church building where countless freight drivers took shelter at night.

Soon after the Civil War ended, a story circulated that the church was haunted. People said that a phantom horse and rider entered the building at midnight. The horse hesitated a moment at the door, then walked slowly down the aisle and stopped at the altar. A whinny was heard, then the dull thud of something striking the floor. Measured hoofbeats retreated up the aisle and left the building. Close to the door of the church, people said they heard a chilling laugh.

Up until the 1930s, when the building was razed, search parties often went out to Sand Springs late at night. They tried to follow the sound of the horse's steps with flashlights, but they never saw a thing.

Only a few persons knew the true story of the unearthly drama that was re-enacted in the building; it was a curious tale of passion, intrigue and revenge that belonged to an earlier era.

In 1848, Wyndham Potter, a wealthy planter from Georgia, settled on a parcel of land near Sand Springs. He had no wife or family, but he brought a large number of slaves with him, including a mulatto woman named Jenny and her quadroon daughter, Carolyne.

Potter built a handsome house and invited his new neighbors to a housewarming at which Jenny presided as hostess. She was assisted by sixteen-year-old Carolyne, a strong, slim beauty who bore a striking resemblance to Potter.

Two years later, in 1850, Potter died. He left the house and a trust fund to Jenny and Carolyne. The rest of his estate, including a small piece of land nearby, went to a nephew.

Charles Potter, the nephew, soon arrived to take up residence on the land he had inherited. Before long, he began appearing in the little church near Sand Springs each Sunday with Jenny and Carolyne.

The pulpit was often filled by a man named Maupins who insisted upon being called "Elder Maupins." He was a formidable figure nearly six feet tall, strong and muscular with black chin whiskers. He had a gaunt and weary wife and two grown sons. Although he was respected by most people, he was not liked by all. His next door neighbor, an old woman whom everyone called "Grandmother," thought Maupins was evil and cruel. As an example, she pointed to the occasion when she saw Maupins shoot and kill his sons' dog simply because it refused to come to him.

Grandmother soon noticed that Maupins was becoming a regular visitor at the home of the mulatto woman, Jenny. After others questioned the propriety of such visits, Grandmother herself confronted Maupins. What was he doing in the mulatto woman's home, she wanted to know. Saving souls, he told her, as God had appointed him to do.

That explanation satisfied everyone ... except Grandmother. Was she the only one who saw the dark looks exchanged between Maupins and Charles Potter in the church? Even Jenny and Carolyne were embarrassed and averted their eyes as Maupins, rising on tiptoe in the pulpit, arms outstretched and trembling, declaimed the evils of sin.

But Maupins did not preach for very long. A country preacher was assigned to the Sand Springs church and after that, Maupins seldom attended services.

Then one day cattle buyers passed through Sand Springs, announcing that horse thieves had raided a community on the Osage River, escaping with twenty head of stolen mules and horses. A posse raced south after the gang. In the exchange of gunfire one officer was killed and another wounded. Supposedly, the lethal shots were fired by a man wearing a high-crowned black hat, a red linsey shirt and dark pants tucked into his boots; he rode a large sorrel mule. It was an apt description of Maupins and his mule, Judy.

Several days later a detective arrived in Sand Springs to inquire about the ownership of a large sorrel mule. Maupins told his wife he had urgent business in the Boston Mountains. After dark, he fled on the mule.

At about the same time the quadroon girl, Carolyne, vanished. Jenny explained that she was awakened at eleven o'clock the night before Carolyne's disappearance by hoofbeats going past the house. The male rider was singing a church hymn as he rode along. Thinking he was a neighbor returning home, Jenny drifted back to sleep. In the morning, however, she awoke to find her daughter's room empty and all of her clothes gone.

The grief-stricken mother was certain that slave runners had abducted her daughter and would sell her into slavery.

Grandmother knew better. "She's run off with Maupins," she whispered. "When you find him, you'll find her."

Years passed and no word of either Maupins or Carolyne reached the community.

The Civil War had brought difficult times to the people of Sand Springs as husbands, fathers and brothers went away to fight, some for the Confederates and others choosing the Union. Charles Potter himself had joined the Confederate forces and rode off with the cavalry that very year. Eventually the parson was the only able-bodied man left in the community. The women helped one another and prayed for the safe return of their men.

Then one Sunday morning in 1863, Elder Maupins appeared in his pew! At the close of the sermon, Maupins leaped to the platform. The startled minister stood awkwardly to one side. Maupins announced that his mother had died in the Boston Mountains and he had been busy settling her estate. He said he was shocked to learn of Carolyne's disappearance, which he attributed to slave traders, and asked the congregation to pray that she might be returned safely to her dear mother. "And let us pray also," he concluded, "for a Union victory!"

Grandmother listened attentively. She claimed that Maupins was an excellent liar.

During the rest of that year and well into 1864, Elder Maupins made frequent long journeys to unknown destinations. Later, Charles Potter returned home in 1865 a colonel, having served the Confederacy with distinction. Maupins returned also.

Someone in Sand Springs discovered that Maupins was a member of a bushwhacker gang that had raided farms and ranches throughout the Finley Creek hills, spreading death and destruction. Maupins denied it and viciously denounced the Rebels. Even staunch Unionists were sickened by his bluster.

Suddenly, Charles Potter sent word to the Sand Springs congregation that on a certain Sunday night when Maupins was preaching, he would ride down the aisle to the pulpit and by looks alone run the Elder out of the church and out of the community . . . forever.

At the appointed hour, the former Rebel officer, in full dress gray uniform, mounted a black horse. Near the close of the service, Potter entered the church and rode slowly down the center aisle. He reined his horse in front of the pulpit. A few people gasped, but many were half asleep and nodding.

Elder Maupins raised both arms to deliver the benediction.

The rider glared at Maupins.

"May the Lord bless you and keep you . . ." intoned Maupins.

Shots rang out from beyond an open window. The young Potter toppled to the floor, fatally shot in the head. The horse stood for a moment, then turned and walked back toward the door and out of the church.

The horrified worshippers neither moved nor spoke. Elder Maupins sank to his knees and asked that they pray for guidance. He had uttered only a few words before he glanced up the aisle to the church door. Then, like a crazed animal, he leaped to his feet and dived through the window from which the shot had been fired.

While the congregation sat in stunned silence, the deacons covered the body of Charles Potter. It would remain in the custody of two of the minister's assistants until an inquest could be held the next day.

In the morning, a jury was convened and witnesses were called. But there were no clues and the identity of the murderer could not be learned. However, the jury did unravel the mystery of Elder Maupins's hasty exit from the church when Ginger, the community's ne'er-do-well, testified.

Ginger admitted that he had drunk too much mountain dew and was seated at the rear of the church. He eventually fell asleep but was jerked awake by the sound of a shot. Glancing up, his bleary eyes focused upon a black horse with saddle and bridle walking toward him. He thought he was having a nightmare, he said, until he saw Maupins in the pulpit.

Ginger went on to say that after the horse left the church and the Elder was kneeling, a young woman—a light-skinned "negress"—stepped through the door. She was dressed like a man in shirt, pants and boots. She pointed a finger at Maupins and issued a bloodcurdling laugh. That's when Maupins dived through the window. Ginger added that as the woman turned he noticed a livid scar on the left side of her face and neck. She glanced down at the body on the floor, then fled.

But still the question remained—who murdered Charles Potter?

Grandmother believed that some of Maupins's raiders had carried out the ambush. Others said the Rebel officer Potter, could have been killed by any Union sympathizer.

Or was the killer Carolyne who had always hated the slave-owning Potters?

On the following Sunday in church, Mrs. Maupins announced that her husband had not returned home and she feared he had met with foul play. Late that afternoon, a search party found a man lying face down in a cedar glade. It was Maupins. His throat was slit from ear to ear; only a bloody piece of flesh had kept his head attached to his torso. A dagger of Mexican art was buried to its hilt between his shoulders. It was impossible to tell how long Maupins had been dead; the searchers concluded that after plunging through the church window, he must have dragged himself along the streambank to the glade where his body was discovered. Curiously, there was no evidence of a struggle, nor of anyone's having been near the body.

After Elder Maupins was buried, Jenny, the mulatto woman, told her neighbors she was selling everything and returning to her people. She kept only two blooded saddle horses.

But why two horses? One would always be rested, she replied. Early one afternoon Jenny headed toward Georgia, riding one horse and leading the other.

A few days following Jenny's departure, a horse trader reached Sand Springs. He reported seeing two black women traveling south on the Wilderness Road. He met them in the Roark Hills, south of the old town of Forsyth. The young woman was dressed in men's clothes and heavily armed. The horse trader recalled that she had a scar on her face.

VANISHED!

Jerrold I. Potter and his wife, Carrie, gazed out the DC-3's window at the rolling Ozark hills 8,000 feet below. They could just make out the doll-sized buildings of Rolla, Missouri. In the distance sprawled the Fort Leonard Wood Army Camp. On that June 29, 1968, the Purdue Aviation Corporation charter flight was carrying the Potters and twenty-one other passengers from Kankakee, Illinois, to a national Lion's Club convention in Dallas.

The flight had been smooth during the hour they had been airborne. In what looked like a fine, cloudless summer day, pilot Miguel Raul Cabeza anticipated no weather disturbances. The passengers, most of them acquainted through the Lion's Club, snoozed or chatted.

As the aircraft passed over Rolla, Jerrold I. Potter excused himself and headed toward the lavatory in the rear tail section. He stopped briefly to talk with James Schaive, president of a Lion's Club in Ottawa, Illinois.

Potter was the quintessential middle-American businessman: a successful insurance executive with a reputation for friendliness and sociability that had brought him membership not only in the Lion's but also the Elks, Moose and the Chamber of Commerce in his hometown of Pontiac, Illinois. He was also in the best of health. Two happily married daughters and a pleasant home life completed the picture of normality.

Mrs. Potter watched her husband walk back toward the lavatory and saw him stop to talk with Schaive. Then she turned to gaze out at the beautiful green countryside below.

Carrie Potter never saw her husband again!

Several minutes later, the plane shuddered as if caught by a sudden wind. It lasted only a few seconds and caused no concern among the passengers.

But when her husband didn't return, Carrie Potter grew nervous. She looked anxiously toward the tail, but saw no sign of her husband. The lavatory door was closed.

Mrs. Potter called a stewardess and asked her to check the lavatory. At about the same time, pilot Cabeza noticed that one of the red "DOOR OPEN" warning signs was flashing. Cabeza asked co-pilot Roy Bacus to check the emergency doors.

Bacus moved quickly but casually so as not to raise concern among the passengers. The stewardess stopped him as he walked down the aisle. "I think a passenger is missing. A Mr. Potter," she whispered, clearly frightened.

Bacus felt a chill. "Are you sure?" The stewardess nodded. She said Jerrold Potter was last seen near the lavatory when the DC-3 was shaken by some force.

"He isn't there now. No one has seen him," she added.

Bacus's gaze swept over the rear passenger compartment area. The exit door near the lavatory was slightly open! That was the cause of the emergency flasher on the flight deck. But since the DC-3 wasn't pressurized, the rush of air coming into the cabin hadn't caused any problems. Bacus then spotted a small piece of chain, used to keep the emergency exit door closed, lying on the floor. He scooped it up and headed forward.

He related the bizarre situation to Cabeza, who speculated Potter may have been thrown against the door as the aircraft lurched and, when the safety chain broke, fell out.

But no one saw him fall. "He has simply disappeared," Bacus emphasized.

Cabeza immediately radioed the Springfield, Missouri, airport about the situation and asked permission to land.

On the ground, mechanics found the emergency door still ajar, the stairs locked in the down position. There was no sign of Potter.

What happened? How could a man be inside an airplane nearly two miles in the air and then *not* be there?

Did Jerrold Potter commit suicide by leaping from the plane? It seems unlikely. From all reports, Potter was happily married, with no financial problems. He seemed to be looking forward to the convention in Dallas with his wife.

Could Potter have somehow mistakenly opened the emergency door, thinking it was the lavatory? Again, this seems improbable. A large white sign with a bright red background, attached to the emergency door, reads "DO NOT OPEN WHILE IN FLIGHT." Although the safety chain had broken, a door handle still had to be turned 180 degrees to allow the locks to be released.

According to Grove Webster, the president of the Purdue Aviation charter company, Purdue Aviation, the door was always locked tightly on take-off. And, he said in a report after the accident, it took a lot of effort to open the hatchway, even on the ground. Air pressure during flight would make the door doubly difficult to budge. Ground mechanics regularly closed the door for stewardesses before take-off. Even after the aircraft landed, many stewardesses could not open the hatch by themselves.

Potter's widow and family members filed suit several months later, charging Purdue Aviation with negligence in maintenance and safety procedures. There was a problem, however. No one saw Jerrold I. Potter fall from the aircraft.

The ground beneath the DC-3's flight path at the time of the disappearance was thoroughly searched, but no body was ever found. To this day, the case remains unsolved.

THE GHOST OF PARIS

Did the village of Paris, Missouri, for nearly seventy years play host to the macabre specter of a woman in black floating along the community's streets? Or was the ghost merely an eccentric female who enjoyed late evening strolls in the fashionable black clothing of decades ago? Those questions have never been satisfactorily answered, but generations in that northeast Missouri community have passed on the legend.

Darcy Ambrose saw the woman first. In the dusk of an October evening, Darcy stood in her front yard calling her children. Suddenly, the stranger swept down the street. She was swathed in black, her wide-brimmed bonnet shielding her face. In her hand she waved a cane. Darcy did not recognize her, but assumed she was a soldier's wife or mother. The Civil War had just ended and relatives swarmed into Paris to greet menfolk home from the battlefields.

The next night the woman in black returned. Darcy and her husband were sitting on the front stoop, talking. The stranger brandished her cane as she passed and the couple shrank into the shadows of their little porch. Then, in the bright moonlight, Darcy noticed that the woman's feet never touched the ground. Although she looked three-dimensional, she *wasn't* real!

Soon the tavern in the courthouse square buzzed with talk of the ghost. For mutual protection, patrons arrived at the tavern in groups of threes and fours and left the same way. Children, scurrying home from after-supper play, burst into hysterics when the stranger brushed past them; three youngsters said they'd heard her long skirts rustling in the wind.

Indian summer lingered well into November. So did the ghost. Frightened residents kept their windows locked, doors bolted and shades drawn. Travelers abroad at night were wary. In several instances, grown men, meeting the ghost, ran down the middle of the street, screaming for help. Although the ghost always swung her cane, she never harmed anyone.

Even when northwest winds stripped the trees, and the snows came, the woman in black didn't leave. Throughout the winter she glided down the icy streets late at night and sometimes peered into an uncurtained window. But when March arrived, she departed.

During the warm springtime and the long hot summer of 1866, the people of Paris almost forgot their ghost. But when the pumpkins ripened in mid-October, she returned and, as before, stayed until spring. For nearly seventy years the dauntless figure in black roamed the village each winter, frightening everyone who saw her.

Who was she? What did she want? Si Colborn edited the *Monroe County Appeal* for nearly sixty years before "retiring" at the age of eighty-two to write editorials and columns. Colborn says he heard the story when he came to Paris in 1920. His late partner at the newspaper, Jack Blanton, often told the tale, sometimes with variations. The woman was said to have had a face that glowed in the dark, and she floated rather than walked.

Colburn, however, said the mysterious figure may have been an actual person, a Paris spinster spurned when her betrothed ran off with another woman. The spinster had been nearly six feet tall, angular and "formidable." Having known the woman, Colborn adds, it is obvious why her husband-to-be thought better of the marriage proposal and left town.

There may be some truth to Colborn's explanation. The figure hasn't been seen since 1934, shortly before the spinster's death at the age of ninety.

But an Associated Press news dispatch in November, 1934, identified the woman as the ghost of a Civil War soldier's jilted sweetheart who swore on her deathbed to haunt forever her faithless lover and the whole town of Paris.

Although there are similarities, the news story seems to be at odds with Colborn's theory. The spinster would have been too young to have had a Civil War sweetheart (she was ten when the war ended).

Whatever the truth of the Paris ghost, the legend that had been passed down for generations disappeared about that time. Perhaps the newspaper publicity represented the last gasp of interest in the subject. At any rate, the streets of Paris, Missouri are safe again, and even the most timid citizen can walk fearlessly through the night.

THE CORPORAL AND HIS LADY

Margaret Baker sat in her dormitory room in Senior Hall, staring at the front page of the newspaper until the print blurred before her eyes.

> Columbia, Mo. Sarah June Wheeler, a student at the Columbia Baptist Female College, died yesterday in Senior Hall, the dormitory in which she resided. The body was found in the bell tower by classmates. An investigation into Miss Wheeler's death has begun ...

> Columbia, Mo. Isaac Johnson, a Confederate corporal, was executed in this city yesterday. He was arrested as a spy in a dormitory room of the Columbia Baptist Female College by General Henry Halleck, commander of the Union forces occupying the city. The Rebel had been sought for weeks ...

Cold brutal facts—the kind you see every day in the newspaper. Margaret read no further. She knew the story by heart. The only thing she did not know was that the unfolding of these tragic events would be recounted over the years, the tale embellished until it achieved legendary status. Even today, new students at the school, now known as Stephens College, hear about the corporal and his lady. And every Halloween at midnight they wait and watch for the ghost of the lovely Sarah June to appear in Senior Hall, searching for her Rebel.

In 1862, the Civil War raged throughout the south. Although Missouri had declared for the Union, General Sterling Price tried to organize a Confederate campaign in the state. But any chance of concerted pro-Southern action ended when he was defeated at Pea Ridge, Arkansas, in March, 1862.

After this decisive Union triumph, General Henry Halleck moved his bluecoats to Columbia. The presence of Halleck's Army of Occupation particularly upset Dr. Hubert Williams, president of the Columbia Baptist Female College, and its dean, Miss Clara Armstrong. The administrators feared for the safety of their young females, and reminded them constantly not to shout from their windows to the soldiers in the streets.

One evening after dinner, Sarah June Wheeler, a student from Independence, Missouri, dashed up to her room in Senior Hall to get badminton racquets for herself and her roommate, Margaret Baker. Rummaging in the closet for the racquets, Sarah did not see the soldier climbing over the sill of her open window. But when she turned, he staggered toward her.

"Please, Miss," he began, "where am I? What is this place?"

His gray uniform was soiled and torn, the rifle in his hands caked with mud.

"A Rebel!" screamed Sarah.

He sprang at her, clapping his hand over her mouth. She struggled to free herself and a moment later the soldier collapsed on the floor. Just then Margaret came in and gasped at the sight of the stranger lying sprawled beside a trunk.

"Oh, my God!" she shouted. "Did the South win the war? Hallelujah!" She leaned out over the windowsill and gave a Rebel shout. Then she slammed the window shut and turned to Sarah. "There's nothin' but damn Yankees out there."

Sarah curled her small hands into fists. She had always tried to be fair, to understand another's viewpoint, and never knowingly to hurt anyone. But she had difficulty accepting Margaret's allegiance to the Confederacy. Yet Margaret could scarcely be otherwise. She was born and raised in Little Rock, and her father, in lieu of paying his daughter's tuition, sent two of his slaves to the college—Lucy Evans and Elijah Patterson. They cleaned, cooked, served and worked in the school's laundry. A number of southern girls took slaves to school and the arrangement benefited the college as well as the girls' parents.

Now Sarah and Margaret knelt on either side of the soldier, loosening his uniform to check for injuries. He didn't appear to be wounded; at least there was no blood anywhere. Sarah put smelling salts under his nose and the Rebel soon regained consciousness.

No, he wasn't ill, he said, only weak from hunger. The women helped him into a chair. Margaret summoned Lucy and Elijah and ordered them to smuggle a tray of food from the kitchen, and to say nothing of the soldier's presence.

After the Rebel had eaten, he introduced himself as Corporal Isaac Johnson, Fifth Cavalry, Mississippi section. He'd fought at Pea Ridge and had just escaped from Camp Douglas, Illinois, traveling by night and hiding by day. His father had been killed in General Grant's bombardment of Nashville, and Isaac was seeking to avenge his death by sneaking into Columbia to kill General Halleck.

Sarah's eyes filled. She understood his bitterness. *Her* father had been killed by Robert E. Lee, and she was so devastated by the loss that she had twice tried suicide.

Sarah's mother had sent her to the Columbia Baptist Female College to keep her occupied.

In the coming days, Sarah would be busy in ways her mother never would have envisioned. Keeping Isaac safe and secure in her room was a constant strain. Whenever anyone rapped at the door, Isaac would leap into the closet to hide behind rows of crinoline dresses, or roll under the bed. Sarah was popular, and her many friends liked to congregate in her room because it was the largest and most beautiful room in Senior Hall. It was directly beneath the bell tower.

Although Sarah enjoyed these visits, she feared the soldier would be discovered. Margaret and the slaves had been sworn to secrecy, yet Margaret often spoke thoughtlessly.

Sarah remained with Isaac as much as possible, often feigning a headache at meal times in order to be with him, and requesting that a tray be sent up later. Though she had never before talked to a Confederate soldier, they argued bitterly about slavery and she even accused him of having precipitated the war. Sometimes he would defend his cause, but more often he would smile and sit down at Sarah's piano to play the old songs he'd learned as a child growing up in Senatobia, Mississippi. His great, gray eyes would sweep over the piano keys, then search Sarah's face. When she knew the songs, she would hum the melodies. In the music and in the softness of his eyes, Sarah found a tenderness, a warmth she'd never known. She was only a little surprised when he declared his love for her.

One day, Elijah, tired of colluding with Sarah, told her it was her duty to turn in the soldier. But she assured the slave that Isaac meant no harm.

Finally word reached General Halleck that a Rebel was loose in Columbia. Knowing the attraction that young pretty women held for bored soldiers, the General suspected that the Rebel was being shielded by one of the students at the college. Perhaps even the college administration was providing protective custody, he thought, for Southern sympathies ran high in the city.

General Halleck paid a call on President Williams and Dean Armstrong and warned them both that he would shut down the college unless the soldier was captured.

That evening the president gathered his young students together and delivered the general's ultimatum. His face was pale; his voice strained. The students were stunned.

Sarah was frightened. Had the slave betrayed her? Or had Margaret's loose tongue revealed Isaac's presence? Margaret had shouted the Confederate victory yell out the window. Had a Union soldier heard the cry and noted the room it came from? How much did General Halleck know?

Sarah urged Isaac to surrender. Escape was hopeless, she said; the city was ringed by Union forces. But Isaac had a better plan. He would flee to Canada disguised in a suit "borrowed" from President Williams's closet.

The next evening, after the students had gone downstairs to dinner, Elijah crept along the corridor, the president's clothing draped neatly over one arm. Sarah waited in her room. After dark, Isaac would be on his way—to freedom, to safety.

But at the close of the dinner hour, throngs of young women barged through Sarah's door, screaming, "Turn him in, Sarah! Turn him in!"

Sarah's thin shoulders trembled and she slumped against the piano. *Someone had seen Elijah delivering the clothing to Sarah's room.*

Sarah searched the crowd for a friendly face. Margaret, her color ashen, pushed her way through the group. She put an arm around her roommate and shouted, "Silence!" Her classmates paid no attention. The clamor rose until President Williams and Dean Armstrong burst in. General Halleck was right behind them.

"This college is closed—absolutely finished!" roared the general. "Now, pack up and leave—everyone!"

Isaac threw open the closet door, faced General Halleck and introduced himself. "Sir, I beg you to let the students stay. I have been hiding here without their knowledge."

General Halleck stepped forward. "I arrest you as a spy."

"But I am a soldier, sir."

"That may be, but you're wearing civilian clothes."

"What does that mean?" asked Sarah.

"It means the firing squad," replied Halleck.

Three nights later, at twilight, Corporal Isaac Johnson was executed in the street beneath Sarah's window. When the last shot rang out, the tower bell began to ring. Above its tolling, Sarah thought she heard her lover's voice. It grew louder and louder.

Sarah rushed out her door and climbed the steps to the bell tower. The air blew fresh and cool against her cheeks. "I'm coming, Isaac, I'm coming!" she called.

Her friends found her later, the stout bell cord around her neck.

Margaret put aside the paper, leaving thumb prints in the ink. She rose from her chair and walked to the window. Stars spangled the sky and a full moon had risen above the treetops, illuminating the cluster of soldiers in the street below. Although the Union troops were bivouacked up on the hill, a night patrol kept guard in the street by Senior Hall. The men's voices rose and fell and now and then broke into laughter.

Margaret lingered for a moment, then turned away.

The tower bell began to toll. And the ghost of Sarah Wheeler, searching for her Rebel, began its eternal wanderings.

THE STRANGER OF KNOB NOSTER

On a night full of fury, when rain lashes the earth and the wind howls in a weird way, the stranger returns. He picks his way down a gutted trail from the top of a hill, or knob, that rises abruptly from the edge of the plain. The man died on this hill many years ago, and the old-timers of Knob Noster claim that his ghost comes back in every storm, his lighted lantern swinging back and forth as he descends.

No one recalls when the stranger first appeared in Knob Noster or where he came from, but he had a wicked reputation. He lived like a hermit on the hilltop and whenever he came down into town to buy groceries, mothers hustled their children inside and bolted the doors. The stranger, with eyes averted, darted up and down the streets, in and out of shops, buying a sack of flour or cornmeal here and a tin of coffee there. His trips were infrequent, however; usually he sent his slave—a pleasant man with a ready smile and friendly ways—in search of the necessities.

One day shopkeepers remarked on the black man's absence; he hadn't been seen for several weeks. Two of the bolder merchants asked the hermit what had happened, but he only turned away, grim-faced. A rumor spread that the hermit had beaten his servant to death, but the villagers were too frightened to investigate.

The following summer brought heat and drought. The knobs glistened in the scalding sun and the grass from the base to the top of the hills shriveled and died. In withered treetops, birds perished for lack of food and water. And barren fields baked, then cracked open.

At last, late one afternoon, thunder clouds began piling up in the western sky. Toward sunset, they became darker and heavier; thunder grumbled far in the distance. A faint breeze turned the poplar leaves. People cast anxious glances at the sky and assured one another, "Rain will surely come this time."

Darkness settled over the valley an hour earlier than usual. The constant lightning turned night into day, and the thunder, closer now, growled like a shackled beast. The approach of this storm, unlike others, brought a curious feeling of dread to the villagers. None expressed it, but all felt a sense of doom as they hurried to the safety of their homes. There, through closed windows, they peered out, watching, waiting for the storm to break.

Suddenly, those who were looking toward the knob saw, between lightning flashes, a glow in the darkness. High up on the knob, the orb swayed back and forth like a lantern being carried. Then a great burst of lightning lit up the entire knob and the figure of a man, doubled over, fighting the wind that tore at his clothes and tugged at his lantern. It was the hermit. Evidently terrified by the wild roar of the storm, he was heading to town for human companionship.

He inched along the trail, the light bobbing beside him. He hadn't gone far when a brilliant blaze of lightning and a cannonade of thunder drove the watchers away from their windows. When they looked again, the lantern light was gone. The rain pounded the earth.

At dawn, a group of men started for the knob. Halfway up the side of the hill, they found the knob dweller. The dead man's face was so contorted with fear that the men staggered back in horror. The body bore no marks of any kind to indicate the cause of death.

Since that time, villagers looking out toward the knob on a stormy night often see a light moving back and forth descending the hill. The elderly and the superstitious shake their heads. They know that on a night full of fury, the hermit walks again.

THE SPINNING WHEEL GHOST

Along the Missouri-Arkansas line, they tell the story of the spinning wheel ghost, a frequent nighttime visitor, whose tormented cries rise above the hum of her wheel. The persistant specter first appeared in February, 1888.

Ruth and Sis Brooks, unmarried, middle-aged sisters, were the first to see it while walking home late at night from a meeting at Mount Zion Church. As they crossed a small ravine close to their house, they heard behind them the distinct hum of a spinning wheel. Looking around, they saw nothing but black tree trunks rising from a quilt of snow. They started to run, the sound buzzing in their ears like a swarm of bees.

When they got to the door of their house, the spinning noise stopped and a woman's wailing filled the air. They rushed inside, slammed the door and threw the bolt.

At first, the sisters kept the incident to themselves. But one night they visited their grandmother. Neighbors had gathered and spent the evening in lively conversation around the blazing hearth. Ruth and Sis told the story of their strange experience. No sooner had they finished than a buzzing sounded from overhead, followed by the sobs of an anguished woman.

Three of the men took lanterns and searched the attic. They found no spinning wheel and no evidence that anyone had recently been up there.

Ruth and Sis were so badly frightened that they refused to stay, and one of the men trudged through the snow with them to their home two miles away.

They never again discussed their adventures, and if anyone mentioned ghosts, Ruth and Sis Brooks changed the subject.

Twenty-six years later, in 1914, Grace Conley was visiting her cousin, Nancy Young and family in the Brooks' old neighborhood. Grace had brought her small daughter, Lucy, with her. One night after Grace and Nancy had put their children to bed, the grownups sat up talking by the fireplace until midnight.

When they retired, Grace and her daughter were given a room that adjoined the dining room. A bed stood in one corner and an ironing board in another; an old-fashioned wardrobe filled the other end of the room, leaving only a narrow passage around the bed. As Grace undressed, she noticed that Nancy had left a can of the baby's talcum powder on the ironing board.

Grace was just dozing off when she heard someone enter her room. Had Nancy come back for the talcum powder? The soft footfalls approached the wardrobe. Nancy must have forgotten where she'd left the can.

"Nancy, the talcum's on the ironing board," Grace said.

There was no reply.

"On the ironing board," Grace repeated.

No response.

"Nancy!" she screamed. Then louder, "Nancy! Nancy!"

A drowsy reply drifted through the wall that separated the hostess's room from that of her guest. "What is it, Grace?" A moment later Nancy pushed open the door to Grace's room. She found her guest sitting up in bed, wide awake. Little Lucy was crying.

"Weren't you just in here?" asked Grace.

"No."

"Someone was," stammered Grace.

The two women lit the lamps and searched the house. All the doors were locked. No one could have entered, for the family's dogs were still sound asleep.

Then from Grace's bedroom came the hum of a spinning wheel . . . and a woman's chilling wail.

Nancy and Grace were terrified. Grace *knew* she could not go back into that room. Sympathizing, Nancy set up a makeshift bed for Grace and Lucy in the living room, and the household settled down again.

Grace was almost asleep when the spinning wheel ghost returned. It came into the living room and walked back and forth beside the bed, waking both Grace and Nancy. As they lit the lanterns again, they could hear from the bedroom the clear hum of the spinning wheel, followed by the cries of the tormented woman.

That was the ghost's final visit of the night. In the morning Nancy told Grace this strange story:

"I had always left my two children to play on the bed in that room while I milked the cows. One evening my sister was here and I left the children in there as usual. When I came back, she had the children in the kitchen, huddled in one corner, and she looked frightened. She said there was 'something' in the room and made me promise never to leave the children in there alone. Of course, after that I never did."

Now Nancy guessed what her sister must have seen or heard. The ghost of an unknown woman was using her spinning wheel to try to attract her loved ones to her, to find her way "back home." Nancy's sister had only tried to protect her from the awful truth: by some mysterious means the restless dead return to walk among us.

MARK TWAIN, PSYCHIC

The literary father of Tom Sawyer and Huckleberry Finn was a dreamer. How else could one man have created characters so real that they've become part of the American experience? The mind of Samuel Clemens, known as Mark Twain, roamed continents and centuries to create his fictional narratives.

But Sam Clemens also had nightmares. In one, he foresaw the tragic death of his own brother.

It all began with Sam Clemens in New Orleans dreaming of Peru. The exotic South American country appealed mightily to the naive Missourian. He had just finished reading a graphic account of one Lieutenant

Herndon's Amazon expedition. So in 1856, Sam left Cincinnati for New Orleans, determined to embark on the next steamer heading for the southern hemisphere. Unfortunately, no steamboats left New Orleans for that port o' call.

With no friends and even less money, Sam turned to a relatively new acquaintance, Capt. Horace Bixby, a pilot on the steamer *Paul Jones* on which Sam had traveled to New Orleans. Sam had struck up an acquaintance with Bixby on the journey, and Bixby had let him take a few turns at the wheel. Now Sam asked his friend to take him on as an apprentice pilot. Bixby agreed—for a fee of $500, $100 to be paid in advance.

Sam steered for Bixby north to St. Louis where the fledgling apprentice borrowed $100 from his sister Pamela's husband, William A. Moffett. The balance was to be paid from Sam's earnings as a cub pilot. For the next eighteen months, Sam learned the art of piloting a steamboat on the Mississippi River, first with Horace Bixby on the *Paul Jones* and later with Mr. Brown, a pilot on the *Pennsylvania*.

While apprenticing on the *Pennsylvania*, Sam found a job on the boat for his brother, Henry. It wasn't nearly as glamorous as life seen from the towering pilot house; it didn't even pay a salary, but Henry was content to be a "mud clerk." There was the promise of promotion, perhaps all the way to first clerk, or purser. Henry signed on early in 1858, his long hours including the time the boat spent in dock at New Orleans or St. Louis, the far ends of its usual Mississippi River run.

Pilots didn't have any duties when the steamers lay in port. In St. Louis, Sam stayed with his sister and brother-in-law. Henry usually visited each night, returning to the boat at midnight. A mud clerk worked from dawn until after dusk each day.

Sam's eerie dream of death came one night before the *Pennsylvania* was scheduled to return to New

Orleans. Henry left about eleven, more solemn than usual. He shook hands all around, as was the custom. His mother, who was staying with the Moffetts, said goodbye to him in the upstairs sitting room. Something made her follow Henry to the head of the stairs where she again bade him farewell. Henry's seriousness was unusual, and his mother noticed it.

Sam awoke before dawn the next day with horrifyingly clear pictures playing in his brain: his brother laid out in a metal coffin stretching between two chairs in the Moffett's sitting room. He wore a suit belonging to Sam. His hands clasped an arrangement of roses to his chest. All the flowers were white, except for one bright red rose in the center.

Sam dressed quickly. Was his brother dead? He honestly didn't know, so real did the dream seem. Rather than go into the parlor and face the ordeal he thought lay ahead, he left the house. The cool air bathed his face as he strode down Locust, and then onto Fourteenth Street. He suddenly stopped. Henry was not dead! Of course, it had all been a bad dream, a nightmare! He ran back to the house, galloped up the stairs and burst into the sitting room. There *was* no casket. Although he still felt a chill at the reality of the dream, Sam's joy was profound. But he couldn't shake the dream's memory, even on the uneventful trip downriver to New Orleans.

On that trip, Sam Clemens had an argument with his master, Mr. Brown (recounted in *Life on the Mississippi*) that led to his dismissal from the *Pennsylvania*.

Fortunately Sam had an irregular job in New Orleans for the times when he was forced into idleness between river trips. He worked as night watchman on the freight dock, his pay $3.00 for each twelve-hour shift. Henry often joined him on his rounds before returning to the boat.

A few days later, with Henry on board, the *Pennsylvania* left New Orleans for St. Louis, while Sam remained behind. The loss of his job probably saved the life of America's greatest humorist.

A few miles below Memphis, the *Pennsylvania's* boilers exploded, scattering debris for hundreds of yards, killing passengers and crew and seriously injuring three dozen people, including Henry Clemens.

Sam was on another steamer about a day behind. As they traveled north, he began hearing the news at towns where they stopped. He finally found Henry on a mattress in a large Memphis warehouse, which had become a makeshift hospital. Around him were the burned and maimed survivors of the explosion, the screams of the dying echoing in the high-ceilinged room. Henry—among the most critically injured—had inhaled scalding steam. Doctors and nurses, forced to pay more attention to those they thought would live, told Sam that Henry had little chance.

Dr. Peyton, however, promised Sam he would take a special interest in Henry and try to save him. Miraculously, Henry responded to the old physician's ministrations, and within a week was pronounced out of danger, although, Peyton warned, he still needed much rest. While Sam sat with his brother one evening, the cries of the injured were particularly disturbing. Dr. Peyton told Sam that he would order one-eighth grain of morphine for Henry, to help him sleep.

Henry did not live to see the next sun rise. The young physician on duty, whether due to a misunderstanding of Dr. Peyton's instructions, or the lack of measuring devices, administered too much morphine. As a result, young Henry Clemens died a few hours later.

His body was carried into what was called the "dead room" and placed in the only metal coffin available, a gift from some Memphis women. That is where Sam found him. At once the dream came back to him in perfect detail. Henry was dressed in one of Sam's suits. As Sam stood near the casket, an elderly woman walked in and placed in the dead boy's hands a bouquet of roses. They were white . . . with a single red rose at the center.

Twain accompanied his brother's body back to St. Louis. When the boat docked, Sam set off for his brother-in-law's office, hoping to find him there, as the business day had just begun. Sam missed him, however, and by the time he got back to the boat, Moffett had already recovered the body, and had it sent on to his home.

Sam raced ahead, wanting to save his mother the trauma of viewing Henry's morphine-twisted face. He arrived just in time to forestall the unloading while he went inside to comfort her. Upstairs in the sitting room, he found two chairs spaced a coffin's length apart, waiting to receive their burden. If he had arrived a few minutes later, the casket would have been positioned on them, the final detail of his dream fulfilled.

Sam Clemens lived for more than half a century. But that premonition of death stayed with him for the rest of his life. Even as a very old man, he could see every detail of the dream—and its tragic counterpart in life— with complete accuracy.

A WARNING FROM THE GRAVE

Henry Burchard and his wife, Harriet, farmed near Kirksville, Missouri. The couple was inseparable; Harriet saw to that. Believing Henry to be "too handsome for his own good," she saved him from the lures of prettier women by accompanying him everywhere he went. Henry reacted with amused tolerance, although sometimes he complained that he couldn't even cut a plug of tobacco on the back stoop without Harriet's banging through the door after him.

Henry had never been unfaithful to his wife. He claimed that she was born jealous. He did have the conversational habit of looking a person directly in the eye, and women usually responded warmly to such attention. He believed it was common courtesy, although an edgy husband observing his own wife speaking to Henry might have had other words for it.

In the winter of 1873, Harriet Burchard died of consumption. She and Henry had just celebrated their thirtieth wedding anniversary. Henry was shocked and saddened by his wife's death, but he often recalled her words, "Man was not meant to live alone." That spring, five months after Harriet's death, Henry married Catherine Webster, a young widow of the community whom he and Harriet had known for several years. After the death of her husband in a farm accident, Catherine had rented out the farm and moved to town where she lived on her rental income and some small savings.

Three weeks after her marriage to Henry, Catherine was home alone when a tremendous crash—it sounded as if rocks were clattering across the roof—shook the house. Catherine dashed outside. Sure enough, rocks of all sizes lay strewn everywhere. Who had thrown them? The nearest neighbor was half a mile away down the dirt road. Catherine gathered up her long skirts and picked her way around the farmhouse. She saw no one.

Then, to her amazement, the rocks at her feet rose slowly into the cloudless sky, hovered above the rooftop and cascaded over the shingles again.

The poor woman, too frightened to move, stood rigid, her hands shielding her face.

That night when Henry arrived home from town, Catherine related what had happened. He told her it was nonsense, that she was just tired and overwrought from the excitement of the wedding. At her insistence, they went outside to look, but the rocks had disappeared. Only clumps of coarse grass edged the foundation. Catherine was more alarmed than ever.

The next night, while the couple slept, their bedclothes were snatched away. Shivering in his nightshirt,

Henry leaped up to find them heaped on the floor at the foot of the bed. Had a breeze blown through the window? No, it was closed, as always, to keep out the bad night air. Had Catherine been restless and accidentally pushed the covers off? Perhaps. But she looked relaxed and peaceful now, sleeping soundly.

Henry put the bedding back on the bed and crawled in. No sooner had he fallen asleep than he was again awakened to find the covers on the floor. Catherine still lay unmoving, her eyes closed, her long hair spread like a fan across her pillow. Henry thought it unlikely that she had kicked off the bedding . . . unless, of course, she was punishing him for not believing her story of the rocks. He remade the bed, taking care this time to tuck in the quilts quite tightly. Now, they could not easily be thrown off.

Eventually, Henry got back to sleep, only to awaken a third time, when his pillow was suddenly whisked out from under his head. He found it on the floor. Catherine must be to blame. After all, she was the only other person in the house. He got up and lit a lantern just as Catherine's pillow flew out from beneath her head and landed at Henry's feet. Her head fell back against the mattress and she woke up, screaming.

Henry stared. What had jerked the pillows from under their heads? Putting down the lantern, he sat on the edge of the bed and took his wife in his arms.

She looked up at him, sleep still in her eyes. "But Henry, why are you up?"

He would not frighten her. "You were restless," he began. "I thought maybe you were having a nightmare. You . . . threw your pillow on the floor." He handed it to her.

"I don't remember."

"No," he sighed. "But now it's very late and we both need sleep." Henry tucked the covers tightly around his wife, extinguished the lantern and got back into bed. Daylight came too soon.

The mysterious events of that night recurred and Henry, unable to explain them, tried to forget. Yet he always woke up when the bedding and his pillow were jerked from the bed. Catherine, on the other hand, usually slept on, and he envied her.

Then came the night Henry would never forget. Unable to sleep, he was in bed reading by dim lamplight. Catherine slept soundly beside him. Suddenly, invisible hands rolled back the bedding to reveal a message on the underside of a white coverlet: "These things shall continue forever!"

With a chill Henry recognized the handwriting. Harriet, his first wife, had delivered a warning from the grave. Now they were to remain inseparable for all time!

Chapter VIII. Nebraska

"Mrs. Buterbaugh worked her way through the crush of students and entered a room at the end of the hall. She had taken only a few steps when she stopped, overcome by a strong, nauseating odor. . . . Mrs. Buterbaugh stared through the glass window into a world she had never seen. There were no familiar landmarks. No streets. No buildings. Madison Street, less than a half block from her building, wasn't there. Neither was the Willard sorority house directly across the expanse of lawn. The secretary realized she had stepped backward in time, had walked into a scene that belonged to the past."

"A JOURNEY THROUGH TIME"

A JOURNEY THROUGH TIME

Just before nine o'clock on a bright October morning in 1963, Mrs. Coleen Buterbaugh left her secretarial office to do an errand for her boss, Dean Sam Dahl. Classes at Nebraska Wesleyan University were changing and students shuffling in and out of various rooms clogged the hallway. From behind one closed classroom door, Mrs. Buterbaugh heard the light, metallic music of a marimba.

Mrs. Buterbaugh worked her way through the crush of students and entered a room at the end of the hall. She had taken only a few steps when she stopped, overcome by a strong, nauseating odor she couldn't identify. She coughed and choked until the air cleared. Silence enveloped her; the noises in the hall behind her muted.

The secretary's eyes took in the scene before her. At a bookcase against the back wall, a tall young woman stood with her right arm reaching up, as if for the top shelf. But the figure was frozen in place. Mrs. Buterbaugh felt lightheaded and put her hand on the back of a chair to steady herself. She realized she'd never seen the woman before, not anywhere on campus. Strangely attired, she wore a long-sleeved white blouse, long, dark skirt, coarse stockings and sturdy oxfords. Her bushy hairdo hardly looked contemporary.

With mounting horror, Mrs. Buterbaugh realized the woman was not real. Gradually, the figure faded. Now the secretary saw only the bookcase. Yet she had the feeling she was not alone in the room. She was being studied by someone. She glanced toward the walnut desk and the leather chair to her left. She felt a presence. But she couldn't see anything!

Sunlight, streaming through a large, low-silled window, bleached the desk top and the bare wooden floor. Mrs. Buterbaugh stared through the glass into a world she had never seen. There were no familiar landmarks. No streets. No buildings. Madison Street, less than half a block from her building, wasn't there. Neither was the Willard sorority house directly across the expanse of lawn. The secretary realized she had stepped backward in time, had walked into a scene that belonged to the past.

She stumbled into the hallway and was surrounded again by noisy students. Marimba music filled her ears. Her apparent excursion into another dimension had taken place within a few minutes.

Mrs. Buterbaugh was disturbed by the incident. It was unlike anything that had ever happened to her and she was determined to solve the mystery. Who, or what, had she seen in that room? How could the present-day campus buildings and streets have vanished before her eyes?

She searched the faces in old yearbooks and campus histories, and questioned elderly faculty members. A 1915 photograph in the university files showed the campus as she had seen it during that strange interlude. Finally she identified the ghost at the bookcase. It was a female music professor who had taught at the college from 1912 to 1936. Most astonishing was the fact that the teacher had died in that room just before nine on that long ago October morning. Mrs. Buterbaugh had been transported backward through time to the moment and place of the teacher's death.

THE GRINNING SKELETONS

He knew he couldn't make it. Darkness had set in, the horse was nearly exhausted, and Fremont was still at least five miles distant. As the storm spilled its fury upon the earth, Jacob Meyer hunched low in the saddle, knees pressed against the steaming flanks of his mount. He winced as the rain lanced his back. The prairie had become an inland lake into which the horse had already stumbled once, but regained its footing.

In the next flash of lightning, Meyer caught a glimpse of an old, abandoned shack. He recalled having seen it before. It had stood for years, wind and rain nibbling away at its foundation until the rickety walls leaned at a crazy angle. The chimney had been toppled by the storms and the windows shot out by thieves. But on this May night in 1877, the dilapidated structure was the refuge Meyer sought. He'd tie up for awhile, then swing on into town. His wife wouldn't worry. She'd know he had taken shelter.

Meyer tethered the horse to a nearby cottonwood tree, then sloshed to the cabin's door. It sagged and he had to lift it from the bottom to open it. Once inside, he shivered, wet clothes pasted to his body, water running into pools at his feet.

He sat on the floor, squeezed shut his eyes for a few moments of rest. His back and shoulders ached. As a young man with a fast, sure-footed pony, he could have made it home to Fremont. But Meyer and his horse were no longer young, and he was wise enough to honor his own, and his mount's, limitations.

When Meyer opened his tired eyes, he sensed presences around him, just as he always sensed the presence of his wife when she approached silently and stood behind his chair while he was reading. Meyer squinted into the darkness. He couldn't see anything, but a rattling sound assaulted his ears. Was someone sleeping in a corner of the room and snoring in peculiar fashion? He had met no one on the prairie and he hadn't noticed a horse tied up outside.

Then a flash of lightning illuminated the cabin's single room, and Meyer saw the occupants clearly. Three hideous skeletons stood in a row in front of the fireplace, facing him. The two taller skeletons stood at each end, the shorter one between them. Father, mother and child? Meyer felt droplets running down his cheeks and knew it wasn't rain. He pulled his cap low over his eyes to shut out the gruesome sight.

But as if to command his attention, the skeletons rattled louder. When Meyer looked again, the bony figures shimmered and glowed in a pale blue light, their jaws twisted into sickly grins. They jerked like puppets on a string, the bones of their feet dangling several inches above the floor. Meyer thought he saw ribbons of flesh still clinging beneath the empty eye sockets of the child. His stomach churned, a lightness came over him and he passed out.

He never remembered staggering from the cabin. When he regained consciousness, he was lying in the sodden grass halfway between the door of the shack and the tree where he had tied the horse. The moon had risen and stars sprinkled the sky.

When Meyer related the experience next day, the villagers were horrified. For weeks afterward they talked of nothing else, speculating upon the identities of the skeletons. Were they the remains of murdered settlers?

No one knew. But no one in the area ever again went inside the abandoned shack on the outskirts of Fremont.

THE TERROR OF OMAHA HEIGHTS

Irish coffee laced with gossip. That's what an invitation from Bridget O'Hanlon always implied, and Henrietta Hale was looking forward to a pleasant afternoon with her friend. She could not know how terrifying the visit would turn out to be.

Dried leaves crackled under her feet and the wind tugged at her shawl as she hurried along the streets of Omaha Heights on that November day in 1888. Bridget heard her friend's steps on the walk and threw open the door. "Sure, and begorra, Henny, you're looking fit! Do come in!" She helped her guest with her shawl and bonnet and then said abruptly, "Now I've got some work to finish, but I won't be long."

Henrietta watched her hostess vanish up the staircase. Bridget was well-meaning, but distracted, often leaving her guests to fend for themselves while she finished a chore in another part of the house. Casual acquaintances thought her rude, but close friends learned to be tolerant of her disconcerting ways. Henrietta was a close friend.

Henrietta went directly to the sitting room at the rear of the house and settled into a Morris chair by the window. No sooner had she sat down than she heard a knock at the front door. Was another visitor expected?

She listened a moment for Bridget's steps on the stairs, then went to the door herself. No one was there. She closed the door, but before she could lift her hand from the knob, the knocking came again, more insistent than before. Henrietta opened the door a second time.

She looked up and down the street which, at this hour, was deserted. Unable to account for the sounds, she shut the door and returned to the sitting room.

A moment later, the pounding on the front door shook the walls of the house. Henrietta leaped from her chair and peered cautiously around the doorjamb before stepping into the hallway. The front door stood wide open, and a few leaves had blown in onto the carpet. Yet no one was in sight. At the same time, she heard heavy footsteps behind her in the sitting room. When she turned to look, the front door slammed shut.

Then the cacophony began—footsteps reverberated from the front parlor, the kitchen, the bedrooms, until every room in the house vibrated with the awesome sounds of tramping feet. The dining room chairs rose and crashed against the walls, and agonizing groans and cries rose from the cellar.

Henrietta Hale stood trembling in the hallway. Portraits in heavy frames on the wall opposite her fell to the floor, spraying shards of glass into the air. Terrified, fearing the imminent collapse of the house, she screamed, then fled by the back door. With shocking indecency, she hiked her skirts and ran. Fiendish yells from inside the house followed her as she raced down the street.

That evening Bridget O'Hanlon and her husband, John, called on Henrietta. Bridget carried a pot of Irish coffee. She confessed that she'd heard the commotion that afternoon, but had been too frightened to come downstairs. When the walls started to shake, she said, she'd hidden under the bed.

John explained that five years earlier, when repairs were being made on the house, a human skeleton was found in the cellar. It was thought that a peddler was murdered and dumped into a makeshift grave beneath the kitchen. Shortly after this discovery, the footsteps were heard. From that time on few families remained long in the house.

When the O'Hanlons bought it in 1887, John hired Eddie Warner, a painter, to do some redecorating. Warner worked half a day, then quit because of the strange noises. His successor, Frank Hitchcock, also quit the job prematurely.

Bridget told Henrietta that she and John would be moving out of the house the next day. Although they'd heard raps on the door and footsteps on the stairs many times, recent noises had become more terrifying.

Was the old peddler banging on the door to announce his presence? Wreaking havoc to avenge his murder? The O'Hanlons thought so, as did Henrietta Hale. So when the O'Hanlons invited her back for a farewell cup of Irish coffee, she sent her regrets.

THE CRY ON BLACKBIRD HILL

On October 17, 1933, scores of interested people gathered at Blackbird Hill on the Omaha Indian reservation. There they ate a bountiful picnic supper and sat silently in the moonlight, waiting. Hours passed, the crowd sat, and no sounds were heard save the occasional cry of a night hawk. Finally, the women packed up the food baskets, and the disappointed multitude dispersed.

What were the people hoping to hear? A woman's piercing scream as she fell to her death in the Missouri River!

The story begins on a bright fall day in 1849. A band of Omaha Indians was hunting along the Missouri River north of Decatur. Near Blackbird Hill they came upon an emaciated white man, his feet bare and bleeding, his body barely covered by rags of clothing. The man was delirious and unable to speak coherently.

The Indians carried him back to their camp and summoned the medicine man. As the stranger lay on a pallet in the wigwam, the medicine man sprinkled dried herbs over the hot coals of his fire. Then, fanning the smoke over the prostrate form, he rubbed his forehead and murmured incantations.

The man eventually recovered and stayed with the Indians until he regained strength enough to travel. Before he left he told his hosts a strange story. He had been born and raised in the East. After he finished his schooling, his father sent him abroad on a business trip. On the way home he was shipwrecked and five years went by before he got back to the United States. Only then did he learn the sad news. In his absence, his mother had died and his sweetheart, who had promised to wait for him, had married his best friend and moved west.

The brokenhearted young man set out to find his girl. If he could locate the couple perhaps he could persuade the husband to release his wife. The hopeful traveler joined the wagon trains carrying prospectors to the California gold fields. He searched all the way to the coast, but in all the changing sea of faces, he saw not one he recognized.

Bitter and discouraged, he headed home. Sailing down the Missouri River, he landed one evening at the foot of Blackbird Hill. A well-worn path wound up the bluff to a cabin where, incredibly, the man found his sweetheart. She confessed that she had never stopped loving him, but, when he failed to return, had supposed him dead. She told him that when her husband got home later in the evening, she would ask to be released from her vows. They planned to leave together in the morning.

When the husband returned, he didn't see the stranger waiting in a grove of trees near the cabin. Hearing his wife's plans, he pleaded with her to stay. When she refused, he became enraged and, overcome by jealousy and anger, attacked her with his hunting knife. Her screams were silenced; the blows to her breast pierced her heart. The husband dropped the knife, gathered his bleeding and barely conscious wife into his arms, and raced for the cliff. With scarcely a moment's pause, he leaped with her toward the river below, her final scream of agony lingering in the cool air.

From his hiding place, the former sweetheart witnessed the murder-suicide. Numbed by grief and shock, he lapsed in and out of consciousness. Then he wandered aimlessly, ill and starving, until found by the Indians.

When he left his hosts, who had saved his life, he returned to his home in the East. But he never forgot his harrowing experience. Blackbird Hill too was marked forever with the horror of the murder. The grass stopped growing on the trail from the cabin to the cliff. And the belief persists that each year on October 17, a woman's chilling scream can be heard at the top of the hill.

THE HAUNTED SODDY

Late one summer evening in the mid-1880s, two Phelps County farmers were heading home from a board meeting at Phelps Center, the newly-established county seat. Both had spent the daylight hours cultivating corn, and now they nursed their weariness in silence on the wagon seat. The owner of the wagon had left his double-shovel plow in the wagon box. It clattered from side to side as the wagon bounced over ruts in the road.

On a lonely lane half-a-mile south of the present village of Funk, a supposedly empty sod house on an abandoned farm hunched by the side of the road. Its owner, driven out by the devastating grasshopper plague of 1874, had gone east. As the farm wagon creaked past the empty hut, wild, terrifying screams sounded from within. The farmers' hair stood on end.

The chilling cries spooked the horses, and they broke their traces and bolted. The wagon, propelled by some unseen force, sped backward so fast that the wheels nearly tore from the axles. The men clung to each other and to the edge of their seat. Just in time they ducked as the plow sailed over their heads. Then they too were hurled into a field. Holding on to each other for support, they limped home. The horses had beaten them there and paced nervously outside the barn.

In the morning, neighbors found the wagon in a ditch with the rear wheels crushed. The plow was located behind the soddy. The two farmers never could explain their harrowing experience, but the people of the area didn't question their story. They were highly respected, not given to hysterics.

As word of the haunted soddy spread, no one ever traveled that lane again. People went miles out of their way, if necessary, to avoid it.

A few years later, a bachelor named Larson rented the farm. A pleasant man with a warm smile and a firm handshake, he made friends quickly. Neighbors warned Larson that the soddy was haunted, but he laughed. He could live with ghosts, he said. They might even be welcome companions on long winter evenings when only the howl of a blizzard and the cry of a hungry coyote punctuated the silence.

Larson worked the farm with diligence, planting, cultivating and harvesting each crop in its time. In the evening hours, he improved the soddy itself; he replaced the rotted leather hinges on the door, squared the windows and sealed up cracks in the earthen blocks. The rhythm of Larson's life, ordered by the seasons, moved in calm, predictable fashion.

Then one summer night he dreamed that he was running through an empty prairie, with a herd of wild horses thundering after him. There was no tree to climb, no shack to duck into. He screamed, but only the wind answered. Just before the beasts trampled him to death, he fell, waiting to feel the weight of the wild animals that would crush him.

Larson awoke in a cold sweat. He could not recall a nightmare more vivid nor frightening. Sitting on the edge of his bed, he rubbed life back into his arms and legs. Then he heard the galloping horses again, thundering toward the soddy. His nightmare had come to life! The walls and floor vibrated as the beasts whinnied and circled.

Larson, steadying himself on tables and chairs, staggered to the door and cracked it open. Amazingly, the night was soundless. A full moon hung in the sky and a soft breeze murmured in the cottonwoods. He stepped out onto the stubble of grass, welcoming its prickliness on his bare feet.

There were no horses, no hoof prints. Where had the beasts gone? And why had they come? Larson wondered if he were losing his mind. Yet he was certain he had not imagined the incident.

The next night he stayed up, drinking coffee, pacing the floor, waiting for the horses. Again they came. He could not see them, but he heard them clearly, stampeding around the hut. When he went outside, again, all was quiet. There was nothing in sight to account for the commotion.

Night after night the phantom horses returned and night after night Larson was awakened by their arrival. But then a new sound filled the house—a low cooing. He never heard it in the daytime, only at night when he tried to sleep. Was it perhaps the call of a mourning dove nesting nearby? Hardly. With mounting horror, Larson realized the sound was issuing from the earthen walls of his home. He tapped, he probed. The walls were solid and he could find no source for the sounds.

But a night's sleep was becoming impossible. Now something dragged the quilts off the sleeping man; doors between rooms were thrown open and banged shut by invisible hands. Larson's eyes became puffy from wakefulness and he jumped whenever a bird sang in a treetop. His neighbors, meeting him in the village and noting the change that had come over him, asked if anything was wrong. He always shook his head no.

At the start of the next planting season, weeds and shrubs took over the fields behind the soddy. Larson had fled.

The next tenant . . . and the last . . . was also a bachelor. Nels was a giant of a man who liked nothing better than to sit in the gathering dusk and play his violin after a long day of field work. When he first moved in, a couple of neighbors called to tell him the story of the weird goings-on in and around the soddy. They did not go into great detail, however, for fear of upsetting the big Swede.

Nels listened attentively, snapped his wide red suspenders, and said, with a grin as wide as the Platte River, "We drink." Sitting in the sun of the open doorway, the three men consumed many mugs of coffee and discussed the crops and the weather. Before the guests went home, they knew that once again they had a fine friend living in the soddy. They hoped Nels would stay and prosper.

Like his predecessor, Nels worked the farm with care and made more improvements in the house. Things went well for the first few months.

Then one night, just before crawling into bed, Nels glanced out a window. He caught his breath, rubbed his eyes and looked again. A huge fire burned in the barnyard, the flames leaping higher than the tallest cottonwood. Nels felt his stomach tighten and pain shoot down his spine. The barn would go and with it his stock—a few cows, the team of oxen and the horse. Then he saw that the flames hadn't yet reached the front of the building. Maybe he could get to the barn door and save at least the horse.

He dashed out, his nightshirt flapping, and ran so hard his chest ached. With both hands, he pulled open the heavy barn door. At that moment, a strange feeling came over him. He was not hot; no smoke filled his nostrils. The flames didn't crackle or give off heat. The fire was gone!

Inside the barn, the animals slept. Nels sagged against the door as he looked around. There was no sign of burned grass anywhere. Oddly, his eye caught the glitter of a $20 gold piece. What good fortune! He bent over to pick it up, then saw it was nothing but an old rusty two-cent piece. He took it back to the house anyway.

Nels made a fresh pot of coffee and sat up the remainder of the night pondering the significance of the phenomenon he'd witnessed. He had seen the fire with his own eyes. How had it disappeared? Why hadn't it scorched the earth and the barn siding? Perhaps it wasn't fire. But then, what was it? Nels found no answers. Finally he eased back into bed and, exhausted, fell asleep.

The mysterious fires continued to erupt every week, lighting up the night sky. And each time Nels rushed outside, the flames vanished before his eyes.

Late on a November night, when hoarfrost powdered the corn stubble and winds tore the last fluttering leaves from the trees, Nels became even more apprehensive. Normally an easy-going, relaxed man, he realized how much he had changed since the fires had started. And now: this new feeling of absolute terror and dread. He felt lightheaded and his hands trembled. Deciding that perhaps he was coming down with the flu, he went to bed early.

At three-thirty in the morning, Nels was jarred awake by violin music. Wild, savage notes seemed to pour out of the corners and walls of the tiny room. Nels strugged out of bed and lit a lantern. On the floor against the far wall his violin stood upright, the bow moving deftly, expertly over the strings.

Nels saw the violin clearly. No one was near it. Not anyone he could see. He started toward it, but a force of some kind held him back. It was as if he were pushing against a solid wall.

Dropping onto the edge of the bed, Nels swung his head down between his knees to keep from fainting. The playing continued, swinging from one tune into the next. Nels didn't remember going back to sleep. The last piece he recalled hearing was "The Little Old Sod Shanty on the Claim," a song written in 1871 and popular with the settlers.

At dawn, Nels stretched himself awake and laughed heartily at his nightmare of the previous evening. It had seemed so real, like the nightmares he used to have as a child. He got up to make his coffee and then stopped. The violin lay on the floor where it had been played. It *hadn't* been a nightmare! The instrument's case stood open in the corner. Nels felt sick.

Later that day, he put the violin away and locked the case. Then he threaded the key onto a length of twine and tied it around his neck. Now nothing could get at the instrument without breaking the lock or smashing the case.

That night, Nels was again awakened by the chilling music. He groped for the metal key on his improvised necklace. It was secure. He knew then that the thing had smashed the case to get at the fiddle. Pulling the covers over his head, he tried to shut out the sounds that assaulted his ears.

In the morning, Nels again found the violin on the floor. But the case was locked and showed no signs of having been tampered with! Fearful of what might happen next, Nels moved out of the soddy that night. Before he left, he told his neighbors about the incidents. No one ever moved into the place again.

As late as 1895, ghastly noises still issued from the once again dilapidated and deserted sod house. Eerie lights were seen flashing in the weed-choked fields. The children of Funk sat silent and breathless as their mothers talked of the ghostly phenomena. And the young men of the neighborhood, like their fathers before them, traveled out of their way to avoid passing the haunted soddy on the lonely dirt lane.

ALMA'S NIGHTWALKER

At eleven o'clock on a March night in 1902, H.S. Wetherald hung up his green eyeshade and turned the key in the door of the newspaper office. It had been a long, hard day, but this week's issue of the Alma *Journal* would be special. Former Congressman Ashton C. Shallenberger was home on a visit and Wetherald had written a long story on that event in addition to his weekly editor's column.

As Wetherald started down the moonlit street, he turned up his overcoat collar against the raw wind. March was always a restless month on the prairie, the wind soughing and moaning over the snow-filled fields, then doubling back, in an afterthought of fury, to lash the shops that huddled shoulder-to-shoulder on Alma's business street.

At the end of the first block, the editor saw *her*—a tall, young woman dressed all in black. She emerged from a dark alley and crossed in front of him. Wetherald stopped short to avoid a collision. He knew everyone in town. But this woman was a stranger. In fact, she didn't look quite real. In her long, somber garb, she floated past him and vanished.

Wetherald rubbed his tired eyes. Where could she have gone? Hallucination? That was it. He'd been working too hard.

But it wasn't Wetherald's weary mind playing tricks on him. He had seen a ghost. It would return.

The next night, Congressman Shallenberger, on the way to a party in his honor, parked his carriage and proceeded on foot to the host's house. He sensed someone following him. He spun around. The black-robed figure of the woman floated toward him. Shallenberger fled in the opposite direction.

Several nights later, Frank Griggsby, the carriage dealer, met the phantom woman. Hands in pockets, he was whistling a jaunty tune as he strolled down the street. When the figure in black brushed past him, the whistle froze on his lips.

He raced after the thing and had almost caught it when a horse and buggy clopped into an intersection and stopped. The figure lifted from the pavement and appeared to sail through the body of the horse. Griggsby dashed around the buggy and sprinted on.

He ran faster and faster and was closing the gap when a boy on a bicycle suddenly appeared between him and the figure. The youngster, startled by his predicament, lost control and crashed into a hitching post.

Griggsby stopped long enough to see that the child wasn't seriously hurt. When he glanced up, he saw no trace of the mysterious lady in the dimly-lit street. With a sense of relief, he trudged homeward.

But his relief was short-lived. He had gone only two blocks when he again felt something behind him. A glance over his shoulder confirmed his fear—the figure was swooping toward him, her black shawl flapping, her arms flailing the air. Griggsby ran until he reached his house. He threw open the door, slammed it shut and slid the bolt. Sinking onto the sofa, he lay motionless while his wife rubbed the pains out of his legs.

Wiley Schwartz, deacon of the Methodist Church, thought the ghost was a colorful invention like Paul Bunyan. It gave the people something to talk about other than the harsh, drab weather.

At least, that's what he opined one night at prayer meeting. An hour later, he had changed his mind. He had started home on foot and had gone only a few steps when he felt a presence behind him. He looked back. Like a giant blackbird in the moonlight, the specter was bearing down upon him. Schwartz ran harder than he'd ever run in his life. Inside his house, he collapsed.

From that night on, whenever the subject of ghosts came up, Schwartz remained silent.

When the winds of winter relented and the melting snow ran in rivulets under a warm spring sun, the citizens of Alma talked of the price of new farm wagons and the prospect of a bountiful harvest.

Like all the villagers, H.S. Wetherald, Ashton Shallenberger, Frank Griggsby and Wiley Schwartz welcomed the spring. But the unforgotten fears of the nightwalking woman in black remained a tiny, unmelted patch of ice in the shadowed recesses of their souls.

THE BATES HOUSE

It was past midnight on that fall evening in 1879 when Benjamin Brill drove his gig toward Dakota City. As he passed the Bates House, he saw a glow in a second-story window. Strange. For the last seven years, the old hotel had stood vacant, bats and owls its only tenants. Were new owners moving in?

Brill stopped. As he gazed at the light, it wavered and moved from room to room. More startling was its bluish cast, unlike any light the man had ever seen.

He got out of his carriage, pushed open the heavy front door.

"Hello!" he called.

Silence.

He called again.

The staircase loomed before him, its treads broken, the banister smashed and hanging askew. Once the Bates House had been the pride of Nebraska Territory, the place where the U.S. District Court met each spring and fall. But time and vandals had erased all evidence of its early grandeur.

Brill loaded his revolver. Then, looking anxiously around him, he picked his way up the stairway. In the hall at the end of the landing burned the ball of blue light he had seen through the window. Oddly, it did not flame.

From somewhere deep inside the old structure came the sudden sound of music—sad notes in a minor key. Whether sung or played, Brill couldn't tell. He stopped to listen. There was something mysterious about it. Like a chilling wind, it came from nowhere and everywhere.

At that moment, a being swathed in a white flowing garment crossed the landing, carrying a lamp.

Brill felt his scalp prickle. At first, he thought it was a real person. But then standing at the head of the landing, he watched the strange figure sweep into a room and out again, go in and out of the next room . . . and the next . . . and the next.

What did it want? It seemed to be searching for something, moving all the while to the accompaniment of the sad, humming music. Brill, more fascinated than fearful, called to the figure. But it brushed, unseeing, past him, intent only upon its own incomprehensible mission.

Finally, the figure slipped into a room near Brill and hovered in a corner, while in the hallway, the blue light again appeared, rolling like a ball up and down the corridor. When it reached a point a few feet above the floor, it wailed. As if by prearranged signal, the figure in the room kneeled, than sank prostrate to the floor. The light paused at the doorway, trembling and wailing.

Benjamin Brill stood against the opposite wall. His finger closed on the revolver's trigger.

As the light in the doorway floated into the room, Brill followed it. Peering around the doorjamb, he saw the blue ball of light change into a slender taper. He rubbed his eyes. Was he imagining it? As he watched, the taper materialized into a being, clothed, like its companion, in a long white garment. The figure on the floor rose and the two stood side by side. Then they swept out of the room, past a startled Brill and down the hallway.

At the far end of the hall, both figures sank to the floor and began a hideous chant that bristled the hairs on the back of Brill's neck. When he saw them rise and head toward the north end of the building, he turned again to follow. But it was too late. They had vanished.

Where had they gone? Who were they? What did they want? Brill searched the entire building, but found no sign of any living thing.

Outside again in the gig, Benjamin Brill gazed blank-eyed up at the hotel, a derelict hulk limned by moonlight. He heard no sounds anywhere, not even the whisper of wind in the trees. Only the strange blue light throbbed behind a sagging window pane . . . .

Chapter IX.
Ohio

"One afternoon in March, while her son napped, Geraldine Todd decided to investigate the noises. Opening the trap door in the kitchen, she descended the rickety stairs. A single bulb cast a dim light; the earthen floor was damp, the air musty. Geraldine shivered and looked cautiously around.

From the ancient furnace, heating ducts spread in all directions like the tentacles of a giant octopus. In a corner, Geraldine spotted a pile of broken furniture—chairs with splintered legs, smashed chests and tables. But what Geraldine saw sticking out of the rubbish caused her to scream and race back up the stairs. It was a hideous human hand, gnarled and bloody, which appeared to stand upright, at rigid attention . . ."

"THE HAUNTED CELLAR"

GIRL OF THE LILACS

For some men there is only one woman. It is as if love, once given, is expended and cannot be given again. Frank Burbank was that kind of man. Ethel Hanley was the woman he loved. She loved him in return. This, then, is their love story, one that transcended even death.

Our story begins one day in late May, 1900. Frank, a surveyor in the Bucyrus office of the Ohio State Highway Commission, was inspecting land a few miles beyond town that the Highway Commission had arranged to buy. The acreage was part of a farm owned by a Mr. Hanley. Frank's assistant, Ted Davis, accompanied him.

As the men tramped across the fields, Frank felt the sun burn the back of his neck above his shirt collar. The heavy heat felt like July. Spring had come early; the daffodils and tulips had already finished blooming and were now replaced by climbing roses and clematis.

Frank led the way up a hill. At the crest, the men paused to catch their breath. Laughing voices came from a white clapboard house a short distance away. The house was bordered by flowers and shrubs. But what caught Frank's eye was the girl, radiant in a white ruffly dress. Hair the color of corn silk spilled over her shoulders, and in her arms she cradled a huge bouquet of white lilacs.

It was several moments before Frank saw the photographer with the black cloth draped over his head. The girl was having her picture taken. A woman stood watching in the doorway of the house and two small children romped playfully at the photographer's feet.

Frank then noticed a wooden sign nailed to a nearby tree. It read, "Cold Buttermilk Served." He turned to his companion. "Ted, I won't be going back to Bucyrus," he said, jerking his thumb at the sign. "I have to get my daily glass of buttermilk."

Frank never drank buttermilk. Ted knew it. He laughed and reminded his boss that there'd be a full moon that night. Then he set off alone back down the path.

Mr. and Mrs. Hanley greeted Frank warmly and invited him to stay for dinner. Although they knew the surveyor only by reputation, they admired him. Everyone in the small town knew Frank Burbank to be a hardworking and dependable young man who was saving for further schooling; he planned to become a civil engineer.

As Mrs. Hanley bustled around the kitchen, she explained that the photographer had been engaged to take her daughter's graduation picture. The final stitching of the white organdy dress hadn't been done, she said, but that wouldn't show in a photograph. There were many other preparations also to be made for the occasion. Mrs. Hanley was cheerful and easy-going, without pretension, and Frank liked her immediately. She put him at ease and so did her daughter, Ethel. At the dinner table Frank couldn't take his eyes off Ethel, and wondered if the others noticed.

After the meal Frank offered to help with the dishes, but Mrs. Hanley wouldn't hear of it. Instead, he played with Ethel's little brother, Sammy, and the child's orphaned cousin, Addie, who lived with the family.

Later that evening, Frank and Ethel walked down to the meadow and sat on the stone foundation wall of an old hay barn. The rocks held the heat of the day and in a number of places wild roses grew, covering the crumbling wall with splashes of pink and red. The lambent light of the moon bleached Ethel's hair bone-white, and when she caught Frank looking at it, she unpinned the bun and the long locks cascaded down her back.

The gesture made a statement, wove a spell.

Ethel finally broke the silence. "Frank, when will you be leaving Bucyrus? I mean, when will you finish your surveying work?"

Frank detected the slightest tremor in her voice and chose his words with care. Placing one of Ethel's hands between both of his, he told her. "I could stay here, Ethel, in Bucyrus, as long as you want me to."

She smiled up at him and he took her in his arms.

Frank accompanied the Hanleys to the graduation exercises. Ethel, as valedictorian, gave the class oration, and Frank thought she looked lovelier than ever in her white dress with the blue sash. Tucked into the sash was a spray of white lilacs he had given her that afternoon. Lilacs and Ethel . . . they naturally belonged together. The thought of one reminded him of the other. Lost in these pleasant thoughts, Frank wasn't aware of what Ethel was saying up on the stage. He was certain of only one thing: he was going to marry Ethel Hanley.

The next day Frank asked Ethel's father for his daughter's hand in marriage. He could scarcely conceal his disappointment when the farmer asked him to wait two years. Ethel was only seventeen. Hanley felt nineteen was the proper age for a bride; Ethel's mother had been that age when Hanley married her.

"If you'll wait two years, son," he told Frank, "I assure you I'll give my consent." He extended his hand and Frank took it.

Frank Burbank moved to Cincinnati that fall to study engineering. He was twenty-eight. He found a room in a small boardinghouse and worked nights at a newspaper office to earn part of his expenses. The acute loneliness he felt at first was eased by his immersion into his studies and by Ethel's frequent letters. The night before he left Bucyrus she gave him her graduation picture. Frank kept the picture on his bedside table, and every time he looked at the smiling girl in white he was intoxicated by the perfume of the flowers she held in her hands. It was as if the lilacs had come to life within his room.

Ethel filled her days to exhaustion so they would pass quickly. She helped with the housework and the care of the younger children, and performed many of the farm chores. She bore her father no grudge for his refusal to permit her marriage because she knew he had acted with her best interests in mind.

Two years later to the day, Frank Burbank returned to Bucyrus, a bona fide engineer. Ethel met his train with the buggy. As they drove up the hill toward the Hanley farm, the horse needed a strong hand on the reins.

"That's a new horse, isn't it?" said Frank.

Ethel laughed. "Yes, and he's so silly he shies at his own shadow. Don't you, Bill?"

Frank grew uneasy. Skittish horses were always undependable.

The Hanleys rejoiced in Frank's homecoming and set the wedding date for Ethel's birthday, the fifth of June, two weeks away.

The following Sunday afternoon Ethel planned to show Frank a small house that was for sale out on Mansfield Road. Her father had taken the horse out that morning to drive her mother to church in Greggsville. Would Bill be too worn out to be hitched up again so soon?

Her father didn't think so, but he gave her a warning. "Ethel, that horse is really jittery. For being twelve years old he acts like a two-year-old. Better let Frank drive. And tell him to be careful."

Frank would be careful. Of course.

Ethel went upstairs to change into the new dress she had bought to surprise Frank. It was white with a lace-trimmed ruffle at the waist. Then she put on her new hat, a pale blue straw with loops of blue satin ribbon decorating the brim. As a final touch she pinned a spray of lilacs to the ribbon.

Frank caught sight of Ethel starting down the stairway and his eyes shone with love. She ran toward him and he took her into his arms.

The air was still and the sun warm, a perfect day for a drive. Spring had been unseasonably long again and, in the protracted heat, the flowers had begun to lose color. The snowy apple blossoms had turned brown and the lilacs in the dooryards were starting to fade.

Setting off down the turnpike, Bill jogged along at a steady, comfortable pace. Frank held the reins loosely. Ethel sat beside him, commenting on the scenery and the houses they passed.

They hadn't gone far when Frank pulled to the side of the road to permit a fringed-top surrey to pass. A young woman with fiery red hair and a large green bow on her hat waved from the front seat. "Hello, Ethel!" she called.

Ethel returned the greeting. After the surrey had gone by, she turned to Frank. "That was my school friend, Zella Murdock. You met her at the graduation dance. Remember?"

"I saw only one girl at the dance," Frank grinned and reached to squeeze Ethel's hand. "But a red-haired girl driving a white horse is a good luck omen. We should make a wish."

They both laughed. Frank commented on the newly-painted silo on the Hawkes's farm and the nice condition of the Murdock home directly across the road. It was neat and attractive, but he promised Ethel that one day they'd have an even finer place.

Just beyond the two farms was Hawkes's Hill. At the bottom, a stone bridge spanned a narrow brook choked with weeds. As the horse started the descent, a boy on a bicycle shot across the highway from a side road. Frank tightened the reins. Bill shied and snorted, then reared up and leaped forward, snapping the horizontal crossbar of the buggy to which the harness traces were attached. The crazed animal, wild with fright, plunged down the hill and the careening buggy slammed against a parapet of the bridge. Ethel was thrown from her seat. Her head struck the coping of the bridge. She died instantly.

Frank Burbank left Bucyrus after Ethel's funeral. For three years he moved around the country, working in one city after another, trying in vain to shake his sorrow. But grief never left him; always he carried in his mind the picture of his beloved lying crumpled in his arms at the foot of Hawkes's Hill.

Then one day in Winnipeg, Frank wrote to his former boss, Will Taylor, in Bucyrus. Was there an opening in the State Highway Commission? If so, he wanted it; he didn't care what the job was.

Frank returned. He kept the books for the Highway Commission, did occasional surveying and on Sundays took long walks alone in the countryside.

Except for visits to the Hanleys, Frank saw few people socially. Mrs. Hanley often remarked to her husband how much Frank had changed. He never smiled and the light had gone out of his eyes; his whole face seemed immobilized, as if set in concrete.

One day in October, when the maples flamed in the woodlots, Frank walked along the highway's edge. A buggy pulled up beside him and a young woman called out. "Hello there. Aren't you Frank Burbank?"

He nodded and she smiled down at him. "I'm Zella Murdock. I'll be happy to give you a ride into Bucyrus."

Frank didn't know if she had changed, but he doubted that he would have recognized her had she not introduced herself. "I'm going to Hanleys for supper, Miss Murdock."

"Get in," she said. "I'll be glad to drive you there."

The waning light gilded wisps of red hair that curled beneath the brim of her hat. Frank hopped up beside her and the horse trotted down the road.

After supper, Frank sat in the kitchen watching the children play and listening to Mrs. Hanley's small talk that once made him feel so comfortable. Now the words seemed harsh and distant. Part of the time he sensed that she was questioning him, but his thoughts were elsewhere. When he left, he stopped at the lilac bush beside the millstone. Snapping off a bare twig, he passed it beneath his nose and muttered, "The scent of lilacs is strong tonight."

From the darkened doorway, Mrs. Hanley saw and heard and was perplexed.

No one was surprised when the marriage of Zella Murdock and Frank Burbank took place. Zella was spoiled and headstrong and always got what she wanted. In Frank she got a consort with whom she had three children. That was all. Never did she capture his heart, nor even share his thoughts; she seemed not to care for such depth of intimacy.

Zella had inherited wealth and, with hired help to care for the large house and to look after the two little boys and their sister, she devoted her time to various clubs and social activities. She organized her life around her own interests and left Frank to his own devices.

The first thing Frank did upon moving onto the Murdock farm was to plant white lilac bushes. Some he bought from nurseries, some he bought from farmers who were thinning out dooryard hedges and others he dug up from old, abandoned places back in the hills. In every free moment he wandered the hills and the valley of the Scioto River, mumbling to himself and searching for yet another lilac bush.

On a raw March day filled with wind, Frank went to Hanleys to help unload fertilizer. By late afternoon the men finished the work and Frank climbed into his buggy to leave. As he was about to drive off, he thought he saw a woman standing down by the old hay barn foundation. Tying the reins to a hitching post, Frank started down the path. He had gone only a few steps when he was overcome by the heady perfume of lilacs. He turned to look back at the big lilac bush. The branches were bare.

When he looked again toward the place where the barn had stood he saw the figure clearly. A young girl in a white dress and a wide blue hat smiled up at him. He cried out and ran toward her. But the apparition faded, swallowed by the shadows of the coming night. Frank Burbank sat for a long time on the cold stones of the crumbling wall, his head cradled in his arms.

The hunting was good that fall, with quail and partridge plentiful. One November afternoon Frank took his gun and his setter, Sport, out to try his luck. The air was clear and crisp and the excited dog raced on ahead. When Frank reached a dense thicket at the foot of the hill on which the Hanley farm lay, he whistled for the dog.

The setter came bounding to his master, then cowered at Frank's feet. With hackles raised, he trembled and whined. Frank looked in the direction the dog was staring. A girl in a white dress was coming toward them down the steep hill. She approached slowly, her feet not quite touching the ground. The network of branches and twigs that blocked her way never bent to permit her passage; the apparition passed right through them. Then, for just a moment she stood smiling, a luminous figure pierced by sapling twigs.

Frank once asked Mrs. Hanley if she had ever been aware of her daughter's presence.

The woman nodded. "Once I thought I saw her walking down by the ruins of the old hay barn." She sighed and looked away. "But I guess it was just a trick of the moonlight."

When Frank Burbank's daughter, Joan, turned eighteen, Zella gave a dinner-dance in her honor. Before the guests began to arrive, Frank wandered into the dining room. Joan stood there by the bay window. Her father thought she looked lovely in her new apple-green silk gown and told her so.

"Daddy," Joan began softly, "something strange is going on in the garden. For the last hour a woman has been walking out there by the white lilac hedge. She looks young and she's wearing a white dress and a big hat. She seems to float in and out of the lilacs. At first I thought it was one of my friends playing a joke on me, but when I went out to check there was no one in sight. Yet I'm sure I saw her. I was standing right here watching."

The doorbell rang and Joan hurried to the door. Frank heard the exchange of greetings, but did not go to meet the guests. People often oppressed him, even his own children whom he loved. The soft, fragrant air of

May always made him restless, and at times his loneliness seemed unbearable. He stared now at the dark window panes until Zella came for him.

After dinner, more guests arrived and the dancing began. Frank knew the party would last far into the night for Zella was a tireless hostess. He slipped unnoticed out the back door and for a while walked aimlessly. Then he struck out along the brook that skirted Hanley's hill. Far ahead he saw a light in their kitchen.

Before Frank realized how far he had come, he reached the thicket at the base of the hill. He stopped suddenly. Before him the girl in white was dancing on the hillside. With her arms extended, she glided in and out among the trees.

Frank's eyes misted and his heart ached with a young man's desire. Tonight Ethel would not elude him. He sprang forward and the figure floated backward. He fought the prison of branches, his eyes riveted on the apparition that kept receding farther up the hillside. He had almost reached her when she raised her arm and tossed something toward him. The object fell in the soft earth at his feet. He picked it up, but when he raised his head she was gone.

Frank Burbank looked down at his trembling hand. He held a spray of lilacs—white, fragrant blooms, newly cut.

H. P. AND SON

Cleveland businessman H. P. Lillibridge was at his desk on that morning in 1887, dictating a letter, when he saw the image of his son, Joe, his face covered with blood.

Lillibridge paled and put a hand to his throbbing head. When his secretary asked if he were ill, he said no. But he *knew* Joe, somewhere at sea, was seriously hurt.

Lillibridge hurriedly finished his dictation and went home to lunch.

He picked at his meal, then took a brisk walk to calm himself. He and his son were unusually close. They shared the same likes and dislikes, habits and opinions, and often, each knew what the other was thinking and feeling. People often remarked that they seemed more like brothers than father and son. Joe captained a freighter as his father had in his own youth; each had started as a common sailor. Lillibridge wrote to his son regularly, and Joe, who had no time for long letters, kept a daily log that he mailed to his father whenever he was in port.

Back at his office, H. P. sat at his desk and wrote a detailed account of the incident. Putting the paper in an envelope, he sealed it with his private seal and addressed it to himself. Then he sent for the cashier.

"Willis," he began, tapping the envelope against his fingers, "please seal this in a large envelope, address it to yourself and put it in the safe."

"Yes, of course, sir."

"Right away, please."

"I understand, sir," said Willis, taking the envelope.

But Willis didn't understand. He'd never before been asked to carry out such an odd assignment. A letter in the safe with the money and important papers? And doubly sealed? Why? Willis remarked about it to the secretary. She too was perplexed. She told Willis that Mr. Lillibridge had seemed confused that morning and she wondered if he'd had a stroke.

Days passed and every time Willis opened the safe he saw the large envelope and pondered its contents.

Seven weeks after Lillibridge wrote the letter, Joe Lillibridge's log arrived from Melbourne, Australia. Lillibridge called his brother, who was one of his partners, to his office, then summoned the cashier to bring the sealed letter from the safe.

Willis delivered the envelope, leaving a damp thumb print in one corner. Standing to one side of the desk, he watched Lillibridge slit the envelope cleanly with a silver opener. Lillibridge shook out the sheets of paper, adjusted his glasses and began reading in a clear voice. His letter told of "seeing" a mutiny on his son's ship during which Joe was struck by a piece of iron pipe as he started down a hatchway, then struck a second time as he got to his feet. He wrote that he saw Joe's face badly injured and bleeding profusely.

Lillibridge put aside the letter then turned to his son's log. Lillibridge's brother and the cashier paled as they listened to Joe's account of the mutiny; it paralleled the father's account in nearly every detail. Allowing for time and date differences, the father had "seen" his son's apparition at the exact time of the mutiny.

Four years later, in 1891, Joe Lillibridge died of sunstroke. But his close association with his father extended beyond the grave. Lillibridge said he frequently received messages directly from Joe and often saw his ghost. On one occasion the apparition spoke, warning his father to avoid an unsound business deal. Lillibridge heeded the advice, which proved to be beneficial.

H. P. Lillibridge and his son Joe remained "close" for many years to come, thereby convincing the elder Lillibridge that the bonds between parents and children do indeed transcend death.

THE HAUNTED CELLAR

The first-floor apartment at 4207 Mason Court S. E. wasn't the nicest address in Cleveland, but music student Thomas Todd signed the lease anyway. It would be an affordable and fairly comfortable place for himself, his eighteen-year-old wife, Geraldine, and their two-year-old son, Anthony, Todd surmised.

The young family moved in during November, 1957—and fled for their lives in March, 1958! It seems that they were regularly awakened by strange moans and groans and piercing screams rising from the cellar.

One afternoon in March, while her son napped, Geraldine Todd decided to investigate the noises. Opening the trap door in the kitchen, she descended the rickety stairs. A single bulb cast a dim light; the earthen floor was damp, the air musty. Geraldine shivered and looked cautiously around.

From the ancient furnace, heating ducts spread in all directions like the tentacles of a giant octopus. In a corner, Geraldine spotted a pile of broken furniture—chairs with splintered legs, smashed chests and tables. But what Geraldine saw sticking out of the rubbish caused her to scream and race back up the stairs. It was a hideous human hand, gnarled and bloody, which appeared to stand upright, at rigid attention. The body to which the hand was connected was covered with debris.

Safely up the stairs, Geraldine heaved the two-by-four trap door back into place, slumped into a rocker and sobbed.

When Thomas returned home, Geraldine stammered out her story. Thomas took his wife into his arms to comfort her; of course her imagination had gotten the best of her, he thought.

That evening, while preparing supper, Geraldine was standing on the trap door. Suddenly, the door lifted and sent her sprawling to the floor. Thomas leaped down the stairs to catch the intruder. But no one was there. He returned upstairs and nailed the trap door shut.

The next day the Todd family moved out of the Mason Court apartment and into the Woodland Avenue Hotel.

Friends of the young couple, hearing the frightening tales of the haunted house, were skeptical and wanted to experience it for themselves. On March 31, the Todds took fifteen people to the apartment. As the group gathered in the kitchen, the trap door raised with such violent force that the wood ripped and the nails bent!

The visitors rushed into the living room for safety. But to their horror, they saw two small holes in the floor—human fingers waggling through the openings!

At ten o'clock that night, the Todds and their friends fled. Thomas called the Cleveland Police Department. Patrolmen Edmund Sinton and John Mancuso visited the Mason Court house and saw the damaged trap door and the holes in the floor. They searched the place thoroughly, but found nothing.

"But I did hear sounds like someone shoveling dirt in the cellar," Mancuso later recalled.

The two officers described the Todds as sincere, religious people who found comfort in verse five, Psalm 91 (the "Psalm of Protection"): "Thou shalt not be afraid for the terror by night."

Yet once the officers suggested that the couple return to the apartment, Thomas Todd cowered. "This house is haunted and I won't stay there another second," he told the policemen.

Nevertheless, after the couple had moved out, Thomas remained curious about the phenomenon in the house. One day he stopped by the old neighborhood to talk with some of the other residents. The woman next door told him he had done the right thing in leaving. She said that years ago a quarrelsome couple had lived in the house and, in a fit of rage, the husband had killed his wife. At least, that was the rumor. The man had disappeared and the woman's body was never found. Since that time, a succession of renters had occupied the apartment, but none of them had stayed for long.

Five years after the Todd's departure, in September 1963, ghost hunter Hans Holzer investigated the house for a possible program on the "Mike Douglas" television series. Holzer was accompanied by a television cameraman and George Condon, a Cleveland newspaper columnist. The three men found the house in a dilapidated state, the boarded-up windows and weed-choked lawn suggesting that no one had lived there for some time. There was no electricity or heat in the place and the interior reeked of urine and garbage.

The men settled themselves in the dark front room and Holzer called out to the ghost of the murdered woman whose name was supposedly Edna. Nothing. Holzer called again. Then he commented that without a medium he might not be able to make contact with the ghost.

But Holzer did make contact with *something*. Stepping into a back room, he flashed his light across the floor. Suddenly the light illuminated a shapeless form beneath a dirty blanket. Holzer approached cautiously and the cameraman moved in closer. The ghost hunter jerked off the blanket and jumped back. There, on the cold floor sprawled a local bum sleeping off an old-fashioned bender. And beside him, curled in a corner, his head thrown back against the wall in a stuporous pose, sat his buddy with an empty wine jug.

Holzer threw down the blanket and the three men hurried from the house. Yet he remained convinced that the derelicts were *not* the only occupants of the place. He later told Condon that if one were to dig in the cellar, they would find the body of Edna.

But no one ever searched the place again. The abandoned house, located in a rough and rundown neighborhood, repelled everyone, especially the Todds. Although the couple told the story of the haunted cellar for years, they never set foot in the house again.

The Reformed Hobo

The hobo wasn't sure how many miles he had ridden before he decided to go back. He couldn't say exactly why. There was something in young Sam's face that disturbed him, something that communicated an unspoken need. The hobo recalled that he had been about Sam's age when his own father had died. When the train slowed at a pasture crossing, he jumped off and hitchhiked back to Willis, Ohio.

As he traveled the miles back to Willis, the weary hobo reflected on the bizarre events of the day before. It seemed as if it was all part of a weird dream, yet as he recalled the man's voice and his invitation and the entire evening's events, he realized that everything had indeed taken place.

During a driving rainstorm the previous night, the hobo had crawled off a freight train in Willis. Shivering in a light jacket and thin pants, he sloshed through the deserted rail yard. Suddenly, someone spoke to him. "It's sure a bad night."

The hobo looked up to see a man wearing a slicker with a rain hat pulled low on his forehead.

"You got a place to stay?" asked the man. "If you don't you'd better come home with me for the night."

The hobo thanked the man and then followed him down the street. Neither of them spoke. After walking two blocks, the man in the slicker turned and walked up to the porch of a house. Stepping aside, he told the stranger to go on in.

A woman and her two children were preparing dinner in the kitchen. Giving the tramp a quick smile, she indicated a chair just inside the back door. She motioned to her daughter Lucy to set another place for dinner.

When the hobo sat down, he felt the water draining out of his cracked and weathered shoes; he hoped the puddles on the floor wouldn't be noticed. He glanced nervously toward the door. Where was the man?

"I ain't meanin' to make work for ya, ma'am," the tramp said. "A gentleman brought me here. He said to go in. He went around the other side of the house."

The woman nodded. "We don't eat fancy, but we can always feed an extra," she remarked as she stirred extra carrots and onions into the skillet.

Silence descended upon the room as the hobo sat quietly and observed the young family finishing their dinner preparations. The only sound to be heard was that of the skillet sizzling in a wreath of smoke.

"Where you headed?" the woman asked.

"Out west. Gonna get me a job," the hobo volunteered.

"Doing what?"

The hobo's cheeks reddened. "Whatever work I can git."

Lucy clattered the plates and silverware onto the table. Her little brother Sam carefully set out the bread and butter and pulled up the chairs. The hobo kept his eyes fixed on the door. What had happened to the man who had brought him here? He told him he'd join him in a few minutes. In the silence, the hobo started to count the place settings—there were only four! Wasn't the other fellow going to join them?

The woman noticed the visitor's agitation. As they ate, she spoke openly to the hobo. "It was my husband brought you here. He likes to wander around the rail yard on stormy nights. Most times he brings a tramp or two home with him. But don't be nervous—it's fine that you're here. Enjoy your meal."

The stranger stared into his lap, his fingers rolling the paper napkin into a tight, damp ball. He had followed a man down the street and now the man had disappeared. The hobo heard the snap of wood in the kitchen range.

When he looked up, he saw young Sam's eyes upon him, eyes that seemed too old for such a small, sad face.

After the meal was finished, the woman orchestrated the cleanup. Once everything was away, she called to Sam. "Son, show our guest to the spare room."

Our guest. The tramp liked the sound of the term "our guest." No one had ever called him that before.

The guest room was spotlessly clean and the bed comfortable. Yet for some reason the hobo could not sleep. As he was just dozing off, he heard footsteps coming down the hall. They stopped at his door. Soon they resumed, walking away in the distance. Then they returned. The hobo thought it was probably one of the children sleepwalking, and he rolled over in bed.

Some time later, the tramp heard the footsteps again, heavier this time. They stopped outside his door. Then came a knock so hard that it shook the door. He got up, cracked open the door, but saw no one. The knocking came again. This time the tramp threw open the door. No one was there. He glanced up and down the corridor. But just as he was shutting the door, something cold and wet brushed past him. He quickly climbed back into bed, but did not sleep.

In the morning, a warm sun shone. The hobo, bone-weary from lack of rest, thanked his hostess and set off for the depot. He reached the tracks as a westbound freight rumbled in. The tramp spotted an empty boxcar with a partially-opened door. He was just about to leap aboard when he heard a voice behind him.

"Here's your cap, mister."

The hobo turned around. Sam, squinting into the sunlight, held forth the old, sweat-stained cap.

"Thanks, kid."

The train was picking up speed. Another open boxcar hove into view. Sam just stood there, watching.

"I've been meanin' to ask you something kid," the hobo shouted above the din of the moving train. "But if it 'tain't none of my business, you tell me."

Sam remained motionless.

"I was wonderin' why your old man never came back last night. Did I do something to offend him? Or was that him banging on my door all night long?"

Sam's eyes widened. He spoke loudly and without emotion. "My father's dead mister. He was killed in an accident in this here rail yard almost six years ago."

The hobo just stood there. Then, unconsciously, as the train moved away, he returned Sam's friendly wave. "So long, kid!" he bellowed as he leaped aboard the last box car.

Within a few moments, all the hobo could hear was the screeching of the train's wheels on the polished rails. In the billowing smoke from the engine, young Sam was lost to sight.

By the time he returned to Willis, the hobo knew exactly what he was going to do. The ghost of Sam's father had paid him a visit the night before for some inexplicable reason. Now the hobo had to go back and find out why.

The widow took the hobo in and said he could stay until he found work. At first he was nervous about trying to sleep in that bedroom with its eerie footsteps passing in the night. But he soon discovered that the ghost only walked on stormy nights. Was it the old trainman looking in on his family? The tramp thought it was and was pleased.

The hobo helped around the house, and taught young Sam to fish and hunt. In the evenings, he entertained Sam and Lucy with stories of his travels around the country. Before long he landed a job as a fire-builder in the round house at the Willis rail yard and married a young woman from the community. The reformed hobo saw Sam regularly, and for the rest of their lives, they remained the closest of friends. All on account of a friendly invitation from a rail yard specter.

HOUSE OF EVIL

In 1864 Hannes Tiedemann and his wife Luise realized a lifelong dream—the construction of their turreted home at 4308 Franklin Boulevard N. W. in Cleveland. The "castle," as they called it, had been planned and built exactly to their specifications. The Tiedemanns were overjoyed!

Some local residents claim, however, that the old couple liked their house *too* much—so much that they *never* left, even though they are long since dead and buried in Riverside Cemetery!

Bizarre stories of psychic disturbances have always been told about this mansion on "Millionaire's Row." Doors fly off their hinges without being touched, lights go on and off by themselves and chandeliers rotate when the air is still. Mirrors fog for no apparent reason and voices murmur in empty rooms. From time to time a woman in black is seen peering out a narrow window in the front tower room.

The history of the Franklin castle is a mixture of fact and legend, blurred by incomplete or missing records. It is known, however, that the Tiedemanns lived in the house for nearly thirty-three years; that Hannes built his fortune from wholesale grocery and liquor businesses; and that, in his later years, he became a bank executive.

In 1881 Tiedemann's fifteen-year-old daughter, Emma, and his eighty-four-year-old mother, Wiebeka, died in the house. Tiedemann listed Emma's cause of death as diabetes.

In 1883, three more children in the family died. Their father claimed they had been ill, but neighbors suspected there was more to the deaths than that.

The grief-stricken Luise Tiedemann busied herself with her house, adding secret passageways, hidden rooms and turrets and gargoyles that made the house appear very much like a legendary "haunted castle." She even installed a huge ballroom on the fourth floor.

After Luise's death, Tiedemann sold the place to a family named Mulhauser, remarried and moved elsewhere, outliving every member of his family. Hannes Tiedemann died in 1908.

In 1913 the Muhlhauser family sold the castle to the German Socialist Party who used it solely for meetings and parties. The Socialists owned it for fifty-five years, and for most of that time the house was considered unoccupied.

Yet a Cleveland nurse recalled caring for an attorney who supposedly lived at 4308 Franklin Boulevard in the early 1930s. She remembered being terrified by the late night sound of a small child's crying. The servants refused to talk about it, dismissing the cries as those of a cat. But forty years later, the nurse told a reporter that she would "never set foot in that house again."

In 1968 Mrs. James C. Romano bought the Tiedemann castle and she, her husband and six children moved in. Mrs. Romano had always admired the huge stone house and planned to open a restaurant in it, but quickly changed her mind.

On the day they moved in, their two sets of twins, ages two and three years old, went upstairs to play. Soon they came down to ask if they could take a cookie up to their friend—a little girl in a long dress who was crying. This happened a number of times, but every time Mrs. Romano went up to check no one was there.

Mrs. Romano sometimes heard organ music, although there was no organ in the house. In bed late at night, she would hear heavy tramping as if an Army platoon was marching on the third floor where her two grown sons by a previous marriage slept. Sometimes, when no one was on the third floor, she heard voices and the clink of glasses. She finally refused to set foot on that floor (and the fourth floor) alone, and forbade the children to play on either of those floors.

Mrs. Romano's fears about the third floor may have been well-founded. Barbara Dreimiller, a Cleveland writer, also had a chilling experience there. During a visit, she and three friends just reached the third floor when they saw a vaporous object, like a blanket of fog, ahead of them.

The friends hung back, but Ms. Dreimiller walked toward it. Before she could reach it, her vision began to fade. Her friends pulled her free of the sickening cloud just before she passed out. They later searched the room, but found no source of the strange vapor.

One Halloween the telephone awakened Mrs. Romano at midnight. She picked up the receiver and heard, "Can I sleep with you tonight?" The voice, she recalled, sounded as though it came from a grave. She screamed and dropped the phone. After that incident she vowed never to answer the phone when she was alone in the house.

"A week later," Mrs. Romano said, "I woke up from a deep sleep and found myself in the middle of the floor screaming so loud I lost my voice. And someone was screaming with me! ..."

Mr. Romano, who is an electrician, rewired the house. Yet light bulbs burned out in a week's time and fixtures burst into flames.

Finally, Mrs. Romano consulted a Catholic priest. He told her she was possessed, at times, by the spirit of Luise Tiedemann and that it was the ghost of little Emma Tiedemann who slammed doors and raced up and down the stairs. The priest felt there were many evil entities in the house and advised the family to leave.

Mrs. Romano's grown sons needed no urging. They moved out after something pulled the covers off their beds in the third-floor bedroom.

In spite of the disturbances, Mr. Romano remained calm and philosophical about the house. "When you buy a castle," he said, "you get the ghosts. It's Halloween at our place 365 days a year."

His wife never adopted such a casual attitude. She felt certain the house held a dark and brooding secret, but she was too upset to try to learn what it was. "It isn't something to mess with," she said.

Eventually she became physically ill and admitted the house was getting the best of her. In September 1974, the Romanos sold the place to Samuel Muscatello.

The new owner turned the castle into a "Universal Christian Church," and, to raise money, opened the house to tours.

A Cleveland disc jockey and a photographer emerged from their tour visibly shaken.

The disc jockey would not discuss his experience, but he turned down an offer of three hundred dollars to spend the night in the castle.

The photographer said he was sitting downstairs with the owner when he heard a woman's voice call his name. He leaped up the stairs but found no one. The only other people in the house were two floors higher and their voices could not be heard.

John Webster, a Cleveland radio station executive, told psychic investigators Richard Winer and Nancy Osborn Ishmael that when he visited the castle to gather material for a special program on its hauntings a large tape recorder was torn from his shoulder and thrown down the stairs where it smashed into pieces.

During the visit of a Ted Ocepec, a television news cameraman, a hanging lamp turned in a slow circle. Traffic vibrations? Ocepec didn't think so. "I just don't know," he said, "but there's something in that house."

Even owner Muscatello grew uneasy. He heard strange sounds and discovered articles taken from one place and put down in another. His plans for the church did not work out and he sold the castle.

In 1978, former Cleveland Police Chief Richard D. Hongisto and his wife, Elizabeth, bought the castle. They thought the twenty-room home, with its beautifully carved paneling and original wood plank floors, would be a perfect place to live, easily spacious enough for the large parties they liked to give.

Yet less than a year later the Hongistos abruptly sold the old mansion to George Mirceta, a buyer who was unaware of its haunted reputation. He had bought the Gothic castle for its solid construction and architectural whimsy.

Mirceta lived alone in the house and conducted tours on weekends. At the end of each two-hour tour, he passed out cards and asked the visitors to jot down phenomena they had observed—some reported seeing a woman in black in the tower room; others saw a woman in white. Still others complained of becoming temporarily paralyzed or of finding themselves babbling incoherently.

Mirceta told reporters that he heard babies crying and saw chandeliers swaying. Still, he claimed to be unafraid—he would not live there, he said, if the castle were haunted. "There has to be a logical explanation for everything," he rationalized.

THE GROCER

When Reuben Weisgerber, the grocer, died, the businessmen on St. Clair Street in Cleveland were saddened. Reuben had been one of them. Although a somewhat egotistical man, he had always worked hard and was well respected. He was also a faithful husband who loved his wife, Rosa, deeply and promised never to leave her. He died poor, but his widow did not complain.

With help from her children, she operated the grocery store and earned a modest living.

Yet Rosa was grief-stricken. During long, sleepless nights, she wept, believing that if she could see her beloved Reuben once more to say goodbye, then she could accept his death.

On the evening of July 13, 1870, Rosa visited Silvie Heitman, a spiritual medium who lived nearby. Although Rosa did not know Silvie, she had heard favorable reports of Silvie's success in contacting the dead. Rosa was determined to see her husband one last time!

The two women shared a pleasant conversation over cups of coffee, then Rosa asked Silvie if she could show her a sign of Reuben. Silvie closed her eyes and entered a light trance. Soon a pale gray light filled the room. Out of the light stepped the figure of Reuben Weisgerber. His lips did not move, but the apparition looked so real that the astonished widow shrank in horror. The figure faded and Rosa collapsed in a chair. Too frightened to return home alone, she asked Silvie if she might spend the night.

At one o'clock in the morning, Silvie was awakened by a bright yellow light in the room. It shimmered against the walls and the ceiling, turning everything to starburst gold. Silvie looked toward her guest's bed and saw that it was empty.

Rosa, wearing only her corset and nainsook corset cover, was walking back and forth at the far end of the room. Silvie thought Rosa was sleepwalking and called to her, but the widow paid no attention. Then, in the brilliant glow, Silvie saw that something invisible was dressing the widow. Unseen hands slipped the muslin petticoat and the percale house dress over Rosa's head and smoothed them into place. Rosa flopped into an armchair and something unrolled her cotton stockings up her legs and guided her feet into the pointed toe oxfords.

Silvie called out again, but Rosa did not answer. The light went out and the guest was gone.

Later that morning, the medium went to Rosa's house. The widow remarked that the only thing she recalled of the night's incident was finding herself at the bedside of her husband's mother who was suffering from a sudden illness. She did not know how she got dressed, how she reached her mother-in-law's place, or how she arrived later at her own home.

Silvie told Rosa that Reuben's spirit had returned to send her to the aid of his ailing mother, but the widow found the story preposterous.

That evening Silvie suggested that the two of them go out for a walk. She thought the cool night air would refresh and relax Rosa after her harrowing experience. Rosa readily agreed.

The women had walked only three blocks when Rosa glanced back over her shoulder. She stopped and seized her friend's arm. "There he is!" she exclaimed. "Do you see him?"

"Of course," said Silvie, patting Rosa's arm. "He's been following us the whole way."

The apparition looked almost real in a long grocer's apron that reached to its knees.

The widow shuddered and drew closer to her companion. Both turned instinctively toward Mrs. Weisgerber's house.

Inside the house, tables and chairs rose in the air, turned over and crashed to the floor. Bureaus danced and pictures flew off the walls. Cups and saucers and plates sailed out of the china cupboard and spun crazily in the air. Window shades rolled noisily up and down. Blue lights flashed an eerie glow upon the flying objects. And the face of the grocer appeared everywhere in the house—on the walls, on the ceiling, on the floor and even on the crashing furniture.

Rosa never recovered from the shock.

For months afterward, the widow complained that her dead husband followed her everywhere she went.

Driven mad by Reuben's shadowy presence, Rosa would often scream into the air.

Each morning as she plodded down St. Clair Street to open the grocery store, passersby noticed her stony gaze and heard her ravings. Those who knew her shook their heads and said to one another, "There goes Rosa Weisgerber. She isn't right in the head, you know."

Poor Rosa. She hadn't realized, when Reuben promised never to leave her, just how doggedly he would keep his vow.

THE ETHEREAL INNKEEPERS

Shutters bang on windless nights. Stairs creak. And floorboards groan. At first, Mary Stevens Sweet thinks the noises are natural complaints of the rambling, old house settling down for the night. It is the late 1920s and Mrs. Sweet has just taken over the management of the historic Buxton Inn in Granville, Ohio.

Several weeks later, Mrs. Sweet senses a presence on the upstairs balcony early in the morning, peering over the railing to the lilac bush below. In the evening, she feels something following her into the ballroom where once the night was filled with fiddle music and the rhythmic stamp of dancing feet performing the old quadrilles.

Before long, guests reported being awakened to find a forlorn, transparent figure leaning on the bedpost. Others become startled when they spread their hands to the fire on the hearth and see a pair of pale, indistinct hands beside their own.

Mrs. Sweet knows now that the inn is haunted!

The Buxton Inn was built in 1812 by pioneer Orrin Granger, who left Granville, Massachusetts, to seek a better life for his family. Originally, the building served as a post office and stagecoach stop. Stage drivers cooked their meals in the massive open fireplace in the basement and bedded down there on straw pallets. Through the years throngs of travelers of all sorts crowded the old inn, leaving the residue of their memories and emotions imprinted on the structure. Given such circumstances, identification of a ghost is usually impossible.

But identification came soon, in an unexpected way. Mrs. Sweet's son, Fred,who lived with his mother in the inn, crept downstairs one night to raid the pantry. He reached for the pie shelf, but it was empty. A ghost stood in the larder, devouring the last wedge of apple pie!

Sensing the young man's disappointment, the ghost drew up two chairs and in a thin, reedy voice introduced himself as Orrin Granger, the builder. The apparition then regaled Fred with tales of the olden days when carriages rolled along the Granville Pike and stopped at the Buxton Inn for bumpers of cider and rashers of bacon.

After a period of time, the friendly ghost confided that it approved of the way Fred's mother was running the place, retaining the nineteenth-century atmosphere and blending it with new, attractive furnishings and tasteful food.

"No need for me to hang around any longer," the ghost said. With a wave of his hand and a gentle smile, the ghost was gone.

But it didn't go far. Years later, a psychic glimpsed the ghost of Orrin Granger in the house. She described a gray-haired gentleman, a country squire type, who wore knee breeches and white stockings and was sometimes dressed in blue.

In 1972, Orville and Audrey Orr purchased the Buxton Inn from Nell Schoeller. The Orrs had heard tales of a ghostly *lady* in blue haunting the old hotel, but were determined not to forfeit the purchase because of a "spook" wandering the premises.

Orr, a soft-spoken former minister, spent two years restoring the inn to its original state, even to the vivid pink clapboard siding. During that time he hired several young carpenters to do finish work on the house, and one summer evening as they packed their tools for the day, Orr told them the stories he'd heard about a ghostly lady in blue and how she had frightened unsuspecting guests by appearing suddenly in their rooms. The workmen laughed and said they didn't believe in ghosts. They demanded proof.

"Proof" was not long in coming. One day an attractive young woman in a blue dress opened the second-floor stairway door, walked across the back balcony and started down the stairs. Then she evaporated before the workmen's eyes. The startled carpenters fled. The ghostly lady repeated her visit the next day and every evening thereafter, promptly at six o'clock. The workmen began leaving earlier each day.

Who is this mysterious lady in blue? She's generally believed to be Ethel Houston "Bonnie" Bounell, the establishment's vivacious innkeeper from 1934 until her death in 1960.

"Bonnie" Bounell was a popular woman whose elegant looks lent an air of sophistication to the Buxton Inn. In her earlier years she had been a singer of light opera. Those who had known her remembered her hats and her lovely pastel dresses. Blue was "Bonnie's" favorite color.

More specific information hinting at the ghost's identity came later from Mayree Braun, a Cincinnati medium and a founding member of the Parapsychology Forum of Cincinnati, who once toured the house. Although the Buxton Inn was unfamiliar to her and she knew nothing of its history, Mrs. Braun reached some startling conclusions. She reported seeing, clairvoyantly, a woman in blue, from modern times, accompanying her and Audrey Orr from room to room. The psychic said the ghostly lady was beautifully dressed, had once been on the stage and obviously liked hats. Mrs. Braun also remarked that the spirit was pleased with the restoration work the new owners were doing, especially the work done in the ballroom. The medium had unknowingly described "Bonnie" Bounell.

While medium Mayree Braun had identified this "lady in blue" as "Bonnie" Bounell, Peggy Little, a Columbus area psychic and member of the British Spiritualist Church, told a reporter that the ghost of a lady she had seen in the inn was wearing blue clothing of an *old-fashioned* design. Although unable to see the bodice of the gown, she did see the long, blue-gray skirt and heard the rustling of its folds as the wearer swept across the floor. Mrs. Little also saw a white cap on the woman's head. She thought it was Mrs. Orrin Granger, the wife of the original owner of the inn. Or was it "Bonnie" in an elegant gown?

Orr himself admits to psychic abilities and has witnessed unexplained incidents in the house. During the long renovation period, he often heard footfalls on the stairs and the slamming of doors in upstairs rooms when no other human being was around. Sometimes he even heard the clinking of coins on the pegged wooden floors.

Orr has never been fearful, but once he did lose his patience. He had spent an entire evening alone in the inn and was preparing to leave when someone opened the front door, walked upstairs and across the second-floor balcony, opened the back door and proceeded down the back staircase. An incredulous Orr searched the house, but could find no one. All the doors were bolted and every window latched. The Buxton Inn was secure. Or was it? Tired and exasperated, Orr shouted to his "guest," "If you want this place, you can just have it." Later Orr rethought his offer and refused to give up that easily.

On many occasions he has encountered a shadowy male figure in various parts of the house. Orr finally decided that this was probably the ghost of Major Buxton, inn operator from 1865 until 1905, and the person for whom it was named. Fortunately for Orr, the ghost of Major Buxton seems quite harmless.

"When we first purchased the building, employees would even set a place for the Major at the table," Orr told a news reporter. "One waitress claims to have seen the Major sitting in a rocking chair before the fireplace."

The Grangers, "Bonnie" Bounell, and Major Buxton may be the most prominent ghosts who haunt the Buxton Inn. But some say that there are other "visitors" whose identities may never be known.

Orr operates his pub, The Tavern, in the original basement of the house. Here, where stage drivers cooked and bedded down a century ago, psychics have observed many spirits, especially between 9:30 and 11:30 at night when the energy level in the inn slows down.

Mrs. Little has seen ghosts congregate on the stairs during the evening hours. "It's almost as if they were a wall of feeling . . ." she told a reporter.

Newspaper photographer Gordon Kuster, Jr., and freelance writer Mary Bilderback Able, of Granville, might agree. They're convinced that there's something eerie at the Buxton Inn. Kuster, visiting the inn in 1979, observed a pitcher fly off a table and crash to the floor.

There's something about the Buxton Inn, then, that seems to attract or retain its old caretakers. Perhaps someday the Grangers, "Bonnie" Bounell and Major Buxton will be joined by Mary Sweet and the Orrs as they all continue to "manage" the affairs of the Buxton Inn.

THE TALE OF THE TROUBLED TEENAGER

A microwave oven is on. A television set blares forth. And the upstairs shower is running.

Typical activities in your house? Of course. But not in the home of John and Joan Rupard and their six children in Columbus. Their microwave oven and their television set are both unplugged! And the shower turned itself on with no one near the faucets!

In early March, 1984, the Rupard family began to be plagued by these and other strange goings-on. Furniture overturned, eggs splattered against walls and lights came on by themselves.

Rupard initially called an electrician. The man couldn't stop the appliances from operating without electricity. He even tried taping the light switches in the OFF position, but the tapes mysteriously vanished and the lights came back on.

All of the incidents occurred only when Lisa, the Rupard's fourteen-year-old adopted daughter, was in the house. At first, it was thought that Lisa was causing these things to happen when no one was watching. But on one occasion—while she was sitting in the living room—objects flew out of the kitchen! Lisa herself was struck by a flying candlestick, a clock and a wall hanging which soared through the air.

The Columbus police were called, but they could do nothing. The Rupards then invited news reporters to their home. Forty of them showed up for a press conference!

Mike Harden, a *Columbus Dispatch* reporter, claimed he saw a telephone leap into the air and a cup of coffee sail off a table and smash against the fireplace. And Fred Shannon, a veteran photographer on the *Dispatch*, captured on film what appears to be the flying phone.

"After seeing this, it made a believer out of me on psychokinetic energy," Shannon reported.

Mrs. Rupard told Harden they had taken Lisa to a neurologist and a neuropsychologist, neither of whom could help. "They cannot see any reason she should be doing this," she added.

But a parapsychologist from the Psychical Research Institute in Chapel Hill, North Carolina, believed that the family was beset by Recurrent Spontaneous Psychokinesis (RSPK), a condition often triggered unconsciously by a teenager who is under a lot of unrelieved tension and stress.

Lisa's mother acknowledged that her daughter was very upset because she had just recently discovered that she was adopted and, as a result, was feeling very anxious about her life.

The debate raged in the Ohio newspapers and electronic media for weeks. Many believed Lisa's tale of travail; others felt the entire incident was a hoax. Shannon stuck close to the girl and her family. He believed Lisa's story.

"I know what I saw," he explained, "and I do not think that Lisa has been orchestrating any of these strange goings-on."

Eventually, Lisa was taken to the Chapel Hill Psychical Research Institute to be tested there. The same unusual phenomena—flying objects and the like—occurred there as well, leading researchers to conclude that Lisa herself was the cause of the incidents.

By the summer of 1984 Lisa Rupard was no longer plagued and battered by flying objects. That ordeal was over for her. But perhaps new challenges would await her—the staff at the Psychical Research Institute came away from their experiments convinced that Lisa Rupard is psychic!

THE PIRATE'S MISTRESS

The bottom lands of the Scioto River valley in central Ohio are rimmed by forested cliffs lush with undergrowth.

Many years ago travelers reported seeing the ghost of a lithe, young girl gliding among the trees. And at night they heard screams coming from the vicinity of a ruined mansion, followed by silence, another shriek, and then stillness. Some said the ghost was the spirit of the little Spanish girl that John Robinson was supposed to have murdered. At least they thought he had killed her. Searchers never did find her body though.

John Robinson entered this wild, inhospitable country in 1825. He arrived at Delaware, Ohio—at that time a village of a few log huts strung along a portage between the Ohio River and the town of Sandusky on Lake Erie—with a party of trappers.

Robinson himself was not a trapper, nor was he friendly with any of his traveling companions. He left them without so much as a goodbye or a wave of the hand, stopping for the night at the local tavern, two heavy packs in tow.

The villagers were suspicious. Most foot travelers crossing the wilderness carried the lightest of loads. And while the tavern keeper, the blacksmith and the stable boy welcomed the stranger and asked about his plans and what assistance he might require, Robinson remained silent and disdainful.

In the morning, the newcomer rented a saddle horse and set out to explore the bottom lands and bluffs of south Delaware County. In the depths of the nearly impenetrable forest, Robinson found the retreat he sought, a vast acreage of high bluff country that afforded a splendid view of the valley below. He took title to the property that night and as soon as the deed was executed, he began designing a mansion grander than any home in Ohio.

Once the plans were ready, Robinson hired an army of stone and brick masons. They blasted from a hillside, cut and laid the rock with utmost precision. Stone by stone, foot by foot, the magnificent building rose in the forest. A master craftsman, Robinson finished the interior himself, carving mantels and cornices and the balustrade for the staircase from virgin oak and embellishing them with intricate patterns of astonishing beauty.

Soon wagons arrived, bringing furnishings imported from Europe—heavy brocade draperies, gilded tables and chairs, desks and chests, and trunks filled with linens, silver and dainty bone china. One large chest held easels, canvases, brushes and oils, while other chests contained books for the library. Such opulence had never before been seen in the wilderness!

Behind the house a mausoleum was built for the owner's final resting place.

When everything was finally finished, Robinson paid his bills in full—in gold pieces! Now the villagers knew the contents of the leaden sacks Robinson had dragged into the tavern. The workmen were dismissed and the new homeowner retired within his house and bolted the door.

And Robinson's door remained closed while the little community waited for an invitation to the housewarming that never took place. Masons and carpenters who had worked on the house were angered; local officials who had helped Robinson procure the land were puzzled by the rejection. An occasional neighbor who stopped by the mansion to welcome its owner to the area was rudely turned away.

But one day Robinson summoned a workman to make some repairs in the house. The man noticed the walls of the rooms were covered with the owner's paintings, sweeping landscapes of rolling hills and baronial castles and great medieval halls reminiscent of England. Robinson indicated that he worked at his easel every day from morning to night.

But the one painting that astonished the workman covered an entire wall of the library. Its setting was the deck of a pirate ship. Dark, heavy-bearded sailors gathered at one side of the vessel, the officers at the other. In the center, the captain struck a swashbuckling pose, sword and pistols at his side, a bold and crafty look on his bronzed face. It was Robinson! Even in the dim light, the likeness was unmistakable.

Rumors flew. A pirate captain in Delaware County? What did it mean? Romantically-inclined persons pondered chests overflowing with gold. And silver. Perhaps even rare jewels and gems. Others viewed Robinson as the black sheep of an aristocratic English family to account for his other paintings with their typically English scenes.

When Robinson wasn't painting, he would roam the forest, searching for rare stones and unusual rocks. A neighbor sometimes caught sight of him studying a specimen, turning it over in his strong hands.

Then one day local residents glimpsed a stranger in the woods near the Robinson mansion—an exotic young girl, small and dainty with hair and eyes as black as the raven's wing and a pale complexion faintly tinged with olive. In her brocade gowns with the lace-trimmed sleeves, some said she resembled a Spanish countess. There was a certain nobility in the tilt of her head and the way she moved through the light and shadow of the forest. Like Robinson, who had arrived two years earlier, the girl's presence was unexplained. Not a single trader had met her on the portage paths.

Rumor had it that the señorita served as a model for the artist's paintings, that her portrait would be his masterpiece, the crowning achievement of his life's work.

Sometimes, in the waning light of summer afternoons, Robinson and the girl would be seen seated side by side on a stone bench in a clearing at the brow of a hill. But more often the girl was alone, darting like a small bird among the trees, or wandering the willow-fringed banks of the Scioto River.

When the days shortened and the leaves fell, the girl was seen no more. Yet she was heard. Night after night her chilling cries shook the forest and trembled above the valley floor. Word spread that Robinson beat her severely when she displeased him. The settlers were alarmed, yet unwilling to interfere.

Early snows laced the barren trees and filled the forest. The land lay silent. The great stone house was silent too. Sinister.

The girl's cries no longer pierced the night air. It was as if they too had been stifled by the snows. Throughout the long winter, the villagers spoke of Robinson and his companion, of the strange goings-on. Not once that winter had the pair been observed.

With the coming of spring, the snows melted and the river ran full; the trees leafed out and the birds returned. But no sound came from within the mansion. Weeds choked the path to the front door, and vines and lichen clung to the damp foundation stones. Over all there was an air of desolation.

At last a few hardy farmers banded together and approached the house. They banged on the stout oak door. No one came. Using a fallen tree as a battering ram, they crushed the door and entered. There was no sign of life anywhere. Only the signs of a furious struggle.

In the library, filled with Robinson's books and paintings, chairs and tables were overturned; the easel lay smashed on the floor. One wall bore the bloodied prints of tiny, slender fingers! Just above the bloodstains hung the lifesized portrait of the Spanish girl.

As the men stared with disbelief, the colors of the painting intensified—the eyes flashed darkly and the lips moved as if to speak. The farmers, mute with horror, turned and ran back to the village. By nightfall everyone in Delaware had heard that the mansion was haunted. And the midnight stillness of that night and every night to come was pierced by the mournful cries of the sad little stranger.

As the days passed, search parties scoured the woods of Robinson's estate for some trace of the girl. Only her portrait and a few of her belongings left in the house testified to her life.

Robinson's disappearance was just as mystifying. He left the forest as stealthily as he had come into it. His hand-carved and gruesomely-chased casket was found in his workshop. Behind the house the mausoleum was filled with snakes.

Neighbors eventually swarmed over the pirate's mansion, determined to unearth the fortune they believed he had taken in plunder and buried in the earth. For months zealous plowmen and woodcutters swung picks, spades and shovels, overturning stones, uprooting young trees and even undermining the foundation of the house. Others ransacked the interior of the house, tearing out the handsome paneling, pulling down the hand-carved staircase and stripping the walls bare in their frenzied search for bags of gold.

Yet not a single coin was ever found.

Time and neglect eventually finished what the treasure hunters had begun, and the mansion was reduced to rubble.

Only the ghost of the young señorita lingers. Legend has it that the wraith still walks the banks of the Scioto River in the twilight of a summer afternoon. And sometimes, in the gathering gloom, a scream shatters the stillness and echoes down the valley floor.

THE HEADLESS BIKER

Have you ever wanted to confront a ghost? Are you brave enough to sit in a darkened car on a lonely road at night and summon the specter of a *headless motorcyclist*?

That is exactly what Richard Gill did on the twenty-first day of March, 1968, near the small Ohio community of Elmore. What Gill and a friend found on that vernal equinox evening made the men believers in things unseen.

The subject of the ghost tale is a motorcyclist who met an untimely death shortly after World War I. The young man had received his mustering-out pay and immediately purchased a shiny new motorcycle to impress his girlfriend. He had not seen her since his discharge from the Army. But when he arrived at her secluded farm home, he found she was engaged to another man. In his fury, the rejected suitor leaped aboard the cycle and roared off into the night. A few yards from his girl's driveway, the road curved before crossing a bridge. Somehow, and nobody knows just what happened, the man lost control of the cycle. Man and machine went careening into the ravine.

They found the young man and his cycle . . . both in pieces. The rider had been decapitated and the motorcycle's headlight wrenched off.

On the anniversary of the cyclist's death—each March 2l—visitors to that bridge are said to be able to see the motorcycle leave the deserted farmhouse's driveway, speed around the curve and disappear halfway across the bridge.

Richard Gill had heard the story from several people, including his friend who related one version at the Bowling Green University Student Union.

Together the men arrived at the haunted bridge well after dark, equipped with two cameras—one a movie camera, the other a still camera set up to take time exposures—and a tape recorder. They parked their car on the far side of the bridge, opposite the farmhouse, with the vehicle pointed toward the bridge. The men also put the cameras on the far side of the bridge in a position to capture on film anything that might move toward it.

In the car, Gill followed the procedure said to attract the ghost—he blinked the car lights three times and then honked the horn three times. As if on schedule, a light appeared, roared down the farmhouse driveway and headed toward the waiting men. It vanished midway across the bridge.

Buoyed by their success, the observers decided to tie a string across the bridge. In this way they hoped to find out if a physical object was hurtling down the road.

They repeated the ghost-summoning procedure and, just as before, the light traveled its curious route, then vanished. The string remained intact.

Still mystified, but determinedly curious, the pair decided to go one step further . . . and it almost proved fatal!

Their plan: while Gill summoned the specter, his friend would *stand* in the road halfway across the bridge.

On cue, the specter again repeated the performance. When his friend did not return to the car, Gill investigated. He found him in a ditch by the side of the road, soundly beaten! The battered fellow didn't know what had attacked him nor how he had gotten off the bridge. He had no recollection of the event at all.

For their fourth and final experiment—and by this time most ghost hunters would have given up—the men moved the car to the side of the bridge nearest the farmhouse, still pointing toward the bridge. They blinked the lights three times, honked three times and the light began its journey. As the light moved up behind the men, they started the car moving forward. The light overtook them, passed *through* the vehicle and disappeared on the bridge. The men kept going, convinced that *something* uncanny was happening that night.

And what did the cameras and tape recorder document? The movie film was blank. The tape recorder picked up some unusual, high-pitched noises. The still camera recorded a light source of some kind. Whether it was the ghost light, or something else, Gill and his friend couldn't determine.

But they never returned to the Elmore bridge on the occasion of the vernal equinox or any other time: apparently their ghost-confronting days were over.

OLD RARIDAN

Ancient tales of those mysterious places where animals go to die have always intrigued the "highest" animal of all. Whether it is the "elephant's graveyard" or the dying place of the bison, men for centuries have searched for the one spot within each region toward which old and wounded beasts struggle, driven by some instinctual urge during their final days.

Do such places actually exist? Or are they solely mythical?

In southern Ohio, somewhere within present-day Jackson and Pike counties, old-timers will tell you there *was* such a graveyard for the magnificent gray wolf. Its name was originally "Great Buzzard's Rock," but later generations knew it simply as "Big Rock."

The earliest explorers found this high granite, flat-topped hill a dying place of wolves. Bones of hundreds of the animals lay strewn on its surface. Buzzards floated in the skies above, waiting for new arrivals.

Until the end of the Revolutionary War, wolves in the region were of little concern to man. There were few people, and the occasional explorer shot a wolf only when it posed a threat. All that changed, however, as civilization edged westward. Pioneers began pushing into the fertile Ohio River Valley, bringing livestock and villages with them. Wolves had no place in the frontier settlement.

For one thing, they began to prey on livestock as pioneers killed deer for meat, diminishing the herds that were the wolves' source of food. Countering these depredations, settlers started slaughtering wolves whenever and wherever they could. Every new settlement pushed the wolves farther west.

Each wolf pack had its own leader. In about 1796, settlers began to notice that one pack of several dozen wolves followed a magnificent gray wolf. They called him Old Raridan, the king of wolves.

How he got his name isn't known. Only that this awesome beast, larger and more powerful than his comrades, often prowled in the distance after wolves had killed a farm animal. He knew what the hunters' guns could do and always kept himself out of range.

To avenge the increasingly frequent raids by Old Raridan's pack, groups of a dozen or more pioneers would set off after him, their hounds baying in pursuit. Although many wolves and hounds were slain, Old Raridan always eluded capture. His fatally wounded followers made their painful way to Big Rock to die.

Not even the bravest farmer dared follow a dying wolf to that strange and haunted dying place. Nor would a tracking hound approach it.

As the fame of Old Raridan grew, so did the number of hunters seeking to put an end to his murderous ways. His time was running out. Every man wanted to be known as the one who killed the King of the Wolves.

At last, only a few tough old wolves survived, among them Old Raridan and his mate. The bones of their followers littered Big Rock. Then, sometime in 1801, word spread through the Ohio Valley that only Old Raridan and his mate still lived. Hatred for the old wolf, fanned over many years, became a fury so intense that even the godly preachers prayed for his death. People talked of little else. Even women and children took part in the feverish search for Old Raridan.

Vastly outnumbered, Raridan found even his skill and cunning, learned through hundreds of battles, could not save him. An army of men with dozens of hounds now stalked the woods, searching him out.

And then it happened. Hunters cornered the king and his mate in some low hills near the Ohio River. The wolves killed several hounds, but in the process the she-wolf was wounded. Old Raridan would not leave her. Instead, they turned in the direction of Big Rock.

The hounds held to the trail as the day-long hunt wore on. For every wound the hounds inflicted, one of their number lost his life.

Just a mile from Big Rock, the hounds encircled the pair. Old Raridan let out a howl that froze the marrow in the pursuing hunters' bones, and then he rushed the dogs.

The fight was merciless. Old Raridan, protecting his mortally wounded mate, slashed in fury, moving inch by bloody inch to the foot of the trail leading to Big Rock's summit. Then the baying hounds, through some instinctual fear or compassion, fell back.

Suddenly a shot rang out. The she-wolf dropped, a bullet in her heart. A second shot: Old Raridan's right hip exploded in a sickening shower of flesh and bone. The warrior staggered toward his companion, his life flowing from a dozen wounds.

He raised his ragged gray head, once majestic and unbowed, now a mass of bloody fur, and surveyed the men who had destroyed his empire. His stare became a final challenge. "Here I am," he seemed to say. "Take me!"

Not more than fifty paces distant, the hunters could easily have finished off their quarry. Yet each stood welded to the earth, weapons stilled.

The old wolf turned toward the trail. Though it disappeared into heavy brush, he knew his destination was close. "Ooooooowwwwwwwwhhhhhoooooo!" Old Raridan raised his voice in one last cry. From the top of Big Rock floated an answer, almost an echo, yet more ethereal. It seemed to give the old wolf new energy, for he gently fastened his powerful jaws around the nape of his mate's neck and began to drag her up the trail . . . to the dying place of the wolves.

What is known of Old Raridan's final battle is based on legend. No hunters ever spoke on the record about their experiences that day. It is doubtful that anyone would have believed the tale. Something beyond human understanding had taken place in the wilderness.

Old Raridan is more than a folktale to many who have seen his specter prowling his old forest kingdom. When the moon is full, his awesome cry still drifts with the wind across Big Rock. And on its summit, the shadowy form of a giant beast stands proud against the darkening sky.

Chapter X. Wisconsin

"Summerwind. The name evokes a picture of a stately home, light and airy, expansive windows open to the breeze. So it once was. But now this mansion, on the shore of West Bay Lake in Wisconsin's Vilas County, is a dilapidated hulk, its windows broken, its roof rotted and its dormers filled with bats. Summerwind is the most notorious haunted house in Wisconsin ...

For six months in the early 1970s, Arnold Hinshaw, his wife, Ginger, and their six children lived at Summerwind. Within these few months, Arnold was driven mad by ghosts and his wife attempted suicide ..."

"SUMMERWIND"

SUMMERWIND

The name evokes a picture of a stately home, light and airy, expansive windows open to the breeze. So it once was. But now this mansion, on the shore of West Bay Lake in Wisconsin's Vilas County, is a dilapidated hulk, its windows broken, its roof rotted and its dormers filled with bats. Summerwind is the most notorious haunted house in Wisconsin.

The mansion was built in 1916 by Robert P. Lamont, who later became President Hoover's Secretary of Commerce in 1929. For years, it was the Lamont family's summer home, a quiet haven in the north woods far from the hustle and heat of Washington, D. C.

Upon Lamont's death, Summerwind was sold ... and sold again. The house has had a number of owners, yet is still known locally as the "Lamont place." Nothing out of the ordinary ever happened there ... or did it?

For six months in the early 1970s, Arnold Hinshaw, his wife, Ginger, and their six children lived at

Summerwind. Within these few months, Arnold was driven mad by ghosts and his wife attempted suicide.

From the day the Hinshaw family moved into the house they saw vague shapes flitting down the hallways and heard voices mumbling in dark corners. And every evening while they ate dinner, the ghost of a woman the family called Mathilda floated back and forth beyond the French doors to the living room.

For a brief time Ginger wondered if they were all imagining these things; but after numerous unexplained occurrences, she decided they were *not* imagining things. These occurrences included: a new hot water heater broke down, but started working again before a repairman could be called; the same thing happened with a new water pump. Other appliances failed, too, then mysteriously fixed themselves.

Windows and doors that were closed at night were open in the morning. A heavy window in the master bedroom, without sash weights or pulleys, was difficult to raise. One morning Arnold closed the window and started downstairs. Remembering that he'd left his wallet on the dresser, he returned to the bedroom. The window was open! In desperation, he drove a spike into the window casing. The window stayed closed. Months later, the spike was removed with a crowbar, but no nail hole could be seen!

On one occasion when Arnold went out to start his car to go to work, it burst into flames before his eyes. No one was near it and the cause of the fire was never determined. Other cars that the Hinshaws owned seldom started. An auto mechanic could find no mechanical problems to explain the breakdowns.

The couple hired subcontractors to undertake restoration projects in the house, but invariably the workers failed to show up, pleading illness or non-delivery of materials. A few told Ginger that they refused to work on *that* house.

The couple then realized that they would have to do the work on the house themselves.

One day they began painting a closet. A large shoe drawer was installed along the closet's back wall. The Hinshaws removed it in order to prevent the paint from sticking. Behind the drawer they discovered a dark space. It aroused their curiosity.

Ginger got a flashlight and Arnold wedged himself into the opening up to his shoulders. He beamed the light back and forth, then suddenly backed out of the opening. He was speechless—a corpse was jammed into the compartment!

Because there was a lot of plumbing and structural material in the way, Arnold couldn't squeeze far enough into the opening to be sure. The Hinshaw children then arrived home from school, and their parents told them about the bones. Ginger said a bear had been trapped in the wall while the house was being built.

Their daughter Mary volunteered to crawl into the space with the flashlight. Moments later she yelled out. She saw a head of dirty black hair, a brown dried-up arm and part of a leg.

The other children, thinking it was a game, wanted to see the bones too. Each of them took a turn. Each one emerged serious and quiet. Ginger made them promise never to say a word to anyone.

After the children had skipped off, Arnold and Ginger speculated on how the body had gotten there. Arnold suggested there may have been a murder while the house was being built and the body was dumped there. But the Hinshaws did not call the police, figuring nothing could be done about the crime since so many years had elapsed. Besides, most of the crew who had worked on the house and known about the crime would probably be dead anyway.

About this time Arnold began to stay up late and play the Hammond organ the couple had bought before moving into Summerwind. He always enjoyed playing in the evenings; it was a relaxing hobby. But now Arnold's playing became a frenetic jumble of melodies and chords, growing louder by the hour. Ginger pleaded with him to stop, but he said the demons in his head demanded that he keep on playing. Night after night, the family was kept awake until dawn by the awful music. The children were so frightened that they huddled together in one bedroom.

Arnold's breakdown came quickly, followed by Ginger's attempted suicide.

While Arnold was in treatment, Ginger and her children moved in with her parents who lived in Granton, Wisconsin. Ginger and Arnold were eventually divorced, and after Ginger regained her health she married George Olsen. Her new life was happy and tranquil, and the days at Summerwind seemed only a distant nightmare.

But the past came rushing back . . . too soon.

Ginger's father, Raymond Bober, a popcorn vendor, announced that he was going to buy Summerwind. He and his wife Marie would open a restaurant in the mansion, and eventually turn it into an inn. Its beautiful north woods location on a quiet lake would attract many guests.

Ginger was horrified. Although she had never given her parents all the details of her frightening experiences in the house, she begged them *not* to buy it. But Bober's mind was made up. He knew the place was haunted and he said he knew who the ghost was—Jonathan Carver! According to Bober, the eighteenth-century English explorer was searching for an old deed to the land granted him by the Sioux Indians in return for negotiating peace between two warring nations. The grant supposedly took in most of the northern third of Wisconsin. The deed was locked in a black box and sealed in the foundation of Summerwind. Carver's ghost sought Bober's help in locating it.

But how did Bober know this? From communicating with Carver through dreams, hypnotic trances and the Ouija board, he claimed. At least that's what he wrote in his book, *The Carver Effect*, published in 1979 under the name Wolffgang von Bober.

Shortly after Bober bought Summerwind, he, his son Karl, Ginger and her new husband, George, spent a day inspecting the mansion. The group was just leaving the second floor when George spotted the closet at the end of the hall. He began pulling out drawers and looking behind them. Ginger begged him to stop.

George dropped his flashlight and asked what she was talking about. Until now, Ginger had never told anyone about the discovery of the corpse. Sitting in the kitchen later, fortified by hot coffee, Ginger told the entire story.

Undaunted, the men gathered lanterns and returned to the closet. Ginger's brother, Karl, insisted on going into the space first. In a moment he backed out. It was empty!

Ginger's father and her husband also inspected the area. They saw pipes, beams and insulation . . . but no body! Where had it gone? Who had removed it? Why? Or, had there ever been a body there in the first place?

Over Labor Day weekend Karl traveled alone to Summerwind. He had gone to get a repair estimate on the well and also to look for an exterminator who could rid the house of bats. He thought he might even trim some trees and tidy up the lawn if the good weather prevailed and he had time.

It started to rain the first day and Karl ran upstairs to close a window. In the dark hallway, a deep voice called his name. The young man spun around. The voice repeated the greeting. Karl saw no one. Perhaps it was a friend outside. Karl looked out a window onto the courtyard, but saw no one.

Karl closed the window and went downstairs. When he reached the living room, he heard two shots. A heavy caliber pistol, he surmised. Close by. Was someone hunting on the property? Karl started for the back door.

Once in the kitchen Karl found the room filled with the acrid smoke of gunpowder. Someone had fired from *inside* the house! But an intruder could never have entered or escaped without being heard; the back door always stuck and had to be noisily pushed open or slammed shut and the other doors were all barred on the inside. Karl made a thorough search of the kitchen. He discovered two bullet holes in the door leading to the basement. But the holes were *old* ones that had been worn smooth on the edges! Karl left the house that afternoon.

In his book, Bober wrote that the original owner of the house, Robert Lamont, whom he called Patterson, had fired two shots at a ghost. But that had been decades ago!

Bober's attempts to renovate the house were as futile as those of his daughter. Workmen refused to stay on the job, complaining about being watched by evil eyes. Bober's wife, Marie, understood that complaint. She was always uneasy around the house. Every time she sat in the sunny courtyard she felt someone watching her from the windows of the master bedroom.

On one occasion, her husband found one of the windows open that he knew he had closed a few minutes before, but he never mentioned it to Marie for fear of alarming her.

Most disturbing to the new owners was the apparent shrinkage and expansion of the house. Bober would measure rooms one day and then find their dimensions different the next. Usually his measurements were larger than those given on the blueprints of the house. Sometimes Bober estimated he could seat 150 people in his restaurant, but after he laid out the plans on the blueprints of the house, he realized the place would seat no more than seventy-five!

Photographs taken by the same camera in the same position and only a few seconds apart likewise displayed incredible distortions of space. The living room in particular seemed to enlarge.

Once Bober compared his pictures of the living room with those Ginger had taken before she and Arnold and the children had moved into the mansion. Ginger's pictures showed curtains at the living room windows which she removed after she moved in. Those same curtains reappeared in her father's later photographs!

If the ghost of Jonathan Carver wanted help in locating his deed, why did he manifest himself in such diabolical ways? Bober explained that Carver did not want any improvements made in the property and that he resented anyone living in the house or renovating it in any way.

The Bobers never attempted to stay in Summerwind overnight. Instead, they cooked and slept in a camper on the grounds. And Bober spent many days searching the basement and chipping away at the foundation in efforts to locate the black box containing Carver's deed.

Will Pooley, a freelance writer, visited Summerwind in the fall of 1983 to gather the facts. His research had revealed that even if Bober had unearthed Carver's deed, it would have been worthless! Not only had the British government ruled against an individual's purchase of lands from the Indians, it was also later determined that the Sioux had never owned land east of the Mississippi River anyway! In addition, although the original deed was apparently found in an old land office in Wausau, Wisconsin, during the 1930s, historians argue that it is very unlikely Carver ever traveled as far north as Vilas County. Thus, how could the deed have gotten into the foundation of a house built 136 years after the explorer had died?

Pooley talked to dozens of local residents who had some connection with Summerwind. They revealed the history of the house as they knew it.

For example, Herb Dickman of Land O'Lakes helped pour the foundation for the Lamont mansion in 1916; he recalled that the only thing they put in there was stone. There was no black box containing a deed. Dickman also lived in the house for three months after it was finished. He said nothing unusual ever occurred.

Gene Knuth, resident of the area for over sixty years, told Pooley that kids only started calling the mansion haunted after it had been abandoned and became dilapidated. It never had that reputation while it was occupied.

Carolyn Ashby of Land O'Lakes lived in the mansion as a child during summers in the early 1940s. She didn't remember any ghosts, but admitted that the place seemed spooky, especially at night, because of its large number of rooms.

Other neighbors told writer Pooley that the Bobers spent less than two full summers on the estate. After Bober abandoned plans for his restaurant, he tried to get a permit to operate a concession stand near the house, but a local ordinance prohibited it.

There is some uncertainty as to whether Bober ever actually owned Summerwind. One area resident told Pooley that Raymond Bober had tried to buy the property on a land contract, but was unsuccessful.

Is the mystique of the haunted house based upon publicity and the deterioration of a once-magnificent home? Summerwind's neighbors think so. And they resent strangers tramping over their lawns and driveways and knocking at their doors. Today, even chartered buses disgorge ghost hunters upon the grounds of the Lamont mansion.

And what do the visitors see? Only the gray skeleton of a Victorian relic rotting in a grove of pines. Yet, when winds whine through the shattered windows and doors creak on rusty hinges and bats fly low in a sullen sky, it's easy to believe that something lurks behind those weathered walls.

But, of course, everyone knows there's no such thing as a ghost. As longtime area resident Gene Knuth remarked—"I don't believe in ghosts, but I've been afraid of them all my life."

THE TWICE DEAD GHOST

Is it possible to murder a ghost with a shotgun blast—or at least scare it enough so that it leaves the house it is haunting . . . permanently?

A modest, two-story farmhouse a few miles south of Portage was home to August and Patricia Heinz in 1925. The Heinzes and their children—seven-year-old Freddy, his older sister Elizabeth, eleven, and Charles, age nine—had moved into the house in 1915. During their ten-year occupancy, nothing untoward had happened.

All that changed during the summer and fall of 1925.

The trauma which would soon envelop each member of the Heinz family began ominously in February when a mysterious fire destroyed one of their barns. Another barn burned in June. The origin of both fires was never discovered.

Then one evening in late June, as the family gathered around the dining room table for supper, they heard footsteps descending from the second floor. Each member of the family was at the table.

Charles and his father investigated but found, as expected, no one else about. The footsteps resumed almost as soon as the family regrouped around the table— and would continue, off and on, for the next three months.

Yet the most bizarre incidents of the haunted summer centered on a broom Mrs. Heinz kept in the enclosed summer kitchen. The room could be reached only through an outside door.

Nearly every morning Mrs. Heinz discovered the broom was missing. Family members usually found the broom stashed in some remote corner of the farm property, or else in a different room of the house. Was one of the Heinz children up to mischief? Each child steadfastly maintained they had no connection with the roving broom, and their parents believed them.

With the family growing weary of searching for the broom each morning, Mr. Heinz decided to shackle the broom to the wall with a solid chain and lock the summer kitchen door. The next morning the chain was broken, the broom missing ... but the kitchen door was still locked! Mr. Heinz had the only key. The broom was outside in the yard!

The final encounter with the "thing," as the Heinz children took to calling their unseen guest, started after August Heinz had returned from a hunting trip. A neighbor had been with him, and he stayed for supper with the Heinz family. Soon the meal was interrupted by footsteps on the staircase. August reluctantly told the visitor about the family's resident ghost.

The neighbor thought for a long time and announced that possibly he might "scare" the ghost out of the house. He picked up his unloaded shotgun, crept toward the stairs, leaped around the corner and with a wild scream pulled the trigger. Unexpectedly, a blast shattered a wall, sending pieces of plaster and wallpaper flying in all directions! The "unloaded" shotgun wasn't unloaded!

Freddy and young Charles believed they heard a moan after the shotgun discharged, and later nearly everyone in the family heard groans and cries, like those of someone in pain, coming from the fruit cellar.

Could they have "killed" the ghost? It doesn't seem possible that something already *dead* could die a second time. But from that night on, the Heinz family was never again plagued by their unbidden visitor.

THE PHANTOM CONGREGATION

A few miles from Amery, Wisconsin, down a winding country lane, past trim farm homes and grazing cattle, and perched atop a windswept knoll, there stands an old Lutheran church. Its profile juts sentinel-like over the rolling fields, casting its shadow over a century-old cemetery. The church, painted a brilliant white, is a plain structure, a large cross affixed to an outside wall near the main door the only decorative touch. A bell tower rises dramatically, its spire visible for miles in any direction. A more modern, single-story addition housing offices and classrooms angles away from the main church.

Like hundreds of other country Protestant parishes across the Midwest, the church was founded by pioneer Scandinavian immigrants during the last century. At this place near Amery, Norwegians first assembled for worship in 1870. The old ways die hard. Church services weren't offered in English until 1941.

But this church is very different from any other rural house of worship.

Within its walls are trapped phantom worshippers who speak in subdued tones.

And once, in that majestic steeple, the heavy iron bell tolled *all by itself*.

At least four persons, including the church pastor, have witnessed the peculiar incidents. They are all hard-working, practical people not prone to belief in ghosts, phantoms and bells that ring by themselves. Yet each of these people never ventures forth into the church alone . . . at night.

The phantom congregation was first heard twenty years ago. Mrs. Barbara Anderson, now a middle-aged farm wife with grown children, was the church organist in the early 1960s. She had always been reluctant to enter the church at night, but never out of fear of anything unseen. Even in rural areas, women hesitated to travel alone after sunset. She set aside daylight hours in which to practice at the organ.

Mrs. Anderson didn't think anything peculiar could happen during the day. Then she heard the voices.

The encounter is etched upon Barbara Anderson's memory as if it had happened only yesterday.

"It sounded like people talking, so loud I could almost hear what they were saying. The first time, it was just kind of a mumbling though. I didn't even bother to go downstairs to the basement where the voices were coming from. I thought it was just somebody in the church."

The voices continued as Mrs. Anderson tried to concentrate on her music. Her curiosity got the better of her. She got up from the organ bench and walked downstairs into the basement meeting room. It was empty.

"I even went to the outside door to look into the churchyard because the voices were so loud," Mrs. Anderson explained. Except for the old parishioners buried in the nearby cemetery, she was quite alone.

On two separate occasions, when she knew she was alone, Mrs. Anderson heard clear, distinct conversations in the church. But at other times, on other days, the voices seemed distant and muffled.

Each time she heard the voices, Mrs. Anderson packed up her sheet music and left for home.

Barbara Anderson told no one of her experiences. Fifteen years passed before she found out another church parishioner had also heard voices in the lonely church.

Sheila Larsen is an active member of the church. She volunteers countless hours to help operate the small country parish on a tight budget. One of her jobs in past years was to help prepare the annual financial report.

On the first Friday night of a December in the early 1970s, Mrs. Larsen and another woman sat in the church office poring over ledgers and balance sheets. A small electric space heater warmed the small room, while an electric mimeograph machine hummed in a corner, churning out pages of figures which would be discussed later that week by the congregation. It was well past ten o'clock and Sheila and her friend were anxious to finish the job and return to their families.

Ever so slowly, almost without a conscious realization of *when* it started, the women became aware of a low murmuring of voices coming from somewhere deep within the darkened church. The women thought they were alone; no one else had been scheduled to use the church that night. The voices grew more distinct over the next few minutes as the listeners anxiously stared through the open office door and down the dim hallway. The sounds seemed to be coming from the basement, which is used as a meeting hall and recreation room.

"You couldn't hear what they said, but it was loud enough so that we thought a meeting was going on," Mrs. Larsen remembers.

The mysterious conversation even seemed to get louder, as if someone turned up the volume on some unseen radio. But there was no radio, or any other cause for the voices.

"We went downstairs to see what was going on," Mrs. Larsen related. "Of course, there was nobody there. We came back upstairs and went back to work. But the voices began again, just as before. We hurried up and got our work done and left!"

The voices still drifted through the church as the women scurried from the building.

To this day, Mrs. Larsen cannot explain what happened to her that night ten years ago. She tried to rationalize the experience. Was it the wind? No, the evening air was quiet and cold. Passengers in a passing car? Highly doubtful since the church office in which Mrs. Larsen worked is some distance from the highway and all the doors and windows were locked. The nearest house is several hundred yards distant, save for the parsonage across the road. And no one was home there that night.

When Barbara Anderson and Sheila Larsen first compared notes, they were struck by the similarities of their experiences: the voices always faded as the women neared the apparent source; the voices seemed to be part of a rather large gathering; and both men and women appeared to be speaking, although specific words could never be distinguished.

And then there is the church bell. It rings. By itself. The ponderous, iron instrument hangs in the church steeple. A long, heavy rope twists downward from the bell to the bottom of a narrow stairway adjacent to the choir loft. The door to the staircase is usually kept locked to keep curious youngsters out of the musty, dimly-lit tower.

The bell's strange behavior began in early June, 1981. At the parsonage across the road, three people were in the yard—Rachel Halvorsen, Barbara Anderson and the church pastor, the Rev. Elizabeth Robinson, a young woman not long out of the seminary who was serving her first congregation in the Amery church. She and her husband lived in the church-owned house.

The trio had been talking only a short while when the clear, clanging ring of the church bell drifted across the road. The Rev. Robinson and Mrs. Anderson stared at each other, then at the bell tower. Though neither could believe her ears, they agreed they had heard the bell. The church was empty, or so they thought. Rachel Halvorsen heard nothing.

As Barbara Anderson recalled, "I don't know if it rang once or twice. Although the other woman with us didn't hear it, we all decided to go over and see who was there."

They thought perhaps a youngster had gotten locked in the church and was using the bell to summon help. Or . . .

"We went down into the basement," Anderson related, "to the kitchen, the bathrooms, everywhere. We even went upstairs to the balcony to see who pulled the rope. But the door to the steeple was closed and the rope was not moving."

There is nothing that can move the bell save a solid tug on the rope. Yet, Mrs. Anderson and the Rev. Robinson heard the bell ring, a soft pealing, as if someone had pulled gently on the bellcord.

Could the women have been mistaken? Was it, perhaps, a cowbell off in the distance?

"Women in rural areas know the difference between a cowbell and a church bell!" stated the Rev. Robinson emphatically.

And what she heard that evening was most definitely a church bell . . . her church's bell . . . rung by unseen hands!

The history of the church is an unexceptional chronicle. To the best of anyone's knowledge, there have been no spectacular or peculiar deaths to account for a possible haunting. The only unusual legacy concerns the graveyard adjacent to the church. In a previous era, persons who died by their own hand were buried *outside* a fence that enclosed the legitimately deceased members of the parish. Over the years, the wooden picket fence collapsed several times and eventually was taken down so that those who died natural and unnatural deaths now mingle freely in the earth.

Similarly, hauntings seem to center on certain people who may be sensitive to paranormal events. Perhaps Sheila Larsen, Barbara Anderson and the Rev. Elizabeth Robinson are three of those rare individuals.

For her part, however, the Rev. Robinson doesn't believe in ghosts. "I don't think that when people die their spirits float around."

But, she trusts the witnesses who heard the voices in the church and of course, what she heard for herself—the toll of the church bell.

How does she explain the events? She can't. Although she remains skeptical, the Rev. Robinson is open to the possibility that the voices in the church may be of a paranormal nature. "After all," she said, "I haven't heard them."

Barbara Anderson and Sheila Larsen have. And they know *something* not of this world is congregating in their church. And summoning others to join them with a toll of the bell.

THE HAUNTED TENANT

Bob Lambert really didn't want to go upstairs.

The clouds had been lowering all that humid August afternoon, and now the weather bureau had issued a severe storm warning.

He waited. Perhaps the rain wouldn't come. Perhaps it would skirt Shorewood to the south. He sat nervously in his lower floor apartment, occasionally glancing out the window. He just knew he would have to go upstairs. If only Ginny were here. Maybe she couldn't protect him, but at least she would be around in case . . . anything . . . should happen.

But why should it? It was 1980 after all and ghosts and spirits and "things that go bump in the night" belonged to another era. But there were the footsteps.

For a time Bob thought they couldn't harm him or Ginny, but now he wasn't so sure.

"Come on, grow up," he said to himself. "It's silly to think that ghosts come out only during thunderstorms."

At the first sign of rain, Bob decided that he would close the windows in the upstairs apartment, just as he had promised the tenants he would do. And nothing would happen.

Shortly after three o'clock, the rain started. Now Bob had no choice. He started up the staircase, and stopped.

"I'm coming up to close the windows," he shouted to the empty apartment. Farther up the stairs, Bob again paused. "I'm going to shut the kitchen windows first," he called out. If something was around, Bob didn't want to take the chance of surprising it. He hesitated a moment, reflecting on the five years he and Ginny had spent in their Shorewood apartment.

Up until that afternoon, the Lamberts had lived in relative peace with the "ghost" upstairs. In fact, the couple had grown accustomed to the footsteps, as if they belonged to another member of their family. But the noises only occurred when *no one* was home in the upstairs apartment.

The tenants had keys to each other's apartment in case of an emergency. At first, Bob or Ginny would climb the stairs each time the footsteps started in order to check on their source. But the footsteps always stopped before either of them reached the apartment.

The ghost only made one appearance over the years, as far as the Lamberts knew. Yet it was a visit which provided a clue to the specter's identity.

Dottie Rosmund, the upstairs renter at the time, was bathing. Her husband was out for the evening. Suddenly, the air chilled. From the bathroom door a light, gray mist hovered in the air, the vague outline of a man billowing upward from the cloud. He was staring straight toward Dottie! She watched horror-stricken as the mist evaporated. The Rosmunds moved out of the apartment a short time later.

Had Dottie Rosmund actually caught a glimpse of the ghost? She may have. Bob Lambert later discussed the peculiar episodes in the apartment with his landlady. She informed him that one of her sons, who had been raised in that house, was very sickly as a child and was confined for most of his life to a bedroom on the second floor. He died shortly after his mother moved to a new home. She told Bob that it might be her son's ghost who was prowling the second floor apartment.

Bob flipped on the apartment lights, but a few seconds later they dimmed and went off. His flashlight was downstairs and he had no idea where the upstairs tenants kept their candles. He would have to make do. Although it was only midafternoon, the dark sky had turned the apartment into a jumble of shadows.

He closed the kitchen windows and started down the long, narrow hallway toward the bathroom. He noticed something palpable in the air, something more than the watery humidity of a typical late August afternoon. It was a sense of being followed, of knowing that he wasn't *really* alone.

The bathroom door was closed, but Bob knew the window was probably open. He hesitated. A little voice inside him—and he was never quite sure where it came from—told him not to open that door. A feeling of dread, almost a sense of immediate danger, swept over him. The tiny hairs on the back of his neck stood at rigid attention. He could feel the sweat starting to drip down his chest.

He slowly took his hand from the door and backed away. Then, quickly, he closed the bedroom and living room windows and raced for the staircase. As he passed the hallway, he looked toward the bathroom. The door

stood wide open! It had been firmly closed a minute before
... and the wind was coming from the wrong direction
to have blown it open. Had the landlady's son returned?

Bob Lambert didn't wait around to find out. He
never wanted to visit that apartment again!

THE SPIRIT OF ROSSLYNNE MANSE

THE TIME: A Sunday afternoon in October, 1981.

THE PLACE: The sprawling campus of St. John's
Military Academy in Delafield, Wisconsin.

THE EVENT: Fire departments from Delafield and
nearby Wales, with the Army Corps of Engineers assisting,
are gathered around an old house in the center of campus.
Rosslynne Manse, once the home of former Academy
president Sidney Thomas Smythe, is set ablaze to enable
firefighters to practice fire-control techniques.

The last traces of the old mansion disappear as smoke
and flame devour the rotting wood and sagging roof. Only
the massive stone blocks used in the foundation, and as
supports for the porch pillars, remain.

Uninhabitable after years of neglect, and too costly
to renovate, Rosslynne Manse becomes a mere memory
for the thousands of young men who passed through the
gates of St. John's Academy. But for a handful of others
who knew of the peculiar ghost story connected with the
mansion, Rosslynne Manse will live on.

A silver shovel turned the first piece of earth for the
fourteen-room house, planned around a massive stone
fireplace, which was modeled after one which Dr. Smythe
had seen as a child in his uncle's Scottish home. Even the
name of the home, Rosslynne Manse, originated in
Scotland, "manse" being the old Scottish term for a
clergyman's home.

Beautiful porches stretched across the front and rear portions of the house, the latter enclosed by pillars wedged atop hand-hewn stone blocks. The Smythe family lived in the first two stories, reserving the large room on the third floor as a sort of clubroom for senior cadets who frequented the house in great numbers. Dr. Smythe insisted on knowing each student personally, and as many as fifteen to thirty cadets dined at the house each week.

In fact, according to legend, Dr. Smythe placed a large, leather armchair in front of the huge picture window which overlooked the Academy grounds. Supposedly the elderly Dr. Smythe wanted to keep an eye on "his" campus. But strange events occurred within the house itself that defied even the doctor's most rational explanation.

Mrs. Sidney Smythe was sewing in the upstairs hallway on a November evening in 1905. Her children, Betty and eight-year-old Charles, were in bed. A grandfather clock near the stairway to the second floor chimed eight o'clock, reminding Mrs. Smythe that her husband would be coming home soon. He would expect a light meal. She put down her sewing materials, descended the stairs and started toward the kitchen.

The house had a rather large entrance hall which extended directly into a living room with two large windows, one facing east, the other south. A rocking chair was situated so that it commanded a view out the south window.

As Mrs. Smythe walked toward the living room, her gaze shifted toward the rocking chair. In the chair sat a man, well-dressed but extremely pale. She later said that the man appeared to be in the last stages of some fatal disease.

Mrs. Smythe backed up a step or two, bumping into the clock. As she reached out to steady the instrument, she looked back into the living room. The man had vanished!

It wasn't until the next morning that Mrs. Smythe told her family about the incident. Even then she didn't show any fear, but coolly described the man's appearance, and disappearance, as if the specter had been an old family friend in for a visit.

The Smythes knew that their house was not the first built on that particular parcel of land. A family named Ashby had owned a house there some time before, but the Smythes did not know anything about the Ashby family or what had become of them. Now they wanted to find out, sensing a solution to the mystery of the man in the chair. An answer came the following summer.

An old gardener, who worked for the Smythes, had also known the Ashbys. One day while he was planting shrubs near the Rosslynne Manse porch, Mrs. Smythe asked him about the Ashbys. The gardener told her about the family, including the fact that Mr. Ashby had a son-in-law who had died of tuberculosis of the lung. Mrs. Smythe pressed the gardener for details of the dead man's appearance—they matched exactly the figure she had seen in the rocking chair!

Twelve years later, Charles Smythe, then twenty years old, also encountered the Ashby's ghostly son-in-law. The rest of the family was attending a function at the school one evening, leaving Charles alone in the house. When they returned, Mrs. Smythe noticed a visibly shaken Charles seated in the living room. At his mother's urging, he recounted the following strange experience:

"I was upstairs reading. The dog, Jack, was lying at my feet. After a bit, I decided to go into the lower hall for some reason or other, and started downstairs, the dog preceding me.

"When I reached the lower landing, I looked toward the window, and there I saw the same man whom mother had seen in 1905. This time he was standing with his feet apart, hands behind his back, and facing the window. I could not see his face entirely.

"At this instant, the dog, who had advanced to the center of the room, uttered a ghastly growl. It was partly a choked snarl, and partly a moan, as if the animal was in terror. He was crouched down, ears laid back, teeth bared, and was staring at the figure by the window.

"I glanced down for a second toward the dog, and upon looking up the figure was gone. I searched all around, the dog following me, trying vainly to pick up a scent; there did not seem to be one. I found nothing."

Betty Smythe, who was upstairs as her brother told their mother about the bizarre event, noticed the dog sniffing around, going from room to room, whining. He seemed to be searching for something.

Neither Mrs. Smythe, nor her son Charles, sought an explanation for the phenomena they witnessed. And to this day no one knows why the Ashby's son-in-law found it necessary to "return" to his former home. There were no other ghost sightings ever reported in Rosslynne Manse.

The "spirited" area is now an open field on the campus of St. John's Military Academy. The old maple trees and majestic oaks that once shaded the Smythe house are gone, along with the last vestiges of the great mansion. Young cadets march across the site of the old house every day, unaware of the peculiar events which transpired there nearly eight decades ago.

The Wandering Dead

The recent Hollywood film "Poltergeist" popularized the idea that the wrath of the dead might be visited upon the living if a burial ground is disturbed. The unwitting family in the movie lived in a house built on a graveyard. A series of catastrophic events—including the kidnapping of their young daughter by spirits and a nightmarish march of ghosts down their staircase—eventually drove the family from the house.

The movie was fiction, of course. But, is it possible that a haunting as in the film "Poltergeist" can actually happen? In fact, yes—events like those described in the movie *did* occur in Wausau, Wisconsin, during the early 1970s!

The split-level home in a Wausau subdivision looked ideal to Harry and Jackie Fischer when they first saw it in 1972. Although the house was no different in appearance from the other dwellings in the neighborhood, the couple felt fortunate to find a place they could decorate and complete to their own tastes. The last thing on their minds, and they would have laughed at the idea, was that the pleasant house could be haunted.

For Jackie Fischer, a hint of evil in the house came shortly after they moved in. Pots and pans rattled in the kitchen cupboards, soda bottles on the counter swayed—and sometimes moved—and a ringing, like that of a tiny bell, floated through various rooms.

The couple dismissed the events as coincidences, or vibrations from passing cars, until Jackie's father had a peculiar encounter with his radio. He was spending a few days with them, and had settled down one evening with his radio. He just finished tuning in a station when a high-pitched whine erupted from the speakers. At almost the same instant, a lighted candle, sitting on the coffee table in front of him, rose straight into the air, flipped onto its side so that it pointed directly at his heart and then settled back on the table!

He reported the incident to Jackie. She looked at her husband. They both shook their heads.

Soon, the couple realized that what was happening had an origin beyond their comprehension. Various household items began sailing through the air, the radio periodically changed stations or emitted the same sound Jackie's father had heard. The local radio-TV repairman couldn't find anything mechanically wrong with the radios.

The small hallway just inside the front door, with short flights of stairs leading up to the first floor or down into the lower level, seemed to be the center of a physical presence. The Fischers decided this after their cocker spaniel started to act particularly sensitive there. The dog often sat in the hall, staring intently down the steps to the basement. Her hair stood on end, as she growled her distress at whatever it was that she "saw." She refused to go down the stairs by herself.

A complete inspection never turned up anything, but that didn't satisfy the cocker spaniel. She would be back in the hallway, growling and barking a few hours later.

The incidents occurred sporadically that first year. Days or weeks would go by with little activity. The Fischers almost began to believe there really was a natural cause for everything that happened.

Until the footsteps began.

That was in the second year, 1973, and the couple had grown accustomed to the occasional flying candle, or to their cocker spaniel growling into the basement. The soft treading began at night, in the basement, and proceeded up the stairs, across the landing and up to the first floor. Then, nothing more until the next night when the episode would be repeated. But not every night, making the occurrences even more disturbing.

Accompanying the footsteps was a gradual increase in the ghostly activity. A warm bath suddenly turned icy ... lights flickered on in the middle of the night ... and doors opened and closed of their own will. Like the gradually increasing beat of a tribal drum, the house began to vibrate with the hauntings.

Jackie Fischer remembered a particularly unnerving evening in 1975. She was in the bathroom preparing to shave her legs when the safety razor floated straight up and shot past her head. It missed her by only a few inches. Never before had the family been physically threatened. The Fischers now felt the entity haunting their house had turned against them.

In that same year, the footsteps multiplied in frequency. On one occasion, Harry Fischer grew so irritated at the incessant stomping that interrupted his sleep that he got out of bed, crept from his room and into the hallway. He threw on the lights, hoping to catch a glimpse of their unseen visitor. Instead, the lights flickered off, almost as if they had been candles blown out by an unfelt wind. But the lights worked again the next morning!

Then a second, potentially serious, attack by the entity occurred. A fire broke out in the Fischer's basement. Fortunately, it was discovered early and the fire department was able to extinguish it. The firefighters determined the blaze had been caused by a faulty battery charger. The Fischers disagreed—the charger wasn't even plugged in!

In desperation, the couple turned to their pastor. His blessing, they hoped, would rid the house of its evil.

It didn't work. On the afternoon following the minister's visit, Jackie was washing clothes in the downstairs utility room. She heard a thump—thump—thump from the storeroom a few feet away. The timid cocker spaniel sat at her feet, growling at the noise.

Jackie walked over and pushed against the door. It hit against something solid—an object that shouldn't have been there. Jackie scooped up her dog and flew up the stairs.

A later inspection of the room found no reason for the door to have hit anything. Indeed, it always swung open easily before and after that day.

The experiences proved to be too much for the Fischers. They decided to sell, and were fortunate to find a couple they knew, Jim and Mary Strasser, willing to buy the house. The Strassers knew of the problems the Fischers had encountered, but they thought there was a reasonable explanation.

Whatever haunted the house, however, would not let Jackie Fischer escape without one last jolt. A few days before they were to leave, Jackie awakened before dawn to let the dog outside. As she entered the kitchen and turned on the light, a gray mist evaporated in a far corner. Jackie was convinced it was the "residue" of whatever shared the house with her and Harry.

The Strassers lived peacefully in the house for a time, but then they too became targets of the resident ghost.

As with the Fischers, the episodes began infrequently and then grew in number and intensity. First, a loud humming, almost like a song, according to Jim Strasser, was heard in the house. Strasser said it seemed melodic, although it was never loud enough to be heard distinctly. Possibly an Indian chant, he speculated.

The Strasser's three-year-old daughter, Lorrie, complained that someone squeezed her toes while she slept. When she changed bedrooms, the pinching stopped. But the footsteps, floating objects and evaporating mists repeated their appearances for the Strassers.

The entity in the house went one step farther with the Strassers—it made an appearance in Jim Strasser's sleep! In the nightmare, Jim saw himself as an old Indian, wrapped in a blanket, choking to death. He awoke trying to catch his breath.

There was never any *physical* harm done to either family. But both couples *knew* there was something in the house.

What was it?

A local historian's research showed that the house had been built over an ancient Indian burial ground.

Perhaps the restless spirits of the ancient dead were showing their anger at having their graves desecrated. The Fischers recalled that the hauntings were particularly noticeable between the end of October and Thanksgiving, the usual time for Indians to gather in large numbers to celebrate the harvest.

As strange as it sounds, this explanation may prove to be accurate. To date, neither the Fischers nor the Strassers have come up with a better one.

THE ASTHMATIC APPARITION

One chilly midnight in early December, 1913, Max Kubis couldn't sleep. It wasn't just the relentless wind slamming against the house, piling the falling snow into ever deeper drifts. Something else kept him awake. From somewhere below his second-story bedroom, a faint scraping noise prevented his slumber.

It seemed at first nothing out of the ordinary—perhaps one of the family's numerous cats. The house was locked tight against the Milwaukee winter, and animals become bored during the long inside months just as their masters do. A frolic late at night was not unusual for the Kubis cats—yet the rhythmic sounds of this disturbance puzzled Max. Felines are sporadic creatures, their activity coming in bursts followed by silences. The noises that reached Max's ears seemed human, like someone moving about in the darkness, their slippered feet sliding across the oak floors.

Max carefully lifted the blankets and eased out of bed. His wife, Julia, slumbered peacefully over on her side of the fourposter. His feet found the carpet slippers. He threw a robe around his shoulders as he moved across the room. The mantel clock downstairs was completing its midnight tolling.

His stealth wasn't necessary. At the instant his hand found the bedroom door, a vicious pounding at the distant front door aroused the entire household. Julia sat up in bed, eyes wide and questioning. The couple's daughters, Helen and Armilla, called out from their bedroom.

Before Max could answer the midnight commotion, however, the front door crashed open and somebody walked from the hallway into the kitchen.

By this time, the family found itself huddled in the upstairs hall, staring down the darkened staircase toward the unseen caller.

"Who's there? What do you want?" Max Kubis demanded, his strong voice betraying only the slightest trace of fear.

After a few seconds of silence, Max, followed by his wife and daughters, moved toward the stairs, flipped on the lights and made their way to the first floor. The little troupe searched through the front parlor, closets and kitchen. There was no trace of anyone.

The Kubis family knew very little about their new house, except that it had been, until her recent death, the lifelong home of Mrs. Alex Pickman. They had only recently moved back to the state after a brief stay in Everett, Washington, having come originally from the small west-central Wisconsin town of Independence.

Some time later, on a night when the thermometer hovered well below the freezing mark, Mrs. Kubis climbed out of bed in the early predawn hours to add wood to a bedroom stove. She was halfway across the floor when the distinct image of an elderly woman materialized beside the woodstove. Her hands were held out toward the warmth of the blaze as if trying to ward off the chill of the room. The apparition vanished as Mrs. Kubis drew near.

Could this old woman and the nocturnal prowler be Mrs. Pickman? When Mrs. Kubis described the apparition, a neighbor said it matched the former owner even down to the dowdy housedress the vaporous figure had worn. Furthermore, Mrs. Pickman had told her husband and relatives that she intended to return to her Milwaukee home as a ghost. Although she had been buried in Omaha, Nebraska, she had obviously kept her promise.

During the following weeks, in the hour between midnight and one a.m., there were repeat performances of the door opening and closing, footsteps pacing about and, most disconcerting of all, the heaving of labored breathing. That settled it, the neighbors told Mrs. Kubis. Mrs. Pickman had had a severe asthmatic condition!

Each night for weeks to come, just after the stroke of midnight, old Mrs. Pickman came back to visit. Once she became confused, apparently, and showed up at a neighbor's house. That distraught family called their minister to come and spend the rest of the night with them!

One night Mrs. Pickman went too far. Helen and Armilla were fast asleep when they were jarred awake by the heavy thud of a falling body hitting their bed, followed by the scrambling of someone trying to crawl under the covers. The girls fled screaming from the room, quite convinced that the old lady had jumped into bed with them!

That was enough! The following morning, Max Kubis packed up his family and belongings and moved. In their rush to leave, however, the family left behind their mantel clock. When Julia Kubis returned for it the next day, she found it stopped . . . at midnight!

THE TEETOTALING POLTERGEIST

Tim and Louise Mulderink are an energetic young couple who always dreamed of owning a restaurant. In November, 1982, they bought a 125-year-old house in Plover, Wisconsin. As they would discover, not all the former residents of the attractive, two-story clapboard dwelling had moved out. Someone they couldn't see opened the front door, knocked glasses off the bar, tramped the upstairs rooms and turned lights on and off.

At first, Tim and Louise were so busy remodeling that they didn't notice any peculiarities. They put in new wiring and plumbing, installed a new roof and insulated the walls. Tim, who had an extensive background in food management and catering, did much of the planning, including the conversion of the former garage into a kitchen. Louise, a vivacious, willowy blond, supervised the redecorating of the house. The main color scheme of petal pink and burgundy created an elegant ambience for fine dining.

The Mulderinks named their restaurant the Sherman House to identify it with the famous Sherman House restaurant in Chicago, their hometown. They also wanted to honor Eugene A. Sherman, the most historically significant of the home's previous residents. Sherman had operated a sawmill and general store in Plover, moving into the house in 1891. Now, nearly a century later, the Sherman House restaurant was ready for its first guests. The well-attended grand opening in April, 1983, pleased Tim and Louise.

A month later, Louise was standing behind the bar, facing a glass-shelved, glassware storage cabinet, when a glass exploded.

"It just shattered," Tim remembered. "Louise never touched it. There was glass on the bar, everywhere." The glass had been in the center of a row of glasses. Had a vibration of some sort caused it to break? Tim didn't think so, or other glasses in the cabinet would have broken also.

Shortly afterward, two women in the bar ordered drinks. No sooner had the bartender set the first drink down, when the glass exploded, showering one of the women with liquid and glass fragments. Fortunately, she wasn't hurt. The bartender, a waitress and Charles Grachan, Louise's father, witnessing the incident, said no hands had been touching the glass.

On a Friday night, Paul, one of the dishwashers, experienced a similar incident. Five minutes after he pulled a rack of glasses out of the machine to air dry, he heard a loud popping noise. Tim, who was standing nearby, said, "What are you doing, Paul? Breaking glasses?"

"I didn't even touch it," Paul said, holding a stack of plates he had just removed from another machine.

On another day, during the lunch period, a fourth glass exploded, throwing shards into the liquor and ice bins. "The pieces looked like a windshield somebody'd taken a sledge hammer to," said Louise.

By this time, Tim, convinced that the glasses were defective, talked to the company representative. The man could not explain the explosions; he said that an occasional glass shatters, but it is highly improbable for several glasses to do so.

Meanwhile, the heavy front door developed a will of its own. It opened six or eight inches by itself. Tim discounted an air current caused by the kitchen exhaust fan because doors between the kitchen and entrance lobby are always kept closed. There was never any wind on days the door swung open, and the Mulderinks never found anyone who might have opened it as a prank, or carelessly failed to shut it.

The restaurant opens at four-thirty on Sundays, and one afternoon Louise's father was alone in the house answering the telephone and taking dinner reservations. Suddenly, he heard someone unlock the front door and open it. He called out jokingly, "Come in, Mr. Sherman. I'll buy you a drink."

No one came in. Thinking it must be a cleanup man, Grachan went to check. The door was open just wide enough for a person to slip through, but no one was in the house.

"Only a few people have a key to that door," Mr. Grachan said. "Whoever opened it had to have a key. I heard it click."

But that was not the end of Mr. Grachan's experiences. Late one evening, he, Tim and a friend named Rick were lounging after hours in the bar. At midnight, the mantel clock in the center of the top shelf behind the bar began striking the hour. The men looked up at the clock and counted. It struck thirteen!

"I've had enough for tonight," Mr. Grachan said. He had bought the clock new in April of 1983, and this was the third time it had struck an extra hour. He had examined the battery-operated device carefully, but could find nothing wrong with it. "I'm not scared of anything," Mr. Grachan explained, "except anything I can't see. I have trouble with that."

Corinne, the cleaning lady, felt the same way. A religious woman who always carried her Bible with her, she reported to work early each morning ... until she quit. "Whatever is in there," she told Tim, "I can't work there any more."

"She was scared out of her wits," Tim said, shaking his head. "She would constantly talk about kitchen pots clanging or shadows in the bar; when she was near the entrances she could see shadows going by."

Tim thought it was probably the wind and the old house creaking, although he admits that the structure is quite solid.

Even though other employees besides Corinne were nervous about working in the house, Tim and Louise were not inclined to accept a supernatural basis for the incidents. Tim, especially, sought logical explanations for everything—but never found them. Louise, however, soon experienced an incident that changed her mind. It frightened her so badly that she refused, afterwards, to stay alone in the house.

That night, while John, another dishwasher, finished up in the kitchen, Louise emptied the cash register and went upstairs to the office to count the money and put it in the safe. She kept the office door open. Suddenly, it closed. She got up to open it. Returning to her task, she heard footsteps cross the hall. Then she noticed that the door to the banquet room opposite—which was always kept closed—was open.

Louise raced downstairs to ask John if he had come up. No, he said, he had not left the kitchen. Louise went back upstairs, turned on the banquet room lights and checked the room. Nothing was disturbed. By the time she returned to counting the money, John was ready to leave.

"I counted very fast," Louise remembered, "put everything in the safe, made sure the back (fire escape) door was locked, turned off the light in the office, and made sure all the upstairs lights were off. John and I walked out the door together and he got in his car and left. My car was parked in the back so I had to walk around the building and ... I heard this tapping on the upstairs window.

"I got in my car, locked all the doors and backed the car up to see if the branches of any trees were scraping the window. No, the branches can't hit the window. I looked up and the office light was on. I knew I'd turned all the lights off and I wasn't about to go back in. So I went home and woke Tim up. I had to tell him what happened."

In the morning, the office light was off!

Louise said her father had a similar experience while managing the restaurant while she and Tim were out of town. Mr. Grachan finished counting the money, put it in the safe and turned off all the lights. While walking to his car, he looked up and saw the office light burning. He went back inside and the light was off.

Louise was not the only one who heard footsteps. One Friday night Tim and Louise and four of the employees were gathered in the kitchen when they heard distinct thumping noises overhead.

"Stop talking for a minute!" someone shouted. Heavy footsteps crossed the upstairs hall as if to enter the banquet room. Tim searched the entire upstairs. He found nothing.

On a fall night in 1983, Louise witnessed a second disturbing incident. She was upstairs when the fluorescent lights in the office flickered, but did not go out. Then Louise heard a tinkling noise. On the back of the office door is a rack holding lightweight metal clothes hangers. As Louise turned from the safe, she noticed the hangers swinging back and forth, including one that held a shirt of Tim's.

"It was as if somebody had brushed past them," she said. But she was alone. No air was moving, nor was the air conditioner running. Louise could find no explanation for the movement of the hangers.

"I went home and told Tim that the ghost was here again," she said.

But *who* is the ghost?

The Mulderinks still hope to find out. Wendell Nelson, a Portage County historian, provided the couple with much background information on the house and its residents. And Louise also gathered information from customers familiar with the place. The only person known to have died in the house was a two-day-old infant.

However, all of the families who had lived in the house were Methodists and teetotalers. Especially the Pierces who owned the house from 1903 until 1945. James W. Pierce was a grocer in Plover. The deacons and the mens' club met in his house, and Mrs. Pierce regularly entertained the ladies' sewing circle. Louise thought the Pierces were probably offended by the transformation of their homestead into a restaurant. Especially after she and

Tim unwittingly converted Mr. Pierce's old bedroom into a bar!

"He's probably just having kittens over that!" exclaimed Louise.

Does the ghost of James Pierce haunt the house? If so, he was there long before the Sherman House began operations. The Mulderinks believe the house has been haunted for at least twenty-five years. The last residents, the William Sowiaks, who owned it from 1957 to 1982, also witnessed strange phenomena. When the Mulderinks bought it, Tim and Louise became acquainted with Mike Sowiak, son of the owners, who had grown up in the house. Mike told them this story:

The rear portion of the upstairs banquet room was once Mike's bedroom. (Tim and Louise had removed the wall between two bedrooms to create the private dining area.) The Sowiaks had a friendly dog who was also fearless . . . except at certain times when it refused to go upstairs. It would stand at the foot of the stairway and bark and howl. Once, Mike pushed the dog up a couple of steps, but it came right back down.

In the 1970s, Mike married and moved to Chicago. Each time he and his wife, Sue, returned to visit Mike's parents, they slept in Mike's bedroom. But they got little rest. The couple would hear someone enter the room and approach the bed. It was as if a parent were coming in late at night to check on a sleeping child. But no one was ever there.

After a few such nocturnal checks, Sue refused to sleep in the room anymore. Mike stuck it out until one night when something awoke him. He refused to say what had frightened him.

A few sensitive patrons of the Sherman House may suspect that someone invisible may be watching them in the oak-trimmed bar or in one of the comfortable dining rooms. But luckily, since the bar glasses shattered, there have been no further incidents involving customers.

They also know that the front door, secure as it seems, may open mysteriously at any time ... that someone prowls the banquet room upstairs ... that the mantel clock in the bar can't be depended upon to chime the correct hour. And that the woman who lives next door may greet Tim and Louise in the morning by asking, "Did you know your office light was on all night?"

Meanwhile, the Mulderinks are working hard to complete the restoration of this lovely vintage home. Eager to forge a link with the past, they've named the various dining rooms in honor of previous residents and they are collecting pictures of the families. They have little time to ponder what their resident ghost might do next.

Louise's father, who believes in ghosts, offers the last word. "He's just a nice, friendly guy."

And hopefully an asset to the restaurant business.

BARTHOLOMEW RUDD'S CHRISTMAS GUEST

Bartholomew Rudd trudged silently homeward through the steady snowfall blanketing the little Mississippi River town of Fountain City. The midnight Christmas Eve church services had been beautiful, as they always were. Though the temperatures hovered below the freezing mark, a spiritual warmth lightened Bartholomew's stride.

Not a soul moved abroad. He had bid his fellow churchgoers a last "Merry Christmas!" and turned toward his own home at the edge of town, amusing himself by glancing now and then toward the rooftops. Expecting to see what? St. Nicholas? Silly of him. In the silent world of a snowy Christmas Eve, his mind fastened on childish fantasies.

A taciturn man who had remained a bachelor for all his fifty-three years, Rudd would spend the holiday alone. Or so he thought.

He wondered if the families in the snug little houses he passed felt as content as he did. Here and there a few candles still flickered in darkened windows. Rudd chuckled to himself. Perhaps the children had prevailed upon their indulgent parents to place a beacon to guide St. Nicholas. Or, he noted wistfully, families awaited the late arrival of friends with whom they would pass a festive Christmas Day.

Rudd quickened his step as the snow began to fall more heavily, muffling him in a soundless, white cocoon. Yet he seemed to hear footsteps behind him. He stopped to listen, but the silence fell as deep as the snow. He started to turn around, but thought better of it. Nothing back there, he thought, why trouble myself?

He resumed his pace ... and soon he knew it was not his imagination. Someone *was* following him. The crunch of boot against snow was unmistakable.

Rudd walked faster. He was not a particularly brave man. By the time he reached the familiar stone steps of his house, he was panting. He flew up the stairs, stopped short to catch his breath and listened again. Stillness. The man must have turned off.

Rudd then noticed a peculiar thing. Although the snow was swirling about him, obscuring even the corners of his own house, not a flake had fallen on him. His coat was only lightly covered when it should have been soaked. How odd. Hatless, Rudd felt the wet flakes pelt against his head, but when he reached up to touch his hair, he found it quite dry.

Summoning all his courage, he turned quickly toward the street. There was no trace of a living soul. Perhaps no one had been behind him after all. Perhaps the swirling snow, the crackling caused by the freezing temperatures and his own elation after church had combined to create the delusion.

Lost in these perplexing thoughts, Rudd let himself in the front door. Agatha, his aged tabby cat, rubbed against his leg as he removed his coat and scarf in the chilly hallway. An involuntary shudder rippled through his body as he placed the garments on a hall tree. Was it the bleakness of the house? Or the chill remaining from his curious journey home?

He quickly mounted the staircase to his study. The hearth fire kindled before he left should still be blazing, and he anticipated that its warmth would be enough to rid him of the cold that had suddenly seized him.

"Barty!"

The voice came from the rocking chair near the fire. Bartholomew let out a cry at the unexpectedness of it. He peered cautiously toward its source. A man rose and held out his hand.

"Andrew!" Rudd stuttered. "Andrew Putnam! Here in Wisconsin! But how?"

Rudd and Putnam had been childhood friends, growing up with the rugged Wisconsin territory. Although they had remained in touch through an occasional letter, each had gone his separate way. Rudd had remained in Fountain City, while Putnam went to Washington, D.C., and now held a position in the Andrew Johnson administration.

Rudd's amazement at the thoroughly surprising visit of his old friend evaporated quickly as they chatted about their mutual delight in being able to spend the holidays together. His harrowing walk home faded from his mind.

After quickly apprising each other of their individual triumphs and failures, Rudd remembered that he was hungry. He prepared a modest supper for himself and his guest, accompanied by glasses of ale. Try as he might, Bartholomew could not persuade Putnam—quite chilled from the long walk, he said—to leave the warmth of the fire, so they ate before it.

They talked for nearly two hours before retiring. They would talk again in the morning, Rudd promised.

Putnam didn't reply, but simply turned toward the guest room door Bartholomew indicated.

Rudd did not sleep well that night. Either the lateness of their meal—nearly two in the morning—or his strange feeling earlier of being followed, caused him to remain awake until nearly dawn.

At nine o'clock, the sharp voice of his housekeeper aroused him from fitful slumber. Breakfast would be ready shortly, she announced. Rudd dressed quickly and on his way to see if Putnam was awake, passed by the open door of the study. The sight of that tidy room nearly staggered him. Surely it was not possible! On the small fireside table stood the remains of the post midnight repast: two tall glasses, two plates. But one of the glasses was still brimful of ale and one plate heaped with food.

Barty rubbed his eyes and pinched himself, but the scene didn't change. One of the meals had been completely untouched. He could not evade the inescapable conclusion.

Doubting his own memory of the previous evening, Bartholomew hastened to the guestroom. He rapped loudly. When no voice answered, he threw open the door. Inside all was as it had been for months. No signs of recent human occupancy had disturbed the room.

Bartholomew flew down the stairs. Perhaps his old friend had become ill, or was angry at something that had been said last night.

He found Mrs. Fitzsimmons, his housekeeper, at the kitchen stove. What about his guest? he demanded. Had she seen him leaving the house? The portly woman stared back at her distraught employer. She had seen no one all morning, she said. And no, she had not made the bed or in any way tidied up the guestroom.

Bartholomew spent the rest of Christmas Day wandering through the house with the faint hope that he might somehow fit the pieces of this puzzle together. Night came and still he could not throw off the dread that seemed to etch ever deeper into his mind. He felt he was going mad.

He was only vaguely aware of the knock at his front door early the next morning. He had fallen asleep in his study, in the very same chair Andrew Putnam had sat in (or had he?) the night before. He shook off the remnants of sleep and started for the staircase.

Mrs. Fitzsimmons met him at the top step and handed him the envelope, postmarked Washington, D.C. He tore it open and stared at the telegraphed words:

Sir: The family of Andrew H. Putnam, Esq. wishes to inform you of his death on the first of December, 1866. We know you join us in mourning his passing.

A.H. Putnam Family

Rudd walked back into his study and collapsed in the chair. The letter fluttered from his grasp. The footsteps following behind him in the snow, an old friend who insisted on staying near the warmth of a fire, a supper never consumed . . . of course it was now clear. Bartholomew Rudd had passed Christmas Eve with a dead man!

THE NODOLF INCIDENT

Southwestern Wisconsin is speckled with unique geographic formations—deep valleys called coulees, and towering bluffs and limestone outcroppings. There are pockets of wilderness virtually untouched by the outside world, small villages and isolated farmhouses recalling a way of life more suitable to the last century.

One of the bigger communities, Platteville, served as an early trading center for the nearby lead miners. Today it is a thriving small city, home of a state university, yet savoring its ties to pioneer history.

Not far from Platteville, a part mystery, part legend remains to be solved. Its origins go back nearly 120 years. Those familiar with the case call it "the strange night" or simply, "the Nodolf incident."

Carl Nodolf was a German-born farmer who settled on a large swatch of land near the base of a towering rock bluff known to this day as The Mound. Nodolf moved into a sturdy, two-story house already situated on the property.

Carl had left his bride-to-be in Germany when he emigrated to the United States. Like many other men creating a new life in an unfamiliar land, he wanted a measure of success before he married. The deep, rich black soil, the spectacular view of the rolling countryside from the house's windows and the dramatic mound towering above it would surely appeal to his betrothed as it did to him. He had fallen in love with the region.

Prospering, Carl returned to Germany in the late 1860s. When he arrived, he found his sweetheart had died in a diphtheria epidemic only weeks before.

Anguish replaced Carl's hope. Only two of his bride-to-be's family had survived: her mother and a sixteen-year-old sister, Louise. Gradually he realized that his dream of a farm and family in Wisconsin could still be fulfilled. He could ask Louise to come with him to America. Yet he didn't feel it proper to rush into a marriage.

Finally, both Louise and her mother accompanied Carl back to Wisconsin. Carl and Louise fell in love and were married soon after their arrival in Platteville. Their first child, a daughter named Minnie Louise, was born three years later. Louie, their first son, was born two years after that.

Louie was two years old, Minnie just turned five when "the strange night" began. All day a wicked storm had been moving toward the Nodolf farm. Near dusk, the blackened clouds loomed directly overhead and the wind increased to gale proportions.

Carl and Louise tucked their two children into an upstairs bedroom, then securely locked each bedroom window shutter. Downstairs, Carl slid the shoulder-high bar across each door. They shuttered each window tightly against the storm.

Still they hesitated to retire. Lightning ricocheted across the night sky. The wind howled more like a November blizzard than a June thunderstorm. An occasional wolf howled near the house. Too near, Louise thought.

Shortly after midnight, Carl finally decided the house was secure and, with Louise leading the way up the stairs with the lantern, the couple prepared for bed. They tucked the blankets around the children's shoulders and retired for the night.

A few hours later, a deafening blast of thunder awoke Louise. At the same instant, she heard little Minnie's voice crying for help. Louise quickly lighted the lantern and ran into the children's bedroom. Both children had vanished.

By this time Carl was at her side. Together they searched the upstairs. "Carl," Louise said, "they must have become frightened and gone downstairs."

The couple rushed after them, calling the children as they descended. No voices answered. When they reached the front room they stopped, unbelieving. Between the cracks of thunder and pounding wind, faint voices could be heard . . . from outside the house!

Carl threw off the heavy bar blocking the door and swung it open. On the steps, shivering in their nightwear, stood Minnie and Louie. Carl scooped them up in his muscular arms.

"Wrap them up," Louise said. "I'll get their dry . . ."

He stopped her. "Louise, you don't have to get dry clothes. The children aren't wet!"

Despite the heavy downpour, battering even now against the stone walls, neither Minnie nor Louie had as much as one drop of rain on them. It was as if they had been standing in some invisible shell on the doorstep of the house. Handing the children to Louise, Carl checked each shuttered and locked window, the bolted doors. All were secured *from the inside.* "How did they get out there?" he demanded. "That's not possible!"

When their parents asked them what happened, neither Louie nor Minnie could answer. Stuttering badly, they tried to recall the last few hours. The children stuttered for the rest of their lives, the only two of the eight Nodolf children to do so.

Neighbors offered many theories to explain the strange evening. Perhaps one of the parents was a sleepwalker who had picked up the children and put them outside while under the influence of some strange dream. Others with more vivid imaginations suggested gypsies, known to frequent that neighborhood, could have broken into the house, snatched the children and then been scared away, leaving the youngsters to be found on the front doorstep. Given the facts, however, there seems to be no rational explanation.

The old stone house, now crumbling and vacant, huddles forlornly at the base of The Mound. More than a few people familiar with the Nodolf incident have stood on the expansive lawn, under one of the nearby oak trees, and gazed up at the structure. The question on their lips is always the same: What really happened on "the strange night" so long ago?

THE RETURN OF THE HANGED MAN

The Walker House is Wisconsin's oldest inn. It was built in 1836 in Mineral Point, then the "metropolis" of the lead region in the southwestern corner of the state. The handsome three-story stone building, with its two-story addition at one end, has a decidedly continental flair.

Tucked into a hillside and set off by a row of sentinel-like trees, it could have been a baron's hunting lodge. Heavy, rough-hewn beams, with the bark still on them, give character to the ceilings of the main-floor rooms. A massive bar and walls adorned with hunting trophies dominate the upstairs tavern.

From the start, the Walker House did a brisk business. Wisconsin's territorial officers were sworn in at Mineral Point the same year the inn was built, and the little village teemed with politicians traveling back and forth between their temporary capital at nearby Belmont and their home regions. Cornish miners, frontiersmen and speculators poured into town, eager for the riches that the lead and zinc deposits promised. At night, the men crowded into the Walker House, jostling one another for drink, food and perhaps a bed on the top floor.

On November 1, 1842, a "customer" of a different kind patronized the Walker House. He was a murderer who would hang early that afternoon from a scaffold erected in front of the inn. His name was William Caffee and he'd been convicted of shooting Samuel Southwick to death during an argument.

A crowd of 4,000 turned out for the hanging, men crowding the narrow streets, mothers with children and picnic baskets camped on the hills ringing the town. The execution was a macabre affair with the condemned man sitting astride his casket and beating out the rhythm of a funeral march with two empty beer bottles. Such a nonchalant and contemptuous attitude toward his own death brought Caffee a sort of posthumous fame, even in this country of tough, two-fisted mining men. No one who witnessed his execution would ever forget him. Just to make sure his memory would be preserved, Caffee's ghost came back after his death and settled into the Walker House.

The strange goings-on became widely known to the community some time after 1964. In that year, Ted

Landon and several partners bought the old inn. It had closed its doors in 1957 and stood vacant for seven years, ruined by neglect and vandalism. Landon, an Iowa County social worker and local artist, could not bear to witness further destruction of the historic building. He and his associates restored the Walker House to a modern-day restaurant.

A crew of young people dug out dead trees, replaced 800 window panes and built a native stone fireplace in the first-floor Pub. Oak planks from an abandoned barn became the Pub's walls. The owners worked along with their youthful assistants, putting in untold hours of grueling labor renovating the main floor and making the Walker House safe again for occupancy.

By 1972 one dining room had been refurbished, and the Walker House opened for business, serving Cornish style luncheons and dinners. The next year, another dining room was opened, and in 1974, the second-floor tavern was ready for guests.

Landon and his partners had great hopes, but the business did not go well. Four years later, in 1978, they sold the Walker House to Dr. David F. Ruf, a general practitioner from Darlington, Wisconsin.

At the time Dr. Ruf took over, a student from Madison was living in a second-floor apartment at one end of the building, above the office. He wasn't happy with the room, however, because at night his doorknob would turn constantly. He also heard strange noises that he couldn't identify. After countless sleepless nights, he moved out.

Walker Calvert could understand the student's fear. Calvert, a distant relative of the inn's builder, had just been hired by Dr. Ruf as manager and chef, and almost immediately began to witness peculiar incidents.

In the main dining room, adjoining the office, a small wooden door covers a rectangular, floor-level opening concealing water pipes, and when it is removed, one can peer inside and look straight up to the second floor. One day Calvert saw the door fly out of its place, slide along the wall and drop down on the floor!

"Just like someone grabbed it, slid it over and set it down out of the way," he explains, shaking his head. He saw the phenomenon several more times as did waitresses and diners. It usually occurred in the late afternoon or early evening.

The phenomenon played itself out during the summer of 1978. At least, Calvert never saw the door behave strangely after that date. But he did see, or experience, something else in the dining room. On three different occasions, Calvert found himself talking to someone ... except no one was there.

"I didn't know I wasn't talking to a real person," he says. He couldn't describe the "person" to whom he thought he was speaking, nor recall the conversations, even at the time they occurred. It was almost as if he'd been hypnotized. Waitresses who would hear two voices talking before they entered the room, then find Calvert quite alone, substantiated the story. They said the disembodied voice was always male.

The main dining room was not the only haunted area. In the kitchen, the morning banging and clanking of pots and pans created a din ... except that no pans were being used at the time. Sometimes, the noises seemed to come through the exterior wall, but nothing outside could explain such a racket.

One of the older women became so frightened she refused to work alone in the kitchen. Calvert understood. "When I was in there, I always felt that someone was following me around," he confesses.

The waitresses felt the same way. Several of them told Calvert they would fix drinks, turn around and bump into someone definitely solid ... but no one was ever there. Sometimes they saw a white shape.

One waitress scoffed at the ghost tales. Soon afterward, while she was in the kitchen, her ponytail shot straight up in the air! The girl hollered, "Get away!" Her ponytail remained upright a moment, dropped limply and again was yanked up. She quickly became a believer in the supernatural.

Frightened women customers also related that they felt their hair being lifted when no one else was around.

"The ghost was *always* doing something," Calvert goes on. "It was is if he tried to prove to everyone in the Walker House that he was there."

Heavy breathing and footsteps scared a number of employees. On one occasion, the bartender in the second-floor barroom stooped to check his supply of glasses in a cupboard below the counter. Hearing heavy breathing, he froze. He thought he knew who it was . . . "Leave me alone!" he yelled. As he straightened up, gripping the edge of the counter, he heard the breathing become shallower and the footsteps move away. "He was badly scared," Calvert says. "He came downstairs whiter than a sheet."

The bar is directly above the Pub room on the main floor. Many times diners heard footsteps directly overhead, even when someone stood in the upstairs hall to confirm that it was empty. The footsteps always made Calvert nervous. On a December morning, just before the Walker House closed for the winter season, Calvert was working alone in the office. He heard someone approaching. The footsteps stopped at his open office door.

"I turned around to look," Calvert begins, "and all I heard was a deep groan. Then a howl. I ran out of the building. It scared me to death. Anytime I was alone in the building, the ghost would do something. He'd always get me nervous and then he'd quit bothering me."

There is one incident that Walker Calvert will never forget: the summer morning in 1981 when he felt trapped in the root cellar. Access to this cellar is through the back exterior wall of the Pub. The cellar is insulated, electrified and encased in rock, which, of course, makes it soundproof. A set of old, no-longer-used log steps, not connected with the cellar, is on the other side of one wall.

While Calvert was in there alone, he heard someone climbing these rough log steps, then running down them, over and over again, like a child at play. The sounds came clearly to his ears, as if the person were right beside him. He was badly frightened. When he emerged from the cellar, he asked someone to check all the doors and windows. Everything was locked; the building was secure. No one could have gotten in.

The ghost of William Caffee developed quite an affinity for doors and locks. He often tried to keep customers and employees out of the Walker House. It was as if he resented crowds of people. Several times, either in early morning or late at night, there would be the sound of keys jiggling in the front door lock. Or a door that was unlocked would suddenly be locked.

"Sometimes at night the waitresses and I would start to leave and find the door locked," Calvert recalls. "The door we used has a deadbolt lock opened with a key. We'd have to get the key and unlock the door to get out of the building. There was no way that door could have gotten locked. *I* didn't lock it. And *I* had the only key." He shook his head. "It's a terrifying feeling when you're locked in a building."

Calvert's wife, Linda, co-manager of the Walker House, saw shadows from time to time, but didn't try to explain them. When Calvert told her about being locked in the building, she found the story hard to believe.

Then one spring day, Linda and her husband were inside preparing to open for the season. One of the entrances has a set of doors—an exterior door and an interior door, creating a small airlock vestibule between them. The outside door was seldom used and always kept locked. The interior one had been sealed in plastic to keep out cold, wintry drafts. When Calvert removed the plastic and Linda opened the door, someone hollered, "Hello!" Linda jumped back, terrified. They could see no one in the vestibule.

It is curious, perhaps, that the ghost was not actually seen until 1981. Appropriately, Walker Calvert saw him first. Just before sunset on a crisp October evening, Calvert went upstairs to check the door that opens from the far end of the barroom onto a porch, containing an L-shaped wooden bench and an attractive tree that grows up through a hole in the floor. An exterior wooden stairway leads up to the porch from the ground.

As Calvert opened the door to the porch, he noticed an old man sitting on the bench barely two feet away. He looked three-dimensional, but Calvert says he knew immediately the man was not real. He had no head! A black felt hat rested on his shoulders and his body was clothed in a gray miner's jacket and denim pants.

"He was just a rumpled, funny-looking old man," Calvert says. "His clothes were pretty nice, but they were old, dusty and wrinkled. He was sitting on the bench facing me. I knew right away it was Caffee. But I didn't reach out to touch him. I didn't want to get that close." What he did do was glance down and lock the porch door and when he looked up the old man was gone.

Surprisingly, Calvert was not in the least upset by this encounter. "I'd had so many connections with him that I didn't think much of it," he confides.

Because Calvert had heard that ghosts of hanging victims often appear headless, he was certain that it was the ghost of William Caffee. But was the murderer an old man when he died? Historical records do not reveal his age.

The same week that Calvert saw the old man, a waitress saw the ghost of a young man on the second floor. He had a head. He stood by the bar for a moment, then vanished.

If the headless ghost was Caffee, who was the younger ghost? Another "version" of Caffee? Perhaps. Parapsychologists say a ghost can come back at the age he or she feels. It's not unusual for someone who died at an advanced age to return as a young person. Thus, it's possible that Caffee chose to manifest himself as a young man to the waitress.

To Calvert's knowledge, the ghost of William Caffee never harmed anyone, nor was he a threat to the Walker House in any way. He never smashed dishes or tried to set fire to the place. The ghost did get irritated, however, by large crowds. Caffee's last earthly sight, of course, was the raucous throng pushing against the scaffold, eager to see him swing. Caffee had been brandishing beer bottles just before he mounted the scaffold for his early afternoon hanging. Could that account for the beer bottles that sometimes flew into the air and crashed to the floor during busy lunch hours at the restaurant?

Caffee's ghost was certainly prankish, and, at times, downright frightening. Yet perhaps he was only trying to be "helpful," rattling pans in the kitchen, checking out the bar and locking up at night. On the morning he surprised Calvert in the office, he may have wanted to do nothing more than look over the books. It's not always possible to understand a ghost.

And what does Walker Calvert make of all this?

Before he went to work at the Walker House he scoffed at the supernatural. "Absolutely no way," he says, shaking his head.

And now?

Calvert leans back in his chair and smiles. "Now, I'm sure it's all possible."

A MOTHER'S DREAM

The bond between a mother and her child is often beyond comprehension—a slight, unexpected stirring from the baby's nursery can awaken her from deepest slumber, an almost sixth sense warns of imminent danger to her little one. But does that sense of peril end at what is taken by most to be death? Or can a mother commune with her child even as he lies in the grave?

In the nineteenth century, cholera was a disease that terrified parents of small children, the word itself inspiring unspeakable horror. For decades, the nearly-always fatal intestinal infection swept across various regions of the United States, leaving hundreds dead in its wake. Not until well into this century were cholera epidemics brought under control, and even today the word evokes images of slow, agonizing death.

Few people escaped its fatal snare. Little Maxie Hoffman, five years old, was one of the lucky ones. He would not have survived, however, if his mother had not believed a most incredible dream.

Maxie lived with his parents, brothers and sisters on a small Wisconsin farm. Early in 1865, shortly after his fifth birthday, he contracted cholera. The doctor looked in on him, but he knew little about the disease and even less about a cure. All he could do was make the child comfortable and offer his sympathies to the family. And, he added, pray that no one else in the family contracted "the yellow death."

Maxie died three days later. His small body was placed in a simple pine coffin. His father used part of the family's savings for silver handles on the casket. Maxie was buried only a hundred yards from his home, in the country cemetery.

On the night following his death, Mrs. Hoffman awoke wild-eyed, screaming in panic. Her husband reached to console her as she sobbed out the nightmare that had been more vivid than life.

"It was Maxie ... in his coffin," she stammered. "But, oh dear God, he was alive!" She collapsed against her husband. "He ... he was trying to get out. I *saw* him. His hands were under his right cheek. He was twisted. Oh! He's alive ... I know it!" she wailed. "We must go to him ...!"

Mr. Hoffman said he understood. The agony had been great for both of them. As the youngest child, Maxie had a special place in their hearts. The dream was no doubt the result of the emotional strain both of them had been under. Maxie wasn't alive, he told her soothingly, and digging up his body would only add to her sorrow.

But Mrs. Hoffman's dream reappeared the next night. The details were the same as the night before. Maxie twisted in his coffin, his tiny hand clenched tightly under his head.

This time, Mr. Hoffman agreed to her pleadings. He sent his eldest child to a neighbor's house for help. Together the men would exhume Maxie's body. Mr. Hoffman believed this was the only way to persuade his wife that her son was dead, as horrifying as the experience would be.

It was well past one o'clock in the morning when they raised the coffin from the earth. As his neighbor held the lantern high, Mr. Hoffman pried off the lid. His wife huddled close with two of the older children.

A gasp arose nearly simultaneously from their lips. Maxie's body was twisted to the right side, and his hand was clenched under his right cheek! Just as his mother had dreamed!

The child showed no signs of life. Nevertheless, Mr. Hoffman scooped the boy's still form up into his arms and rode to the doctor who had pronounced Maxie dead just two days earlier.

Answering the banging on his front door, the physician drew back from the bizarre group on his doorstep: Mrs. Hoffman, the neighbor who had come to the family's aid and Mr. Hoffman, his dead son Maxie cradled in his arms.

Reluctantly at first, but at the family's insistence, the physician tried to revive the child, if only to please the distraught mother. Then he detected something. A faint heartbeat, an unnatural warmth in the frail body.

The minutes passed. At last, nearly an hour after he first began, the doctor knew the boy lived. Maxie's eyelids fluttered open. The overjoyed parents, almost afraid to hope, hovered near while the doctor coaxed some brandy down the child's throat, then placed heated salt bags under Maxie's arms, a common restorative in those days.

Within the week, Maxie Hoffman, healthy and normal, played cheerily with his brothers and sisters. He would remember nothing of his own "death."

An explanation? We can only guess that Maxie was one of those rare medical cases in which an individual showing no apparent signs of life has been pronounced dead only to revive later. In pioneer days, the technology for assessing life was limited to the stethoscope and a doctor's intuition. The child was fortunate indeed. His mother's dream saved him from death *after* burial.

And what became of Maxie Hoffman? He lived until the age of eighty-five and died peacefully in Clinton, Iowa. The silver handles from his "first" coffin always held a place of prominence in Maxie's home.

The Psychic Detective

There is no reliable evidence that the master of Victorian detection, Sherlock Holmes, ever visited America, let alone Milwaukee. More's the pity, for Holmes missed the opportunity to meet a man of that city whose abilities to solve seemingly impenetrable crimes nearly matched his own.

Arthur Price Roberts, known as "Doc" or "Professor" to his friends, was the man once known as America's preeminent psychic detective. Like the fictional Holmes, Doc Roberts was often called upon by authorities and private clients to help unravel intricate criminal puzzles. But unlike Holmes, who solved his famous cases through the powers of observation and deduction, Roberts apparently employed only his own amazing psychic powers.

Doc Roberts was a son of the British Isles, born in Denbeigh, Wales, in 1866. He emigrated to this country as a young boy, settling first in Fox Lake, Wisconsin, with an uncle. As a teenager, he headed for Blanchard, North Dakota, and a job herding cattle. There, he once said, he first became aware of his psychic powers. A man named Wild lost some money and Roberts said he "saw" a picture in his mind of its hiding place.

Incredibly, Roberts remained an illiterate all of his life. He feared an education would destroy his psychic abilities!

Arthur Price Roberts rose to fame shortly before the turn of the twentieth century and continued his celebrated career for over forty years. Most of his psychic puzzle-solving took place in Wisconsin, although he occasionally helped to solve cases elsewhere in the United States.

Doc Roberts also possessed Sherlock Holmes's ability to startle visitors by correctly surmising their background, current difficulties and other personal information. In 1905, he took on the case of Duncan McGregor, a Peshtigo, Wisconsin man, who had been missing for a number of months. His distraught wife sought Roberts out when authorities reached a dead end in their investigation.

Mrs. McGregor said later that Roberts met her at the door to his home and proceeded to accurately identify her and the cause of her distress. There is no evidence that Roberts either knew of the case or had ever seen the woman before.

He concluded their brief meeting by saying that he could not help her at that time. She should come back in a few hours, he said, giving him time to concentrate on the case first. Roberts—in an unusual step for him—then went into a sort of trance. Normally, when asked to put his abilities to work, he received a mental picture immediately.

The trance apparently worked. Mrs. McGregor returned early that evening. Gently, Roberts revealed that her husband had been murdered, but he would not identify the individuals responsible. "The testimony I could give would not be admissible in court," he apologized. But he hastily added that the body of her husband was in the Menomonee River near Milwaukee, snarled in some sunken logs that prevented it from rising to the surface.

Mrs. McGregor alerted police who dragged the river at the location specified by Roberts. They found McGregor's body, but it took them some time to retrieve it. The man's clothing was caught on water-logged timbers on the bottom!

Not even geography constrained Doc Roberts's psychic senses. In one of his more dramatic cases, he found the body of a missing man in Arizona . . . without ever leaving the comfort of his Milwaukee home!

In this case, a wealthy Chicago financier, J.D. Leroy, had sought Roberts out. Leroy's brother had vanished on a trip to Albuquerque six months before. The police didn't have a clue to the man's whereabouts.

Enter Doc Roberts. He disclosed that the man had been murdered and his body dumped in Devil's Canyon in Arizona. He then described for J.D. Leroy the area in which his brother's remains would be found.

A few weeks later Roberts received a letter from Leroy. Police had found his brother's corpse *in Devil's Canyon* only a few hundred feet from the very scene Roberts had pictured. The body bore signs of foul play.

In yet another instance, without leaving Wisconsin, Roberts tracked a murder suspect to Canada. The psychic was visiting Fond du Lac when police in that city approached him for help on an old, unsolved murder case. Their search for a suspect had been stymied.

Roberts listened carefully to their story, then held up his hand for silence. He proceeded to describe the murder victim in the greatest of detail. Although the police were amazed, the cynics still weren't satisfied. They claimed Roberts really hadn't revealed anything that could not have been known from studying published accounts of the crime.

But what happened the next morning surprised even the harshest critics. Doc walked into police headquarters and asked to look through their mug books, collections of photographs of known criminals. He sat for hours scanning the rough faces as he slowly turned the pages. At last he called detectives over and placed his finger on the picture of one man, known to officers as a petty criminal. "That's your killer, gentlemen!" he exclaimed. And, he added, police could find him in Canada . . . working for the Royal Canadian Mounted Police!

Fond du Lac police notified their Canadian brethren of the man's name and description and said he was wanted for murder. The Canadians found him . . . in Canada . . . working for the Mounties. When arrested, he confessed to the Fond du Lac murder.

In a dramatic case, Doc Roberts saved a man from the electric chair. The family of Chicagoan Ignatz Potz asked Doc for help. Potz was awaiting execution after being convicted of murder. He claimed that, although he was present at the killing, he took no part in it.

Roberts went to work and uncovered evidence supporting Potz's claims. The death sentence was commuted to life imprisonment.

Roberts made headlines in the mid-1920s in two separate crime investigations. He was consulted by Northwestern National Bank officials following a robbery in 1925. Based on a séance Roberts held, a suspect was identified and arrested. Unfortunately, the man was later acquitted for lack of admissible evidence.

One of Wisconsin's most famous murder mysteries also involved Roberts. The body of Clara Olson was found in a shallow grave near Mt. Sterling, Crawford County, on December 2, 1926. After her husband, Erdman Olson, became the prime suspect in the murder, he dropped from sight. Doc Roberts predicted that Erdman would never be found alive. He wasn't ... and the case remains unsolved.

Arthur Price Roberts's crowning achievement came in the months of October and November, 1935. Milwaukee was rocked by a series of bombings that held the city in the talons of terror for over a week. Roberts correctly predicted not only the bombings, but the final terrific blast ... which proved to be an accidental detonation caused by the terrorists!

The incredible episode began unfolding on October 18, 1935. On that Friday afternoon, Roberts told a group of acquaintances that the city would experience several bombings in the very near future. His audience wanted desperately not to believe this awful prediction, but they were too familiar with Roberts's uncanny accuracy to dismiss his words.

On Saturday night, October 26, the Shorewood Village Hall was dynamited at 7:23 p.m. The estimated five sticks of dynamite ripped a hole in the building's foundation and splintered a tall, white column. The explosion was felt for blocks around. Windows were blown out in scores of homes and offices. The explosion caused a fire that consumed what remained of the structure at 3930 North Murray Avenue.

Less than twenty-four hours later, investigators had just begun their investigation when two more explosions shook the city. This time the targets were two branch offices of the First Wisconsin National Bank. At 6:40 p.m., October 27, a hole was blown in the rear wall of the Citizens Offices of the large bank at 3602 North Villard. Damage was limited to the rear of the building and shattered windows for several blocks.

Forty minutes later, the east side offices of the First Wisconsin National Bank at North Farwell and East North Avenue were the target of the dynamiters' wrath. There was no damage to the building, although eight cars in a parking lot were demolished. In both of the bank explosions, witnesses saw the alleged suspects flee in a small gray automobile.

By this time, Milwaukee realized a maniac may have been set loose upon the city. Dozens of federal, state and local investigators converged on the explosion sites.

So far, there had been no serious injuries, but officials feared the next bombing might cause a loss of life. They posted guards at all governmental and bank buildings since these seemed to be the targets. Investigators theorized that the bombers may have mistaken the Shorewood City Hall for a bank building.

The city was tense, fearful as the first of the week passed uneventfully. Police had determined that the dynamite in the early explosions had been stolen from a Public Works Administration project on October 3. One hundred and fifty pounds of explosives had been taken, along with 450 fuse caps and 200 feet of fuse. Authorities were now even more concerned. That much dynamite could cause enormous destruction.

The terrorists struck again on Thursday, hitting two police substations. Once again, good fortune prevented personal injury. Damage was extensive but not critical.

So far, Arthur Price Roberts had been proven correct. Police knew that and, in desperation, turned to him for advice. He told them the last explosion would erupt on Sunday, November 3, somewhere south of the Menomonee River. Could he identify the criminals? Did he know precisely where the explosion would occur? No, Roberts said. Regretfully, that was all the information he could "see."

That Sunday an army of police officers flooded the city south of the river. Sharpshooters kept watch from rooftops. Every officer was told to shoot first and ask questions later. As the countdown to Roberts's predicted catastrophe began, all suspicious persons were questioned and abandoned buildings searched.

Somehow the police missed the old shed behind the house at 2121 West Mitchell. Inside, two young men with long petty crime records hunched over an awesome arrangement of dynamite and fuse caps. They were concocting their "final surprise" for Milwaukee.

Something went wrong. Whether the youthful bombers mis-set a timing device or just grew careless no one knows for certain. At 2:40 p.m. on Sunday, November 3, 1935, an estimated forty sticks of dynamite exploded in that shed, leaving only a gaping hole in the earth, charred rubble and smoking timbers.

The two men inside—twenty-year-old Isador Rutkowski and sixteen-year-old Paul Chovenee—were blown to bits. Tragically, nine-year-old Patricia Mylanarek, of 2117-B West Mitchell, also lost her life. She was in her second-story bedroom, overlooking the makeshift bomb factory, when it exploded. The blast collapsed her bedroom walls on top of her.

At least ten other persons were injured, the fronts of buildings were blown out for a hundred yards around the shed and windows were knocked out of houses for several blocks. One witness said the area looked like a war zone.

Rutkowski, the apparent ringleader, was an unemployed auto mechanic with a police record. He was identified through parts of his body, including his head, which was found against a garage thirty feet away. A later investigation showed he had some imagined grievances against bankers.

Chovenee's death was not discovered until the next day when his father reported him missing, saying he had last seen him with Rutkowski. His father identified swatches of his son's hair and scalp, along with the remnants of a blue jacket.

An additional two boxes of dynamite were found intact in the building rubble, miraculously surviving the massive destruction. Police said that had they exploded, the results would have been catastrophic.

The death of Rutkowski ended the bombing terror in Milwaukee. Investigators were unanimous in their opinion that Rutkowski and Chovenee had been preparing another bomb when it accidentally exploded. Arthur Price Roberts's premonition was accurate. He had even predicted the final *unintentional* bombing!

Doc Roberts was probably frightened on occasion by the future he "saw." Whether that applied to his own mortality is not known.

A small dinner party was given in his honor in November, 1939. He told the gathering how very pleased he was with the tribute and proceeded to reminisce about his own incredible life. He was nearly seventy-three years of age and though he seemed to be in good health, his psychic senses told him otherwise.

As the dinner group planned for their next meeting, Roberts expressed his regrets. "I won't be with you beyond January 2, 1940," he confided with a tinge of sorrow.

On the morning of Tuesday, January 2, 1940, Arthur Price Roberts died peacefully in his sleep.

The man who had called Milwaukee home for nearly fifty years was buried the following Friday in Wanderers' Rest Cemetery, ending the career of America's most amazing psychic detective.

Bibliography

Illinois

BOOKS

Allen, John W. *Legends and Lore of Southern Illinois.* Carbondale: Southern Illinois University, 1963.

Brandon, Jim. *Weird America.* New York: E. P. Dutton, 1978.

Bruce, H. Addington. *Historic Ghosts and Ghost Hunters.* New York: Moffat, Yard & Co., 1908.

Dorson, Richard M. *Regional Folklore in the United States—Buying the Wind.* Chicago & London: The University of Chicago Press, 1964.

Drake, S. A. *Myths and Fables of To-day.* Boston: Lee and Shepard, 1900.

Gaddis, Vincent H. *Mysterious Fires and Lights.* New York: Dell Publishing Co., Inc., 1968.

Hintze, Naomi A. and Pratt, J. Gaither, Ph.D. *The Psychic Realm: What Can You Believe?* New York: Random House, 1975.

Holzer, Hans. *Psychic Investigator.* New York: Hawthorn Books, Inc., W. Clement Stone, Publisher, 1968.

Illinois A Descriptive and Historical Guide (American Guide Series). Chicago: A. C. McClurg and Co., 1939.

Lamon, Ward Hill. *Recollections of Abraham Lincoln 1847–1865.* Chicago: A. C. McClurg and Co., 1895.

Lindley, Charles, Viscount Halifax. *Lord Halifax's Ghost Book.* New York: Didier, 1944.

Murphy, Gardner, M.D. and Ballou, Robert C., compilers and editors. *William James on Psychical Research.* New York: The Viking Press, 1960.

Rogo, D. Scott. *The Poltergeist Experience.* New York: Penguin Books, 1979.

Sibley, Mulford Q. *Life After Death?* Minneapolis: Dillon Press, Inc., 1975.

Smith, Susy. *The Enigma of Out-of-Body Travel.* New York: Helix Press/Garrett Publications, 1965.

Smith, Warren. *Strange Hexes.* New York: Popular Library, 1970.

Strange Stories and Amazing Facts. c. 1976 Reader's Digest.

Tyrrell, G. H. M. *Apparitions* (Revised Edition). Collier Books, New York: The Macmillan Company, 1963. (original copyright by The Society for Psychical Research, 1953).
Walker, Danton. *I Believe in Ghosts*. New York: Taplinger Publishing Co., 1969.
Winer, Richard and Osborn, Nancy. *Haunted Houses*. New York: Bantam Books, July 1979.
Winer, Richard. *Houses of Horror*. New York: Bantam Books, 1983.
Winer, Richard and Ishmael, Nancy Osborn. *More Haunted Houses*. New York: Bantam Books, 1981.

PERIODICALS

Biederman, Pat. "Spirit abounds in town of mediums." *U.S.A. Today*, June 2, 1983.
Burkholder, Alex A. "April's Hand of Death." *Firehouse Magazine*, April 1983.
Geist, Bill. "Resurrection Mary." *U.S. Catholic*, August 1979.
Harris, Jesse and Neely, Julia. "Southern Illinois Phantoms and Bogies." *Midwest Folklore*, Fall 1951, vol. 1, No. 3.
" 'Haunted' house conquered by TV announcer." *The Commercial Appeal* (Memphis, Tennessee), November 1, 1978.
Hudson (Wisconsin) *Star-times*, February 18, 1870.
"Peculiar Experiences Connected With Noted Persons" (Apparition of the Dead Two Years Before the Death of the Percipient). *Journal of the American Society for Psychical Research*, Vol. 15, 1921.
"Priests rid tavern of ghost." Des Moines *Tribune*, February 7, 1980.
Swarbrick, Fran. "He spent night, but was he alone?" Rockford (Illinois) *Register Star*, November 1, 1978.
_____ "Groans, forms haunt Slave House's attic." Rockford (Illinois) *Register Star*, October 9, 1977.

UNPUBLISHED WORKS

Bloomington, Indiana. Indiana University Folklore Archives.
Federal Writers' Projects Mss. for the Works Progress Administration for the State of Illinois, various dates.

INDIANA

BOOKS

Anderson, Jean. *The Haunting of America*. Boston: Houghton Mifflin Co., 1973.

Brandon, Jim. *Weird America*. New York: E. P. Dutton, 1978.

Edwards, Frank. *Strangest of All*. New York: The Citadel Press, 1956.

Ellis, Edward S. *The History of Our Country, Vol. III*. Cincinnati: The Jones Brothers Publishing Company, 1918.

Gaddis, Vincent H. *Mysterious Fires and Lights*. New York: Dell Publishing Co., Inc., 1968.

Historical Hannah House. undated brochure, no publisher given.

Indiana: A Guide to the Hoosier State. New York: Oxford University Press, 1941.

Keel, John A. *Our Haunted Planet*. Greenwich, Conn.: Fawcett Publications, Inc., 1971.

Smith, Susy. *Life Is Forever*. New York: G. P. Putnam's Sons, 1974.

Smith, Warren. *Strange Hexes*. New York: Popular Library, 1970.

Stuart, Rory, ed. *The Strange World of Frank Edwards*. New York: Berkley Medallion Books, Berkley Publishing Corp., c. 1977 Lyle Stuart, Inc.

Winer, Richard and Ishmael, Nancy Osborn. *More Haunted Houses*. New York: Bantam Books, Inc., 1981.

PERIODICALS

Boudreau, George, ed. "Haunted Andrew House?" *OldLetter*. La Porte: La Porte County Historical Society, October 1982, Issue 12.

Clements, William M. And Lightfoot, William E. "The Legend of Stepp Cemetery." *Indiana Folklore*, various issues.

Coffeen, Bob. "Up and Down Town with the Town Crier." The La Porte *Town Crier*, November 6, 1975.

George, Philip Brandt. "The Ghost of Cline Avenue." *Indiana Folklore*, various issues.

Hall, Steve. "Horrors Haunt Hannah House?" The Indianapolis *News*, October 27, 1981.

Heady, Linda. Forum The Reader's Corner. The Indianapolis *Star*, September 5, 1976.

"Historic Hannah House For Sale." The Indianapolis *Star*, February 22, 1981.

Johansen, Marguerite Bell. "Dunes Woman." *Dunes Country Magazine*, Winter 1982.

Lecocq, James Gary. "The Ghost of the Doctor and a Vacant Fraternity House." *Indiana Folklore*, various issues.

O'Dell, Vicki L. "The Haunted Bridge." *Indiana History Bulletin*, v. 41, 1965.

472

Sander, David. "Diana of the Dunes: The Real Story." *Dunes Country Magazine*, Summer 1981.
Spiers, Al. "Diana of the Dunes—Michiana's Original Streaker?" *News-Dispatch* (Michigan City, Indiana), March 13, 1974.

UNPUBLISHED WORKS

Bloomington, Indiana. Indiana University Folklore Archives.
Marshall, Lyn. "The Andrew House." La Porte, Indiana, n.d.

IOWA

BOOKS

Baule, John A. *The Ham House and the Life of Its Builder*. Booklet written for the Dubuque (Iowa) County Historical Society, n.d.
Ebon, Martin, ed. *Exorcism: Fact Not Fiction*. New York: New American Library, Inc., 1974.

PERIODICALS

"The ghost of Simpson College." Des Moines *Register*, November 8, 1979.
Grant, Donald. "Strange Knocking From Table; Family Prays, Calls Spiritualist." Des Moines *Register*, September 11, 1940.
"A Haunted House," *Weekly Gate City* (Keokuk), August 17, 1899.
Hopson, Julie. "Tales to make your blood run cold." Des Moines *Register*, October 31, 1976.
Lackey, Patrick. "Stuart, the friendly Iowa ghost." Des Moines *Register*, April 22, 1977.
Monson, Val. *Des Moines Tribune*, October 30, 1980.
Ryder, T. J. "Spending the night with 'spirits.' " Des Moines *Register*, October 31, 1978.
Shanley, Mary Kay. "They didn't believe in ghosts either." Des Moines *Register*, October 28, 1973.
Worrel, Elaine V. "The Ghost Was a Stranger," *Fate*, April 1972.

UNPUBLISHED WORKS

Conaway, Minnie. "The Great Mystery." Paper submitted 1936 for Federal Writers' Projects (Folklore), Decatur, Illinois.

KANSAS

BOOKS

Harter, Walter. *The Phantom Hand and Other American Hauntings.* Englewood Cliffs, New Jersey: Prentice-Hall, Inc., 1976.
Hollenberg Pony Express Station. Topeka: Kansas State Historical Society brochure, n.d.
Kansas: A Guide to the Sunflower State. (American Guide Series). New York: Viking, 1939.
Montgomery, Ruth. *A Search for the Truth.* New York: William Morrow & Company, Inc., 1967.
Reid, Chick. "Legend of White Woman Creek" (condensed by Daniel Brown) in *History of Early Greeley County, Tracks, Trails and Tribulations,* Vol. 1, Tribune, Kansas, 1981, (no publisher given) Greeley County Historical Book Committee.
Smith, Warren. *Strange Hexes.* New York: Popular Library, 1970.

PERIODICALS

Elmer, Timothy R. "Ghostly deeds haunt ancient Topeka home." Topeka *Capital-Journal,* October 31, 1981.
Findley, Rowe. "The Pony Express." *National Geographic,* July 1980.
Maxwell, Bob. "Ellis County's Own Ghost (1867–1919–1967?)." *Heritage of Kansas,* Vol. VIII, No. 1, 1975.
"This Ghost Enjoys Tickling Sleepers' Feet." Des Moines (Iowa) *Register,* March 25, 1940.

UNPUBLISHED WORKS

Koch, William E. The William E. Koch Folklore Collection, Kansas State University, Manhattan.

MICHIGAN

BOOKS

Anderson, Jean. *The Haunting of America.* Boston: Houghton Mifflin Co., 1973.

Dorson, Richard M. *American Folklore*. Chicago: The University of Chicago Press, 1959.
————— *Bloodstoppers and Bearwalkers*. Cambridge: Harvard University Press, 1952.
Hamlin, Marie Caroline Watson. *Legends of Lé Detroit*. Detroit: Thorndike Nourse, 1884.
Skinner, Charles M. *Myths and Legends of Our Own Land*, Vol. II. Phila.: J. B. Lippincott Co., 1896.
Steiger, Brad. *Real Ghosts, Restless Spirits and Haunted Minds*. New York: Award Books, 1968.
Stuart, Rory, ed. *The Strange World of Frank Edwards*. New York: Berkley Medallion Books, Berkley Publishing Corp., c. 1977 Lyle Stuart, Inc.
Walker, Danton. *I Believe in Ghosts*. New York: Taplinger Publishing Co., 1969 (a re-edited version of *Spooks Deluxe*, published in 1956).

PERIODICALS

Johnston, Nina E. "The Haunted Camp." Saginaw *Daily Courier*, March 6, 1889.
Journal of the American Society for Psychical Research, Vol. 57, 1963. (original account in New York *Mercury*, September 13, 1851).
"A Lake Huron Ghost Story," from the New York *Sun* by way of the Saginaw *Courier*, August 30, 1883.
Steiger, Brad. "Stories of Ghosts, Witches and Demons." c. 1971 by *Scholastic Magazine* (originally entitled "Horrible Hag of Detroit" in *Strange* magazine c. 1966. c. 1971 by Eugene Olson and Popular Library).
Volgenau, Gerald. "Of things that go bump in the night . . ." Des Moines *Register*, March 4, 1979.

UNPUBLISHED WORKS

Detroit, Michigan. Wayne State University Archives.

MINNESOTA

BOOKS

Barnouw, Erik. *The Magician and the Cinema*. New York & Oxford: Oxford University Press, 1981.

Brown, Raymond Lamont. *Phantoms of the Theater*. Nashville & New York: Thomas Nelson Inc., 1977.

Minnesota A State Guide (American Guide Series). New York: The Viking Press, 1938.

Potter, Merle. *101 Best Stories of Minnesota*. 1931 printed by the Harrison and Smith Co., Minneapolis, Minn.

Smith, Susy. *The Enigma of Out-of-Body Travel*. New York: Helix Press/Garrett Publications, 1965.

PERIODICALS

Gendler, Neal. 'A ghost may be a projection of a living person through telepathy.' Minneapolis *Tribune*, October 30, 1977.

_____ "Who's haunting our house? Albert Lea family wonders." Minneapolis *Tribune*, October 30, 1977.

Giese, Don and Farmer, Bill. "Elusive Phantom 'Haunts' St. Mary's." St. Paul *Pioneer Press*, February 24, 1969.

Giese, Don and Farmer, Bill. "Newsmen Spend Sleepless Night." St. Paul *Pioneer Press*, February 27, 1969.

Giese, Don and Farmer, Bill. "What Haunts Summit Avenue Mansion?" St. Paul *Pioneer Press*, February 6, 1969.

"The Haunting of St. Mary's: Fables and Facts." *Nexus* (St. Mary's College, Winona, Minn.), October, 1967.

Hudson *Star-times*, March 28, 1873.

The Minneapolis *Journal*, February 6, 1924; February 7, 1924.

The Minneapolis *Morning Tribune*, February 6, 1924; February 7, 1924.

Mulvaney, Maureen. "Legendary Spectre Still Skeleton in SMC Closet." *St. Mary's Cardinal*, October 31, 1979.

UNPUBLISHED WORKS

Nelson, Jake. "Forty Years in the Roseau Valley." n.d. ms. courtesy Roseau County Historical Museum & Interpretive Center, Roseau, Minn.

Selected Oral History Tapes: Iron Range Research Center, A Division of the Department of Iron Range Resources and Rehabilitation, Chisholm, Minn.

MISSOURI

BOOKS

Anderson, Jean. *The Haunting of America*. Boston: Houghton Mifflin Co., 1973.

476

Brandon, Jim. *Weird America*. New York: E. P. Dutton, 1978.
Collins, Earl A. *Folk Tales of Missouri*. Boston: The Christopher Publishing House, c. 1935.
──── *Legends and Lore of Missouri*. San Antonio: The Naylor Co., c. 1951.
Fornell, Earl Wesley. *The Unhappy Medium* (Spiritualism and the Life of Margaret Fox). Austin: University of Texas Press, 1964.
Gaddis, Vincent H. *Mysterious Fires and Lights*. New York: Dell Publishing Co., Inc. 1968.
Greenhouse, Herbert B. *In Defense of Ghosts*. New York: Simon and Schuster, Inc., Essandess Special Editions, 1970.
Heywood, Rosalind. *Beyond the Reach of Sense An Inquiry Into Extra-Sensory Perception*. New York: E. P. Dutton & Co., Inc., 1961.
Hintze, Naomi A. and Pratt, J. Gaither, Ph.D. *The Psychic Realm: What Can You Believe?* New York: Random House, 1975.
The Hornet Ghost Light One of Nature's Unexplained Mysteries. brochure published by the Neosho (Missouri) Chamber of Commerce, n.d.
Moore, Tom. *Mysterious Tales and Legends of the Ozarks*. Philadelphia: Dorrence & Co., 1938.
Neider, Charles, ed. *The Autobiography of Mark Twain*. New York: Perennial, 1959.
Prince, Walter Franklin. *The Case of Patience Worth*. New Hyde Park, New York: University Books, c. 1964 (by University Books, Inc.); c. 1927 by Boston Society for Psychic Research.
Randolph, Vance. *Ozark Magic and Folklore*. New York: Dover Publications, Inc., 1964. (book originally titled *Ozark Superstitions* published by Columbia University Press, 1947). c. 1947 by Columbia University Press. Dover edition by special arrangement with Columbia.
Rayburn, Otto Ernest. *Ozark Country*. New York: Duell, Sloan and Pearce, 1941, from the American Folkways Series edited by Erskine Caldwell.
Schurmacher, Emile. *More Strange Unsolved Mysteries*. New York: Paperback Library, c. 1969 by Coronet Communications, Inc.
Sibley, Mulford Q. *Life After Death?* Minneapolis: Dillon Press, Inc. 1975.
Skinner, Charles M. *American Myths and Legends*. Philadelphia and London: J. B. Lippincott Company, 1903.

PERIODICALS

Gannon, Robert. "Balls O'Fire!" *Popular Mechanics*, September, 1965.

Goodavage, Joseph F. "skyquakes, earthlights, and e.m. fields." *Analog Science Fiction/Science Fact*, September, 1978.
Herbert, Amanda. "Ghostly alumna haunts Senior Hall, seeks lost lover every year, story says." *Stephens Life*, October 27, 1977.
Rand, Willard C. "Spook Light." Kansas City *Star*, October 21, 1973.
Springfield *Republican*, January 5, 1896.

UNPUBLISHED WORKS

Koch, William E. William E. Koch Folklore Collection, Kansas State University, Manhattan, Kansas.
LaZebnick, Jack. "The Ghost of Senior Hall," an original play written in 1983 to commemorate sesquicentennial of Stephens College, Columbia, Missouri.

NEBRASKA

BOOKS

Kettelkamp, Larry. *Haunted Houses*. New York: William Morrow & Co., 1969.
Rogo, D. Scott. *Parapsychology A Century of Inquiry*. New York: Taplinger Publishing Co., 1975.
Steiger, Brad. *Real Ghosts, Restless Spirits & Haunted Minds*. New York: Award Books, 1968.
Welsch, Roger L. (compiler) *A Treasury of Nebraska Pioneer Folklore*. Lincoln: University of Nebraska Press, 1939.

PERIODICALS

"Ghost Failed to Scream, Upsetting Old Tradition," *The* New York *Times*, October 22, 1933.

UNPUBLISHED WORKS

Federal Writers' Project, Works Projects Administration Collection for the State of Nebraska, Nebraska State Historical Society, Lincoln, 1940.

478

Ohio

BOOKS

Anderson, Jean. *The Haunting of America*. Boston: Houghton Mifflin Co., 1973.

Dorson, Richard M., collector & editor. *Negro Folktales in Michigan*. Cambridge: Harvard University Press, 1956.

Fort, Charles. *The Complete Books of Charles Fort*. New York: Dover Publications, Inc., 1974.

Holzer, Hans. *Psychic Investigator*. New York: Hawthorn Books, Inc., W. Clement Stone, Publisher, 1968.

Reynolds, James. *Ghosts in American Houses*. New York: Farrar, Straus and Cudahy, 1955.

Webb, David K. Ohio Valley Folk Research Project, The Ross County Historical Society, Chillicothe.

Winer, Richard and Ishmael, Nancy Osborn. *More Haunted Houses*. New York: Bantam Books, Inc., 1981.

PERIODICALS

Abel, Mary Bilderback. "Ghostly Guests linger at an inn in Granville." Columbus *Dispatch Magazine*, June 24, 1979.

Condon, George E. "Ghastly Labor and Ghostly." *The Plain Dealer* (Cleveland), September 3, 1963.

———— "Ghost Hunt Yields Bodies," *The Plain Dealer* (Cleveland), September 16, 1963.

Dawson, Carol A. "Death Calls for Grandpa." *Fate*, April 1972.

Dolgan, Robert. "Priest sets bail benefit in castle." *The Plain Dealer* (Cleveland), April 13, 1975.

Dorn, Clyde; Berg, Susan Marie; Stephenson, Dave. "Beyond Incredible." *The Ohio Magazine*, November 1980.

Dreimiller, Barbara. "Franklin Castle's fright-seeing tour." *The Plain Dealer* (Cleveland), February 28, 1975.

"Ghosts drive family from home." Eau Claire *Leader-Telegram*, March 10, 1984.

Henkle, Rae D. "A Native Ghost." *The Ohio Magazine* (vol. 4), 1908.

Hudson *Star and Times*, August 19, 1870.

Journal of the American Society for Psychical Research, vol. 2, 1908.

Journal of the Ohio Folklore Society, December 1972.

Kaib, Tom. "A Tale for Halloween." *The Plain Dealer* (Cleveland), October 28, 1973.

Kay, Leslie. "Old castle's present, past riddled with fiction, fact." *The Plain Dealer* (Cleveland), May 11, 1975.
The Plain Dealer (Cleveland), January 20, 1975; July 23, 1975; June 6, 1978.
Schwartz, Donald M. "Ghost's work on film, photographer says." St. Paul (Minnesota) *Dispatch*, March 7, 1984.
"Strange things happen to family when daughter is in the house. St. Paul (Minnesota) *Pioneer Press*, March 9, 1984.
Sweet, Fred. "The House The Ghost Built." *Alumni Bulletin*, Denison University, May 1932 (vol. 23, No. 9).

WISCONSIN

BOOKS

Collections of the Minnesota Historical Society, Vol. I. St. Paul, Minnesota, 1902. (published by the Society).
Fiedler, George. *Mineral Point A History*. Madison: The State Historical Society of Wisconsin, 1973.
Skinner, Charles M. *American Myths and Legends*. Philadelphia and London: J. B. Lippincott Company, 1903.
Stewart, Jim and Shirley. *Easy Going A Comprehensive Guide to Grant, Iowa and Lafayette Counties*. Madison: Tamarack Press, 1976.
The Story of Mineral Point 1827–1941. Compiled by the Workers of the Writers' Program of the Work Projects Administration in the State of Wisconsin 1941. Published by the Mineral Point Historical Society, 1979.
Stuart, Rory, ed. *The Strange World of Frank Edwards*. New York: Berkley Medallion Books. Berkley Publishing Corp., c. 1977 Lyle Stuart, Inc.
von Bober, Wolffgang. *The Carver Effect*. Harrisburg, Pa.: Stackpole Books, 1979.

PERIODICALS

Bennett, Joan. "Ghostly events change Granton man's life." Eau Claire *Leader-Telegram*, March 29, 1980.
Brennwald, James. "Ghost story adds dash of color to Big Foot beach." Beloit (Wisconsin) *News*, April 15, 1981.

480

"The Ghost of Rosslyne Manse." *Journal of the American Society for Psychical Research*, vol. 8, 1924.

Hollatz, Tom. "Summerwind is not empty." Lakeland *Times* (Minocqua, Wisconsin), December 11, 1980.

"House Haunted in 1830's Still Stands Near Mound." Platteville *Journal*, 1974.

Hudson (Wisconsin) *Star-times*, February 20, 1867.

Jensen, Arlene. "Puzzling phenomena haunts tavern." Kenosha *News*, June 27, 1983.

Kluever, Michael H. "Shy Shorewood ghost." Milwaukee *Journal*, September 11, 1980.

———. "Stepfamily—Who was that mysterious guest?" Milwaukee *Journal*, July 29, 1982.

Kluever, Mike. "Ghostly guest plagues owners of modern ranch." Milwaukee *Sentinel*, November 1, 1978.

Pooley, Will. "Haunted? Once called Summerwind, an old house stirs controversy." Milwaukee *Journal*, October 30, 1983.

"Terrifying Tales of 9 Haunted Houses." *Life* magazine, November 1980.

UNPUBLISHED WORKS

Rohde, Roswell B., letter to Robert Gard, March 27, 1955.

Madison, Wisconsin. State Historical Society of Wisconsin. Van Antwerp Folklore Collection. Wisconsin Mss. QW.

Place Names in
Haunted Heartland

The authors are interested in hearing from readers who may have an interesting ghost story to tell, either from personal experience or one based on legend or folklore. If you would like to share your ghost story, send the information to: Michael Norman and Beth Scott, c/o Stanton & Lee Publishers, Inc., 44 East Mifflin Street, Madison, Wisconsin 53703. All requests for confidentiality will be honored.